A REPORT FROM THE

CHILDREN'S DEFENSE FUND

INTRODUCTION BY MARIAN WRIGHT EDELMAN

BEACON PRESS
BOSTON

Beacon Press
25 Beacon Street
Boston, Massachusetts 02108-2892
www.beacon.org

Beacon Press books are published under the auspices of
the Unitarian Universalist Association of Congregations.

06 05 04 03 02 01   8 7 6 5 4 3 2 1

ISBN 0-8070-4215-3
ISSN 1084-3191

Children's Defense Fund ®

Dedication

In the last year of the 20th century, some of the great advocates for children passed on. They inspired and touched so many lives and brought America closer to realizing its best self. This book is dedicated to them.

Gary Bellow, Harvard Law professor, brilliant lawyer for the poor and pioneer in legal services and legal clinical education. He was a partner in CDF's first office in Cambridge/Somerville, Massachusetts.

Gwendolyn Brooks, the first Black person to receive a Pulitzer Prize. She was the first visiting poet at Haley Farm, CDF's center for spiritual renewal and leadership development, where she read to local schoolchildren and met with Black women leaders seeking to prevent teen pregnancy.

Dr. Alonzo Crim, superintendent of schools in Atlanta and first Black school superintendent in a major Southern city, Mott Foundation board member, and strong leader for excellence in education.

Mrs. Annie Devine, Mississippi trailblazer for voting rights who challenged the racially discriminatory Mississippi Democratic Party at the 1964 Democratic convention in Atlantic City and a leader in the Child Development Group of Mississippi Head Start program.

Dr. Annie Dyson, pediatrician, philanthropist, educator, mother, and chair of the board of the Hole in the Wall Gang. She organized all the medical support for the 1996 Stand For Children at the Lincoln Memorial.

Darryl Evers, lead plaintiff in the lawsuit to desegregate Jackson, Mississippi public schools, and son of civil rights martyr Medgar Evers and former NAACP chair Myrlie Evers-Williams.

David Liederman, passionate voice and leader for children and the poor, especially those in child welfare systems, head of the Child Welfare League of America for 15 years.

Mrs. Mary O. Ross, Spelman graduate and long-term president of the Women's Division of the National Baptist Convention. She garnered support for CDF's efforts to prevent teen pregnancy.

Helen LaVon Taylor, early childhood educator for over thirty years and associate commissioner of the Head Start Bureau in the Department of Health and Human Services Administration for Children, Youth, and Families.

Sister Mary Geraldine Tobia, saintly, tireless worker for families and children, co-director of the Center for Family Life in Sunset Park, Brooklyn, where she devoted her life to providing a unique combination of 24-hour service, advocacy, and community development work dedicated to realizing the families of Sunset Park's full potential.

Albert Turner, trusted colleague of Dr. Martin Luther King, Jr., a leader of the voting rights march from Selma to Montgomery, and Alabama field secretary for the Southern Christian Leadership Conference.

Elizabeth Wickenden, brilliant expert on social welfare policy, "Wicky" was the leading partner in CDF's first office of juvenile justice headed by Judge Justine Wise Polier. They conducted research and surveys which led to CDF reports and advocacy on Children in Adult Jails, Children of Women Prisoners, Children Without Homes, and Unclaimed Children in the Mental Health and Child Welfare System.

Acknowledgments

Special thanks to Susanne Martinez, Senior Vice President for Programs and Policy at the Children's Defense Fund, who guides the preparation of this annual State of America's Children Yearbook and with quiet effectiveness coordinates all of our policies and programs. We're deeply grateful for her leadership.

Susanne Martinez oversaw development of this book and provided overall editorial direction with assistance from Kinda Serafi and Deena Maerowitz. Sandra Won was the principal editor. Many individuals at CDF and elsewhere contributed to the content and may be contacted for further information about their subjects. CDF contributors include Deborah Weinstein, Arloc Sherman, and Daniel Hatcher (family income); Margo Edmunds, Gregg Haifley, Martha Teitelbaum, Bill England, Claire Lutz, Lisa Alfonso-Frank, and Desmond Brown (child health); Helen Blank and Karen Schulman (child care); Kinda Serafi, Deena Maerowitz, and Judith Keenan (education); MaryLee Allen and Mary Bissell (children and families in crisis); Jill Ward, Jesselyn McCurdy, and Dawnyel Pryor (juvenile justice and youth development). Data were produced and analyzed by Paul Smith and Janet Simons. Cindy Rigoli managed production. Anourack Chinyavong designed the cover. Lisa Clayton Robinson also contributed to the editing. Joanne Pittman, Martha Espinosa, Jennifer Hutsal, Autumn Dickman, Cynthia Kirkland and Kalpana Bhandarkar provided administrative and other support.

Feroza Fitch of Lexicon Graphics provided typesetting and design services.

The creation, publication, and distribution of this book were underwritten by an endowment gift from the DeWitt-Wallace Reader's Digest Fund.

Media inquiries should be directed to Gigi Hinton.

Contents

It's Time!

*"O Lord, how long shall I cry for help, and you will not listen?
Or cry to you 'Violence!' and you will not save? Why do You make me see
wrong-doing and look at trouble? Destruction and violence are before me; strife and
contention arise. So the law becomes slack and justice never prevails."*

The prophet Habakkuk's complaint to God

*"Write the vision; make it plain on tablets, so that a runner may read it.
For there is still a vision for the appointed time... If it seems to tarry, wait for it;
it will surely come, it will not delay. Look at the proud!
Their spirit is not right in them, but the righteous live by their faith.
Moreover, wealth is treacherous; the arrogant do not endure."*

God's reply to Habakkuk

"In our own time revive it; in our own time make it known."

Habakkuk's plea to God

It's time! It's time to build a mighty movement to Leave No Child Behind® in the richest and most powerful nation on earth. I hope you will be a part of it.

It's time! An incredible magical moment in history which few human beings have been blessed to experience. A new millennium. A new century. A new decade. How will we say thanks to God for the earth, nation, and children entrusted to our care? How can we make "hope and history rhyme" in poet Seamus Heaney's marvelous words?

It's time! A time of political transition. A new president who repeatedly has used CDF's trademarked mission words and promised to Leave No Child Behind®. A new Congress. Hundreds of new state, county, and city officials throughout our nation.

It's time! The wealthiest time in American history. A $10 trillion American economy. Eight years of unprecedented economic growth. A projected multi-trillion dollar federal budget surplus over the next 10 years. Number one in billionaires and millionaires. The top Gross National Product in the world. Many state budget surpluses. Hundreds of billions of dollars of state tobacco settlement monies. Billions more dollars still unspent by some states from welfare and child health legislation.

It's time! An era of stunning American intellectual, technological, and scientific achievement: 168 Nobel prize winners in science this past century. We've sent humans to the moon, spaceships to Mars, cracked the genetic code, amassed tens of billions of dollars from a tiny microchip, and discovered cures for diseases which give hope to millions if they can access treatment. We can transmit information faster than we can digest it and buy anything we desire instantly on-line in our global shopping arcade. Why can't we teach all our children to read by fourth grade?

It's time! Unrivaled American military leadership in a globalizing world. An arsenal of nuclear warheads that exceeds by at least 5,000 our agreed upon needs under the Strategic Arms Limitation Treaty. A conventional military force of questionable suitability for the unconventional wars that spread across the world. An arms export business that exceeds $50 billion a year. A military budget five times that of Russia, eight times that of China, twice that of all the other NATO countries combined, and twenty times the combined spending of the seven "Rogue States" (Cuba, Iran, Iraq, Libya, North Korea, Sudan, and Syria) we have designated as our principal enemies in a post-cold war era. Our president proposes spending $618,000 a minute, $6.25 billion a week, and $27 billion a month to maintain our military defenses. We can kill more people quicker and at once than ever before through nuclear arms, chemical warfare, and assault weapons. Even children can become mass killers at home and child soldiers around the world.

It's time! A churning new world order is being born. Changing rules of doing global business are creating important new questions, challenges, and opportunities. Who will gain and who will be left behind? Will the life chances of the poor, women, and children be enhanced or exploited? Will powerful corporate interests eviscerate or respect democratic nation–state decision making processes? Will multinational conglomerates be accountable to or run roughshod over communities and citizens in pursuit of quicker and bigger profits? Will the changing nature of work and the demands of the new economy strengthen or weaken family and community life and job security? Will cultural homogenization and corporate branding contribute to or detract from the rich diversity of the world's peoples? How can we close the spiraling digital, health, income, and education divides between the rich and the poor of the world and at home? Can we develop a concept of enough for those at the bottom and at the top so that the common good, stability, and our children's futures will be preserved?

Just four wealthy Americans possess greater wealth than the GNP of the 34 least developed nations in the world with over 650 million people. *Harper's* magazine estimated in 1997 that 240,183 people could be fed for *one year* with the food we Americans *waste* in *one day*. The gaping divide between rich and poor nations is mirrored in the gap between rich and poor in our own country. The wealth of these four richest Americans exceeds that of 14 million American families combined, exceeds the revenues of 24 state governments with 42 million citizens, and could lift 12 million children out of poverty five times over.

Since 1979, the top 5 percent (3.6 million) of American families saw their average income increase by $101,000 or 66 percent, while the bottom 20 percent (14.4 million families) lost $184 a year from their average income of $13,500 in 1999 dollars. In 1999, chief corporate officers' pay ballooned by $1.8 million to a new high of $12.4 million each, six times what they made as recently as 1990 and 475 times more than the average blue-collar worker. They made 800 times more than the average child care worker who helps shape children in the formative early years and earns $7.42 an hour, $15,430 a year. They made 315 times more than the average public school teacher who earns $39,300 a year.

Between 1999 and 2000, the U.S. economy grew by half a trillion dollars, the largest single-year jump ever recorded. This increase alone was 13 times the amount needed to end child poverty in America which afflicts over 12 million American children — one in six. Although 78 percent of poor children lived in households where someone worked in 1999, their increased work effort did not get them ahead.

The decline in eligible people receiving government health, child care, food, and cash assistance following the 1996 welfare law because of poor state outreach, impenetrable state bureaucracy, and the welfare law's exclusion of legal immigrants pushed thousands of already poor children into deeper poverty: 26 percent (2.4 million) of poor children lived in extreme poverty in 1999, compared to 21 percent in 1996 after accounting for taxes, cash, and noncash income.

> "America, at its best, is compassionate. In the quiet of America's conscience, we know that deep, persistent poverty is unworthy of our nation's promise. And whatever our views of its cause, we can agree that children at risk are not at fault."
> --President George W. Bush, Inaugural Address, January 20, 2001

Homelessness blights our national landscape and stalks even those who work every day. Rents have increased at twice the rate of inflation and available housing units have declined. Less than 30 percent of low-income renters get any housing subsidy. Emergency shelter needs rose in 25 cities the Conference of Mayors reports. High child care and housing costs not only leave many families homeless and hungry, they cause many families to break up. I heard heartbreaking stories of Chinese families in New York City who sent their young children back to China for many years because both parents worked long hours and could not find or afford reliable child care. I heard about working parents forced to place their children in foster care or unable to have them return home because they were homeless. In Phoenix, Arizona I visited a large school

Choices: Tax Cuts for the Wealthy or Investments in Children and Families

President Bush is proposing a $1.6 trillion tax cut over 10 years which will dramatically increase the gap between the rich and poor — already the largest in history — unless it is scaled back and better targeted on middle- and low-income families and their children.

The top 1 percent of families with incomes over $373,000 would receive 45 percent of the benefits; the top 5 percent (with incomes over $147,000) would receive 52 percent; those in the bottom 60 percent (with incomes below $44,000) would receive 28.4 percent of the benefits; those in the bottom 20 percent (with incomes below $15,000) would receive 0.8 percent.

53 percent of Black and Hispanic families with children would receive no tax relief. This includes 6.1 million Black children (55 percent of all Black children) and 6.5 million Hispanic children (56 percent of all Hispanic children).

For the $1.6 trillion tax cut President Bush says we can afford, we could close the child poverty gap, make all the investments children need to be healthy and educated, and have billions of dollars left over.

A Refundable Child Tax Credit to Help All And Not Just Some Children

President Bush is proposing to double the Child Tax Credit from $500 to $1,000 and lift the ceiling of those eligible from $110,000 to $200,000 in recognition of the cost of raising children. We support this if he extends it to all children by making the Child Tax Credit *refundable* to families without federal income tax liability but who do pay payroll and other taxes. Unless the tax is made *refundable*, more than 16 million children will be left behind in families for whom the $1,000 benefit would make the most difference. A working family with income between $15,000 - $20,000 needs help with the cost of raising their children more than a family with a $200,000 income. If the tax is made refundable, two million children would be lifted out of poverty — one-sixth of all poor children — a giant step towards CDF's goal of reducing child poverty by half by 2004.

for homeless children, wondering the entire time why in the name of God decent housing, jobs, and job training for parents were not the highest priorities? Shelters are no places for children who are daily humiliated when peers learn they have no home. In inner-city schools I heard about children who changed schools every few months as their parents tried to stay one step ahead of the landlord making a good education impossible. School mobility rates — the number of students who change schools in a year — of 60, 70, and 80 percent are not uncommon, educators told me. I've talked to mayors about the increase in homeless families during a time when the economy is "as good as it gets" and I get angry as many states clamor for more federal money without accountability when they have

billions of unspent block grant funds to help children and working families. It's shameful that some states are failing to inform eligible working families about available food, health, housing, and child care benefits, and are creating complicated application procedures that families can't figure out and renewal barriers which contribute to child and family poverty.

It's time for a profound culture change among state and local governments — and all of us — if children are to thrive and working parents are to become self-sufficient. Every governor needs to lead this culture change and show that states can and will more efficiently help their own children being left behind.

It's Time! It's Time to Heed Dr. King's Warning and Realize His Dream

*"Woe to the legislators of infamous laws ... who refuse justice to the unfortunate and
cheat the poor among my people."*
(Isaiah 10:1-2)

*"We read the Gospel as if we had no money and we spend our money
as if we know nothing of the Gospel."*
Jesuit theologian John Haughey quoted in the *Biblical Jubilee
and The Struggle for Life* by Ross Kinsler and Gloria Kinsler

*"The fundamental problem for the poor in our country is not homelessness.
It's not AIDS. It's not hunger. It's not any one, or even any combination, of the many targets of our
charitable work. The fundamental problem is an economic, governmental, social, and
religious system that undergirds inequality, and creates injustice."*
Dr. David Hilfiker, "Justice and the Limits of Charity," author, *Not All of Us Are Saints*

The day after Dr. King's assassination on April 4, 1968, the pent-up rage, hurt, and grief of poor Black communities exploded in riots across America. As smoke swirled through the air of Washington, D.C., I visited several public schools to urge children not to loot, risk arrest, and jeopardize their futures. A 12-year-old boy looked me straight in the eye and said, "Lady, what future? I ain't got no future. I ain't got nothing to lose."

He spoke much truth — a truth I and many others have spent the 33 years since Dr. King's death trying to change. I never dreamed it would be so *hard.* That child's truth is a truth Dr. King died trying to *get* us to do something about. He reminded us of the parable of the rich man Dives and the poor man Lazarus in a sermon at the Washington National Cathedral the Sunday before his death. "Dives did not go to hell because of his wealth," Dr. King said, "but because he refused to see and help his brother." He feared America could make the same mistake and warned that our wealth could be either our opportunity or our downfall. He called for a Poor People's Campaign to help bridge the gulf between the haves and the have nots. "The question is whether America will do it. There is nothing new about poverty. What is new is that we now have the techniques and the resources to get rid of poverty. The real question is whether we have the will."

That is still the real and even more urgent question in a $10 trillion American economy that has tripled in real value since Dr. King's death. Although America has made enormous racial and economic progress in many areas, huge inequalities remain. In 1968, 11 million American children — 15.6 percent — were poor; in 1999, 12.1 million American children —16.9 percent — were poor.

Child poverty is not an act of God. It is our moral and political choice as a nation as our great progress in decreasing poverty among the elderly shows. In 1968, 25 percent of those 65 or over were poor; in 1999, 9.7 percent were poor. Although the senior poverty rate decreased more than 60 percent over this period, the child poverty rate increased 8 percent. The child poverty rate used to be one-third less than the senior poverty rate; now it is three-fourths more.

Economist Rebecca Blank points out that if we asked churches to pay the costs of just three government programs for the poor — welfare for families, disability payments for the poor, and food stamps — every single church, synagogue, mosque, and other religious congregation in the country would have to come up with an extra $300,000.

Choices: Military Defense and the Domestic Defense of Children

Instead of spending the $4 billion appropriated in Fiscal Year 2001 to build new F-22s, we could:

◆ provide all eligible 3- and 4-year-olds a Head Start and nearly double the number of infants and toddlers in Early Head Start; or

◆ provide 1.2 million children in working families quality child care; or

◆ enable 5.7 million youths to participate in the 21st Century Community Learning Centers after-school program; or

◆ provide 2.8 million uninsured children health coverage.

Instead of spending $2.9 billion in FY 2001 to build 42 F/A-18 E/F Navy Super Hornet planes or spending the same amount to build 12 C-17 Air Force Airlift Aircraft, we could:

◆ provide 250,000 children a Head Start; or

◆ provide 860,000 children in working families quality child care; or

◆ enable 4.1 million youths to participate in the 21st Century Community Learning Centers program; or

◆ provide 2 million uninsured children health coverage.

Instead of spending $1.7 billion in FY 2001 on the construction of 20 V-22 Navy Osprey aircraft, we could:

◆ provide 150,000 children a Head Start; or

◆ provide 510,000 children in working families quality child care; or

◆ enable 2.4 million youths to participate in the 21st Century Community Learning Centers program; or

◆ provide 1.2 million uninsured children health coverage.

Child hunger was virtually eliminated in the 1970s thanks to the events set in motion by an outraged Senator Robert Kennedy. After seeing the bloated bellies of hungry children on his visit to the Mississippi Delta in 1967, he returned to Washington determined to do something about it. His passionate concern catalyzed a series of changes that led to an expansion of child and family nutrition programs during the Nixon administration years. He encouraged doctors to go out into poor communities to examine children and to document hunger. He convinced Agriculture Secretary Orville Freeman to reduce food stamp barriers after sending Freeman's disbelieving staff to see first hand that there really were people in Mississippi with *no income*. He encouraged CBS' *60 Minutes* to do a documentary and encouraged fellow senators to hold hearings to make visible the existence of hungry children across America. Hearing my despair later that year over the continuing suffering of Mississippi's poor after his

earlier visit, he told me to tell Dr. King to bring the poor to Washington to make their needs visible and to make our political leaders act. We both feared the Vietnam War was diverting more and more attention from the struggle against poverty at home.

How sad to see the success in ending child hunger in the 1970s reversed during the Reagan years as a result of massive tax breaks to the rich and the biggest military build-up in history. These unfair choices were paid for by tens of billions of dollars of cuts in safety net programs for poor children and families and a huge national debt we are still paying the interest on to the tune of $400 billion a year. The interest on the debt alone is enough to lift every child from poverty and to pay for all their health care, child care, education, youth development, and after-school programs we are calling for in the comprehensive Act to Leave No Child Behind. The Act

A t a Stand For Children Child Care Rally in Benton County, Oregon, child care provider Carry Hector said: "For the past five years I have been a director at a local quality child care center in Corvallis. Every day I watch 50 young children, infants through school age, come to my center learning the most valuable skills of their lives. I love what I do, but honestly, it is a struggle. I watch my parents struggle with the rising cost of tuition. Just two weeks ago, a parent's tuition check bounced, and another owes me $48 but only has $45 until she gets paid. Should I take this woman's last dollar? Should I dis-enroll a single parent for lack of payment? Or should I wait until her tax return comes in and she can pay me? These two are lucky. Many more cannot even afford to enroll because the cost is too high. My staff struggles, giving everything they have to the children. They work long hours and can barely make a living in a profession they love. When we can't afford to buy glue, crayons, paper, or basic developmental materials, it is often teachers who on their limited salaries go and purchase these items. The salaries at our school range from $6.50 to $7.40 per hour. I'd love to pay more, but it is all I can afford to continue providing this service to Benton County communities. The last time I had a teaching position open, I had two qualified applicants. When I told them what the pay was, they both declined the position. What other choice does this leave me? I have a bachelor's degree in pre-school education from Oregon State University and I have worked with children and families for over eight years. I agonize and lose sleep over keeping my staff and replacing those who cannot afford to stay in the profession. Like other directors I've spoken with, I too often struggle to find enough money for payroll. As a provider, I bring home $300 per *month* if I am lucky. Given how important early childhood education is in the lives of all our children, I don't think it should be this way. The issue is not about paying teachers what they deserve because that is impossible. It is about keeping qualified people in the profession of early childhood education for the safety and health of all of our children."

incorporates CDF's policy vision of what any great nation should assure all its children.

If at this turn of an era we let our nation repeat the unjust economic choices of the 1980s as some of our political leaders seek to do, shame on us! If you and I don't stand up and courageously speak for the millions of children left behind right now after eight years of prosperity, who will?

America is jeopardizing its future and its soul.

◆ Every 44 seconds, an American baby is born into poverty.

◆ Every minute, a baby is born without health insurance.

◆ Every 2 minutes, a baby is born at low birthweight.

◆ Every 11 minutes, a child is reported abused or neglected.

◆ Every 2 hours and 20 minutes, a child or youth under 20 is killed by a gun — 10 every day!

Each of these statistics is a real child like Antonio. Maria, his young mother, was sent home with Antonio the day he was born. Only she didn't have a home. She was a single parent with no extended family support. But she loved her baby and within the limits of public assistance found a small room. About three months later, Maria called the health clinic to report her baby was sick. The nurse told Maria to bring him in. Maria said she didn't have transportation. The nurse asked for the baby's symptoms, and upon hearing that the baby had diarrhea for two days, concluded he had a flu virus that was going around and advised the mother to keep the baby hydrated. "Feed the baby liquids every hour. Pedialyte or apple juice is good." Maria went to the refrigerator. She certainly didn't have Pedialyte, apple juice, or even ice. In her cupboard, she did have tomato sauce, so she filled the baby's bottle with tomato sauce and stayed up all night, feeding him every hour on the hour. The sodium content of the tomato sauce accelerated Antonio's dehydration and by morning his tiny body was lifeless. Should any parent in rich America have to watch a child die because she does not have enough food or cannot afford transportation to get needed health care?

Poor Children Come In All Colors and Live in Every Family Type and Region

78 percent	live in families where somebody worked all or part of the time in 1999, up from 61 percent in 1993.
57 percent	live in female-headed families, up from 45 percent in 1969.
37 percent	live in married-couple families, down from 38 percent in 1988.
43 percent	live in two-parent or father-only families, down from 55 percent in 1969.
62 percent	are White, up from 60 percent in 1969.
31 percent	are Black, down from 39 percent in 1969.
29 percent	are Hispanic, up from 14 percent in 1973.
3 percent	are Asian or Pacific Islander.
30 percent	live in young families, headed by a person younger than 30.
57 percent	live in suburban and rural areas, down from 67 percent in 1969.

A three-person family was poor in 1999 if it made less than $13,290. The average poor family with children had just $9,211 in total income: $768 a month, $177 a week, or $25 a day.

69 percent	of that income was from work — $ 6,322 a year, $527 a month, $122 a week, or $17 a day.
15 percent	of that income was from welfare — $1,400 a year, $117 a month, $27 a week, or $4 a day.

A Texas mother with an $8 an hour salary and no health insurance described her stressful dilemma when her daughter woke her up in the middle of the night gasping for breath saying her inhaler was broken. The mother had to debate whether to rush her child to the emergency room or to an all-night drugstore for an over-the-counter remedy she prayed would work. She realized later that for $88 she was gambling with her child's life. Should any parent or child face this draconian choice in rich America? Why doesn't every 6- and 16-year-old have Medicare-type health coverage from birth as every senior citizen has Medicare when they reach a certain age?

"We are obliged to make sure that every child gets a healthy start in life. With all of our wealth and capacity, we just can't stand by idly...We must make sure that every child in America has access to quality health care. We owe them nothing less. It has to be done. It is our responsibility to do that for our children."
—Secretary of State Colin Powell, Address at Republican National Convention, July 31, 2000

Through CDF's Community Monitoring Project, which documents the impact of the 1996 welfare changes on poor mothers and children, we learned of a 45-year-old North Carolina mother with an 11-year-old daughter who had left welfare for a job. She was working 38 hours a week at $6 an hour and was proud to have been named employee of the month. After leaving welfare she lost her housing and was living in a transitional homeless shelter with her daughter. She had no health insurance and has been unable to pay medical bills for herself or for her daughter. She earned a few dollars more than the official poverty line but not enough to make ends meet. Why should a parent working hard every day be unable to find a stable place to live with her child?

It's time to end child poverty as we know it beginning with reducing it by half by 2004. If President George W. Bush seizes the opportunity and makes his proposal to double the Child Tax Credit from $500 to $1,000 *refundable*, two million children could escape poverty immediately — one-sixth of all poor children. If he and Congress fail to pass and make the Child Tax Credit refundable, 16 million children will be left behind — one in four of all children.

The Mission of the Movement to Leave No Child Behind. What You Can Do

O God, grant us Your vision in our time
Help us to write it so large that even a runner can see it.
Make it so compelling that even a cynic will pause,
so convincing that a skeptic will risk trying to bring hope to others,
and so inspiring that the committed will stand courageously in faith
leaving the results to You.

My prayer to God today

During his great life, Dr. King shared his dream of an America that would judge children not by the color of their skin, the stylishness of their clothes and cars, or the size of their bank accounts, but by the content of their character. In March 1968, Senator Robert Kennedy urged us in a University of Kansas speech not to surrender "community excellence and community values to the mere accumulation of material things," and said the Gross National Product (GNP) was a very poor measurement for what is important in life. He said it did not count the health of our children, the quality of their education, the joy of their play, the strength of our marriages, the intelligence of our public debate, the integrity of our public officials, or our courage and wisdom. "The GNP measures everything," he said, "except that which makes life worthwhile."

It's time. It's time to redefine the measure of success at this turning point in history. It's time to lead our children out of the wilderness of poverty, violence, greed, selfishness, triviality, banality, and materialism into a promised land of hope and opportunity and community. We can do this by setting forth a comprehensive national vision of what it means to Leave No Child Behind; by breaking the vision down into manageable goals for action each year; by building a visible, persistent, and powerful witness of presence in support of sensible and just policies for children; and by organizing powerful well trained grassroots and grasstops networks. We must not let the words Leave No Child Behind become a fig leaf for unjust political and policy choices that in fact will leave millions of children and the poor behind, turn the clock of child progress back, and widen the chasm between the have-too-muches and the have-too-littles.

Never has the time been riper to set forth a big moral and policy vision for children. Never has the time been riper for child advocates to seize the mantle of leadership to build a nation fit for children. Never has the time been riper to transform America's shameful child neglect and poverty into a bounty of hope and opportunity for the world to see and emulate.

The real challenge is not *what* to do for children but *how* to build the spiritual and civic will to achieve what all children need for all children. How do we build a broad-based movement to Leave No Child Behind that has the transforming power of the civil rights, anti-war, and environmental movements of the 1960s and 1970s? How do we evoke in the American people the same deep ingrained national commitment to voteless children that existed to protect elderly Americans from poverty, hunger, and social isolation? How do we move children's needs to the top of community, state, and national agendas regardless of who is in office? How do we mobilize and organize a critical mass of Americans to demand concrete major actions from policy makers and then hold them accountable? How do we present a bold, visionary, and comprehensive agenda that covers all of children's needs, rather than piecemeal, fragmented incremental steps that do not resonate beyond the beltway, state capitals, or policy wonks? How do we bring together disparate child advocates and service providers (child care, child welfare, child health, education, youth development, juvenile justice, and violence prevention) with powerful mainstream networks (faith, women, parents and grandparents, youths, and health professionals) to support, strengthen, and achieve an inspiring big vision to protect the whole child and family

We Cannot Afford Not to Invest in Our Children ...

◆ A dollar invested in good early childhood programs for low-income children saves $7.00.

◆ A dollar invested in immunizations against diptheria, tetanus, and whooping cough saves $23.00.

◆ A dollar spent in the Women, Infants and Children (WIC) nutritional program saves $3.07 during a baby's first year.

◆ The average cost of providing a year of Head Start for one child is $5,403.

◆ The average cost of keeping a person in prison for a year is $20,000.

◆ Every year we allow a child to grow up in poverty costs $9,000 in lost future productivity over his or her working life.

and to rebuild community and a sense of common space and purpose as a nation?

It's time. It's time to assure every child a *Healthy Start,* a *Head Start,* a *Fair Start,* a *Safe Start,* and a *Moral Start* and successful passage to adulthood. It's time to withdraw our permission from America's official child neglect and abuse and to sow seeds of hope and empowerment in communities, schools, congregations, and homes all across America until they grow into a mighty torrent of demand for justice. We *can* stop our leaders from investing in prisons and death and start them investing in life — in health care, early childhood and parent training and support, and education. We *can* stop them investing in what we know does not work — missile defense systems, F22s, juvenile detention centers, and boot camps — and start them investing in what does work: Head Start, immunizations, after-school programs, and parental jobs with decent wages that lift them from poverty. We *can* stop our leaders from passing another round of unjust tax cuts and increased welfare for rich corporations and individuals and start them closing the fairness gap by investing in targeted tax policies which offer middle- and low-income families relief.

That is what this movement to Leave No Child Behind will do with your help.

The Vision: As we enter the 21st century, America's strength reflects our courage, our compassion, our hard work, our moral values, and our commitment to justice. Today, we can extend the American dream of our forefathers and foremothers to every child and family. We have the know-how, the experience, the tools, and the resources. And we have the responsibility as mothers,

fathers, grandparents — concerned and sensible people across the country.

We can build a nation where families have the support they need to make it at work and at home; where every child enters school ready to learn and leaves on the path to a productive future; where babies are likely to be born healthy, and sick children have the health care they need; where no child has to grow up in poverty; where all children are safe in their communities and every child has a place to call home — and all Americans can proudly say "We Leave No Child Behind."

Our mission and vision in the months ahead is to do what it takes to meet the needs of children and their parents by building on the strengths and sense of fairness of the American people, learning from the best public and private ideas and successes, and moving forward to a renewed commitment to all our children.

A Key Policy Pathway: Working with a range of national, state, and local child advocacy networks and members of Congress, CDF has developed the comprehensive Act to Leave No Child Behind as a key way to embody this vision and to move forward for children. Any state or local community should feel free to adopt such a comprehensive approach. The Act gives the President, Congress, and all Americans the opportunity to:

◆ Ensure every child and their parents health insurance.

◆ Lift every child from poverty — half by 2004; all by 2010.

◆ End child hunger through the expansion of food programs.

◆ Get every child ready for school through full funding of quality Head Start, child care, and preschool programs.

◆ Make sure every child can read by fourth grade and can graduate from school able to succeed at work and in life.

◆ Provide every child safe, quality after-school and summer programs so children can learn, serve, work, and stay out of trouble.

◆ Ensure every child a place called home and decent affordable housing.

◆ Protect all children from neglect, abuse, and violence and ensure them the care they need.

◆ Ensure families leaving welfare the supports needed to be successful in the workplace, including health care, child care, and transportation.

The twelve titles of the Act to Leave No Child Behind add up to a comprehensive whole because children do not come in pieces. They live in families and communities who need the capacity to support them. The Act is achievable because it builds on the best ideas for helping children and because we have all the resources we need to provide them. The Act is timely because our nation is at a pivotal point as we debate what kind of moral, community, policy, and political choices we are prepared to make at this turn of century and millennium to realize a more just and compassionate society — one where no child is left behind.

How Will We Achieve Our Vision? *By building a powerful grassroots and grasstops movement across America through Wednesdays in Washington and Back Home and other public awareness and engagement efforts.* In 1964, interracial teams of women with a variety of talents and skills went to Mississippi to bear witness every Wednesday for racial justice and to build bridges between White and Black women across income and racial lines. Each was required to get training and to commit to work back home to inform and mobilize their communities about what they saw and what could be done. On Wednesdays — in Washington and Back Home — we are calling on women (especially mothers, grandmothers, and all those with a mothering spirit), people of faith, youths, senior citizens, child advocates, and concerned citizens from all walks of life to take action for children in this new era until the words Leave No Child Behind and the Act to Leave No Child Behind become reality for every child. Everybody can be a part of the movement who shares our mission.

In addition to Wednesdays in Washington and Back Home we will use every means possible to raise public awareness about children's needs and what can be done, including Stand For Children Day events in all 50 states on June 1st; Child Watch visits to expose community leaders and policy makers to children's needs and what they can do; television, radio, and print media campaigns; town meetings; prayer vigils; study circles; and house parties. Coalition building, nonviolence, media skills and organizing training to build a critical mass of effective advocates will be an ongoing and integral part of our movement building in Washington, at Haley farm, and in states and regions.

A Few Things to Remember and a Few Barriers to Overcome

"I have not the shadow of a doubt that any man or woman can achieve what I have, if he or she makes the same effort and cultivates the same hope and faith."

Gandhi

"In a certain city there was a judge who neither feared God nor had respect for people. In that city there was a widow who kept coming to him and saying, 'Grant me justice against my opponent.' For a while he refused; but later he said to himself, 'Though I have no fear of God and no respect for anyone, yet because the widow keeps bothering me, I will grant her justice, so that she may not wear me out by continually coming.' "

The parable of the widow and the unjust judge (Luke 18: 2-5)

One: We are called to act truthfully, faithfully, and justly and to leave the results to God. Pray always and do not lose heart. I believe God will grant justice to those who cry out day and night as the widow and the unjust judge parable promises. No one can know in advance how or when one will be used, or what one's life will count for in the long run. I read somewhere that the young Pablo Casals, while pouring his life energy into years of practice on the cello, could not guess then that when Franco came to power, he would stop playing for three years and that the silence would be heard throughout Spain as if the streets were full of demonstrators.

Two: Do the thing you think you cannot do as Eleanor Roosevelt urged. Let's constantly challenge our fears. I struggle with my fears every hour of every day and make so many excuses for not answering God's call to be more courageous in standing up for children. I blame other people or lack of time or energy or ability or family to avoid doing what I know needs to be done to build the movement that is required to get our leaders and citizens to hear and to act. I am afraid of failing and looking like a fool. I am afraid of risking CDF's hard-earned credibility built laboriously over nearly three decades. I am afraid of being criticized and marginalized by friends and foes alike. I am afraid of all the back-biting from people who ought to be allies but who are more interested in organizational turf and self-promotion than children and the poor. I'm afraid of getting dragged into partisan politics by some who would rather have a great issue to get the House and Senate back than to win great victories for children and protect the nation's future which require bi-partisan support.

Three: Don't ever give in to despair or fatigue. You are not alone. On a particularly discouraging day, my spiritual director shared a piece of paper by an unknown author about a battle weary soldier asking God for a transfer. That's me! (*See* Request for Transfer *on the next page.*)

Four: Be clear about what you believe in and stick with it. Some of us will do anything to be at worldly tables of power: to be invited to the White House or the governor's house for lunch or dinner or for a meeting.

Some of us think power derives solely from association with political, media, entertainment, and other celebrities. If you are not on television you do not exist and are not important. Before former President Clinton addressed the National Baptist Convention in 1996, while the debate on shredding the income safety net for poor children was at a high point, I am told that the thousands of Black religious leaders rose to their feet in a roar of joy when the presidential seal was attached to the podium. I wondered if the Cross got the same ovation? It's time for congregations to open their doors and hearts to our children and compete with drug dealers and gangs for our children's hearts and souls. It's time for faith in action seven days a week and for religious leaders to challenge rather than mirror the culture which treats children unjustly.

Five: Set priorities and don't weigh yourself down with your own or other people's clutter. I am nearly paralyzed by all the things and tasks I have burdened myself with. Focus. Use what you know works and build on your strengths. The shepherd boy David could not have moved with the heavy armor King Saul offered. He wisely relied instead on the slingshot and stones he had used to slay lions and bears to slay the giant Goliath. Do not let others choose your weapons of battle. Jesus, Gandhi, and Dr. King chose nonviolence rather than the violence the world relies on and chose to return good for the evil their opponents meted out.

Six: Don't wait for or expect all your doubts to ever subside or disappear. They never will. Thomas Merton said, "You do not need to know precisely what is happening or exactly where it is all going. What you need is to recognize the challenges and opportunities offered by the present moment and to embrace them with courage, faith, and hope." Real learning comes through doing. Real relationships and communication are the fruit of common engagement and struggle. Real faith is acting on your concerns. Real success usually comes only after failures and trial and error. Let's believe in the truth of our mission just as scientists believe in a truth they seek to discover through trial and error. It is the seeking and trying that life is about.

REQUEST FOR TRANSFER

To: Commander-in-Chief
From: Battlefield Soldier
Subject: Request for Transfer

Dear Lord,

I'm writing this to You to request a transfer to a desk job. I herewith present my reasons:

I began my career as a private, but because of the intensity of the battle, You quickly moved me up in the ranks. You made me an officer and gave me a tremendous amount of responsibility. There are many soldiers and recruits under my charge. I'm constantly being called upon to dispense wisdom, make judgments, and find solutions to complex problems.

You placed me in a position to function as an officer, when in my heart I know I have only the skills of a private. I realize that You promised to supply all I would need for the battle. But sire, I must present You a realistic picture of my equipment. My uniform, once so crisp and starched, is now stained with the tears and blood of those I have tried to help. The soles of my boots are cracked and worn from the miles I have walked trying to enlist and encourage the troops.

My weapons are marred, tarnished, and chipped from constant battle against the enemy. Even the Book of Regulations I was issued has been torn and tattered from endless use. The words are now smeared.

You promised You would be with me throughout the war, but when the noise of the battle is so loud and the confusion is so great, I can neither see nor hear You. I feel so alone. I'm tired. I'm discouraged. I have battle fatigue.

I'd never ask for a discharge. I love being in Your service. But I humbly request a demotion and transfer. I'll file papers or clean latrines. Just get me out of the battle — please, sir.

> Your faithful, but tired, soldier,
> John/Jane Q. Servant

To: Faithful but Tired Soldier
From: Commander-in-Chief
Subject: Request for Transfer

Dear Soldier:

Your request for transfer has been denied. I herewith present My reasons:

You are needed in the battle. I have selected you, and I gave My word to supply your need. You do not need a demotion and transfer. (You'd never cut it on latrine duty.) You need a period of "R and R" — renewal and rekindling. I am setting aside a place on the battlefield that is insulated from all sound and fully protected from the enemy. I will meet you there, and I will give you rest. I will remove your old equipment and make all things new.

You have been wounded in the battle, My soldier. Your wounds are not visible, but you have received grave internal injuries. I will heal you. You have been weakened in the battle. I will strengthen you, and I will be your strength. I will instill in you confidence and ability. My Words will rekindle within you a renewed love, zeal, and enthusiasm.

Report to Me tattered and empty. I will refill you.

> Compassionately,
> Your Commander-in-Chief, God

Seven: Don't be a sunshine, prime-time only advocate. Don't let political rain and storms stop the movement for our children. A successful movement to Leave No Child Behind requires all-weather advocates who will carry on with discipline and grit whatever the political weather. Advocates who want to play only within the bounds of current political possibility are not wanted. We must change the rules of the political game controlled by a few power brokers hidden from public view. Sprinter-advocates and one-time fast runners who tire out and leave after the first heat need not sign up. Long-distance, steady, persistent runners who will keep moving towards the finish line of justice for children are required. Face time advocates who stand for children when the media is there but are gone when they are not should go elsewhere. Children need advocates who do the hard, quiet, thankless, day-to-day work of building community infrastructure and capacity, putting out alerts and following up with phone calls, preparing for meetings and making sure that action and not just talk results, and who read and catch the devilish details behind politicians' flowery promises. Dabblers stay home. Children need disciplined nonviolent supporters who do not try to steal the children's show for themselves and are devoted to winning for children however long it takes.

Eight: Don't be glum or self-righteous. Henry Ward Beecher said, "I can stand reforms, but I can't stomach reformers." We need some fun in our lives. I sure do! Doing good and helping children and the poor should be joyful. I have to struggle every day to remember this as I get caught up in Washington's policy and political treadmill. We can disagree strongly on policies and priorities with each other and with those who are of a different party, faith, or ideology without being disagreeable or disrespectful or turning political differences into personal vendettas. People who think they are right or know it sometimes tend to be intolerant of those who differ making it more difficult to draw adversaries closer and find common ground. We must make our "enemies" our friends, Abraham Lincoln taught as he invited his strongest opponent to join his cabinet.

Nine: Make integrity our foundation. Integrity and nonviolence must ground the children's movement in the 21st century. We must struggle — sinners and penitents all — to be the change we preach and seek. We cannot call on others — especially our young — to change their ways if we do not change ours or offer a more excellent way. I believe adult hypocrisy is the biggest problem children face in America. "You must watch my life," Gandhi said, "how I live, eat, sit, talk, behave in general. The sum total of all those in me is my religion."

Ten: Stand up and be courageous as God ordered Joshua four times and promised to be with him as he led the Hebrew people out of the wilderness into the promised land. Father Walter Burghardt told a story at Haley farm about a Sufi mystic who complained to God about how terrible the state of the world was and asked God to do something! God replied, "I did. I made you." And God made you and me. God's spirit is planted within enabling each of us ordinary humans to do extraordinary things. God used women marginalized by those in power as mighty instruments for transforming change. Two slave midwives, Shiprah and Puah, shrewdly defied the Pharaoh's order to kill all boy Hebrew babies. Moses' mother, sister, and a Pharaoh's daughter protected the slave baby Moses whom God later raised up to lead the Hebrew people from Egypt. The example of these five women who defied worldly power has been repeated again and again in history as women acted. An American slave woman, Harriet Tubman, ushered slaves to freedom on the Underground Railroad. Another slave woman, Sojourner Truth, consistently spoke out against slavery and unjust treatment of women and vowed to keep her enslavers "scratching." South African women fought and helped win an end to murderous apartheid policies. Dorothy Day, co-founder of the Catholic Worker Movement, dedicated her work and her life to the poor and homeless and speaking boldly about the duty one owed to one's neighbor — "anyone in need." Sister Katherine Drexel used her fortune to educate Black and Native American youths and helped found Xavier University in New Orleans. Jane Addams and other prominent women "settlers" started settlement houses and worked for the poor and for peace.

How America Stands Among Industrialized Countries

The United States ranks:

1st	in military technology
1st	in military exports
1st	in Gross Domestic Product
1st	in the number of millionaires and billionaires
1st	in health technology
1st	in defense expenditures
10th	in eighth grade science scores
11th	in the proportion of children in poverty
16th	in efforts to lift children out of poverty
16th	in living standards among our poorest one-fifth of children
17th	in low birthweight rates
18th	in the gap between rich and poor children
21st	in eighth grade math scores
23rd	in infant mortality
Last	in protecting our children against gun violence

According to the Centers for Disease Control and Prevention, U.S. children under age 15 are:

9	times more likely to die in a firearm accident
11	times more likely to commit suicide with a gun
12	times more likely to die from gunfire, and
16	times more likely to be murdered with a gun

than children in 25 other industrialized countries *combined*.

Of the 154 members of the United Nations, the United States and Somalia (which has no legally constituted government) are the only two nations that have failed to ratify the U.N. Convention on the Rights of the Child.

Poor women in India struggling to feed their children and families walked with empty plates and spoons to protest rising food prices. Rachel Carson's groundbreaking book *Silent Spring* launched the modern environmental movement in the United States. Hundreds of years earlier, courageous environmental pioneer Amrita Devi gave her life to protect the trees in her village because she believed them sacred. Her sacrifice inspired others who repeated her sacrifice and saved the trees and sparked the Chipko Movement in India. Thousands of Chilean women faced death and demonstrated in the streets to demand the resignation of a military junta leader. Black women were the backbone of the American civil rights movement: Mrs. Rosa Parks, Septima Clark, Ella Baker, Fannie Lou Hamer, Mae Bertha Carter, Diane Nash, Victoria Gray, and little girls and boys like Ruby Bridges, the Little Rock Nine, and the Carter children who walked through taunting crowds and sat in hostile classrooms to get a better education. And there are so many more stories to tell and so much more history being made each day right now by ordinary people doing extraordinary things across America and the world. To bring all these growing voices together into a mighty demand to Leave No Child Behind is the challenge before us.

Choices: More Tax Breaks for the Wealthy or Needed Investments in Children

Estate Tax Relief

Instead of eliminating the estate tax which would mostly benefit the very wealthy at a cost of $266.5 billion over the next 10 years, we could:

◆ fully fund Head Start for 3- and 4-year-olds for the next 10 years and fully fund Early Head Start for the last five of those years; or

◆ provide child care assistance for about 60 percent of eligible children from working families for 10 years; or

◆ enable the seven million children ages 5 to 14 home alone after school and millions of other children who need extra help to participate in the 21st Century Community Learning Centers after-school program; or

◆ provide health insurance for every uninsured child for 10 years; or

◆ provide a $1,000 child tax credit over 10 years to the 16 million children who get nothing from the credit now, *helping two million children escape poverty; and* reduce the marriage penalty in the tax code for low- to moderate-income married couples; *and* increase the Earned Income Tax Credit for low-income families with three or more children.

Alternative Minimum Tax Relief

Instead of providing about $300 billion in Alternative Minimum Tax Relief for mostly the wealthy over the next 10 years, we could:

◆ fully fund Head Start for 3- and 4-year-olds for each of the next 10 years and fully fund Early Head Start in three years; or

◆ provide another eight million children in working families quality child care for 10 years; or

◆ serve nearly every child between the ages of 5 and 14 in the 21st Century Community Learning Centers program; or

◆ provide health coverage for every uninsured child; or

◆ provide a $1,000 child tax credit over 10 years to the 16 million children who get nothing from the credit now, *helping two million children escape poverty; and* add three million new subsidized housing vouchers over 10 years to help the almost five million households (including three million children) paying more than half their income on rent.

Capital Gains Tax Relief

Instead of giving this often-proposed tax break of $34 billion* over the next 10 years, we could:

◆ enable Head Start to reach full funding for all 3- and 4-year-olds by the end of the next 10 years; or

◆ provide 910,000 children in working families quality child care every year over the next 10 years; or

◆ enable 4.35 million youths to participate in the 21st Century Community Learning Centers program for the next 10 years; or

◆ provide 2.8 million uninsured children health coverage every year over the next 10 years; or

◆ reduce the marriage penalty in the tax code for low- to moderate-income married couples; *and* make food stamps available to millions of low-income working families, including legal immigrants.

*Amount proposed in the 1999 tax bill vetoed by former President Clinton.

The Children's Charter: President Hoover's White House Conference, 1930

On November 22, 1930, the White House Conference on Child Health and Protection sponsored by President Herbert Hoover adopted a statement of objectives for American children "recognizing the rights of the child as the first rights of citizenship." Participants pledged to 19 aims, including these:

◆ "For every child a home and that love and security which a home provides; and for that child who must receive foster care, the nearest substitute for his own home"

◆ "For every child health protection from birth through adolescence, including: periodical health examinations and, where needed, care of specialists and hospital treatment; regular dental examinations and care of the teeth; protective and preventive measures against communicable diseases; the insuring of pure food, pure milk, and pure water"

◆ "For every child a school which is safe from hazards, sanitary, properly equipped, lighted, and ventilated. For younger children nursery schools and kindergartens to supplement home care"

◆ "For every child a community which recognizes and plans for his needs, protects him against physical dangers, moral hazards, and disease; provides him with safe and wholesome places for play and recreation; and makes provision for his cultural and social needs"

◆ "For every child who is in conflict with society the right to be dealt with intelligently as society's charge, not society's outcast; with the home, the school, the church, the court and the institution when needed, shaped to return him whenever possible to the normal stream of life"

◆ "For every child the right to grow up in a family with an adequate standard of living and the security of a stable income as the surest safeguard against social handicaps"

The statement concludes: "For every child these rights, regardless of race, or color, or situation, wherever he may live under the protection of the American flag."

God Help Us to End Poverty in Our Time

We must pray and act without ceasing. Let our actions be our prayers. Let our voices crying out for just treatment for children be our prayers. Let our walks and vigils around Congress and the White House and state houses and city councils be our prayers. Let our votes and e-mails and letters and phone calls be our prayers.

I end with a prayer to keep us all strong in our struggle until those in power are worn down and commit to ending physical and spiritual poverty in our time.

God help us to end poverty in our time.

The poverty of having a child with too little to eat and no place to sleep, no air, sunlight, and space to breathe, bask, and grow.

The poverty of watching your child suffer and get sicker and sicker and not knowing what to do or how to get help because you don't have a car or health insurance.

The poverty of working your fingers to the bone every day taking care of somebody else's children and neglecting your own, and still not being able to pay your bills.

The poverty of having a job which does not let you afford a stable place to live and being terrified you'll become homeless and lose your children to foster care.

The poverty of losing your job because you cannot find reliable child care or transportation to work.

The poverty of working all your life caring for others and finding you have to start all over again caring for the grandchildren you love.

The poverty of earning a college degree, having children, opening a day care center, and taking home $300 a week or month if you're lucky.

The poverty of loneliness and isolation and alienation — having no one to call or visit, tell you where to get help, assist you in getting it, or care if you're living or dead.

The poverty of having too much and sharing too little and having the burden of nothing to carry.

The poverty of convenient blindness and deafness and indifference to others, of emptiness and enslavement to things, drugs, power, violence and fleeting fame.

The poverty of low aim and paltry purpose, weak will, and tiny vision, big meetings and small action, loud talk and sullen grudging service.

The poverty of believing in nothing, standing for nothing, sharing nothing, sacrificing nothing, struggling for nothing.

The poverty of pride and ingratitude for God's gifts of life and children and family and freedom and country and not wanting for others what you want for yourself.

The poverty of greed for more and more and more, ignoring, blaming, exploiting the needy, and taking from the weak to please the strong.

The poverty of addiction to drugs, to drink, to work, to self, to the status quo, and to injustice.

The poverty of fear which keeps you from doing the thing you think is right.

The poverty of despair and cynicism.

God help us end poverty in our time in all its faces and places, young and old, rural, urban, suburban and small town too, and in every color of humans You have made everywhere.

God help us to end poverty in our time in all its guises — inside and out — physical and spiritual, so that all our and Your children may live the lives that You intend.

Marian Wright Edelman

A 2001 Action Agenda to Leave No Child Behind®
And to Ensure Every Child a Healthy Start, a Head Start,
a Fair Start, a Safe Start, and a Moral Start in Life
and Successful Passage to Adulthood

With federal budget experts projecting a $5.6 trillion federal budget surplus over the next decade, and billions of tobacco settlement dollars available in a post-Cold War era, now is the time to end immoral and preventable child poverty, hunger, homelessness, sickness, and illiteracy in the richest nation on earth. Now is the time to stand up and show our children we truly value them. Now is the time to build a more just and compassionate and less violent society — one where no child is left behind. Together the nation, states, communities, employers, parents, and citizens must:

I. *Ensure Every Child a Healthy Start.* There are 10.8 million uninsured children in America; nearly 90 percent of them live in working families. About six million are currently eligible for health care under the Children's Health Insurance Program (CHIP) and Medicaid. Nearly five million lack any health coverage. We must:

◆ Mount a massive and urgent campaign to reach and enroll every one of the six million children now eligible for CHIP and Medicaid.

◆ Simplify and unify application and eligibility procedures in every state to make it easier rather than harder for children to get health care.

◆ Expand health coverage to every uninsured child and their parents.

◆ Encourage employers to expand coverage for employees and their children and to stop dropping dependent coverage.

◆ Urge every community network — religious, child care, health care, parents, senior citizens, education, grassroots, youths, and corporations — to join in a massive and persistent public awareness and enrollment campaign until every child is provided appropriate health care.

II. *Ensure Every Child a Head Start.* Only three out of five children eligible for Head Start and only 12 percent of children eligible for federal child care assistance receive it. Nearly seven million school-age children are home alone after school and are at risk of tobacco, alcohol, and drug use, teen pregnancy, and violence. Quality preschool, child care, after-school, and summer programs, and public school systems are essential to getting all children ready to learn and achieve and keeping them safe when parents are in the workforce.

◆ Head Start should be increased so that every eligible child can participate by 2005 and 40 percent of eligible infants and toddlers can participate in Early Head Start.

◆ The Child Care and Development Block Grant should be increased to serve all eligible children by 2005 and investments should be made to strengthen the quality of child care.

◆ Congress should increase funding for the new Early Learning Initiative for very young children and significantly increase investments in 21st Century Community Learning Centers and other quality after-school and summer programs.

◆ Every state should provide a high quality comprehensive prekindergarten program for all families who wish to participate and invest more state dollars in quality child care and Head Start programs.

◆ Every business should offer affordable quality child care, flex-time, and paid parental leave options to help employees balance work and family responsibilities.

◆ Federal and state family and medical leave laws should be expanded and strengthened to include paid leave.

◆ As a nation, we need to make sure that every child can read by fourth grade and can graduate from school able to succeed at work and in life.

III. Ensure Every Child a Fair Start. Over 12 million children are poor; 78 percent of them live in working families; 5.8 million of them live in extreme poverty in families with incomes below $6,600. They often suffer hunger, homelessness, and lack other basic necessities. Our nation must commit to doing whatever is necessary to reduce child poverty in America by half by 2004 and end it by 2010. Children should get a fair share of the federal and state budget surpluses, tobacco settlement monies, and be guaranteed the same income and health security as senior citizens. We must:

◆ Ensure work at a decent wage and education and training for parents to improve their earnings.

◆ Make the Child Tax Credit refundable, increase and make refundable the Dependent Care Tax Credit (DCTC) for lower-income families, and expand the Earned Income Tax Credit (EITC) for families with three or more children.

◆ Make sure that every poor family with children currently eligible for nutrition, health, housing, child care, and other assistance gets them. States should immediately use rather than hoard dollars intended to help parents work and become more self-sufficient, reduce their bureaucracies, and create a culture of service among their employees.

◆ Strengthen child support enforcement.

IV. Ensure Every Child a Safe Start and Successful Transition to Adulthood. American children under 15 are 12 times more likely to die from guns than children in 25 other industrialized nations combined. A child is reported abused or neglected every 11 minutes. Children are exposed to relentless glorification of violence in toys and on movie, television, video game, and Internet screens. All children need positive role models in their homes and communities and positive alternatives to the streets.

◆ Parents should be educated about the dangers of owning a gun and be required to store guns locked and unloaded. Manufacturers, sellers, and other adults should be held liable for guns that get into the hands of criminals and children.

◆ Congress should support legislation that will help communities provide positive developmental activities for all youths.

◆ Youth involved in criminal activity should be held accountable for their behavior, but also should be provided appropriate treatment and rehabilitative services to give them the opportunity to turn their lives around to become productive law-abiding adults. And we must invest in children before they get into trouble.

◆ Nonviolence training, conflict resolution, peer mediation, and other activities to prevent all forms of family and community violence should be instilled in our homes, congregations, schools, and communities.

◆ Investments should be made in services and activities to prevent child abuse and neglect, assist families in crisis, and offer ongoing support for birth, adoptive, and kinship care families to assure permanent homes for children leaving foster care.

◆ Partnerships between child protection and substance abuse agencies should be encouraged to expand comprehensive treatment for families with alcohol and drug problems to promote safety and permanent homes for children and recovery for their parents.

◆ Community-based supports for kinship caregivers should be expanded so that they can get help for their children, including ongoing assistance when they commit to care permanently for children who have been in foster care.

V. Ensure Every Child a Moral Start. It is time for American adults to stop our moral hypocrisy and to live the values we want our children to learn. If we want them to stop being violent, then we should stop being violent. If we want them to be honest, then we should be honest. Parents, preachers, teachers, and all public officials must conduct themselves as they would want their own child or any child to emulate. Our children need consistent love, time, attention, discipline, family stability, and limits at home and in school, and they need to see that adults in their nation, private sector, and communities value and care for them — not as consumers and future customers to be exploited or as a non-voting group to be ignored — but as the heirs of America's institutions and values. It is time for all adults to accept their responsibility to be good protectors of and mentors for the next generation.

*Most of these and other proposals are included in the Act to Leave No Child Behind — which lays out CDF's comprehensive policy vision of what a great and sensible nation could provide all its children.

If the World Were a Global Village of 100 People:

About 24 of them would live on less than $1 a day

80	would live outside the developed world
77	would be non-White and/or of Hispanic descent
66	would be either women or children under 15
31	would be children under 15
5	would live in the United States

But those five U.S. villagers would have 20 percent of the total gross domestic product (at purchasing power parity) of the whole world and would expend one-third of the world's total military expenditures. One and a half billion human beings live every day on one-third the amount every American spends on weapons every day.

If the United States Were a Village of 100 Children:

76	would have at least one parent in the labor force
68	would live with two parents
41	would live in a two-parent family where both parents are in the labor force
38	would be minorities
28	would live in a central city
23	would live only with their mother
22	would have at least one parent who graduated from college
20	would have no parent who graduated from high school
19	would live in a rural area
17	would be poor
15	would be Black
14	would be Hispanic
11	would live with a parent who never married
10	would live with a parent who is divorced
4	would live with their father
2	would live with a grandparent

How U.S. Child Safety Net Policies Compare to 23 Other Industrialized Countries

Country	Universal Health Insurance/ Health Care	Paid Maternal/ Parental Leave at Childbirth	Family Allowance/ Child Dependency Grant
Australia	Y	Y	Y
Austria	Y	Y	Y
Belgium	Y	Y	Y
Canada	Y	Y	Y
Czech Republic	Y	Y	Y
Denmark	Y	Y	Y
Finland	Y	Y	Y
France	Y	Y	Y
Germany	Y	Y	Y
Hungary	Y	Y	Y
Ireland	Y	Y	Y
Italy	Y	Y	Y
Japan	Y	Y	Y
Luxembourg	Y	Y	Y
Netherlands	Y	Y	Y
New Zeland	Y	Y	Y
Norway	Y	Y	Y
Poland	Y	Y	Y
Portugal	Y	Y	Y
Spain	Y	Y	Y
Sweden	Y	Y	Y
Switzerland	Y	Y	Y
United Kingdom	Y	Y	Y
United States	N	N	N

Source: Office of Research, Evaluation and Statistics, Social Security Administration, Social Security Programs Throughout the World 1999, August 1999, Summary Table and Individual Entries. Programs characterized by CDF.

Moments in America for All Children

Every second	a public school student is suspended.*
Every 9 seconds	a high school student drops out.*
Every 10 seconds	a public school student is corporally punished.*
Every 20 seconds	a child is arrested.
Every 24 seconds	a baby is born to an unmarried mother.
Every 44 seconds	a baby is born into poverty.
Every minute	a baby is born without health insurance.
Every minute	a baby is born to a teen mother.
Every 2 minutes	a baby is born at low birthweight (less than 5 lbs., 8 oz.).
Every 4 minutes	a baby is born to a mother who had late or no prenatal care.
Every 4 minutes	a child is arrested for drug abuse.
Every 8 minutes	a child is arrested for a violent crime.
Every 9 minutes	a baby is born at very low birthweight (less than 3 lbs., 4 oz.).
Every 11 minutes	a child is reported abused or neglected.
Every 19 minutes	a baby dies.
Every 37 minutes	a baby is born to a mother who is not a high school graduate.
Every 42 minutes	a child or youth under 20 dies from an accident.
Every 2 hours 20 minutes	a child or youth under 20 is killed by a firearm.
Every 3 hours	a child or youth under 20 is a homicide victim.
Every 4 hours	a child or youth under 20 commits suicide.
Every day	a young person under 25 dies from HIV infection.

* Based on calculations per school day (180 days of seven hours each).

25 Key Facts About American Children

3 in 5	preschoolers have their mothers in the labor force.
2 in 5	never complete a single year of college.
1 in 2	will live in a single parent family at some point in childhood.
1 in 3	is born to unmarried parents.
1 in 3	will be poor at some point in their childhood.
1 in 3	is behind a year or more in school.
1 in 4	lives with only one parent.
1 in 5	is born to a mother who did not graduate from high school.
1 in 5	has a foreign-born mother.
1 in 5	was born poor.
1 in 6	is poor now.
1 in 6	is born to a mother who did not receive prenatal care in the first three months of pregnancy.
1 in 7	has no health insurance.
1 in 7	has a worker in their family but still is poor.
1 in 8	never graduates from high school.
1 in 8	is born to a teenage mother.
1 in 8	lives in a family receiving food stamps.
1 in 12	has a disability.
1 in 13	was born with low birthweight.
1 in 15	lives at less than half the poverty level.
1 in 24	lives with neither parent.
1 in 26	is born to a mother who received late or no prenatal care.
1 in 60	sees their parents divorce in any year.
1 in 139	will die before their first birthday.
1 in 1,056	will be killed by guns before age 20.

Educational Attainment of Kindergartners

Of every 100 kindergartners,   88 graduate from high school.

Of every 100 White kindergartners,   94 graduate from high school.

Of every 100 Black kindergartners,   87 graduate from high school.

Of every 100 Hispanic kindergartners,   63 graduate from high school.

Of every 100 kindergartners,   58 start college.

Of every 100 White kindergartners,   64 start college.

Of every 100 Black kindergartners,   53 start college.

Of every 100 Hispanic kindergartners,   33 start college.

Of every 100 kindergartners,   29 complete 4 years of college.

Of every 100 White kindergartners,   34 complete 4 years of college.

Of every 100 Black kindergartners,   18 complete 4 years of college.

Of every 100 Hispanic kindergartners,   10 complete 4 years of college.

U.S. Census Bureau, Educational Attainment, Detailed Tables, Table 1, persons ages 25-29 in March 2000. White and Black races exclude persons of Hispanic origin, Hispanic origin includes persons of any race.

CHAPTER

Family Income

The burgeoning economy has brought unprecedented prosperity to many families, and the nation is more capable than ever of giving all children a Fair Start, free from hardship and poverty. Yet the income gaps that divide rich and poor families remain almost as wide as ever. As America enters the new century, one in six children still lives below the federal poverty line. These children face hardships and heightened risks including low birthweight, dying in infancy, stunted growth in toddlerhood, lower test scores in the elementary school years, fewer completed years of schooling, and lower pay as young adults.

Experience shows that states and communities *can* significantly reduce child poverty by supporting poor parents' efforts to work. When parents get these supports, children are more likely to succeed in life. In rigorously evaluated demonstration programs, when families on welfare were encouraged to go to work and were offered cash payments to supplement their low wages, children performed better in school and had fewer behavioral and mental health problems. Unfortunately, by 2000, few states — if any — had fully embraced this approach to reforming welfare and ending poverty.

In 1999 and 2000, low-income parents did their part in reducing child poverty by spending more time working outside the home. The proportion of poor children who lived in a family where someone worked continued to climb, reaching 78 percent in 1999. Yet, for the poorest families, the higher incomes achieved through longer work hours have been wiped out by declines in government benefits, which followed the national welfare legislation enacted in 1996. In key respects, many poor children are poorer today than before the new welfare law.

Moderate- and middle-income parents are also working longer hours and need different supports. Continuing a trend that began in the last century, mothers spent more time working for pay in 2000, partially to offset their husbands' shrinking paychecks. More work yielded higher incomes, but longer work days took parents away from their children and drained family budgets to pay for child care and other work expenses. The trend has underscored the need for family-friendly employment policies that allow working parents to meet job and family responsibilities.

As 2001 began, the record, decade-long economic boom showed signs of slowing down, raising new questions about how low-income families will fare in a weaker economy. Parents who are now struggling to maintain their jobs and their families will need help even more if the economy declines.

Unmatched Prosperity, Unequally Shared

The nation's economic resources grew rapidly in 1999 and 2000. In 2000, the U.S. economy, as measured by gross domestic product, generated wealth at a rate of $10 trillion of goods and services. From 1999 to 2000, the economy grew by close to half a trillion dollars (in inflation-adjusted 2000 dollars), the largest single-year jump ever recorded.[1] This increase alone equaled 13 times the sum needed to lift the incomes of all below-poverty families with children to the poverty line.[2]

Most families benefited from the prosperity. In 2000, unemployment fell to 4.0 percent, the lowest rate in over 50 years.[3] Income for the typical, or median, family with children reached a record high of $47,949 in 1999 (the latest year for which family income figures are available), and the number of children living in poverty declined by more than 1 million.

Yet the strong economy did little to close the wide gaps in income that divide rich and poor families. In 1999, the wealthiest one-fifth of families received 47.2 percent of total U.S. family income — slightly below the record high of 47.3 percent set in 1998. By contrast, the poorest one-fifth of families received 4.3 percent of the income in 1999.

The poorest one-fifth of American families saw their inflation-adjusted incomes dwindle by 4 percent during the 20 years since 1979 (from $13,504 to $13,320 in 1999 dollars). The middle one-fifth of families gained 11 percent (from $44,030 in 1979 to $48,933 in 1999). Widening the gap between the rich and poor, the richest one-fifth of families gained 42 percent (from $103,972 in 1979 to $147,779 in 1999).

This 20-year trend of widening income inequality marks a departure from earlier decades. From 1949 to 1979, for example, income growth was shared more equally and incomes more than doubled for families at all rungs on the economic ladder.

Wage trends show that education marks a growing fault line in the economy. For all but the best-educated workers, weekly wages lost ground to inflation over the past two decades. For those who had not finished high school the typical (or median) weekly wage of full-time workers declined by 26 percent, after adjusting for inflation, between 1979 and 2000. Wages dropped 13 percent for those with only a high school degree and by 9 percent for those who finished one to three years of college. Wages only rose (by 12 percent) for four-year college graduates.

Racial gaps also persist. While annual unemployment rates hit their lowest point in decades for all racial groups in 2000, unemployment was about twice as common for Blacks (7.6 percent) as for Whites (3.5 percent), a disparity that has barely changed for 47 years. Unemployment was also high for Hispanics (5.7 percent). Similarly, weekly wage levels for the median full-time worker in 2000 were one-third higher for White men than Black men ($669 versus $503) and one-sixth higher for White women than Black women ($500 versus $429).

Promisingly, the wage gaps dividing high- and low-paid workers narrowed in 1997 and 1998. Unfortunately, wage figures for 2000 revealed weak wage growth overall and a return to wider wage gaps. Average wages of non-production workers were under $14 an hour in 2000, up less than one-half of 1 percent from a year before, after adjusting for inflation. Median weekly wage figures showed virtually no growth in buying power except

- Annual income rose to $47,949 — the highest on record — for the typical family with children in 1999. The number of poor children fell by 1.4 million.

YET...

- 12.1 million children — one in six — remain in poverty.

- From 1979 to 1999 — while the United States became 49 percent richer (as measured by inflation-adjusted per capita gross domestic product) — the number of poor children rose by 17 percent.

- An American child is more likely to be poor today than 20 or 30 years ago, more likely to be poor than an American adult, and more likely to be poor than a child living in Canada, Germany, or France.

- Three out of four poor children (78 percent) live in families where someone worked in 1999.

- In 1999, more than 3.6 million children lived in families either paying at least half their income on rent, or living in severely substandard housing.

- Food stamps are reaching fewer needy children. Fewer than 72 children received food stamps for every 100 poor children in 1999, down from 88 children per hundred in 1996.

for the best-paid one-fifth of workers, who gained 3 percent over 1999.

How "Prosperity" Leaves One in Six Children in Poverty

Government poverty figures for 1999 show that over 12 million of America's children lived below the federal poverty level of $13,290 a year for a three-person family ($17,029 a year for a family of four). Although the number of poor children has dropped for six straight years — most recently by 1.4 million children in 1999 — a child is more likely to be poor today than 20 or 30 years ago.

Unequal incomes help explain why so many children remain poor in an era of unprecedented prosperity. If the enormous growth in national disposable income during the last 20 years, which was equivalent to more than $9,500 per person (after inflation) or nearly $29,000 for a family of three, had been evenly shared by all Americans, no family would be poor today.

In addition to unequal income growth, other forces contributing to child poverty include single-parent families (whose numbers grew most rapidly in the 1970s and 1980s but slowed in the 1990s) and the lack of strong government supports for low- and moderate-income families.

America's support for families contrasts sharply with policies in other nations. The U.S. child poverty rate is roughly twice as high as the rates in Canada and Germany and at least six times higher than France, Belgium, or Austria — a result some experts have attributed chiefly to low spending on benefits for non-elderly families.[4]

The possibility of an economic slowdown raises grave prospects for low-income families. Any economic downturn would likely hit children hardest. Economists Timothy M. Smeeding, Lee Rainwater, and Gary Burtless observe, "In a future recession, declines in employment and hourly wages are likely to be particularly severe for low-income breadwinners, boosting the poverty rate, especially among children. Building a stronger safety net in anticipation of the next recession can significantly improve the fortunes of low-wage breadwinners and their families."[5]

Poor and Middle-Income Families Are Working Harder

Mothers are spending more time earning a paycheck, and their efforts have helped many families sustain their income against the weakening wages and fraying safety net of the 1980s and 1990s. But increased work also carries hidden costs for families and children.

Two out of three mothers (67 percent) worked outside the home in March 2000, up from fewer than one in two (49 percent) in March 1979.[6] Fathers' employment rates have changed little, inching up from 87 percent in 1979 to 89 percent in 2000. Employment is up for both single mothers and married mothers and continued to rise in 1999 and 2000 for mothers from both low- and middle-income families. However, the employment surge has been strongest for different mothers at different times and for different reasons.

In the 1990s, the strongest employment gains were among low-income single mothers. In 1979, 42 percent of single mothers in the bottom one-fifth of the U.S. family income distribution (making less than about $17,000 a year) worked. The figure was identical in 1989 and 1993. But after 1993, the figure leapt nearly 19 points to 61 percent by 2000 (those with jobs worked an average of about 35 hours a week throughout the period).

Reasons for the sharp rise in employment include a strong economy and major expansions of government

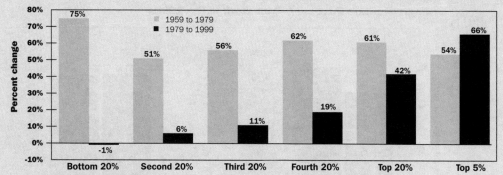

The Rich Have Grown Richer

Change in the Average Income of Rich and Poor Families (in constant dollars), 1979-1999

Legend: 1959 to 1979 / 1979 to 1999

- Bottom 20%: 75%, -1%
- Second 20%: 51%, 6%
- Third 20%: 56%, 11%
- Fourth 20%: 62%, 19%
- Top 20%: 61%, 42%
- Top 5%: 54%, 66%

(Percent change)

Note: The Census Bureau adjusted these figures for inflation using an inflation measure, called the CPIU-XI, which is more conservative than the official inflation measure. If the figures had been adjusted, using the official measure of inflation, they would have shown deeper losses or smaller gains.

Source: U.S. Department of Commerce, Bureau of the Census, Historical Income Tables, at http://www.census.gov/hhes/income/histinc/f03.html. Calculations by Children's Defense Fund.

incentives and supports such as the Earned Income Tax Credit and help with child care and child health insurance for low-income working families. Also, in the 1990s a variety of major welfare changes were adopted at the national, state, and local levels and ranged from increased help with job placement, transportation, or counseling to harsh restrictions limiting access to public assistance even for the neediest families.

Increased employment among single mothers has had a dramatic impact on the lives of poor children. More than three out of every four poor children (78 percent) now lives with somebody who works, according to the latest poverty data for 1999. This figure is up from just 61 percent as recently as 1993. One out of three poor children lives with someone who worked *full time, year round* yet, despite working, the family is still poor. The proportion of poor families with children headed by a worker is at its highest peak in the 25 years for which these figures are available.

Middle-income mothers, especially married mothers, are working harder as well. Unlike single mothers, their greatest employment surge came in the 1980s, not the 1990s. The employment rate of married mothers jumped from 47 percent to 60 percent between 1979 and 1989, then rose 5 more percentage points in the subsequent decade.

One reason for the increased workforce participation of married mothers was to compensate for weaker wages of their husbands. Between 1979 and 2000, among full-time workers with only a high school education, men's median weekly earnings lost one-sixth of their value, after adjusting for the cost of living; among those with no high school degree, median weekly wages lost one-third of their value. Most, but not all, of the losses hit in the 1980s.

Wages for women rose by 16 percent during the same period, although in 2000, their pay ($491 a week) remains far below men's ($646 a week). These wage trends explain why, even during the seemingly prosperous 1990s, married couples' incomes outpaced inflation only for families where the wife worked; for couples where the wife did not work, inflation-adjusted median income declined.

The only group of mothers whose employment increases did not continue in 1999 and 2000 was higher-income mothers. Among mothers in the wealthiest one-fifth of U.S. families, 73 percent worked in March 2000. This was down slightly from 74 percent in March 1999, although well above 57 percent in 1979.

While mothers' increased work helped many families sustain or raise their incomes, there were hidden costs of longer work days, which not only take parents away from their children but also lead to more work expenses such as child care. Paying for child care consumes as much as one-third of an average poor family's income.[7] (For more information, see the Child Care chapter.) The costs of child care and other work expenses such as transportation and medical care increased faster than overall inflation in 2000, according to the U.S. Bureau of Labor Statistics.

With more parents working, the need has grown for family-friendly employment policies in areas such as paid parental leave, quality child care, and safe and healthy after-school activities for school-age children. Working families also need education, job training, and minimum wage policies that can help families earn more without sacrificing even more parenting time.

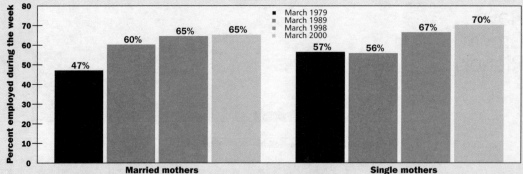

More Mothers Are Working

Married Mothers Increased Their Work Most in the 1980s
Single Mothers Increased Their Work in the 1990s

Percent employed during the week

- March 1979
- March 1989
- March 1998
- March 2000

Married mothers: 47%, 60%, 65%, 65%
Single mothers: 57%, 56%, 67%, 70%

Source: U.S. Department of Commerce, Bureau of the Census, Current Population Survey, March 1979, March 1989, March 1998, and March 2000. Calculations by Children's Defense Fund.

Lack of National Safety Net Means Deeper Poverty and Hardship

While the total number of poor children has declined for six straight years, the children who remain in poverty face a weakened public safety net. During the 1990s, state and federal agencies have increased many forms of help for low-wage working families. But for those who cannot find steady work, help has eroded.

As a result, many poor children have become significantly poorer since the passage of national welfare legislation in 1996. According to a CDF analysis of Census Bureau data, 22 percent of poor children were considered extremely poor in 1996, with incomes below *half* of the poverty line or $6,645 a year for a family of three. This proportion rose to 25 percent in 1997 and 26 percent in 1998 and 1999. (These CDF figures differ from official poverty figures because they account for food and housing benefits and taxes, in addition to cash income, in determining poverty status.)

The Nation Can Do Something about Child Poverty

A dramatic reduction in child poverty can be achieved, if the nation has the will to do it. Parents are doing their part by working more, with the help of a strong economy. When work alone does not lift children out of poverty, a combination of initiatives can help protect children. Child poverty could be cut in half within four years by such attainable measures as doubling the federal child tax credit and extending its availability to the poorest children, replicating anti-poverty strategies that have been shown to work in a number of states, making sure families get the food stamps and other supports they need, and

increasing access to affordable housing. If poor families with children were allowed to benefit from the child tax credit while doubling its size from $500 to $1,000 per child, this initiative alone would cut the child poverty rate by at least one-sixth — almost 2 million children. The child credit can be useful to poor families if it is made "refundable" — available to families as a refund even though their incomes are too low to owe federal income taxes. If more states used approaches similar to the Minnesota Family Investment Program (MFIP) demonstration model, with its goal of helping families gain above-poverty incomes through a combination of work and supports (see box), family incomes would increase nationwide and children's lives would improve. If larger numbers of low-income families received food stamps and subsidized housing, hundreds of thousands of children would be lifted out of poverty. Investments in low-cost child care and other supports would also result in reduced child poverty.

Components of a Family Income Package

Jobs at decent wages, support from both parents, nutrition aid, affordable housing, child care help, health coverage, equitable tax policy, cash assistance — these and more can be part of an income package that enables the poorest families to make ends meet. Work is critical to any strategy that alleviates child poverty, but finding a job is not always enough. Parents with few skills or severe problems such as disability or domestic violence typically work in low-wage, temporary jobs that will not cover the basic needs of families with children. Even above-poverty wages frequently do not supply the basics all children need. Forty percent of all American children live in families with incomes of less than twice the poverty line (or

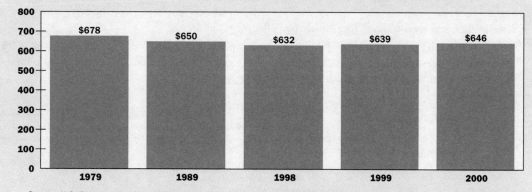

Men's Wages Are Static

Median Weekly Wages of Full-Time Male Workers (in constant 2000 dollars)

1979	1989	1998	1999	2000
$678	$650	$632	$639	$646

Source: U.S. Department of Labor, Bureau of Labor Statistics. Adjusted for inflation with the Consumer Price Index CPI-U-X1. Calculations by Children's Defense Fund.

The Bottom Line: Where Communities Have Boosted Income, Children Have Succeeded; Where Welfare Policies Lowered Income, Children Fared Worse

New research proves that communities *can* reduce child poverty. More importantly, initiatives can help children succeed at school and in life and help their parents work.   One initiative that boosted income was the pilot phase of Minnesota's Family Investment Program (MFIP). A study of MFIP found "some of the most rigorous evidence available to date that *money matters*. For very disadvantaged families (in this case, single-parent, long-term recipients), providing financial support to parents as they move from welfare to work can improve children's outcomes," according to Manpower Demonstration Research Corporation (MDRC), which evaluated the program for the state. Teachers reported that children in MFIP performed better in school and engaged in less "problem behavior" compared with children in a randomly assigned control group, MDRC found.

Operating in seven counties from 1994 to 1997, MFIP offered unusually strong incentives for going to work. Under MFIP rules, families could continue receiving some cash assistance until their income reached 40 percent *above* the poverty line, help with child care, and other needed services. MFIP raised participants' incomes by one-seventh (13 percent) compared with the control group and reduced the estimated poverty rate by one-sixth. Although participation in MFIP's welfare-to-work activities was mandatory and was backed by the threat of benefit cuts, evaluators noted that:

"MFIP's incentives (rather than the participation mandate) were responsible for decreasing poverty, decreasing domestic abuse, decreasing the risk of maternal depression, and improving children's well-being."

MFIP is just one of several recent welfare experiments that illustrate how income-boosting policies can help poor children succeed, while policies that lower family income can have negative effects. CDF analyzed the MFIP findings and 13 other programs evaluated by MDRC. The programs had varied impacts on children: five had mostly good effects (more good impacts than bad impacts), seven had mostly bad effects (more bad impacts than good impacts), and two had no significant effects on children. The programs' impacts on income were also mixed: four lifted participants' average income substantially (by 5 percent or more), four substantially reduced income, and six barely changed income. The connection between income and child well-being was striking.

◆ The four programs that substantially *lifted income* all had mostly *good* effects on children.

◆ The four programs that substantially *reduced income* all had mostly *bad* effects on children.

◆ Programs that barely changed income had no clear pattern of effects on children.

The programs that lifted incomes did so by boosting employment and earnings while providing cash assistance and services that succeeded in "making work pay." Unlike traditional welfare programs, these programs placed a strong emphasis on work.

Yet the research shows that merely boosting employment, without boosting income, did not help children succeed. Programs that boosted employment but caused families to lose income (largely due to lost cash assistance and food stamps) had mostly bad effects on children.

Confirming the importance of easing children's poverty, a 2000 literature review by the National Academy of Sciences concluded that "the persistent economic hardship that affects so many children is likely to be highly detrimental, especially during the earliest years of life."*

This report analyzes 14 rigorously-evaluated U.S. programs begun in the 1990s for which data are available regarding impacts on child well-being and family income. The evaluations compared program participants with families who had been randomly assigned at the start of the experiment to a control group that received more traditional welfare incentives, services, and rules. All reports cited were prepared by Manpower Demonstration Research Corporation (MDRC) and are available at www.mdrc.org.

*Jack P. Shonkoff and Deborah A. Phillips, Editors, From Neurons to Neighborhoods: The Science of Early Childhood Development (Washington, DC: National Academy Press, 2000), p.295.

Programs that lowered families' incomes harmed their children.
Programs that raised families' incomes helped their children.[a]

	Income decreased 5% or more:	Income stayed about the same:	Income increased 5% or more:
Programs with mostly good effects on children[b]	(none)	Columbus integrated case management	Portland* New Hope* MFIP* Atlanta job-focused
Programs with no significant effects on children	(none)	Atlanta education-focused Detroit	(none)
Programs with mostly bad effects on children[c]	Riverside education-focused Grand Rapids education-focused Riverside* job-focused Grand Rapids* job-focused	Oklahoma City Los Angeles Jobs-First GAIN Columbus traditional case management	(none)
Table shows:	4 programs lowered income: all of them had more bad effects than good effects on children	6 programs had little or no impact on income: effects on children were mixed	4 programs raised income: all of them had more good effects than bad effects on children

*Income increase or decrease was statistically significant at the 90 percent confidence level.

(a) Income is employer-reported earnings plus cash welfare and food stamps.

(b) Programs with more significant good effects than significant bad effects.

(c) Programs with more significant bad effects than significant good effects.

Source: CDF compilation of data from Manpower Demonstration Research Corporation.

below $26,580 for a three-person family).[8] The Urban Institute found that half of all children living below two times the federal poverty level in 1999 were in families who had trouble affording food at some point in the prior year. For single-parent families, the proportion with food worries climbed to 60 percent. Almost one-third (31.8 percent) of all single mothers with incomes up to twice the poverty line reported problems paying their housing or utility bills in the previous year.

To the extent that wages do not meet a family's needs, other income components can make a real difference, if they are actually available. The following is a survey of the parts that can make up a family income package, their strengths and shortcomings included.

Jobs at decent wages

A typical man who worked full time and had finished high school earned $594 a week in 2000. A similar working woman earned $421 a week in 2000, about one and a half times the federal poverty level for a three-person family.[9] Even though this woman is not poor by official standards, she would be hard-pressed to afford housing, child care, and other necessities at this rate of pay. In reality, many do not earn as much as the typical full-time working woman who has completed high school. Among the lowest-paid one-fifth of all full-time working women, typical wages were $270 a week in 2000, just under the federal poverty level for a three-person family.[10]

Single-mother families are not alone in struggling to make ends meet. Nearly 30 percent of children in two-parent families live below twice the poverty line and are therefore at risk of hardship. But for the more than one in five American children who live with only their mothers, supports beyond wages are especially likely to be necessary.

Efforts to raise wages: minimum and living wage campaigns: Over the past 30 years, raises in low-wage jobs have not even kept pace with inflation. In the early 1970s, full-time, year-round, minimum wage work would lift a family of three out of poverty. At the current rate of $5.15 an hour, full-time, year-round, minimum wage work only earns three-quarters of the federal poverty guidelines ($14,650 for a family of three in 2001). The federal minimum wage has not been increased since 1997. In 2000, Congress passed legislation that would have increased the minimum wage by $1 over two years, but the increase was tied to costly tax cuts favoring the wealthy, resulting in a veto. According to the National Economic Council, more than 10 million workers would have benefited from the proposed increase, and a third of them would have been parents with children under 18.[11]

While the federal minimum wage slipped farther below poverty, some states increased state minimum wages. Vermont raised its minimum from $5.75 to $6.25 as of January 2001. Rhode Island moved from $5.65 to $6.15 in September 2000. In all, 11 states (including the District of Columbia) have minimum wage laws setting higher rates than the federal wage: Alaska, California, Connecticut, Delaware, District of Columbia, Hawaii, Massachusetts, Oregon, Rhode Island, Vermont, and Washington. Notably, Washington state started annually adjusting its minimum wage for inflation January 1, 2001.[12]

Recognizing the inadequacy of the minimum wage, campaigns have sprung up around the country to persuade local governments to adopt "living wages" — requiring businesses that contract with them or receive tax or other benefits to pay their employees wages more reasonably related to the cost of living. Through October 2000, 53 such ordinances had passed nationwide, including 41 in cities, 10 in counties, one township, and one school board. Wage rates ranged from a low of $6.25 an hour in Milwaukee County to a high of $12 an hour (without health benefits, or $11 if health insurance is covered) in Santa Cruz, California. Santa Cruz was one of 12 living wage ordinances that passed in 2000. Others included Berkeley, Calif.; San Fernando, Calif.; San Francisco, Calif.; Denver, Colo.; Warren, Mich.; Saint Louis, Mo.; Omaha, Ne.; Cleveland, Ohio; Toledo, Ohio; Alexandria, Va.; and Eau Claire County, Wis. By the end of 2000, more than 70 campaigns were underway in other localities.[13] Legislation was also introduced in Congress for a federal living wage, which would require federal contractors to pay at least the poverty line for a family of four, or $8.20 an hour in 2000.

Support from both parents

Almost 23 million children under age 21 live with only one biological parent, about one-quarter of all American children. Of the 14 million single parents, 85 percent are mothers and 15 percent are fathers. Children living with married parents are far less likely to be poor — 8.4 percent of children in married-couple families were poor in 1999, compared with 42 percent of all children living with a single mother.

Family arrangements have become increasingly complex: children are less likely to live with married parents today, but they may be living with both their parents. In the early 1990s, close to 40 percent of the births to unmarried mothers occurred when mother and father were living together (up about 10 percentage points over the preceding decade). Cohabiting relationships tend to be unstable, and unmarried parents living together are about as likely to be poor as single mothers.[14] When parents are poor, they are less likely to marry and less likely to stay together. Noting that married families are much better off financially, bipartisan interest in programs intended to encourage marriage has been growing. The data suggest that helping parents improve their economic prospects is likely to be one of the more effective "pro-marriage" policies and would certainly benefit children. In 2000, the U.S. House overwhelmingly passed legislation to fund $140 million in grants to local programs promoting responsible fatherhood and marriage. The grants would fund job initiatives, counseling, and other services. Similar legislation stalled in the Senate and was not enacted by the end of 2000. Interest remains strong, and action is likely in 2001.

Whether or not they live with both parents, children need their support. While child support payments have increased over time, more than three-quarters of children living with only one parent do not receive any support from their other parent. A new U.S. Census Bureau study about child support found that in 1998, 44 percent of all parents with custody (custodial parents) had no child support orders or agreements, and another 33 percent of parents did not receive payments even with agreements. When families received the full amount due to their children, it made a big difference: the average payment to families who received the full amount was $4,700 in 1997. Yet only 41 percent of families with a child support order received all that was owed. Twenty-seven percent of families with an order for child support received partial payments, averaging $1,900 for the year. The proportion of custodial families receiving any support declined slightly from 1993 to 1997, although the number of families receiving full payments rose by 7 percent.[15]

Government child support enforcement offices help establish paternity and child support orders and collect payments from absent parents. Preliminary reports from FY 2000 show that enforcement officials collected more than $18 billion in child support, a substantial increase over the $15.8 billion collected the year before.[16] In FY 1999, 6.1 million government child support cases had collections out of the total 16.4 million cases, serving 19.76 million children. Almost two-thirds (63 percent) of the child support caseload is made up of current and former welfare recipients, but more than 90 percent of the funds collected in FY 1999 were for former recipients or for families who have never received welfare assistance. Only 9.3

percent of child support was collected on behalf of current recipients of Temporary Assistance for Needy Families (TANF). Current welfare recipients seldom see a direct benefit from collections on their behalf, since the government keeps $1.3 billion out of the $1.5 billion collected as reimbursement for welfare expenditures. Before the 1996 federal welfare law passed, states were required to pass through $50 a month when child support was collected for current welfare recipients; the federal and state governments would split the rest. The 1996 law ended the requirement that any child support be passed along to families receiving welfare, and many states stopped doing so. Former recipients get much more of the support collected on their behalf ($3.8 billion out of the $4.83 billion collected).[17] Through a very complicated distribution system, former welfare recipients get all of the child support that is currently due to them each month, but get only some of the back child support collected. When absent parents owe months or years of back support, child support enforcement officials employ a variety of enforcement tools, such as freezing bank accounts or other assets. In FY 2000, $1.4 billion in overdue support was collected from IRS refunds seized from delinquent parents. Arrearages collected from most sources are paid to families who formerly received welfare benefits. But intercepted IRS refunds, one of the most fruitful sources of back child support owed to former welfare recipients, are kept by the government. The Child Support Distribution Act, introduced in Congress in 2000, would allow families who have left welfare to receive all back child support payments, including those collected from IRS refunds. These changes would help parents who need child support payments to add to usually low wages when they leave welfare. When fully implemented, the proposed changes would provide over $1 billion a year in support for children. The act, which also contained the fatherhood grants discussed

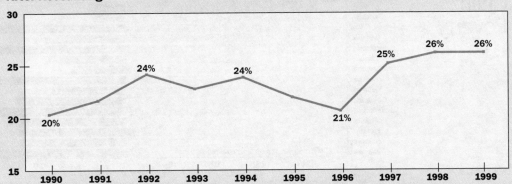

Poor Children Getting Poorer

Percentage of Poor Children Who Live Below Half the Poverty Line After Accounting for Food and Rent Assistance and Taxes, 1990-1999

Source: U.S. Department of Commerce, Bureau of the Census, Current Population Survey for March 1991– March 2000. Calculations by Children's Defense Fund.

earlier, passed the House by a vote of 405 to 18, but was not taken up by the Senate.

While more needs to be done to help low-income absent parents earn more so they can pay support, families leaving welfare will have far more stability if they can rely on child support as a part of their income package.

Help from the tax code

In 1999, the federal Earned Income Tax Credit (EITC) lifted 2.6 million children out of poverty, a bigger impact than all other means-tested programs combined. The EITC is so effective because it provides a tax credit to low-income working families even when their earnings are too low to owe federal income taxes (called a "refundable" credit). More than 16 million children live in these families — one out of every four U.S. children under age 17. Workers with two or more children and 2000 earnings between $9,500 and $12,500 receive the maximum EITC of $3,888. For workers with one child, the maximum payment of $2,353 is available to those with incomes from $7,000 to $12,500. Families with lower or higher incomes receive smaller credits. With two or more children, the credit phases out completely when the family's income exceeds $31,000; for a family with one child, the phase-out point is $28,000. Since most single-parent families with incomes below $9,000 and married couple families with incomes below $12,950 do not have to file federal income tax forms, some may not realize they are eligible for the EITC. Outreach efforts to inform low-income working families about the EITC are very important, especially because families who have not filed for their EITC in the past may receive up to three years' worth of back EITC payments.[18] Preliminary figures for the first eight months of 2000 (for the 1999 tax year) showed that 15.8 million families with children, plus another almost 3 million workers without children, had claimed the EITC. The value of their credits totaled almost $31 billion.[19]

The EITC not only helps to reduce child poverty, it also provides a substantial work incentive. One study estimated that the EITC accounts for about 60 percent of the growth in annual employment by single mothers between 1984 and 1996.[20]

However, the EITC is not as helpful for families with three or more children. Children in larger families are disproportionately poor. Counting the value of the EITC and non-cash benefits, 23 percent of families with three or more children are poor, double the rate of smaller families. To address this problem, legislation with bipartisan support was introduced in 2000 to create a third tier for the credit and include families with three or more children. Another victim of election-year gridlock, the EITC expansion did not pass.

Fifteen states provide EITCs in addition to the federal credit. The District of Columbia, New Jersey, Illinois, and Maine adopted new EITCs in 2000. Ten of the 15 are refundable credits (Colorado, District of Columbia, Kansas, Maryland, Massachusetts, Minnesota, New Jersey, New York, Vermont, and Wisconsin). In 1999, Montgomery County in Maryland became the first county to establish its own EITC. Wisconsin provides a separate and larger credit for families with three or more children.[21] States can use federal welfare (TANF) block grant funds to pay for the refundable portion of any state EITC.

Two other federal tax credits are intended to help families with children. The Child Tax Credit provides $500 per child under age 17. The tax cut plan introduced by President Bush in early 2001 includes doubling the Child Tax Credit to $1,000 per child and increasing the income at which the credit begins to phase out (to $200,000 for

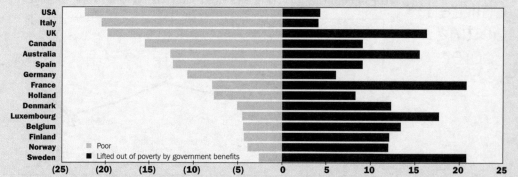

International Child Poverty

Among all children, percent in poverty and percent lifted out of poverty

Legend:
- Poor
- Lifted out of poverty by government benefits

Countries (top to bottom): USA, Italy, UK, Canada, Australia, Spain, Germany, France, Holland, Denmark, Luxembourg, Belgium, Finland, Norway, Sweden

Scale: (25) (20) (15) (10) (5) 0 5 10 15 20 25

Note: For international comparisons, poverty defined as family income below half of national median income.
Source: United Nations Children's Fund, Innocenti Research Centre, "A League Table of Child Poverty in Rich Nations" (June 2000), Figure 9, at http://www.unicef-icdc.org/publications/pdf/repcard1e.pdf

married couples, up from the current $110,000). The Child and Dependent Care Tax Credit allows families with children under age 13 or family members with disabilities to claim some of their expenses for care (as much as $720 for families with one dependent, for example). Neither of these credits is refundable, so they do not help families with wages too low to owe income taxes. If the Child Tax Credit were made refundable, more than 16 million children who get nothing from either the current credit or the proposed expansion would benefit. Doubling the credit and making it refundable would lift 2 million children out of poverty.

Unemployment insurance

For low-income working parents whose jobs are temporary or unstable, unemployment insurance (UI) should be an important protection. But over the years, increasingly restrictive state eligibility rules have made unemployment insurance unavailable to most unemployed workers. In 1999, only 38.7 percent of unemployed workers received UI, compared to three-quarters of the unemployed during the 1974-1975 recession. Part-time, low-wage, and women workers were much less likely to receive unemployment insurance than the average worker. Between 1988 and 1994, for example, low-wage workers (earning less than $8 an hour) were less than half as likely to collect unemployment benefits when compared with jobless individuals who had been earning higher wages (22.5 percent versus 53.5 percent). While 35 percent of unemployed men received UI benefits, only 23 percent of jobless women did.[22]

In the last few years, some states have taken steps to reverse this trend. Twelve states have changed antiquated laws and now allow workers to count their most recent earnings in qualifying for UI benefits, which is helpful to low-wage workers including mothers who have recently left welfare for work. States have also been accepting other reasons for leaving employment, allowing more people to qualify for UI benefits. The majority of states now grant unemployment benefits to individuals who leave work because of domestic violence. North Carolina recently passed legislation making those who leave work because of undue family hardship (including inability to provide child care) eligible for unemployment insurance. Unemployed, low-income, single mothers will be more likely to receive benefits as a result of these changes. At least 13 states increased their unemployment benefits through allowances for individuals with dependent children and/or elders. Connecticut recently raised its weekly allowance from $10 to $15 per dependent. Most states have not provided benefits to people seeking part-time work, a problem for some parents who have worked less than full-time hours and need to continue that arrangement. Nine states allow at least some part-time workers to be eligible for UI benefits.[23]

On the federal level in 2000, a two-year negotiation among state employment security agencies, employer and labor representatives, and the U.S. Department of Labor succeeded in developing a consensus proposal to make changes in the UI system. Several of its provisions would benefit low-income workers, including new federal requirements that states count an applicant's most recent wages and that part-time workers be eligible. While there was hope that legislation based on this agreement would pass in 2000, it did not, and its prospects appear unclear for the 2001 session.[24]

In another federal development, the U.S. Department of Labor issued regulations allowing states to use unemployment insurance funds to pay benefits to parents who take a leave from work to care for a newborn or newly adopted child. In a number of states (including Indiana, Massachusetts, Missouri, Vermont, and Wisconsin), legislation has been introduced to take up this option, but none have yet passed.

Help with housing costs

In order to afford a two-bedroom apartment with a fair market rent at the national median, a worker had to earn $12.47 an hour in 2000, based on the standard definition of "affordable" as rent that does not exceed 30 percent of a family's income. But in 47 states, one-third or more of all renting households did not earn enough to afford the fair market rent for a two-bedroom apartment. For families needing a larger space, it was even tougher. In 49 states, at least 40 percent of all renters earned too little to afford a three-bedroom apartment.[25]

Income gains among low-income households resulted in welcome reductions in the numbers burdened by very high housing costs from 1997 to 1999. Even though the number of housing units affordable to poor families dropped sharply during this period, higher earnings meant that fewer families had "worst case housing needs" — paying more than half their income on rent or living in severely substandard housing. "Worst case needs" is an imperfect measure — for example, it does not count the homeless — but it helps us glimpse at some housing trends. In 1999, 4.9 million renter households had worst case needs, down substantially from the record high 5.4 million in 1997. Of the 10.9 million people living in worst case households, 3.6 million were children, down from 4.3 million children out of 12.3 million overall in 1997.

The good news is that the number of poor renter households dropped from 9 million in 1997 to 8.6 million in 1999. The bad news is that 68 percent of poor renters without housing assistance lived in worst case housing conditions in 1999. The number of families with children suffering worst case housing needs declined by 210,000 to 1.8 million, lower than 1991 levels. Nevertheless, more than 42 percent of families with children living in unsubsidized housing with low but above-poverty incomes had worst case housing needs.[26]

Poor families who paid more than half their income on rent were more likely to work (54 percent had earnings in 1997, rising to 64 percent in 1999) and less likely to receive welfare income (36 percent in 1997 and 31 percent in 1999). From 1991 to 1997, the largest increase of households with worst case housing needs occurred among families with children with full-time workers, 29 percent, compared with a 12 percent increase in worst case households overall. The increase among families with full-time earners was most pronounced in central cities (a stunning 62 percent increase in worst case housing needs), all among minority families (74 percent among Hispanics and 31 percent among Blacks).[27]

From 1991 to 1997, rents rose at twice the rate of general inflation. The number of units that poor families could afford declined by 750,000 from 1997 to 1999, a record 13 percent drop that accelerated a decade-long trend. From 1991 to 1999, the number of units affordable to poor households dropped by 940,000. During the same period, for every 100 families with incomes at approximately the poverty level, the number of units both affordable and available for rent dropped from 47 to 40.[28] While rising incomes have allowed families to pay higher rents, an economic slowdown is likely to reduce the rent families can afford, possibly reversing the recent progress.

Housing hardships are not confined to households living below poverty. Urban Institute's National Survey of America's Families shows that high levels of hardship continue among families with children living below twice the poverty line in 1999. Almost a third (31.8 percent) of single parents with incomes below 200 percent of the poverty level had problems paying their mortgage, rent, or utility bills in the previous 12 months; the same was true for about one-quarter of married parents. Despite two more years of economic expansion, the Urban Institute survey showed little change since 1997.[29]

More than 70 percent of very low-income (below or near poverty) renters received no form of housing subsidy in 1997.[30] In 2000, there were about 4.1 million federally subsidized units with rents limited to 30 percent of household income. These subsidies consisted of public housing (1.1 million units owned by local public housing agencies), project-based assisted housing (1.4 million units in projects owned by nonprofit or for-profit sponsors that are required to rent to low-income households), and tenant-based assisted housing (1.6 million renters who are supplied with vouchers, under the federal Section 8 program, that pay the difference between about 30 percent of the tenant's income and the fair market rent). By the end of 1999, there had been a loss of about 90,000 project-based units, as contracts requiring their use as low-cost housing expired. If similar proportions of units with expiring contracts decide to opt out of the program, by 2004, between 120,000 and 180,000 more low-cost units will be lost. The stock of public housing is also being reduced, as public housing authorities tear down aging units in very poor condition. More than 27,600 units had been demolished by 1999, offset by only 7,273 new or renovated units.[31] After years without increases in tenant-based Section 8 vouchers, in FYs 1999 and 2000, Congress approved a total of 110,000 new vouchers, with another 79,000 added in FY 2001. However, without preventing the continued loss of project-based units, the

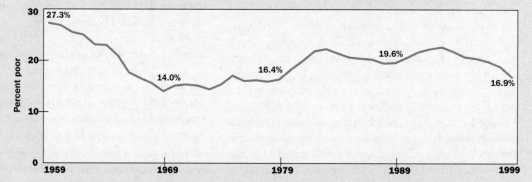

Child Poverty: More Progress Needed

Percent of Persons Younger Than 18 Below Poverty Line, 1959-1999

Source: U.S. Department of Commerce, Bureau of the Census, Historical Income Tables, at http://www.census.gov/hhes/poverty/histpov/histpov3.html.

Poverty Status of Children in America, by Selected Characteristics: 1974, 1989, 1998, and 1999
Persons younger than 18

	Number Poor (in thousands)	Percent Poor			
	1999	1999	1998	1989	1974
All persons younger than 18	12,109	16.9%	18.9%	19.6%	15.4%
White	7,568	13.5	15.1	14.8	11.2
Black	3,759	33.1	36.7	43.7	39.8
Asian and Pacific Islander	361	11.8	18.0	19.8	n.a.
Hispanic (can be any race)	3,506	30.3	34.4	36.2	n.a.
Non-Hispanic White	4,252	9.4	10.6	11.5	9.5
Related to head of household	11,510	16.3	18.3	19.0	15.5
In female headed family	6,602	41.9	46.1	51.1	51.5
All other family types	4,908	9.0	9.7	10.4	8.7
Family member works	8,932	13.3	14.4	13.2	n.a.
Works full time year round	3,812	6.7	7.8	6.1	n.a.
South	4,377	18.4	19.9	22.0	21.2
All other regions	7,133	15.3	17.5	17.4	12.7
Central city	4,938	24.3	27.7	29.0	21.6
Suburb	4,013	10.9	12.2	11.4	9.0
Rural (nonmetropolitan)	2,559	19.3	19.7	21.3	18.1
Under age 6	4,170	18.0	20.6	21.9	16.9
Ages 6-17	7,340	15.5	17.1	17.4	14.9
Comparison: Adults 18-64	16,982	10.0	10.5	10.2	8.3
Seniors 65+	3,167	9.7	10.5	11.4	14.6

n.a. - Data not available.

Source: U.S. Department of Commerce, Bureau of the Census, Current Population Reports, Series P-60, Nos. 102, 171, 207, and 210; and Current Population Survey, March 1990, March 1999, and March 2000. Calculations by Children's Defense Fund.

added Section 8 vouchers will not be enough to offset a net loss of subsidized units in the next few years.

Further, when landlords are able to get higher rents in the private market, it is harder for low-income families to find apartments that will take their vouchers. A recent study of voucher use in Missouri found that the St. Louis County voucher program has a success rate of about 50 percent. In a large public housing agency in Massachusetts, three or four vouchers were issued for every one that was successfully used.[32] To utilize vouchers fully, a combination of approaches is required. In some areas, there simply are not enough units available, because renovation or construction is necessary. But vouchers can be successful if their value is increased to reflect rising housing costs and families are offered help in searching for housing (such as help with transportation and credit checks and more time to look). The Clinton administration proposed a Voucher Success Fund of $50 million for FY 2001 to fund a variety of strategies to make it easier to use vouchers, but the proposal was not enacted.

With low-cost housing in short supply, it is not surprising that the U.S. Conference of Mayors reported that in 1999 to 2000, the average demand for emergency shelter rose in 25 cities surveyed. The extent of the increase is surprising — 15 percent, the highest one-year jump in the last 10 years. Among homeless families with children, who make up 36 percent of all the homeless in the survey, the increase was 17 percent. Twenty-seven percent of requests for shelter by families with children were unmet. Half of the cities indicated that the length of time people remained homeless had increased to an average of 5 months.[33]

The cold winter and rising natural gas prices intensified the housing cost burden for low- and moderate-income families. The cost of natural gas heating rose by 50 percent from the winter of 1999-2000 to the first quarter of 2001. In Chicago, natural gas prices were expected almost to triple compared to a year ago, and the mayor and governor asked the federal government to extend energy assistance funds to families with incomes up to 175 percent of the poverty line, up from the current limit of 150 percent.[34] Some states lowered the eligibility cap, because of insufficient funds. The Low Income Home Energy Assistance Program (LIHEAP), which pays a few hundred dollars towards energy costs for only about 13 percent of the 29 million eligible households, declined from $1.7 billion in FY 1995 to $1.1 billion in FY 2000, but was then increased to $1.4 billion in FY 2001 in response to skyrocketing energy costs.

As housing costs take more of family income, increasing evidence shows that housing subsidies not only help make ends meet, but also help parents find and keep jobs and improve children's behavior and health. In the successful Minnesota Family Investment Program (MFIP) demonstration project, families in public or subsidized housing experienced the biggest gains. An evaluation by the Manpower Demonstration Research Corporation (MDRC) found that long-term welfare recipients who lived in public or subsidized housing increased their employment by 18 percent, which was double the rate for long-term welfare recipients without housing subsidies. Quarterly earnings of MFIP participants in public or subsidized housing rose by an average of 25 percent, while those who did not live in subsidized units gained only 2 percent in earnings.[35] Another study in Boston showed that children in families who had vouchers and moved to neighborhoods with less concentrated poverty had fewer asthma attacks or injuries than comparable families

without vouchers, and boys in families with vouchers had fewer behavior problems.[36]

Food stamps

Between November 1999 and November 2000, the food stamp caseload declined by 437,960 people. The drop continues a multi-year downward trend. In November 1996, the U.S. food stamp caseload included 24.1 million individuals and dropped to 17.1 million in November 2000, a 29 percent reduction.[37] While some of the declining caseload occurred because people earned more and no longer qualified for food stamps, many poor families simply lost access to food stamps. In an analysis of food stamp use from 1994 to 1998, the U.S. Department of Agriculture (USDA) confirmed that the decline was concentrated among households with incomes low enough to qualify for food stamps. The USDA found that more than half of the caseload drop (55 percent) occurred among people with incomes below 130 percent of the federal poverty level, the cut-off for food stamp eligibility.[38] Looking at it another way, the food stamp caseload dropped much more sharply than child poverty did. From 1994 to 1999, child poverty declined by 21.4 percent, while children receiving food stamps declined 36.2 percent.[39]

When the welfare law passed in 1996, even those who favored limiting cash assistance expected that food stamps would remain a safety net for poor families. Instead, food stamps reach fewer needy families than before. In 1995, more than 88 of every 100 poor children received food stamps. In 1999, only 71.5 out of every 100 poor children did.[40] The loss of food stamps is no small thing for low-income families. For the typical single-parent family receiving food stamps in FY 1999, the average benefit was $229 a month; larger two-parent families averaged $274. Food stamps made up more than one-quarter of the single-parent family's income in FY 1999 and more than one-fifth of the married-couple's income.[41]

The decline in food stamp use has been a sobering lesson about the real-world consequences of policy changes. Some of the consequences were intended, if ill-advised. The 1996 law made most legal immigrants ineligible for food stamps, limited food stamps for able-bodied individuals without children to only three months out of 36 if they are not engaged in work, and allowed states to reduce or terminate food stamps if adults do not comply with the rules of cash assistance programs. As a result of the restrictions, the number of households with noncitizens receiving food stamps dropped by two-thirds from 1996 to 1999, even though most immigrants who lost food stamps continued to have low incomes. The overall caseload reduction during the same period was 27.3 percent.[42] The loss of food stamps hit these families hard. A California study shortly after the law was enacted found immigrant families with food hardships serious enough to experience moderate to severe hunger, levels of deprivation four times higher than that of the low-income population as a whole.[43] After an effective effort to expose the hardships endured by young, old, and disabled immigrants, legislation was passed in 1998 to restore food stamp benefits to the immigrants who had arrived in the United States before the welfare law's enactment (August 22, 1996). Advocates have continued to press for a full restoration of food stamp benefits to legal immigrants, including children who arrived after 1996 and parents, whether they came before or after the law passed. While the strongly bipartisan Hunger Relief Act called for restoration of food stamp benefits for legal immigrants, the legislation did not pass in 2000.

Some of the reduction in food stamp benefits, however, was not intended. The implementation of the 1996 welfare law resulted in the loss of food stamp benefits for millions of families when it drastically cut the cash assistance caseload (see discussion on Cash Assistance). Families who receive cash benefits are automatically eligible for food stamps. Families with low wages who do not get cash assistance may qualify for food stamps, but they must apply and document their earnings and income on a regular basis to prove continuing eligibility. Applications and renewals are time-consuming and difficult for parents who cannot take time off from work without risking their jobs. California Food Policy Advocates examined the time it took to apply for food stamps in four counties. To complete an application, families typically had to make between two and three office visits, lasting between one hour and 45 minutes to almost five hours.[44] According to another anti-hunger group, America's Second Harvest, the Illinois firearm application is one page long, and the New York state application to become a school bus driver is only two pages. But the average state application for food stamps is 12 pages long; in some places, there are more than 30 pages to fill out.[45] Unsurprisingly, parents with low-wage jobs are often unable to manage this unwieldy process. As a result, fewer low-income single-parent families received food stamps in 1998 than in 1994.[46]

According to CDF's analysis of its Community Monitoring Project survey findings, among parents who had jobs and did not receive food stamps, almost 30 percent reported problems buying food for their family. In contrast, 20 percent of working former welfare recipients who did get food stamps reported food hardships.[47]

A U.S. Department of Agriculture report about food insecurity and hunger also demonstrates the need for additional help in reaching particular groups of low-income families. While fewer households were unable to afford adequate or nutritious food (were "food insecure") in 1999 compared with 1995, households with incomes between 50 percent and 130 percent of the federal poverty level were more likely to experience food insecurity. Despite having incomes low enough to qualify, food stamp use declined among this group of households during the same period that their food hardships increased. Due to the good economy, there were fewer households with this little income, and food hardships were reduced among female-headed households and among White, Black, and Hispanic families. Also, the prevalence of outright hunger (going without meals because of lack of money) dipped by 24 percent between 1995 and 1999, twice as sharp a drop as for food insecurity overall. Nevertheless, the number and proportion of children, single-mother families, and minorities who report problems affording food is still glaringly high. Thirty-one million people lived in food-insecure households in 1999, including 12 million children. Households with children were food insecure at twice the rate for childless households (14.8 percent versus 7.4 percent). Almost three in 10 (29.7 percent) single-mother households sometimes lacked the money to buy food, and food was at times unaffordable for more than one-third (36.7 percent) of households below the federal poverty level. Black and Hispanic households were more than twice as likely to experience food insecurity as the population as a whole (21.2 percent and 20.8 percent, respectively).[48]

According to a survey of 25 cities conducted by the U.S. Conference of Mayors, requests for food help from families with children rose 16 percent on average in 2000, the biggest increase since 1991. Twenty-one out of the 25 cities reported increased demand from families. Sixty-two percent of those requesting food were either children or their parents, and 32 percent were employed adults.[49] Catholic Charities USA reported a striking 32 percent increase in the number of people receiving emergency food assistance from their agencies nationwide from 1998 to 1999.[50] While increased use of food pantries and soup kitchens helped to alleviate hunger, emergency solutions are not an adequate response to ongoing problems faced by so many low-income and working families.

To help address these problems, the U.S. Department of Agriculture published new rules to encourage states to make it easier for working families to apply for and renew food stamps. Under the new rules, states can verify income and earnings changes as infrequently as once every six months and do not need to require office visits more than once a year. Changes in income may be reported by phone or mail, and reporting forms may be limited to six questions. Until now, many states have required parents to come to the food stamp office every three months, a burdensome requirement for the 42 percent of food stamp

Reports From Struggling Families: CDF's Community Monitoring Project*

To find out more about what has happened to families leaving welfare, the Children's Defense Fund sought the help of more than 180 community agencies in 16 states, who conducted interviews with more than 5,200 people in 1999. CDF analyzed responses from more than 2,000 parents who had left welfare, who were still receiving benefits, or who had never gotten assistance. The individuals surveyed were seeking services at shelters, food pantries, and other agencies. They are among the poorest of the poor, often working, but finding that low-wage work alone is not enough to fend off hardships.

◆ More than half of those who had left welfare since 1996 left for work (either a new job or increased pay), but one-third of them no longer had a job.

◆ When parents had left a job, lack of child care was the reason most often reported for no longer working.

◆ 58 percent of those who were working had family weekly wages below the poverty line.

◆ More than half of the employed parents had been unable to pay the rent, buy food, afford medical care, or had their telephone or electric service disconnected.

◆ Children suffer when their families experience hardships. Working parents without Medicaid were twice as likely as families with Medicaid to report that they were unable to pay for their children's health care.

◆ Despite low incomes, less than a third of the working families were receiving help paying for child care, and half were not receiving food stamps. Nearly a third of the working families had at least one member with no health insurance.

*Children's Defense Fund. *Families Struggling to Make It in the Workforce: A Post Welfare Report.* (Washington, D.C.: Children's Defense Fund, 2000.) Available at http://www.childrensdefense.org

households with children that have earnings. Some states have eased reporting and renewal procedures, although others are reluctant because they fear less frequent reporting will increase federal penalties for errors. State administrators and advocates will seek changes in the federal calculation of state error rates, to make it easier to serve low-income working families who have minor fluctuations in income.

Many working parents need cars to get to work. Yet the food stamp program has excluded families with vehicles worth more than $4,650, a figure that has been raised only $150 since it was first set in 1977. In the fall of 2000, legislation was enacted that gives states the option to ease this limit on food stamp eligibility. For families who receive aid from Temporary Assistance for Needy Families (TANF), and for those who do not get cash aid but receive certain TANF-funded services, states may apply the more generous TANF vehicle rules, currently in effect in most states, to the food stamp program.[51]

With fewer families receiving food stamps because they receive cash assistance, a combination of streamlined application procedures and outreach is needed to make sure eligible families get the help they need. The Food Outreach and Research for Kids Act (FORK) was introduced in Congress in 2000 to provide grants for outreach and systems streamlining. Although it was not enacted, federal funds were appropriated in late 2000 to allow community groups to inform families that they might be eligible for food stamps and to help them apply.

Some states have taken steps to reverse the trend of declining food stamp participation. While food stamps declined 4.4 percent from June 1999 to June 2000 nationwide, 11 states increased participation in the food stamp program. Seventeen states reported spending on food stamp outreach in 2000, up from only nine states in 1999. Activities include hotline numbers, outreach workers in community agencies, eligibility prescreening over the phone, and extended office hours. As of July 2000, 30 states had decided to expand eligibility for food stamps based on families' eligibility for services (not necessarily cash assistance) provided under TANF. Thirteen states were purchasing food stamps with state funds to provide them to income-eligible legal immigrants now excluded from the federal food stamp program.[52]

For millions of children and families who still experience food hardships despite the unprecedented economic boom, restoring and expanding access to food stamps must be a national priority.

Help for children with disabilities

Almost 850,000 low-income children with disabilities received Supplemental Security Income (SSI) in

December 2000. In order to qualify, low-income children must have severe impairments that limit their functioning. After allegations of children inappropriately receiving SSI benefits, the 1996 welfare law restricted eligibility for SSI, especially for children with mental disorders. As a result, the SSI children's caseload dropped by more than 100,000 from its peak of 955,174 children. More than three out of five children receiving SSI live with one parent (almost always the mother). Single mothers caring for children who receive SSI have very little income besides the SSI payment. Almost two-thirds of children on SSI in single-parent families live with a parent who has no earnings because of the time and difficulty of caring for a child with a disability. More than 60 percent of children receiving SSI who live in single-parent families have incomes below $400 a month. Sixty-five percent of children who received SSI got the maximum payment of $512 a month (the amount paid to individuals with no other countable income) in December 2000. The average monthly payment was $447 (families with some income receive less from SSI).

After 1996, 288,000 cases were examined to see if they met the new, more restrictive criteria. Thirty-eight percent were ruled ineligible. Complaints about the decision-making process led to a top-to-bottom review and many children were reinstated. In 2000, mental disorders remained the most frequent diagnosis for children who received SSI, affecting 63 percent of the caseload. Final rules for the children's SSI program took effect in January 2001 and incorporated some of the improved eligibility procedures sought by the families of children with disabilities.

Still, even though most young people receiving SSI now meet tougher eligibility criteria, large numbers have been denied continued SSI after age 18. More evaluation of the criteria is expected, with efforts to continue youths on SSI after age 18 if they are still in school or in a special education program.

Cash assistance

One thing is clear about cash assistance: there is much less of it. From August 1996, when the welfare law was enacted, through June 2000, the number of individuals receiving Temporary Assistance for Needy Families (TANF) has been cut in half, with 6.46 million fewer adults and children receiving cash assistance. In 1999, only 37.8 of every 100 poor children received TANF, down from 57.3 out of every 100 poor children in 1995.[53]

Common points are emerging from the growing library of post-welfare studies. Consistent with CDF's Community Monitoring Project findings (see box), the majority of families work after leaving welfare, but their employment is often unstable and almost always low-paid.

Perhaps most important: families who leave welfare are not all the same. Parents with more education are much more likely to find work and earn more. Those with disabilities, little education, or other barriers will spend much less time employed.

Families leaving welfare: what's been learned

Work patterns: Most studies have found that at least two-thirds of parents who left welfare worked at some point in the year before they were surveyed. Far fewer (between about 35 and 40 percent) worked all four quarters, according to findings from Los Angeles, New York, and Cuyahoga county, Ohio (includes Cleveland).[54]

Earnings: According to state reports, average quarterly earnings for former welfare recipients was $2,027 in the first quarter of employment, rising to $2,647 in the third quarter. These averages were based on 1998-1999 data submitted by 48 states plus the District of Columbia competing for TANF bonuses awarded to states with good records on earnings and work. Unfortunately, even the higher third-quarter wages were only about three-quarters of the earnings necessary to reach the federal poverty level.[55]

Education makes a difference: In a three-city study, 28 percent of mothers who had not completed high school were never employed in the year prior to being interviewed in late 1999, compared with only 13 percent of mothers with a high school diploma or equivalency. Work was steadier for those with more education: those who had finished high school worked 78 percent of the time before being interviewed, while those without a diploma or GED worked 61 percent of the time. Ninety-one percent of those who had not finished high school were poor, compared with 64 percent of those who were high school graduates.[56] In CDF's Community Monitoring Project analysis, three-quarters of those who left welfare for work had finished high school, while only 48 percent of those who left for noncompliance or administrative error had a high school degree.

Health matters: The three-city study also found that 31 percent of the parents who reported fair or poor health were never employed, compared with only 6 percent of parents who reported very good or excellent health. Fair or poor health cut earnings in half ($356 a month versus $718). According to Urban Institute's National Survey of America's Families, one-third of current TANF recipients and one-quarter of former recipients reported that poor health limited their ability to work or were scored as having very poor mental health.

When families leave welfare, they often do not get benefits they are eligible for: As described above, families leaving welfare often do not get food stamps. In the three-city study, fewer than 40 percent continued to get food stamps after leaving welfare, although in most cases they remained poor. Similarly, only about half of those in the Community Monitoring Project sample who had left welfare received food stamps. More families received Medicaid (70 percent in the three-city survey), but still fewer than would be expected based on the families' incomes. Among Community Monitoring Project respondents, 86 percent of current TANF families had Medicaid or other insurance, compared with 59 percent of former recipients. In the Community Monitoring Project, when parents worked and received supports such as food stamps, Medicaid, and child care, they were twice as likely as employed former recipients with no supports to report that paying bills was easier (28 percent versus 14 percent).

Families who are "pushed off" welfare tend to have serious barriers to employment: In the Community Monitoring Project sample, parents whose benefits ended because they missed appointments or did not follow program rules were less likely to have completed high school than current recipients and were more likely to have physical health problems. Similarly, in Utah, one-third of families who lost benefits because of noncompliance said they did not work because of a health condition; one-fifth reported mental problems. In Delaware, families with the least education and work experience were more frequently penalized.[57]

Families who leave welfare sometimes return: Between 22.7 and 35.3 percent of families who left welfare received benefits again at some point within a year of leaving, according to five state and local studies.[58] Among Community Monitoring Project respondents, lack of education and physical disabilities were associated with unstable jobs. Lack of child care was the most frequently cited reason for not working among those who had left welfare. Loss of employment can force families back to welfare if they have not exhausted their time-limited benefits. In the future, when more families hit the TANF time limits, returning will no longer be an option.

When welfare programs result in increased family incomes, children do better: An analysis of 14 welfare experiments shows that when families boosted income through a combination of work and benefits, children's school performance improved and their behavior problems decreased. (See The Bottom Line box.) Unfortunately, few states are investing in this mix of work supports and wage supplements.

These findings offer important lessons as states seek to improve their welfare programs, and as the nation looks towards possible changes in federal law when TANF expires in 2002. Since wages go up when parents have more education or training, a concerted effort should be made to improve educational levels and build skills. But in FY 1999, nine out of 10 participants in TANF work activities held unsubsidized jobs, performed unpaid work experience, or were looking for a job. Less than 1 percent were in on-the-job training, which can be one of the most effective means of building marketable skills. Only 7.2 percent were enrolled in vocational education, with less than 2 percent participating in education related to employment (often high school equivalency training).[59] Some states, including Arizona, Hawaii, New York, Washington state, West Virginia, Vermont, Maine, and Illinois,[60] have recognized the importance of education and allow postsecondary education and/or work-study programs to count as a work activity.

If TANF programs do not identify problems such as disability, domestic violence, or lack of child care or transportation and do not help families solve these problems, more families will be "pushed off" assistance without real prospects of sustained employment. Some states are addressing these problems. In 2000, Tennessee began "Family Services Counseling," which provides intensive help for families with problems such as physical or mental impairments, learning disabilities, domestic violence, or substance abuse. Trained counselors are available to help develop service plans, including changes in work requirements and exemptions from time limits, if appropriate. New Mexico has developed procedures consistent with the Americans with Disabilities Act, permitting adults who receive TANF to establish a Modified Work Participation Agreement, which includes therapies or other support services that count towards the hours of required work. Many states provide substance abuse screening and treatment.

Many families leaving TANF do not earn enough to get out of poverty. Programs that help by raising incomes have a positive impact on children. The most promising approaches combine work with cash and in-kind supports. In 2000, New York committed $45 million for a wage subsidy demonstration program for families with incomes up to 200 percent of the federal poverty level. Many states allow families to combine low-wages with at least modest cash benefits; Illinois, Maine, and Arizona exempt months of such work from the time-limit clock.

State spending on TANF: States need to use TANF funds to provide supports and work preparation for families currently receiving cash assistance and to help low-income families outside the welfare system with a package of work supports. As states have started to provide at least some of these supports, spending has increased. In FY 2000, states used 93.5 percent of the year's TANF allocation. Thirty-six states including the District of Columbia spent at least 90 percent of their total FY 2000 TANF allocation (excluding any bonus funding). Eighteen states spent more than 100 percent of their FY

2000 funds, meaning that they dipped into TANF funds left from prior years.[61]

The nature of TANF spending has been changing. Because the caseload is down, cash assistance declined by $11 billion from 1994 through 2000 and now accounts for less than half of TANF spending (44 percent or $11.4 billion). Child care is the second biggest TANF expenditure at 17 percent or $4.4 billion. Since TANF began, expenditures for work-related activities rose slightly, but are now just 9 percent of the total. Still, of the TANF funds allocated to states in the first four years of the program, about $8 billion remains unspent. Adding together totally uncommitted funds and funds that have been committed but not spent (the latter known as unliquidated obligations), 22 states including the District of Columbia still have left 15 percent or more of the TANF block grant allocated from FY 1997 through FY 2000. Some states label funds as "obligated" because they transfer the funds to counties, even though the counties may have no specific plans to use the money. Some of these TANF dollars may remain unspent.

Moving Forward: A 2001 Agenda for Action

It is time to end child poverty in America. It will not be achieved through one magic step, but it can be done by improving the components of the income package families rely upon. Taking the following steps, child poverty can be cut in half in four years:

◆ **Make tax policies work for children:** By doubling the federal Child Tax Credit from $500 to $1,000 per child and making the credit available as a refund to families with incomes too low to owe federal income tax, at least 2 million poor children can be lifted above the poverty line. The federal Earned Income Tax Credit should be increased for families with three or more children (who are disproportionately poor). States can help by enacting their own refundable tax credits.

◆ **Expand the use of proven anti-poverty strategies:** Programs with the goal of helping families to earn family-supporting wages, with the help of child care, transportation, medical coverage, and wage supplements, can work to increase family income. All states should build programs similar to the Minnesota Family Investment Program demonstration or other programs of similar effectiveness. Make poverty reduction, not just caseload reduction, the goal of TANF by creating a Poverty Reduction Bonus, which would reward states that use these or other strategies for a documented reduction in child poverty.

◆ **Open new gateways to existing supports:** If families received the food stamps, Medicaid/CHIP, child care, child support enforcement help, and Earned Income Tax Credit for which they are eligible, it would be a substantial step towards ending child poverty. Federal and state governments should fund and implement streamlined application and renewal procedures which are designed to meet the needs of working families. Outreach efforts that partner with community-based organizations should help families understand how they can get help with various parts of their income package. Applying or renewing should be possible in convenient locations, open evenings or weekends, and when possible, by phone, mail, or online.

◆ **Expand access to food stamps:** In addition to serving all who are currently eligible, the food stamp program can play a more aggressive anti-poverty role if legal immigrants were once again able to receive them, if the basic meal plan on which food stamp benefits are based were updated to reflect real nutritional needs and current prices (and then adjusted for inflation annually), and if benefits were adjusted to enable working families to receive more assistance.

◆ **Meet the need for affordable housing:** Almost 5 million families pay more than half of their income on rent or live in substandard housing. The nation should add 300,000 more housing vouchers each year for 10 years and create a housing trust fund to increase the supply of affordable housing for families with children. The Low Income Home Energy Assistance Program (LIHEAP) should be expanded so low-income families can better cope with rising heating and cooling costs.

◆ **Make unemployment insurance available to low-wage workers:** A worker's most recent wages should count in determining eligibility, and parents who are forced to leave work for lack of child care or because of domestic violence should qualify for benefits. Workers seeking part-time employment should also be eligible.

◆ **Both parents should support their children:** Federal and state governments should strengthen families by giving both parents the opportunity to improve their job skills and employment prospects. Rules in TANF and other programs that discriminate against two-parent families should be eliminated. States should continue to invest in stronger child support collection efforts and should at least fund demonstration projects in which child support payments are assured by the state when contributions from the absent parent are not available.

◆ **Increase funding for transportation help:** Parents cannot work if they are unable to travel to work or child care. Funds should be added to the U.S. Department of Transportation's Job Access and Reverse Commute grants so communities can improve public transit access. TANF or other funds should be used to help families with the cost of maintaining a car.

◆ **Help families overcome barriers to employment and do not deny help when parents cannot find work or are unable to work:** States must provide trained caseworkers to identify problems and fund services to overcome them. Parents who are willing to work but can-

not find jobs should be able to work at publicly subsidized jobs paying real wages and benefits. Effective education and training should be encouraged, so parents can secure better jobs. Exemptions from time limits should be based on the number of families with problems that make work impossible, and not on an arbitrary percentage of the caseload (currently set at 20 percent).

Endnotes

1. Figures on the size of the economy are calculated from U.S. Bureau of Economic Analysis data and are available on the Internet at www.bea.doc.gov.

2. Unless otherwise noted, poverty and family income figures in this chapter are calculated from Census Bureau data available on the Internet at http://www.census.gov or http://ferret.bls.census.gov/macro/032000/pov/toc.htm.

3. Figures on employment and unemployment of individuals (regardless of family status) in this chapter are calculated from U.S. Bureau of Labor Statistics data available on the Internet at http://stats.bls.gov or http://stats.bls.gov/bls_news/archives/all_nr.htm.

4. Timothy M. Smeeding, Lee Rainwater, and Gary Burtless, "United States Poverty in a Cross-National Context," *Luxembourg Income Study Working Paper No. 244* (Syracuse, N.Y.: Syracuse University, September 2000). Available on the Internet at http://lisweb.ceps.lu/publications.htm.

5. *Ibid.*

6. CDF tabulations of the U.S. Census Bureau's March Current Population Survey.

7. Kristin Smith, *Who's Minding the Kids? Child Care Arrangements: Fall 1995,* Current Population Reports Series P70-70 (Washington, D.C.: Government Printing Office, 2000): Table 14.

8. Sheila Rafferty Zedlewski, "Family Economic Well-Being: Findings from the National Survey of America's Families," Snapshots of America's Families II (Washington, D.C.: Urban Institute, 2000).

9. Bureau of Labor Statistics, "Usual Weekly Earnings of Wage and Salary Workers: Fourth Quarter 2000." Available on the Internet at ftp://146.142.4.23/pub/news/release/History/wkyeng.01182001.news.

10. *Ibid.*

11. National Economic Council, "The Minimum Wage: Increasing the Reward for Work" (Washington, D.C.: National Economic Council, March 2000). Available on the Internet at http://www.chn.org/minimumwage/minwagereport000208.pdf.

12. For state minimum wage information, see U.S. Department of Labor Web site, http://www.dol.gov/dol/esa/public/minwage/america.htm.

13. Association of Community Organizations for Reform Now (ACORN), "Living Wage Successes: A Compilation of Living Wage Policies on the Books" (Washington, D.C.: ACORN, October, 2000). Available on the Internet at http://www.livingwagecampaign.org.

14. Pamela J. Smock, "Cohabitation in the United States," *Annual Review of Sociology* 26 (August 2000). Available on the Internet at http://wwsoc.AnnualRevews.org.

15. U.S. Census Bureau, *Child Support for Custodial Mothers and Fathers,* P 60-212 (Washington, D.C.: U.S. Census Bureau, October 2000). Available on the Internet at http://www.census.gov/hhes/www/chldsupt.html.

16. U.S. Department of Health and Human Services, "HHS Announces New Record Child Support Collections" (Washington, D.C.: U.S. Department of Health and Human Services, January 17, 2001): Press release. Available on the Internet at http://www.hhs.gov/news.

17. Paula Roberts, "The Performance of the Child Support Enforcement System: Two Points of View," (Washington, D.C.: Center for Law and Social Policy, November 2000). Available on the Internet at http://www.clasp.org/pubs/childenforce/Census-OCSE%20Reports.htm.

18. The Center on Budget and Policy Priorities produces EITC outreach materials in many languages. For more information, see their Web site at http://www.cbpp.org.

19. Center on Budget and Policy Priorities, "EIC Participation for Tax Year 1999, by State" in *Help Workers Boost Their Paychecks!* (Washington, D.C.: Center on Budget and Policy Priorities, 2000).

20. Bruce Meyer and Dan T. Rosenbaum, "Welfare, the Earned Income Tax Credit, and the Employment of Single Mothers" (Evanston, Ill.: Northwestern University Department of Economics, and Greensboro, N.C., University of North Carolina Department of Economics, revised October 26, 1998). Available on the Internet at http://www.jcpr.org/wpfiles/meyer_rosenbaum.

21. Nicholas Johnson, "A Hand Up: How State Earned Income Tax Credits Help Working Families Escape Poverty in 2000: An Overview" (Washington, D.C.: Center on Budget and Policy Priorities, November 2, 2000). Available on the Internet at http://www.cbpp.org/11-2-00sfp.htm.

22. Maurice Ensellem and Vicky Lovell, "The Georgia Unemployment Insurance System: Overcoming Barriers for Low-Wage, Part-time and Women Workers" (New York/Washington, D.C.: National Employment Law Project and Institute for Women's Policy Research, December 2000). Available on the Internet at http://www.nelp.org/pub41.pdf.

23. National Employment Law Project, "State Legislative Highlights" (New York: National Employment Law Project, August 2000). Also "Part-time Workers and Unemployment Insurance" (New York: National Employment Law Project, March 2001). Available on the Internet at http://www.nelp.org.

24. National Employment Law Project, "Unemployment Insurance Consensus Offers Significant Federal Improvements" (New York: National Employment Law Project, August 3, 2000). Available on the Internet at http://www.nelp.org.

25. Jennifer G. Twombly, *Out of Reach: The Growing Gap Between Housing Costs and Income of Poor People in the United States* (Washington, D.C.: National Low Income Housing Coalition, September 2000). Available on the Internet at http://www.nlihc.org/oor2000/index.htm.

26. These 8.6 million households were living below 30 percent of their area median income, which is roughly equivalent to below-poverty status. The 42 percent of families with children with worst case housing needs described here as above the poverty line range from 31 to 50 percent of area median income, according to the U.S. Department of Housing and Urban Development.

27. Office of Policy Development and Research, U.S. Department of Housing and Urban Development, *Rental Housing Assistance – The Worsening Crisis,* (Washington, D.C.: U.S. Department of Housing and Urban Development, March 2000). Available on the Internet at http://www.hud.gov.

28. Office of Policy Development and Research, U.S. Department of Housing an/d Urban Development, *A Report on Worst Case Housing Needs in 1999: New Opportunity Amid Continuing Challenges* (Washington, D.C.: U.S. Department of Housing and Urban Development, January 2001). Available on the Internet at http://www.hud.gov. Households described here as at approximately the poverty level have incomes at 30 percent of their area median. Eighty-eight percent of households with incomes up to 30 percent of the area median live below the federal poverty level.

29. *Supra* note 6.

30. Harvard University, Joint Center for Housing Studies, *State of America's Housing 2000* (Cambridge, Ma.: Joint Center for Housing Studies, Harvard University, June 2000). Available on the Internet at http://www.gsd.harvard/edu/jcenter/.

31. *Ibid.*

32. Center on Budget and Policy Priorities, "Section 8 Utilization and the Proposed Housing Voucher Success Fund," (Washington, D.C.: Center on Budget and Policy Priorities, March 2000).

33. U.S. Conference of Mayors, *Hunger and Homelessness in America's Cities 2000* (Washington, D.C.: U.S. Conference of Mayors, December 2000). Available on the Internet at http://www.usmayors.org.

34. William Claiborne, "States, Cities Seek U.S. Aid As Heating Costs Skyrocket," *Washington Post*, (January 7, 2001).

35. Manpower Demonstration Research Corporation, cited in Center on Budget and Policy Priorities, "Research Evidence Suggests That Housing Subsidies Can Help Long-Term Welfare Recipients Find and Retain Jobs" (Washington, D.C.: Center on Budget and Policy Priorities, June 27, 2000). Available on the Internet at http://www.cbpp.org.

36. Lawrence F. Katz, Jeffrey R. Kling, and Jeffrey B. Liebman, *The Early Impacts of Moving to Opportunity in Boston*. Available on the Internet at http://www.wws.princeton.edu/~kling/mto/mto_boston_hudreport.pdf.

37. Food Research and Action Center, "Food Stamp Program Participation," (Washington, D.C.: Food Research and Action Center, February 2001) *citing* U.S. Department of Agriculture, Food and Nutrition Service, *Preliminary Summary of Food Assistance Program Results for November 2000*, February 2, 2001. Available on the Internet at http://www.frac.org/html/news/fsp00novnos.html.

38. Parke Wilde, Peggy Cook, Craig Gundersen, Mark Nord, and Laura Tiehen, "The Decline in Food Stamp Program Participation in the 1990's," *Food Assistance and Nutrition Research Report No. 7* (Washington, D.C.: U.S. Department of Agriculture, Economic Research Service, Food and Rural Economics Division, June 2000).

39. Center on Budget and Policy Priorities, "Child Poverty and Food Stamp Participation," presentation materials (Washington, D.C.: Center on Budget and Policy Priorities, November, 2000).

40. Wendell Primus, "What Do We Know About Welfare Reform and Where Do We Go From Here?" presentation before the Coalition on Human Needs (Washington D.C.: Center on Budget and Policy Priorities, January 2001).

41. U.S. Department of Agriculture, Office of Analysis, Nutrition, and Evaluation, Food and Nutrition Service, "Characteristics of Food Stamp Households: FY 1999" (Washington, D.C.: U.S. Department of Agriculture, July 2000).

42. Randy Rosso and Lisa Fowler, *Characteristics of Food Stamp Households: Fiscal Year 1999*, FSP-00-CHAR (Alexandria, Va.: U.S. Department of Agriculture, Food and Nutrition Service, Office of Analysis, Nutrition and Evaluation, December 2000). Available on the Internet at http://www.fns.usda.gov/oane.

43. California Food Security Monitoring Project and California Food Policy Advocates, "Impact of Legal Immigrant Food Stamp Cuts in Los Angeles and San Francisco" (San Francisco, Calif.: California Food Policy Advocates, May 1998).

44. Mike Meltzer, Susan Chen, Christian Bottomley and George Manalo-LeClair, *How Long Does It Take?* (San Francisco, Calif.: California Food Policy Advocates, 2000).

45. Doug O'Brien, Kimberly Prendergast, Eleanor Thompson, Marcus Fruchter and Halley Torres Aldeen, *The Red Tape Divide: State-by-State Review of Food Stamp Applications*, (Chicago: America's Second Harvest, 2000).

46. *Supra* note 36.

47. Children's Defense Fund, *Families Struggling to Make It in the Workforce: A Post Welfare Report*, (Washington, D.C.: Children's Defense Fund, 2000).

48. Margaret Andrews, Mark Nord, Gary Bickel, and Steven Carlson, "Household Food Security in the United States, 1999" *Food Assistance and Nutrition Research Report No. 8*. (Washington, D.C.: Food and Rural Economics Division, Economic Research Service, U.S. Department of Agriculture, Fall 2000).

49. *Supra* note 31.

50. Catholic Charities USA, "More People Receive Emergency Food in Spite of Strong Economy" (Alexandria, Va.: Catholic Charities USA, December 19, 2000): Press release. Available on the Internet at http://www.catholiccharitiesusa.org/media/releases/2000/121900.html.

51. David Super and Stacy Dean, "New State Options to Improve the Food Stamp Vehicle Rule," (Washington, D.C.: Center on Budget and Policy Priorities, November 28, 2000). Available on the Internet at http://www.cbpp.org.

52. Food Research and Action Center and America's Second Harvest, *State Government Responses to the Food Assistance Gap 2000* (Washington, D.C. and Chicago, Ill.ovember, 2000).

53. Supra note 38.

54. Administration for Children and Families, Office of Planning, Research and Evaluation, *Temporary Assistance for Needy Families (TANF) Program: Third Annual Report to Congress* (Washington, D.C.: U.S. Department of Health and Human Services, August 2000). Available on the Internet at http://www.acf.dhhs.gov.

55. U.S. Department of Health and Human Services, "HHS Awards Welfare High Performance Bonuses" (Washington, D.C.: U.S. Department of Health and Human Services, December 16, 2000): Press release. Available on the Internet at http://www.acf.dhhs.gov/news/hpb1215.htm.

56. Robert Moffitt and Jennifer Roff, "The Diversity of Welfare Leavers," *Policy Brief 00-2* (Baltimore, Md.: Johns Hopkins University, 2000). The three cities in the study are Boston, Chicago, and San Antonio. Available on the Internet at http://www.juh.edu/~.

57. Eileen Sweeney, "Recent Studies Make Clear That Many Parents Who are Current or Former Welfare Recipients have Disabilities and Other Medical Conditions" (Washington, D.C.: Center on Budget and Policy Priorities, February 29, 2000). Available on the Internet at http://www.cbpp.org.

58. *Supra* note 52. The five studies cited are for Arizona, San Mateo, Calif., Washington state, Wisconsin, and Cuyahoga county, Ohio.

59. *Ibid.*

60. Eileen Sweeney, "Welfare and TANF: State Legislative and Administrative Developments During 2000," (Washington, D.C.: Center on Budget and Policy Priorities, October 12, 2000).

61. Ed Lazere, "Unspent TANF Funds at the End of Federal Fiscal year 2000," (Washington, D.C.: Center on Budget and Policy Priorities, January 22, 2001 and presentation, February 23, 2001). Available on the Internet at http://www.cbpp.org.

CHAPTER

Child Health

Millions of children have inadequate health care because they lack health insurance. Uninsured children are more likely to suffer from health problems that could be prevented with routine care. When uninsured children are sick or injured, their care may be delayed because they do not have access to a regular provider. The nation must ensure that every child has health coverage and access to affordable, high quality health care.

Fortunately, the Children's Health Insurance Program (CHIP), enacted in 1997, is beginning to reach children in low-income working families and improve their chances of getting health care when they need it. Largely because of recent CHIP and Medicaid outreach and enrollment efforts, the number of children without insurance coverage has begun to decrease for the first time since 1995. In 1999, 10.8 million children ages 18 and under lacked health coverage, down from 11.9 million in 1998.[1] More than 3 million children have been covered through CHIP, and more than 20 million children have coverage through Medicaid.[2]

Disparities in Coverage and Access to Care

Despite the recent progress in reducing the number of uninsured children, more than 6 million children who are eligible for CHIP or Medicaid are still not enrolled.[3] When children lack insurance coverage, they are more likely to suffer from preventable health problems and from delays in receiving appropriate health care. Studies have shown that low-income, uninsured children are more likely to have eye and ear infections, lead poisoning, serious dental problems, and chronic conditions such as asthma and diabetes. All of these conditions can become more serious when they go untreated.[4]

Racial and ethnic disparities in coverage persist: children of color are more likely to be uninsured. One out of six Black children and one out of four Hispanic children are uninsured, compared with one out of 11 White children.[5] Children in immigrant families are particularly likely to lack health coverage and access to health care.[6] Among families with one or more non-citizen family members, nearly one out of three children is uninsured.[7]

Unfortunately, progress in reducing the number of uninsured children may be hindered by a variety of factors, including the sharp rise in the cost of health care premiums in 2001. After several years of relatively stable rates, increases of 10 percent or more are likely.[8] The increasing costs of coverage will hit lower-income working families hardest as these families face greater difficulties in paying their share of employer-based coverage. More children may then lose employer-based coverage and become uninsured. A downturn in the economy also could affect children's coverage as low-wage workers lose their jobs and their coverage. Thus, the recent gains of CHIP may be lost due to larger economic and market forces.

The nation needs to ensure that every child has health coverage. Every eligible child should be enrolled in CHIP or Medicaid. States have made substantial progress in implementing CHIP but need to do more to reduce administrative barriers, reduce language and cultural barriers, and get the word out to all communities that children in working families may be eligible. Much more needs to be done to streamline Medicaid, to make the Medicaid application process as easy as the CHIP process, and to make sure families stay enrolled from year to year. In sum, every state should be doing everything it can to make sure that every eligible child has coverage.

Progress in CHIP Enrollment

Under CHIP, states have the option of expanding Medicaid eligibility, supporting a separate state program, or using a combination of both approaches. According to the Health Care Financing Administration (HCFA), a total of 3.3 million children were covered by CHIP during fiscal year 2000. Approximately 2.3 million children were enrolled in separate state programs, and about 1 million were enrolled in Medicaid expansions.[9]

Increases in CHIP and Medicaid enrollment have helped to decrease the number of uninsured children from 1998 to 1999. The most substantial gains in coverage in those years were among children in families with incomes below 200 percent of the federal poverty level. Those are the children that CHIP and Medicaid were designed to serve.[10]

What makes states successful with CHIP?

States' performance under CHIP has been, quite literally, all over the map on any dimension that can be measured — eligibility levels, types of programs, implementation timetables, scope of benefits, relationship between CHIP and Medicaid, approaches to outreach, and progress in identifying and enrolling eligible children. Some states have taken major steps to improve coverage, and they have succeeded through a combination of strategies: building on existing children's insurance programs, coordinating CHIP and Medicaid, and simplifying and streamlining enrollment procedures early on.

In the summer of 2000, CDF released a national report, *All Over the Map*, ranking states' progress in increasing children's insurance coverage through CHIP and Medicaid.[11] Based on combined CHIP and Medicaid enrollment, the top 10 states were Alaska, Massachusetts, Maryland, New York, Louisiana, Maine, Missouri, Nebraska, North Carolina, and Arkansas.

Leadership plays a key role in state successes. States with strong public leaders — governors, legislators, and other state officials — set high income eligibility levels, promoted CHIP through highly visible endorsements, and ensured that state agencies became more family-friendly by using strategies such as short applications and simple enrollment processes for both CHIP and Medicaid. Some states have seamlessly coordinated CHIP and Medicaid so families no longer have to go from one agency to another seeking coverage for their children.

Strategic and aggressive outreach efforts have also increased enrollment. States that recognize and respect diversity in communities have succeeded through culturally appropriate outreach efforts involving

◆ The number of children without health coverage dropped from a record high of 11.9 million uninsured children in 1998, down to 10.8 million uninsured children in 1999.

◆ More than 3.3 million children were enrolled in the Children's Health Insurance Program in fiscal year 2000, an increase of almost 1.4 million from the previous year. However, more than 6 million children remain eligible for, but not enrolled in, either CHIP or Medicaid.

◆ In 1998, when compared with babies born to White mothers, babies born to Black mothers were twice as likely to be born at low birthweight, more than twice as likely to die in their first year of life, and more than twice as likely to be born to mothers receiving late or no prenatal care.

◆ In 1998, for the first time in 25 years, the infant mortality rate did not drop but remained at 7.2 infant deaths per 1,000 live births.

◆ Poor children are more than twice as likely as children in higher-income families to have untreated dental cavities.

◆ While one in 10 children and teens suffers from an emotional or behavioral problem that would benefit from treatment, fewer than one in five of these children receive treatment in any one year.

Fewer Uninsured Children in 1999, by Income

The lowest income children had the biggest gains in health coverage

	1998	1999	Gains in health coverage, 1998 to 1999
Total number of insured children	64,133,000	65,550,000	1,417,000
	Percent of children who were insured		
All incomes	84.4%	85.9%	1.5
Under 100% of poverty	73.0	75.1	2.1
100-199% of poverty	76.1	79.0	2.9
200-299% of poverty	86.4	86.6	0.2
300% of poverty & above	93.0	93.5	0.5

Source: U.S. Department of Commerce, Bureau of the Census, Current Population Survey, March 1999 and March 2000. Calculations by Children's Defense Fund.

community-based organizations. For example, Chicago's Alivio Medical Center worked with a local coalition and a Spanish-speaking radio station to promote CHIP through several commercials and public service announcements featuring a popular radio personality.

In North Carolina, the Black Publishers Association developed newspaper editorials about CHIP, and gospel and jazz radio stations helped promote the program. Religious organizations, social service organizations, and the NAACP also helped to spread the word. North Carolina's outreach efforts were so successful that the state ranked in CDF's top 10 states in improving coverage through CHIP and Medicaid during 1998 and 1999.

Unfortunately, in December 2000, North Carolina announced that its funds for fiscal year 1998 were fully spent and CHIP-eligible children would have to go on a waiting list beginning in January 2001. Fortunately, Congress averted the need for waiting lists by passing legislation in December 2000 to redistribute a portion of unspent CHIP funds to states that had already spent their full allotments. The original CHIP legislation allows unspent funds to be reallocated to states that have fully expended their allotments, and although some states had expended their CHIP funding allotments by that time, most had not.[12] The new legislation also gives states more time to use their unspent CHIP funds from fiscal years 1998 and 1999, allowing those states to continue their efforts to expand coverage and get children enrolled.

What impact is CHIP having on states?

CHIP is having a greater impact on states than the program's enrollment figures indicate. CHIP outreach efforts have found more than one new Medicaid enrollee for every CHIP-eligible child, including hundreds of thousands of children who wrongfully lost their Medicaid coverage when states implemented welfare-to-work policies.[13]

There are other impacts as well. States are using social marketing and other commercial techniques to promote a new image for public insurance. Most states gave their CHIP programs appealing names (e.g., Healthy Kids, Hoosier Healthwise, PeachCare). All but 15 states have also renamed their Medicaid programs, and 35 out of 48 states promote their CHIP and Medicaid programs jointly.[14]

Alaska's DenaliCare program has a consumer hotline that refers to the state's eligibility workers as "customer service representatives." Every state and the District of Columbia have mail-in or fax-in applications for CHIP, and 41 states have mail-in Medicaid applications. Every state and the District of Columbia provide CHIP and Medicaid information on a state Web site. Many states also make applications available for downloading through the Web sites, and families can mail or fax them in.

Who Are the Uninsured Children?

Race and Ethnicity

40.8%   are White
31.7%   are Hispanic
19.8%   are Black
5.1%   are Asian or Pacific Islander
2.6%   are American Indian or Alaskan Native

Family Structure

88.5%   have at least one working parent
66.3%   have at least one parent who works full time throughout the year
69.1%   live in families with incomes above poverty
53.5%   live in a two-parent household

Notes:

Children are younger than 19.

Children of Hispanic origin are excluded from the other racial and ethnic categories. Insurance, income, and employment information are for 1999; all other information is for March 2000.

Source: U.S. Department of Commerce, Bureau of the Census, March 2000 Current Population Survey. Calculations by Children's Defense Fund.

California and Pennsylvania are developing online (electronic) application forms.

Marketing studies show that parents are more likely to apply for coverage when they learn about it through a variety of media including television, radio, mainstream and ethnic newspapers. Nearly two-thirds of the states are targeting specific groups through radio or print ads serving racial and ethnic minorities, and California and New York are also using photo novelas (newsprint with pictures and dialogue) with great success in Hispanic communities. Every state is working on outreach activities with community-based organizations, usually schools, child care centers, health care providers, churches, and community groups.[15]

A national study of enrollment barriers found that six out of 10 parents of Medicaid-eligible children did not apply because they believed they made too much money to qualify. Nearly nine out of 10 said they would be willing to enroll their children in Medicaid if they were eligible.[16]

Although media messages help in reaching target audiences, parents are more likely to take action when they get information from friends, family members, and people they know and trust at schools, clinics, and community-based organizations. State officials should do much more to involve influential community members, such as

health care providers, community-based advocates, and religious leaders, in their outreach efforts to working families.[17] More work needs to be done with small businesses and other employers to increase their awareness of the availability and value of Medicaid and CHIP coverage for their employees.

Many parents benefit from personal assistance in completing the applications, especially parents whose first language is not English. Although more needs to be done to improve cultural competence, state officials are beginning to address language barriers in enrollment assistance by working with diverse nonprofit organizations that have racial and ethnic ties to communities. Iowa, for example, has a toll-free telephone number that answers questions and provides application assistance in English, Spanish, Russian, Polish, Vietnamese, and Arabic. Other states have not been as responsive to racial and ethnic minorities. States may have toll-free lines to provide translations, but they are frequently busy or only available for certain hours of the day.

Enrollment barriers

Bureaucratic procedures and excessive documentation are the main barriers to enrolling more eligible children in CHIP and Medicaid. A Kaiser Family Foundation study found that nearly six out of 10 parents with

Using the Internet to Improve CHIP Enrollment

◆ Every state and the District of Columbia have some type of CHIP information on a Web site. Some have a stand-alone site or a site linked through the state's Department of Health Web site, while others have one informational page outlining the program and providing contact information. Some sites take several more clicks to find information than others.

◆ 43 sites have a one-click link to other state health and human services agencies or programs.

◆ 33 states have downloadable applications on their Web site.

◆ 16 states have downloadable applications available in both English and Spanish.

◆ Alaska, Connecticut, and Minnesota have downloadable renewal forms online.

◆ California and Pennsylvania are developing online application forms.

Source: Analysis by Health Division, Children's Defense Fund, December 2000-January 2001. Delaware, Oklahoma, and Utah sites are under construction, and most sites are regularly upgraded and redesigned.

Medicaid-eligible children had tried to enroll in the program but did not succeed because they found the process was too difficult and complicated or their application was denied.[18]

Enrolling in health coverage is confusing enough for privately insured families whose employers provide a benefits counselor to explain what is covered and help them choose a provider and plan. In the private sector, after employees choose a plan, the payments are automatically deducted from their paychecks. Compare this process with CHIP and Medicaid, where low-income individuals have to find out about the program, obtain an application, apply, go through an eligibility determination process, choose a plan, send in monthly payments, and periodically demonstrate that they are still eligible. It should not be surprising that many public programs do not reach full participation.[19]

Program coordination

Almost three-quarters of low-income uninsured children participate in or have family members who participate in the National School Lunch; Food Stamp; Unemployment Compensation; or Women, Infants, and Children's Nutrition (WIC) programs.[20] Collaborative approaches such as "Express Lane Eligibility" have been proposed to accelerate enrollment procedures for uninsured children who are already enrolled in public programs with income requirements similar to Medicaid and CHIP.[21] These approaches hold great promise for increasing the number of children with coverage.

However, in order to make these expedited enrollment approaches work, differences must be resolved among CHIP, Medicaid, and other public programs'

eligibility and confidentiality requirements, immigration restrictions, and other federal verification requirements. Administrative collaboration and reform can be time-consuming and very challenging, but over time, seamless systems can save time and resources and improve families' access.

How can states make it easier for families to enroll?

States must redouble their efforts to promote CHIP and Medicaid as insurance programs, rather than treating families as if they are applying for welfare. The following five steps are key:

◆ Allow self-declaration of income instead of burdensome and unnecessary documentation requirements.

◆ Coordinate CHIP and Medicaid, streamline both programs, and make the enrollment processes similar.

◆ Implement presumptive eligibility for CHIP and Medicaid in every state, allowing children to be enrolled immediately and receive services while their applications are undergoing administrative review.

◆ Implement 12-month continuous eligibility, reducing the administrative burden for families and states and reducing gaps in coverage for children.

◆ Make it easy to renew eligibility by implementing automatic renewals on a yearly basis. This allows families with public coverage to retain coverage the same way that privately insured families do.

Public Accountability: Ensuring Access to EPSDT

The visibility and success of CHIP have brought increased attention to Medicaid. While advocates continue to focus on enrolling children in Medicaid and CHIP, it is equally important to ensure that children get appropriate health care screenings and services after they receive coverage.

Information on access to health services for children enrolled in CHIP will not be available for some time. However, the U.S. General Accounting Office, the Department of Health and Human Services (HHS), and several state Attorneys General have reported that many children are not getting the health services to which they are entitled through Medicaid's Early and Periodic Screening, Diagnosis and Treatment (EPSDT) program.[22] The HHS Office of the Inspector General found that only an estimated 28 percent of children enrolled in Medicaid managed care received *all* of the EPSDT screens, and 60 percent did not receive *any* of the EPSDT services.[23]

EPSDT entitles children under age 21 who are enrolled in Medicaid to receive comprehensive and preventive health care services. As defined by Section 1905(r) of the Social Security Act, these services include:

◆ Comprehensive health and developmental history (assessment of physical and mental health development)

◆ Comprehensive physical exam

◆ Appropriate immunizations (as defined by the Advisory Committee on Immunization Practices)

◆ Laboratory tests (including screening for blood-lead levels)

◆ Health education (educating parents or guardians on childhood development, accident and disease prevention, and the benefits of healthy lifestyles)

◆ Vision services (including diagnosis and treatment for vision problems)

◆ Dental services (including treatment for pain and infections, restoration of teeth, and maintenance of dental health)

◆ Hearing services (including diagnosis and treatment for hearing problems)

◆ Other necessary health care

Monitoring whether children actually receive EPSDT services is very difficult. Under fee-for-service Medicaid, it is theoretically possible to review insurance claims data to determine whether certain clinical services were provided. Under Medicaid managed care, this health care information is not available unless states specifically require clinical data from health plans and clearly specify in advance which formats should be used to produce the data. In other words, the delivery of clinical services such as vision screenings cannot be monitored unless the health plan has set up an automated checklist or tracking system in advance. To hold health plans accountable, states need to insist on provider contracts that specify tracking systems and reporting requirements as conditions of payment.[24]

Because only a small percentage of children have actually received the full array of benefits, lawsuits and disciplinary actions have been filed against state Medicaid offices and managed care organizations. These actions have specifically cited organizations for the lack of screening for lead levels in blood and for the failure to provide necessary dental or mental health services.

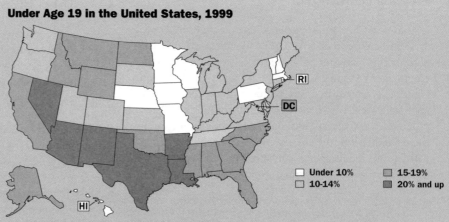

Uninsured Children

Under Age 19 in the United States, 1999

RI

DC

HI

☐ Under 10%   ☐ 15-19%
☐ 10-14%   ■ 20% and up

Source: U.S. Department of Commerce, Bureau of the Census, Current Population Survey, March 1998, March 1999, and March 2000. Calculations by Children's Defense Fund.
Estimates are based on three years of CPS data because of small sample size in some states.
Sorted by rounded percentages of uninsured. Includes children of all income levels.

Streamlining Enrollment in Medicaid and CHIP

States can do much more to simplify and streamline the application and enrollment processes for CHIP and Medicaid and eliminate differences between the programs. Every state and the District of Columbia have a Medicaid program (51), and 19 states have Medicaid expansions under CHIP. In the 32 states with separate CHIP programs, coordination with Medicaid is essential.

Joint Applications

◆ Of the 32 states with separate CHIP programs, 28 use joint applications for Medicaid and CHIP.

Eliminating Face-to-Face Interviews

◆ Eleven Medicaid programs have not eliminated face-to-face interviews from their Medicaid application process (Alabama, Georgia, Montana, New Mexico, New York, Tennessee, Texas, Utah, West Virginia, Wisconsin, and Wyoming). Utah is the only state with a separate CHIP program that still requires face-to-face interviews.

Eliminating Assets Tests

◆ Nine Medicaid programs have not eliminated assets tests from their Medicaid application process (Arkansas, Colorado, Idaho, Montana, Nevada, North Dakota, Oregon, Texas, and Utah). Oregon is the only state with a separate CHIP program that still requires assets tests.

Eliminating Differences Between CHIP and Medicaid

◆ Six states (Colorado, Montana, Nevada, North Dakota, Texas, and Utah) use assets tests for Medicaid but not for their separate CHIP programs.

◆ Six states (Alabama, Georgia, New York, Utah, West Virginia, and Wyoming) use a face-to-face interview for families with children eligible for Medicaid, but not for those eligible for separate CHIP programs.

Presumptive Eligibility

◆ Only 8 states have adopted presumptive eligibility procedures for their Medicaid program (Connecticut, Florida, Massachusetts, Nebraska, New Hampshire, New Jersey, New Mexico, and New York). Five of these states (Massachusetts, Nebraska, New Jersey, New Mexico, and New York) also have it for CHIP. Michigan has it for CHIP only.

12-month Continuous Eligibility

◆ Fourteen Medicaid programs have 12-month continuous eligibility. Twenty-two separate CHIP programs have it. Only 13 states offer it for both their Medicaid and CHIP programs.

Source: Donna Cohen Ross and Laura Cox. *Making It Simple: Medicaid for Children and CHIP Income Eligibility Guidelines and Enrollment Procedures.* Washington, D.C.: Center on Budget and Policy Priorities for the Kaiser Family Foundation, October 2000: Table 2. Available on the Internet at www.kff.org.

Monitoring lead levels

The federal government requires all children in Medicaid to have a blood test for lead by age 2. Despite these requirements, recent studies by the U.S. General Accounting Office have found that most children on Medicaid had not been screened for lead toxicity even though they were more than three times more likely than other children to have high blood-lead levels.[25]

In fall of 1999, Missouri's Attorney General filed suits against two health plans serving children with Medicaid coverage. The suits alleged that the plans had neglected to screen their pediatric patients for lead, which

The Health Effects of Lead Poisoning

Lead poisoning can cause learning disabilities, developmental delays, behavioral problems, kidney damage, and at very high levels, seizures, coma, and death. All children are at potential risk of exposure, and the Centers for Disease Control and Prevention (CDC) estimates indicate that one out of every 20 U.S. children has some lead poisoning without visible signs or symptoms.

According to CDC, children living in poor neighborhoods are at particularly high levels of risk of exposure, and Black children are at five times greater risk of exposure than White children.

The risk of exposure to lead varies significantly in different parts of the country because of the types and age of housing and schools, types of building codes, history of air pollution, industrial pollution, and other factors. The risk also varies significantly within states for the same reasons.

To some extent, good nutrition can offset the effects of exposure to lead. Leafy green vegetables that are high in iron and calcium-rich foods such as milk or orange juice can decrease the absorption of lead, but children with poor diets may not be able to reduce the toxic effects of exposure.

The Department of Housing and Urban Development recommends that any parents who think their homes may have lead should ask a pediatrician to test their young children for lead, even if they seem healthy. If testing shows high levels, treatment involves eliminating the sources of lead in the environment, improving nutrition to limit the lead absorption, and chelation therapy, which allows the body to break down the lead and get rid of it.

Sources: Centers for Disease Control and Prevention, "Recommendations for Blood Lead Screening of Young Children Enrolled in Medicaid: Targeting a Group at High Risk," *Morbidity and Mortality Weekly Report*, December 8, 2000, 49(RR14), 1-13. E.F. Crain, "Environmental Threats to Children's Health: A Challenge for Pediatrics: 2000 Ambulatory Pediatric Association Presidential Address," *Pediatrics*, October 2000, Supplement 106(4):871-875. M. Markowitz, "Lead Poisoning," *Pediatrics in Review*, 2000, 21(10):327-335. Department of Housing and Urban Development, "Protect Your Family From Lead in Your Home." Retrieved from the Internet at www.hud.gov/lea/leadtxe.html on November 13, 2000.

constituted Medicaid fraud because they had not fulfilled the terms of their contracts. In October 2000, the state of Idaho was sued in federal court by 15 state school districts for failing to meet Medicaid lead screening requirements.[26] In August 2000, the mother of a 7-year-old boy filed suit against an Ohio Medicaid HMO for failing to screen her son for lead poisoning.[27]

Federal guidelines require state health officials to develop statewide plans for childhood lead screening and target more resources toward children who are at higher risk. To help states enforce the federal Medicaid requirements, the Centers for Disease Control and Prevention (CDC) and state Medicaid agencies have collaborated with the Center for Health Services Research and Policy at George Washington University to develop sample contracts that can be used with health plans to ensure lead screenings.[28]

Some states, such as Indiana, are using information technology and advanced epidemiological and demographic techniques to identify the geographic areas where children are most at risk (see Streamlining Enrollment in Medicaid and CHIP box). In the long run, investing in information technology can be cost-effective because it will allow states to target scarce resources in those communities where the need is greatest.

Dental care

Public awareness about the role of dental health in general health and well-being has increased significantly, but coverage and use of dental services still lag far behind the rest of medical care.[29] About one out of five children has an untreated dental cavity, and poor children are more than twice as likely as children in higher-income families to have untreated dental cavities.[30] According to researchers at the National Institutes of Health, 80 percent of the tooth decay is found in only 25 percent of children, most of them from low-income families.[31]

The EPSDT benefit in Medicaid includes dental coverage, but fewer than one out of five children in Medicaid receive even a single preventive dental service.[32] Connecticut, New Hampshire, Massachusetts, and Vermont are the only states that report use of dental services in the Medicaid program to be higher than 40 percent.[33]

States are taking a variety of steps to improve low-income children's access to dental services. Many of these steps focus on increasing the number of dentists who accept Medicaid patients. Given the historically low payment rates for dental services under Medicaid, many states are increasing reimbursement levels for dentists to make them more comparable to commercial rates.

Indiana's Award-Winning Tracking System

In collaboration with the Geography Department at Ball State University, the Indiana Maternal and Child Health Program's Health Information Service developed a Geographical Information System (GIS) to target lead screening efforts in the state. Concerned about lead poisoning among young children, the Indiana Legislature was considering universal lead screening throughout the state, at a potential cost of approximately $400,000 per year.

With funding from the Centers for Disease Control and Prevention, the state used GIS software to locate the geographic concentrations of lead exposures. Researchers found that 80 percent of the cases of elevated blood-lead levels were found to occur in six of Indiana's 92 counties, and more than 90 percent of the cases were within 17 counties. The state was able to focus its screening efforts where the need was greatest, thereby saving time and resources.

In 1999, the program won an award from the National Association of State Information Resource Executives for innovative use of technology. The same methodology will now be applied to address other health problems, including infant mortality, cancer, and HIV.

Source: National Association of State Information Resource Executives (NASIRE). 1999 NASIRE Award for Innovative Use of Technology: GIS Childhood Lead Poisoning Prevention Program, State of Indiana. Retrieved from the Internet at www.nasire.org/awards/ 1999awards/99awards.cfm on September 27, 2000.

Washington state provides enhanced reimbursements for dentists who treat Medicaid enrollees. Michigan and Missouri have legislation pending to provide tax credits for participating dentists. Many states are expanding the scope of practice for dental hygienists, allowing them to provide a wider range of services without the supervision of a dentist.[34]

States are also streamlining their procedures for processing Medicaid claims to reduce the administrative burden for participating dentists. For example, Maine developed a single claims form for all dentists, and Florida, Illinois, New Mexico, and North Carolina have set up electronic billing systems, which should save time and increase accuracy.[35]

Minnesota's Medicaid Provider Mandate, enacted in 1994, requires dentists and other providers to treat Medicaid beneficiaries as a condition of participation in health insurance programs for state employees. Other states are developing coalitions or commissions to study the viability of loan-forgiveness programs and other financial incentives to improve provider participation over the long term, to gather more information on the scope of the problem, and to identify successful strategies in improving access to care.

Some improvements are the result of litigation. California, Maine, New Jersey, New York, and West Virginia increased provider reimbursement rates because of lawsuits, and Massachusetts allocated additional funds for the MassHealth dental program after litigation was filed.[36]

Mental health care

EPSDT also guarantees screening, diagnosis, and treatment for mental health conditions. In the mental health area, screenings are particularly challenging because of children's rapid development, difficulty in diagnosing children's behavioral and neurological problems, and a fragmented mental health delivery system. While one in 10 children and teens suffers from an emotional or behavioral problem that would benefit from treatment, fewer than one in five of these receive treatment in any one year, according to the Surgeon General's Conference on Children's Mental Health (http://www.surgeongeneral.gov/cmh/childreport.htm).

Lawsuits have been filed against states and health maintenance organizations because of the lack of needed treatment. For example, in October 2000, the Minnesota Attorney General sued Blue Cross Blue Shield for "denying necessary treatment" to children with mental health problems.[37] In Maine, a class action lawsuit filed in June 2000 alleged that state health officials had not provided services for children diagnosed with severe emotional illnesses or mental health impairments.[38]

The Surgeon General's conference report on children's mental health highlights the "public crisis in mental health for children and adolescents." The report emphasizes the importance of educating families, teachers, health care workers, school counselors, coaches, and faith-based workers to recognize and respond to emotional and behavioral problems. The report also calls for a more coordinated approach of addressing the mental health needs of children, adolescents, and their families.[39]

Federal Legislative Developments

In 2000, several pieces of legislation were passed to improve children's access to health coverage through CHIP and Medicaid, authorize increases in funding for treatment and research on childhood illnesses and disease, and promote efforts to eliminate health disparities across racial and ethnic groups.

In June 2000, Congress enacted legislation allowing school districts to enter into agreements with child health agencies to help inform families of children participating in federal free and reduced-price school lunch programs about CHIP and Medicaid enrollment. As a result, state officials will be able to coordinate and improve outreach efforts to eligible families. This legislation was a major accomplishment in helping public agencies share information about income-eligible children.

In October 2000, former President Clinton signed the Children's Health Act of 2000. The law authorizes funding for research, prevention, and treatment for several medical conditions that affect children, including diabetes, asthma, hearing loss, infant mortality, lead poisoning, oral health problems, and autism.

In November 2000, former President Clinton signed the Health Care Fairness Act, authorizing more than $150 million to create a National Center for Research on Minority Health and Health Disparities at the National Institutes of Health. The legislation is a major step toward meeting the nation's goal of eliminating racial and ethnic disparities in health by 2010. The center will become the lead federal agency in documenting the racial and ethnic differences in rates of diabetes, cancer, heart disease, and other illnesses.

During the fiscal year 2001 budget debate, Congress considered using $1.9 billion in unspent fiscal year 1998 CHIP funds to pay for other federal budget expenditures. The proposal was dropped, thanks in part to members of the child health community who took the position that it was vitally important not to reduce CHIP funding just at the time when states were beginning to show increases in enrollment.

In December 2000, Congress passed the Medicare, Medicaid, and SCHIP Benefits Improvement and Protection Act of 2000. The legislation provided a one-year extension of the transitional Medicaid assistance program, increasing continuity of coverage for families leaving welfare for work. It also authorized schools, emergency food and shelter programs, and housing programs to make presumptive eligibility determinations for children, allowing children to become enrolled immediately in Medicaid or CHIP and receive services while an application is pending administrative review.

The law also allows states to use CHIP allotments from fiscal years 1998 and 1999 through the end of fiscal year 2002. States that have already spent their full allotments will get additional funds from others states' unspent allotments. States that have not yet used their full allotments may keep the remainder of the unspent funds and can spend the money through the end of fiscal year 2002. It is estimated that about 40 percent of the unused money will go to states that have spent their own allotments, and about 60 percent will remain with the states that were slower to launch their programs and implement outreach and enrollment activities.

The year 2000 is also notable for legislation that did not pass. The Family Opportunity Act would have given states the option to allow families who have children with disabilities and who have incomes too high to qualify for

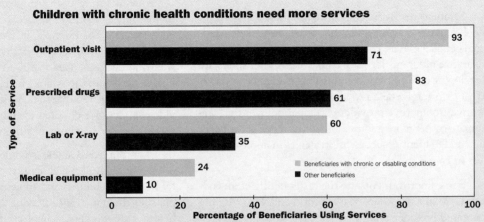

Chronic Health Conditions

Children with chronic health conditions need more services

Source: Center for Health Care Strategies, Inc., The Faces of Medicaid: The Complexities of Caring for People with Chronic Illnesses and Disabilities (October 2000), p. 16; based on U.S. Department of Health and Human Services, Health Care Financing Administration, State Medicaid Research Files for California, Georgia, Kansas, and New Jersey.

Medicaid to "buy in" to the program, which has comprehensive coverage designed for children with special health care needs. The Family Care Act would have provided funding to cover uninsured parents through CHIP or Medicaid if their children were already enrolled in either program. Congress failed to pass legislation that would have given states the option to cover children and pregnant women who are legal immigrants through CHIP and Medicaid, thus allowing states to lift the current ban, which prohibits coverage for five years after admission to the United States.

Congress also failed to pass a Patients' Bill of Rights to provide protections for millions of Americans in managed care. Managed care protections are particularly important for children with special health care needs, including those who have chronic medical conditions and disabilities. Children with chronic and complex medical conditions need access to specialists and improved coordination of care, because they see providers more often than other children and typically see more than one provider for necessary services.

New Regulations on Insurance Claims

In November 2000, the Clinton administration issued new rules requiring private insurers to handle consumer claims faster and more efficiently. The first changes to the insurance claims and appeals process since the 1974 Employee Retirement Income Security Act, the new rules will apply to approximately 130 million privately insured individuals.

Beginning January 1, 2002, urgent claims will need to be reviewed within 72 hours, replacing the current 90-day deadline. Insurers will have 15 days to make decisions on medical procedures that require advance approval and 30 days to review care that already has been provided. Consumers will have 180 days, rather than just 60 days, to file appeals when their requests for care are denied. Thirty-three states already have laws or regulations that require managed care plans to have an appeals process.[40]

Many industry leaders are concerned about the potential increase in litigation, claiming a potential increase in total health care costs. However, most policy analysts and clinicians believe that a fair review process will improve quality of care and therefore reduce the number of lawsuits.

Final CHIP Regulations

On January 11, 2001, HHS published the final regulations for implementing CHIP after a lengthy period of public comment.[41] The final regulations set out HHS policies on enrollment, cost-sharing, benefits, appeal rights, waiting periods for enrollment, coordination between CHIP and Medicaid programs, and other issues.

The policies ease the initial HHS guidelines for waiting periods before enrolling children who previously had employer-based coverage. Other important provisions address procedures to coordinate enrollment between CHIP and Medicaid and requirements for appeals procedures when care is denied under CHIP coverage plans.

Although the published final rules have an effective date of April 11, 2001, on January 24, 2001, the Bush administration delayed the effective date of the published regulations by 60 days beyond the scheduled effective date. Several other regulations released in the final weeks of the Clinton administration also are undergoing review, including rules on Medicaid, privacy of medical records, and environmental issues.

Emerging Issues: Family Insurance Expansions

Many states have expanded health insurance to parents, and more states are considering expansions to include parents as well as other uninsured adults. States may expand Medicaid through a Section 1931 expansion or can apply to HCFA for a Section 1115 waiver for CHIP or Medicaid.

Some studies have shown that children are more likely to be enrolled in coverage programs if their parents are also covered. By allowing an entire family to apply for coverage at one time — similar to private, employer-based dependent coverage — the number of uninsured children may be reduced and their access to health care may be improved.[42]

Three states (Connecticut, Ohio, and Rhode Island) and the District of Columbia have increased eligibility for adults through a Section 1931 expansion of Medicaid. Minnesota, New York, Tennessee, Vermont, and Wisconsin have increased eligibility through Medicaid 1115 waivers. New Jersey increased family coverage using a Section 1931 expansion combined with funding from the tobacco settlement. In addition, Arizona, California, Georgia, and Pennsylvania are developing plans to expand coverage to parents.[43]

In July 2000, HCFA provided written guidance for states that want to expand coverage to parents and other uninsured individuals through CHIP or Medicaid 1115 waivers. To be considered for waivers, states must already be covering children up to age 19 with family incomes of at least 200 percent of the federal poverty level. In addition, states must enroll children on a statewide basis, cannot close enrollment to eligible children or have a waiting list, and must demonstrate that they have promoted

Maternal and Infant Health Indicators, by Race of Mother, 1998

Selected Maternal and Infant Health Indicators, by Race and Hispanic Origin of Mother, 1998

Characteristic	All Races	White	Black	Native American	Asian, Pacific Islander	Hispanic
Percent						
Early prenatal care*	82.8	84.8	73.3	68.8	83.1	74.3
Late or no prenatal care**	3.9	3.3	7.0	8.5	3.6	6.3
Low birthweight***	7.6	6.5	13.0	6.8	7.4	6.4
Very low birthweight****	1.4	1.1	3.1	1.2	1.1	1.1
Births to teens	12.5	11.1	21.5	20.9	5.4	16.9
Births to unmarried women	32.8	26.3	69.1	59.3	15.6	41.6
Births to mothers who have not completed high school	21.9	21.2	26.9	32.7	12.9	49.3
Per 1,000						
Infant mortality rate*****	7.2	6.0	13.8	9.3	5.5	5.8

*Care begun in the first three months of pregnancy.
**Care begun in the last three months of pregnancy or not at all.
***Less than 2,500 grams (5 lbs., 8 oz.).
****Less than 1,500 grams (3 lbs., 4 oz.).
*****Infant deaths per 1,000 live births. These rates are from the linked birth-death files for 1998 and differ somewhat from other infant mortality rates published by the National Center for Health Statistics.
Note: Persons of Hispanic origin can be of any race.
Source: National Center for Health Statistics.

continuity of coverage for eligible children through the application and re-enrollment processes.

Additionally, if states seek to expand eligibility to populations other than low-income children, they must have implemented at least three of the following policies:

◆ A joint mail-in application and a single application procedure for CHIP and Medicaid

◆ Elimination of assets tests

◆ 12-month continuous eligibility

◆ Simplified redetermination (coverage renewal) processes

◆ Presumptive eligibility

States seeking additional CHIP funds to cover groups other than low-income children must first cover the lower-income individuals before extending coverage to higher-income individuals in the group. Waivers must be consistent with the original purpose of the CHIP law.

States cannot reduce benefits, permit higher levels of cost-sharing than the CHIP statute allowed, or use CHIP funds to substitute for other coverage.

Public Health Update: Progress Toward Healthy People 2010 Goals

The national objectives designed to promote health and prevent disease are known as Healthy People 2010. Under the leadership of the U.S. Surgeon General, the nation's primary goals are to increase the quality and years of healthy life and eliminate health disparities by 2010. Reaching this goal will require a national commitment to identifying and addressing the underlying causes of higher rates of disease and disability in minority communities. These areas include poverty, lack of access to quality health services, environmental hazards in homes and neighborhoods, and the lack of effective prevention programs in schools and communities.

Immunization Rates Have Improved Over the Last 5 Years, But Not for Everyone

Percent of 2-year-olds immunized*

	1995**	1996	1999
All races	74	77	80
White	n/a	79	82
Black	n/a	74	75
Hispanic	n/a	71	77
American Indian/Alaskan Native	n/a	80	78
Asian/Pacific Islander	n/a	78	82

*For purposes of comparison across years, the '4:3:1:3' series of vaccinations recommended in 1994 for 2-year-olds by CDC's Advisory Committee on Immunization Practices is used in this table. The series includes the following vaccines: four or more doses of diphtheria/tetanus/pertussis vaccine (DTP); three or more doses of poliovirus vaccine; one or more doses of any measles containing vaccine (MCV); and three or more doses of *Haemophilus influenzae* type b vaccine (Hib).

**Data for immmunization rates by race not available for 1995.

Source: Centers for Disease Control and Prevention, National Immunization Program.

Infant mortality and low birthweight

Great progress has been made in reducing infant mortality over the past three decades. Infant mortality rates have decreased steadily from 25.3 infant deaths per 1,000 live births in 1962 to 7.2 infant deaths per 1,000 live births in 1997. However, in 1998, for the first time in 25 years, the infant mortality rate did not drop; it remained at 7.2 infant deaths per 1,000 live births.[44]

Reducing racial disparities in infant mortality is one of the six priority areas for Healthy People 2010. Despite the improvement in infant mortality rates among both Black and White infants, Black infants still die at more than twice the rate of White infants.[45]

Low birthweight infants are more likely to die than those of normal weight, and the cause of death for Black infants is four times more likely to be related to low birthweight than for White infants.[46] The problem of low birthweight must be addressed in order to improve the national infant mortality rates. Unfortunately, the percentage of infants born at low birthweight (weighing less than 5 pounds 8 ounces) has continued to climb from a low of 6.7 percent of all births in 1984 to the 1998 rate of 7.6 percent of all births. The percentage of low birthweight infants reveals a racial disparity similar to that of infant mortality: infants born to Black mothers are twice as likely to be low birthweight compared to infants born to White mothers.[47] Preliminary data from 1999 suggests there will be no improvement from the 1998 figure.[48]

Reducing disparities in access to prenatal care among racial and ethnic groups may narrow these gaps. At its best, prenatal care can improve the likelihood of normal development by treating maternal hypertension, diabetes, or other potential medical complications; by educating the mother about nutrition and lifestyle (e.g., stop smoking); and by providing the mother with access to social and other supportive services.

Immunization rates continue to improve, but racial disparities remain

In 1999, 80 percent of 2-year-olds were fully immunized against diphtheria, tetanus, pertussis, measles, mumps, rubella, and polio. This represents at least a 40 percent increase over the 55 percent of 2-year-olds who received these immunizations in 1992, when the first reliable national data in several years became available.[49]

To be fully immunized, a child needs a series of vaccinations for different diseases. The national goal calls for 90 percent of 2-year-olds to have the full series of vaccinations, but the goal has not been reached. In general, Black and Hispanic children are less likely to be fully vaccinated compared with White children.

Increases in vaccination rates in the 1990s are due in significant part, together with other immunization initiatives, to the Vaccines for Children (VFC) Program. Implemented in 1994, VFC allows the federal government to buy vaccines at a discount and distribute them to states. States then distribute them free to private physicians' offices and public clinics to administer to children who are uninsured or enrolled in Medicaid as well as to Native American and Alaska Native children. Underinsured children (children with health insurance that does not cover immunizations) can only receive free vaccines through VFC at a federally qualified health center or a rural health center.

Immunization rates vary among racial and ethnic groups, family income levels, and states and cities. States also have different policies for distributing the vaccines: only 15 states are "universal purchasers," meaning that all children can receive the vaccines free, regardless of their insurance status. Even in states with good overall records, rates may be lower in larger cities where there are more communities of color.[50]

Targeted outreach efforts to areas where immunization rates have traditionally been low can help to reduce disparities. Increasingly, states are using information systems, or registries, to help keep track of immunization records for children who see different providers, move, or change coverage or health plans. An increasing financial commitment to registries would be a worthwhile investment, because it would provide accurate coverage records for clinics and providers and prevent duplicative childhood immunizations.[51]

Obesity Is a Growing Problem

The number of overweight children has more than doubled within the past 30 years and now represents about 11 percent of all children ages 6 to 19.[52] According to the CDC, 67 percent of children ages 6 to 19 have a higher intake of fats than the recommended guidelines, and fewer than one out of five eat the recommended five daily servings of fruits and vegetables.[53]

According to one study, almost 60 percent of overweight children ages 5 to 17 already have a risk factor for heart disease, such as high blood pressure or elevated insulin levels, problems more often associated with adults.[54] The highest rates of obesity and being overweight are found among Black female teens, who are far more likely than White female teens to be overweight (16 percent compared to 9 percent, respectively).[55]

Social, cultural, economic, genetic, behavioral, nutritional, and psychological factors all play a role in weight gain. However, physical activity can help to offset the level of calories consumed. In response to a request from former President Clinton, the Secretary of Health and Human Services and the Secretary of Education released a report on how to improve health in children and teens through physical activity and sports. In its call to action, the report documents the health consequences of a lack of physical activity: "soaring rates of obesity and diabetes, potential future increases in heart disease, and devastating increases in health care costs."[56]

The report points out that many aspects of American culture discourage physical activity, including emphasis on cars rather than walking; unsafe community areas and playgrounds; and the appeal of television, video, and computer games. Activity levels vary among racial and ethnic groups: White students (68 percent) are more likely to participate in vigorous physical activity than are Hispanic (61 percent) or Black students (56 percent).[57] These differences are due to variations in access to physical education classes and sports and access to safe recreational areas in neighborhoods and school districts. For example, while it may be appropriate to encourage children to increase their activity levels by walking to school, many neighborhoods are not safe enough for children to walk to school.

The report recommends more school-based and after-school programs, community programs, and health education programs be implemented. These programs can help to improve children's health status, self-esteem, and social

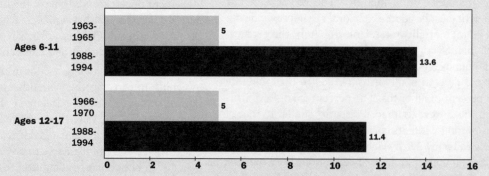

Overweight Children

The percent of overweight children has more than doubled since the 1960s

Ages 6-11
- 1963-1965: 5
- 1988-1994: 13.6

Ages 12-17
- 1966-1970: 5
- 1988-1994: 11.4

Source: U.S. Department of Health and Human Services, National Center for Health Statistics, *Health, United States, 2000* (2000), p. 248.
Note: Overweight is defined as body mass index (BMI) at or above the sex- and age-specific 95th percentile BMI cutoff points, as defined by the CDC. See http://www.cdc.gov/nccdphp/dnpa/bmi/bmi-for-age.htm .

Low-Income Neighborhoods Have Less Access to Healthy Foods

Differences in food resources across different types of neighborhoods have been analyzed by Fannie Mae Foundation researchers. Comparing the Howard University-LeDroit Park neighborhood (a low-to-moderate income, predominantly Black neighborhood in Washington, D.C.) with Georgetown (an affluent, predominantly White neighborhood in Washington, D.C.), the researchers found significant differences in the caliber of food stores and restaurants. The two neighborhoods are roughly equivalent in terms of resident population size and number of households, but they differ strongly from a socioeconomic perspective.

In general, smaller food stores typically have higher prices and less variety than supermarkets. While there are roughly 49 food stores in the Howard University-LeDroit Park neighborhood, all of them are quite small and 40 have fewer than five employees. There are no major supermarkets in the neighborhood. Georgetown, on the other hand, has 3 major supermarkets out of a total of 13 food stores.

This situation fits the pattern observed in cities across the country where lower-income communities are served by small neighborhood stores that typically have higher prices and less variety than the supermarkets that target more affluent markets. Far too frequently, residential location determines accessibility to affordable, quality food.

Contributed by Kristopher Rengert, Fannie Mae Foundation

---

skills and also can help to reduce the number of children who suffer from obesity.

Teen Health

About one out of every six teens ages 15 to 18 lacks health coverage.[58] Compared to insured teens, uninsured teens are five times more likely to lack a usual source of care, four times more likely to have unmet health needs, and twice as likely to have no yearly contact with a physician.[59]

Teens engage in more risky behaviors, including alcohol and drug abuse, cigarette smoking, and sexual activity, than any other age group.[60] All of these risky behaviors jeopardize their health, but teens have the lowest rates of access and use of health care services of any age group.[61]

Teens who have access to school-based health centers (SBHCs) have more health care visits than teens with traditional sources of care.[62] Fortunately, the number of school-based health centers has been increasing, moving from 200 in 1990 to 1,157 in 1998.[63] By increasing the availability of teen-friendly services, the use of health care and health education services may also increase.

Teen smoking

Cigarette smoking increases the risk of lung cancer, heart disease, emphysema, and other diseases and continues to be the leading preventable cause of death in the United States. Despite these risks, each day about 3,000 young Americans become daily cigarette smokers. Almost 90 percent of current and former daily smokers tried their first cigarette before age 18.[64]

The number of teens who tried their first cigarette between ages 12 and 17 increased from 100.9 per 1,000 to 159.2 per 1,000 between 1990 and 1997.[65] In 1999, 35 percent of high school students (grades 9-12) were considered current cigarette smokers (said they smoked on one or more days in the past 30 days prior to the survey). Among high school students who smoke, nearly twice as many Whites are smokers compared with Blacks (39 percent compared with 20 percent) and one out of three Hispanic teens is a smoker.[66]

Since 1995, there has been a gradual rise in the percentage of students who believe that pack-a-day smoking is of "great risk" to the user, signifying that more teens are understanding the dangers of smoking. However, 41 percent of eighth graders, 34 percent of tenth graders, and 27 percent of twelfth graders continue to believe that smoking is not a "great risk."[67] Furthermore, according to the CDC, three out of four teenage smokers have tried to quit at least once — but failed.[68]

Despite state laws making it illegal to sell tobacco products to minors, 24 percent of current high school smokers purchased their cigarettes in a store or gas station, and 70 percent of them were not asked to show proof of age.[69] However, there is evidence that state tobacco control policies may result in lower rates of teen smoking. States with extensive tobacco-control policies, such as New York, Connecticut, California, and Rhode Island, have lower rates of youth smoking compared to states with fewer tobacco-control policies.[70]

Students' Community Service in Health Care

Project Health™ (Helping Empower, Advocate and Lead Through Health) is an innovative, student-driven project that attempts to bridge public policy with community service and to address the health and social needs of the local low-income community. It began as a pilot program of 10 volunteer students from Harvard University and has expanded to involve 230 students from universities in three cities.

One component of the project, FitNut, helps children exercise and learn about the importance of good nutrition, while helping build their self-esteem. A pediatrician, dietician, and physical fitness specialist from Boston Medical Center (BMC) guide the student volunteers.

The Asthma Swimming Program is an effort to strengthen asthmatics' lung capacity through exercise. According to a BMC pulmonologist, lung capacity increased an average of 26 percent among the 18 students who participated in the program during the past year.

Another program, the Family Information Source, is an online interactive computer kiosk in BMC's pediatric clinic that allows parents to access information on illnesses, treatments, physicians, health care coverage, and social services. Other Project Health™ programs focus on literacy, advocacy, and computer training.

Source: Project Health (www.projecthealth.org). Accessed on December 15, 2000.

Births to teen mothers

The birth rate for teens fell once again in 1998 to 51.1 births per 1,000 teen females between ages 15 and 19. The overall birth rate for teens has fallen 18 percent since 1991. During that period, the largest decline was among Black teens, with a 26 percent drop. Since 1991, birth rates for White teens dropped 14 percent, and birth rates for Hispanic teens dropped 12 percent. Preliminary 1999 data show a continuation of these trends.[71]

Although there have been significant declines in teen birth rates, particularly among racial and ethnic minorities, the rates are still too high. In 1998, the teen birth rate for Whites was 45.4 per 1,000 compared to 85.4 for Blacks and 93.6 for Hispanics.[72]

HIV/AIDS

By the end of June 2000, almost 40,000 cases of AIDS and over 13,000 deaths among people under 25 had been reported to the CDC.[73] Many others do not know they are infected, leaving them without adequate medical care.

The number of infants acquiring AIDS during their mother's pregnancy began to decline sharply by the mid-1990s, mainly because infected pregnant women were treated with zidovudine (ZDV) to prevent perinatal transmission of AIDS. In the early 1990s, before the availability of this treatment, an estimated 1,000 to 2,000 infants were born with HIV infection each year.[74]

Similarly, the number of deaths due to AIDS in children under 13 has decreased from 582 deaths in 1994 to 76 deaths in 1999. Cases of AIDS in children under 13 started decreasing from a 1992 high of 947 new cases down to 93 new cases in 1999.[75]

The reported number of AIDS cases varies among racial and ethnic groups. Fifty-nine percent of all pediatric AIDS cases reported to the CDC through June 2000 are among Black children and 23 percent are among Hispanic children.[76] Although Blacks and Hispanics each make up 14 to 15 percent of the U.S. population ages 13 to 19, Blacks account for 50 percent and Hispanics account for 20 percent of the 3,865 AIDS cases ever reported in this age group. [77]

There are also racial differences in education about HIV/AIDS in schools. Overall, 91 percent of U.S. students have been taught about AIDS or HIV infection at school. However, White students (92 percent) were more likely than Black students (87 percent) or Hispanic students (84 percent) to have received HIV/AIDS education at school.[78]

In order to prevent more HIV infections from occurring, the White House Office of National AIDS Policy (ONAP) has called for more collaborative efforts between schools, parents, communities, and health care providers to provide HIV counseling, testing, support services, and prevention education to the teen population.

Environmental Threats and Risks

Lead poisoning

Although most parents and members of the public are not aware of it, lead poisoning may be the most serious and most common environmental health hazard for children. Almost 900,000 children under five currently have elevated blood-lead levels, and more than one out of seven Black children living in older housing have elevated blood-lead levels.[79] The older the house, the more likely it has lead-based paint, which can deteriorate into chips or dust. Lead deposits can be found on floors, windowsills, eating and playing sources, and in the dirt outside the house. Children can swallow lead if they play in dirt or in dusty areas and then put their hands or toys in their mouths.

Lead exposure dropped significantly for all Americans after the Environmental Protection Agency (EPA) banned lead from paint and gasoline in the late 1970s. At that time, nearly 90 percent of children ages 1 to 5 had elevated blood-lead levels.[80] But even after the ban, airborne lead from automobile and truck emissions had already settled in the soil, contaminating residential areas, school playgrounds, and other public areas, especially those previously used for industrial purposes.

Sixty-four million U.S. homes still contain lead paint, and the U.S. Department of Housing and Urban Development (HUD) has identified 5 to 15 million of those homes as "very hazardous." Elementary schools built before 1978 are also likely to contain lead-based paint, and all school buildings and playgrounds should be checked by trained professionals for lead hazards. A 1998 study by the California Department of Health Services found detectable levels of lead in 95 percent of the elementary schools tested, and three out of four schools had levels that were above the EPA's "action level, " meaning steps must be taken to remove lead and safeguard children and the public.[81]

In October 2000, HUD awarded $60 million to reduce lead exposure in housing, affecting 30,000 children in 19 states.[82] In partnership with EPA, HUD has been enforcing the Lead-Based Paint Hazard Reduction Act of 1992 by filing lawsuits against landlords and housing groups who fail to disclose the known presence of lead-based paint. Recent efforts to bring class-action lawsuits against paint manufacturers for concealing the health effects of lead have generally been unsuccessful. However, increased enforcement of regulations, increased implementation of lead abatement programs, and improved risk assessments for children will help to reduce and prevent the toxic effects of exposure to lead.

Asthma

Asthma is one of the most common chronic conditions of childhood, affecting more than 4.4 million children under 18.[83] It is one of the leading reasons for hospitalizations, and the rate of outpatient visits for children with asthma has doubled in the past 25 years.[84]

In addition to genetic factors and allergies, asthma can be triggered by environmental factors such as air pollution and smog, animal hair, dust mites, and cigarette smoke. Symptoms can include coughing, wheezing, and tightened airways and lung muscles. The loss of breath and lung spasms can be very frightening and can be fatal if they are not controlled.

Asthma rates are increasing all over the world, for reasons that are not entirely clear. However, U.S. asthma rates are increasing fastest among children of color in low-income neighborhoods, where indoor and outdoor air pollution are widespread. Nearly half of all the homeless children in New York City are asthmatic, and emergency room and hospitalization rates for asthma are higher for Black and Hispanic children, particularly for those under 4.[85]

Because of the increasing rates of asthma, many providers and schools are improving health education to young asthmatics to reduce asthma attacks and prevent

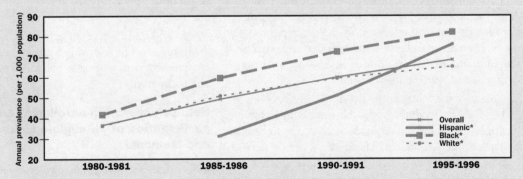

Children and Asthma

The rate of asthma among children has been increasing since the 1980s

Annual prevalence (per 1,000 population)

Legend:
- Overall
- Hispanic*
- Black*
- White*

*The data for 1980-1981 include children of Hispanic origin within the White and Black groups. For subsequent years, Hispanic children are not included in these groups, but are counted separately.

Source: "Measuring Childhood Asthma Prevalence Before and After the 1997 Redesign of the National Health Interview Survey — United States," *MMWR*, Vol. 49, No. 40 (October 13, 2000), pp. 908-911.

unnecessary hospitalizations. For example, after giving patients video cameras to document their experiences with asthma, one physician found that patients were not using their inhalers effectively, took more than the prescribed dose, or stopped using their medications without consulting a health professional.[86] School-based asthma management programs are also effective in helping to monitor the condition; reduce exposure to allergens, pollutants, and stressful situations; and improve the appropriate use of medications.

The Department of Health and Human Services has made asthma a priority area and has developed a strategic plan to reduce the disproportionate rates of asthma among racial and ethnic minorities. Currently, there is no national tracking system on asthma, and a recent report from the Pew Environmental Health Commission found that 27 states lack adequate systems to monitor its incidence.[87] It is vitally important to develop better information systems to monitor rates across the country, because asthma is affected by environmental and many other factors.

Racial Disparities and Environmental Justice

Differences in health status are influenced by economics, geography, culture, language, and race. Racial and ethnic minorities have different rates of disease, different levels of severity of disease, and differences in access to care. [88] The U.S. Surgeon General is leading the national initiative to reduce these disparities by 2010 by developing better information on disparities in health status, by investing in more research to determine genetic differences, and by examining social and behavioral aspects of health (see http://raceandhealth.hhs.gov).

One underlying reason for health disparities is exposure to environmental toxins and hazards in communities of color. For several years, research on the environmental components of racial disparities has been supported by the National Institutes of Health (NIH).[89] A growing movement known as "environmental justice" has brought national attention to the disproportionate number of industrial plants, waste facilities, and other potential polluters that are located in low-income neighborhoods and communities of color.

Many of the communities that have been exposed to higher levels of pollutants may be more vulnerable to health problems because of inadequate access to health care, poor nutrition, and other factors associated with low-income communities. They may also have limited involvement in the political process and may not be aware of their exposures. To assist communities in developing better information on their risks of exposures and potential

health effects, the National Library of Medicine provides training for historically Black colleges and universities and American Indian colleges to use NIH data bases and to develop tracking systems for environmental exposures in their communities. Several colleges and universities are adding environmental justice programs to public health and medical school curricula.[90]

Advances in information technology allow state and local agencies to track locations where children who have developed certain diseases live and then disseminate this data. The Pew Environmental Health Commission estimates that a nationwide network will cost $275 million annually — less than one-tenth of one percent of the $325 billion that chronic diseases annually cost the United States in health care and lost productivity.[91]

A national study sponsored by NIH, EPA, CDC, and the Department of Energy called for more research to develop guidelines to protect the public interest when policy-makers weigh the possible environmental risks of a new facility against the positive benefits, such as jobs and tax revenue, that a facility might provide to the community.[92] Standardized health data is urgently needed to correctly identify high-risk groups and monitor the effectiveness of health interventions that target those groups.

Moving Forward: A 2001 Agenda for Action

Every child should have affordable health coverage and access to health care. The nation also should take active steps to extend coverage to all uninsured adults, beginning with uninsured parents. CHIP and Medicaid expansions have increased eligibility for millions of children, but too many barriers remain for families who try to enroll in public programs. Bureaucratic red tape, inefficient and intrusive administrative procedures, and complicated applications can leave many eligible children uninsured. Streamlining and simplification, which lead to improved efficiency, reduced administrative costs, and peace of mind for parents, are well worth the time and effort.

Every child deserves to grow up in a safe and healthy environment. The following is an action agenda for child and public health advocates and for all citizens who care about children.

Help to ensure full enrollment and participation of all eligible children in CHIP and Medicaid

◆ Continue to raise public awareness about CHIP and improvements in Medicaid.

◆ Find new partners in outreach efforts to ensure that every low-income working parent knows about the availability of CHIP and Medicaid. Involve schools, child care centers, health care providers, businesses, civic organizations, and the faith community in outreach events.

◆ Increase the availability of applications through community-based settings and state Web sites.

◆ Engage community-based organizations in outreach, particularly in racially and ethnically diverse communities, and ensure that outreach funding is adequate.

◆ Provide funding for application assistance, including culturally appropriate translation services and applications in languages spoken in the community.

Streamline, simplify, and coordinate enrollment in CHIP and Medicaid

◆ Implement express lane eligibility in every state, in order to accelerate enrollment in CHIP and Medicaid for children who are already enrolled in public programs with similar income requirements, such as free and reduced school lunch, food stamps, and WIC.

◆ Work to ensure that every state eliminates assets tests and allows self-declaration of income.

◆ Eliminate the face-to-face enrollment requirement for Medicaid in the seven states that still require it (Alabama, Georgia, Montana, New York, Texas, West Virginia, and Wyoming).

◆ Implement 12-month continuous eligibility for CHIP and Medicaid in every state. (In 37 states, 12-month continuous eligibility is not available for one or both of the programs.)

◆ Raise Medicaid income eligibility levels to make them consistent for all children ages 18 and under within a family. Families are confused when one child is eligible for coverage and another is not, when children within the family are eligible for different programs, or when a child loses coverage after a birthday.

◆ Make sure that the same health plans and providers participate in both CHIP and Medicaid. This will allow children in the same family to receive preventive services and health care from the same provider even if their eligibility changes or if one of the children is covered by a different program.

◆ Make it easy to renew eligibility through self-declaration or automatic renewal.

◆ Monitor the impact of cost-sharing (premiums and co-payments) on families in determining whether they continue to participate in CHIP.

Improve accountability for CHIP, Medicaid, and managed care

◆ Make sure that every state's CHIP benefits match the needs of children, including coverage for dental, mental health, and vision care. Help to ensure that prescription drug coverage, durable medical equipment, and coordinated disease management programs for chronic conditions are covered in CHIP programs with minimal or no co-payments.

◆ Support a strong, enforceable consumer protection law that is responsive to children's health care needs. Access to pediatric specialists and sub-specialists, timely referrals, less waiting time for referrals, 24-hour advice lines, and coordination of care should be included.

◆ Push health plans participating in CHIP and Medicaid to issue report cards on child and teen immunization rates, well-child visits, vision and hearing checkups, waiting time for appointments, and other standardized indicators of quality and access to children's health care.

Intensify efforts to reduce racial and ethnic disparities in health status and access to care

◆ Develop benchmarks and set goals to improve the health status of every community, particularly among racial and ethnic minorities.

◆ Recognize diversity and improve cultural sensitivity and cultural competence in all systems that serve children and families.

◆ Incorporate translation services, use multilingual print materials, and recognize cultural traditions when providing health care for racially and ethnically diverse consumers.

◆ Increase the diversity of the health care workforce by using incentives to encourage minority students to enter the health professions.

Work to reduce children's exposures to air pollution, lead, pesticides, and other environmental hazards

◆ Visit www.scorecard.org to find out about environmental hazards in your community.

◆ Call the National Lead Information Clearinghouse at 1-800-424-LEAD for more information about lead poisoning prevention.

◆ Urge local health and education officials to participate in lead abatement programs for substandard housing and elementary schools.

◆ Consult with local officials to have the soil and water in playgrounds and schools tested by professionals.

◆ Visit the EPA Web site (http://www.epa.gov/children/whatyou.htm) to find out how to protect children from environmental threats.

Endnotes

1. U.S. Bureau of the Census, "Current Population Survey," March 1999 and March 2000. Calculations by the Children's Defense Fund.

2. U.S. Department of Health and Human Services, Health Care Financing Administration. Medicaid data are from "HCFA 2082 Reports, August 15, 1999 and January 27, 2000" and CHIP data are from "Aggregate Enrollment Statistics for Federal Fiscal Years 1999 and 2000." Uninsured data are from U.S. Bureau of the Census, "Current Population Survey," March 2000. Calculations by the Children's Defense Fund.

3. U.S. Bureau of the Census, "Current Population Survey," March 2000. Calculations by the Children's Defense Fund.

4. Paul W. Newacheck, Dana Hughes, et al., "The Unmet Health Needs of America's Children," Pediatrics 105, no. 4 (2000): 989-997. See also, American College of Physicians-American Society of Internal Medicine, No Health Insurance? It's Enough to Make You Sick: Scientific Research Linking the Lack of Health Coverage to Poor Health (Washington, D.C.: American College of Physicians-American Society of Internal Medicine, 1999). Available on the Internet at http://www.acponline.org/uninsured/lack-exec.htm.

5. Supra note 3.

6. Henry J. Kaiser Family Foundation, Key Facts: Race, Ethnicity and Medical Care (Menlo Park, Calif.: October 1999). Available on the Internet at http://www.kff.org. See also, Molly Joel Coye and Deborah Alvarez, Medicaid Managed Care and Cultural Diversity in California. Report prepared by The Lewin Group for the Commonwealth Fund (February 1999). Available on the Internet at http://www.cmwf.org.

7. Supra note 3.

8. Center for Studying Health System Change, "Tracking Health Care Costs: An Upswing in Premiums and Costs Underlying Health Insurance," Data Bulletin No. 20 (Washington, D.C.: Center for Studying Health System Change, November 2000).

9. Health Care Financing Administration, "Aggregate Enrollment Statistics for Federal Fiscal Years 1999 and 2000." Available on the Internet at www.hcfa.gov.

10. Supra note 1.

11. Margo Edmunds, Martha Teitelbaum, and Cassy Gleason, All Over the Map: A Progress Report on the State Children's Health Insurance Program (Washington, D.C.: Children's Defense Fund, August 2000). Available on the Internet at www.childrensdefense.org.

12. Genevieve Kenney, Frank Ullman, and Alan Weil, Three Years into SCHIP: What States Are and Are Not Spending, New Federalism Series A, No. A44 (Washington, D.C.: Urban Institute, September 2000).

13. U.S. General Accounting Office, Medicaid Enrollment: Amid Declines, State Efforts to Ensure Coverage After Welfare Reform Vary. Report to Congressional Requestors, GAO/HEHS-99-163 (Washington, D.C.: U.S. General Accounting Office, September 1999); U.S. General Accounting Office, Medicaid and SCHIP: Comparisons of Outreach, Enrollment Practices, and Benefits, GAO/HEHS-00-86 (Washington, D.C.: U.S. General Accounting Office, April 2000).

14. Kaiser Commission on Medicaid and the Uninsured, Marketing Medicaid and SCHIP: A Study of State Advertising Campaigns. Prepared by Lake Snell Perry and Associates and Health Management Associates (Washington, D.C.: Kaiser Commission on Medicaid and the Uninsured, October 2000). Available on the Internet at www.kff.org.

15. Ibid.

16. Kaiser Commission on Medicaid and the Uninsured, Medicaid and Children: Overcoming Barriers to Enrollment. Findings from a National Survey (Washington, D.C.: Kaiser Commission on Medicaid and the Uninsured, January 2000). Available on the Internet at www.kff.org.

17. Ibid.

18. Ibid.

19. Jack Meyer, "Employers' Current Role in Health Care and Other Health Coverage Options" (presentation at the Alliance for Health Reform Briefing on Employer-Sponsored Health Insurance Coverage, Washington, D.C., October 20, 2000).

20. Genevieve M. Kenney, Jennifer M. Haley, and Frank Ullman, Most Uninsured Children are in Families Served by Government Programs, New Federalism Series: National Survey of American Families, No. B-4 (Washington, D.C.: Urban Institute, December 1999).

21. Children's Partnership and Kaiser Commission on Medicaid and the Uninsured, Putting Express Lane Eligibility Into Practice: A Briefing Book and Guide for Enrolling Uninsured Children Who Receive Other Public Benefits into Medicaid and CHIP (Santa Monica, Calif. and Washington, D.C., November 2000). Available on the Internet at www. childrenspartnership.org and www.kff.org.

22. U.S. General Accounting Office, Medicaid and SCHIP: Comparisons of Outreach, Enrollment Practices, and Benefits, GAO/HEHS-00-86 (Washington, D.C.: U.S. General Accounting Office, April 2000); U.S. General Accounting Office, Medicaid Enrollment: Amid Declines, State Efforts to Ensure Coverage After Welfare Reform Vary. Report to Congressional Requestors, GAO/HEHS-99-163 (Washington, D.C.: U.S. General Accounting Office, September 1999).

23. U.S. Department of Health and Human Services, Office of the Inspector General, Medicaid Managed Care and EPSDT, Report No. OIE-05-93-00290 (Washington, D.C.: U.S. Department of Health and Human Services, May 15, 1997).

24. Sara Rosenbaum, Colleen A. Sonosky, Karen Shaw, and Marcie H. Zakheim, Negotiating the New Health System: A Nationwide Study of Medicaid Managed Care Contracts, Third Edition (Washington, D.C.: The George Washington University Center for Health Services Research and Policy, June 1999). Neva Kaye and Cynthia Pernice, Medicaid Managed Care: A Guide for States, Fourth Edition (Portland, Maine: National Academy for State Health Policy, March 1999).

25. U.S. General Accounting Office, Medicaid: Elevated Blood Lead Levels in Children, GAO/HEHS-98-78 (Washington, D.C.: U.S. General Accounting Office, 1998); U.S. General Accounting Office, Lead Poisoning: Federal Health Care Programs are not Effectively Reaching At-Risk Children, GAO/HEHS-99-18 (Washington, D.C.: U.S. General Accounting Office, January 1999). Both reports are available on the Internet at www.gao.gov.

26. Associated Press, "State Sued over Alleged Failure to Meet Medicaid Requirements," (October 4, 2000). Retrieved from the Internet at www.nexis.com/research on October 9, 2000.

27. Mark Moran, "Parent Sues HMO in Lead Poisoning Case," WebMD Medical News, August 10, 2000. Retrieved from the Internet at http://cleveland.webmd.com/content/article/2792.353 on September 4, 2000.

28. George Washington University Center for Health Services Research and Policy, Sample Purchasing Specifications: Childhood Lead Poisoning (Washington, D.C.: George Washington University, November 1998). Retrieved from the Internet at www.gwu.edu~chsrp/sps/lead/nov98/index.html on November 7, 2000.

29. U.S. Department of Health and Human Services, Office of the Surgeon General, Oral Health in America: A Report of the Surgeon General (Washington, D.C.: U.S. Department of Health and Human Services, May 2000). Retrieved from the Internet at http://www.nidcr.nih.gov/sgr/execsumm.pdf on September 15, 2000.

30. National Center for Health Statistics, Health, United States, 2000, With Adolescent Health Chartbook (Hyattsville, Md.: National Center for Health Statistics, 2000): 269-270.

31. K. N. Kaste et al., "Coronal caries in the primary and permanent dentition of children and adolescents 1-17 years of age: United States, 1988-1991," Journal of Dental Research 75, Special No. (1996): 631-641. U.S. General Accounting Office, Oral Health: Dental Disease Is a Chronic Problem Among Low-Income Populations, GAO/HEHS-00-72 (Washington, D.C.: U.S. General Accounting Office, April 2000): 7. Retrieved from the Internet at www.gao.gov/ new.items/he00072.pdf on February 2, 2001.

32. U.S. Department of Health and Human Services, *Children's Dental Services Under Medicaid: Access and Utilization. Report of the Office of the Inspector General*, OEI-09-0-93-00240 (San Francisco, Calif.: Regional Office of the Department of Health and Human Services, 1996).

33. U.S. General Accounting Office, *Oral Health: Factors Contributing to Low Use of Dental Services by Low-Income Populations*, GAO/HEHS-00-149 (Washington, D.C.: U.S. General Accounting Office, September 2000).

34. Jane Perkins and Justin Short, *State Initiatives to Improve Access to Dental Care* (Chapel Hill, N.C.: National Health Law Program, October 2000). Retrieved from the Internet at www.healthlaw.org on November 6, 2000.

35. *Ibid.* See also, Center for Health Care Strategies, *States' Approaches to Increasing Medicaid Beneficiaries' Access to Dental Services, Informed Purchasing Series* (Princeton, N.J.: Center for Health Care Strategies, November 2000).

36. *Supra* note 34.

37. "Hatch Says Blue Cross Shirks Care: Insurer Contends It Covers 94% of Requests for Help," *St. Paul Pioneer Press* (October 4, 2000).

38. National Center on Poverty Law, "Parents Challenge Maine's Failure to Provide In-Home Behavioral and Mental Health Services to Children Receiving Medicaid." Retrieved from the Internet at http://www.povertylaw.org/casesasp/abstract.asp?chno=52951 on February 12, 2001. See also, Edmund S. Muskie School of Public Service at the University of Southern Maine, "Maine's Plan Development Work Group for Community-Based Living." Retrieved from the Internet at http://community.muskie.usm.maine.edu/whatsnew.htm on December 1, 2000.

39. U.S. Department of Health and Human Services, Office of the Surgeon General, *Report of the Surgeon General's Conference on Children's Mental Health: A National Agenda* (Washington, D.C.: U.S. Department of Health and Human Services, January 2001).

40. Geraldine Dallek and Karen Pollitz, *External Review of Health Plan Decisions: An Update* (Washington, D.C.: Prepared for the Kaiser Family Foundation by the Institute for Health Care Research and Policy, Georgetown University, May 2000).

41. *Federal Register* 66, no. 8: pp. 2489-2688.

42. Leighton Ku and Matthew Broadus, *The Importance of Family-Based Insurance Expansions: New Research Findings About State Health Reforms* (Washington, D.C.: Center on Budget and Policy Priorities, September 5, 2000). Available on the Internet at www.cbpp.org.

43. *Ibid.*

44. National Center for Health Statistics, "Deaths: Final Data for 1998," *National Vital Statistics Reports* 48, no. 11 (2000).

45. *Ibid.*

46. *Supra* note 44.

47. National Center for Health Statistics, "Births: Final Data for 1998," *National Vital Statistics Reports* 48, no. 3 (2000).

48. National Center for Health Statistics, "Births: Preliminary data for 1999," *National Vital Statistics Reports* 48, no. 14 (2000).

49. U.S. Department of Health and Human Services, Centers for Disease Control and Prevention, "National, State, and Urban Area Vaccination Coverage Levels Among Children Aged 19–35 Months — United States, 1999," *Morbidity and Mortality Weekly Report* 49, no. 26 (July 07, 2000): 585-9. U.S. Department of Health and Human Services, Centers for Disease Control and Prevention, "Vaccination Coverage of 2-year-old Children — United States, 1993," *Morbidity and Mortality Weekly Report* 43, no. 39 (October 7, 1994): 705-709. Calculations by the Children's Defense Fund. While the immunization rates in 1992 and 1999 are from two different surveys, they have been roughly comparable when measured in the same year.

50. National Conference of State Legislatures, "Childhood Immunizations: States Tackle Costs, Education, Disparities," *State Health Notes* 20, no. 335 (October 23, 2000): 3-6.

51. K. J. Rask et al., "Measuring Immunization Registry Costs: Promises and Pitfalls," *American Journal of Preventive Medicine* 19, no. 3 (April 2000): 262-257.

52. National Center for Health Statistics, *Health, United States, 2000 With Adolescent Health Chartbook* (Hyattsville, Md.: National Center for Health Statistics, 2000): 248.

53. Centers for Disease Control and Prevention, National Center for Chronic Disease Prevention and Health Promotion, Division of Adolescent and School

Health, "Poor Nutrition." Retrieved from the Internet at www.cdc.gov/nccd php/dash/nutrition.htm on November 13, 2000.

54. David S. Freedman, William H. Dietz, Sathanur R. Srinivasan and Gerald S. Berenson, "The Relation of Overweight to Cardiovascular Risk Factors Among Children and Adolescents: The Bogalusa Heart Study," *Pediatrics* 103, No. 6, (June 1999): pp.1175-1182.

55. National Center for Health Statistics, *Health United States 2000, With Adolescent Health Chartbook* (Hyattsville, Md.; National Center for Health Statistics, 2000): Table 69.

56. U.S. Department of Health and Human Services and U.S. Department of Education, *Promoting Better Health for Young People through Physical Activity and Sports: A Report to the President from the Secretary of Health and Human Services and the Secretary of Education* (Washington, D.C.: U.S. Department of Health and Human Services and U.S. Department of Education, December 2000).

57. U.S. Department of Health and Human Services, Centers for Disease Control and Prevention, "Youth Risk Behavior Surveillance — United States, 1999," *Morbidity and Mortality Weekly Report* 49, no. SS-5 (June 9, 2000): 89.

58. *Supra* note 1.

59. Paul W. Newacheck et al., "Adolescent Health Insurance Coverage: Recent Changes and Access to Care," *Pediatrics* 104, no. 2 (August 1999): 195-202.

60. Karen M. Wilson and Jonathan D. Klein, "Adolescents Who Use the Emergency Department as their Usual Source of Care," *Archives of Pediatric Adolescent Medicine* 154 (April 2000): 361-365.

61. *Ibid.*

62. T.M. Anglin, K.E. Naylor, D.W. Kaplan, "Comprehensive School-based Health Care: High School Students' Use of Medical, Mental Health, and Substance Abuse Services," *Pediatrics* 97, no. 3 (1996): 318-30.

63. Making the Grade, *National Survey of School-Based Health Centers, 1997-98* (Washington, D.C.: Making the Grade, The George Washington University, 2000). Retrieved from the Internet at http://www.hfni.gsehd.gwu.edu/~mtg/FS/fsmap.html on July 31, 2000.

64. Centers for Disease Control and Prevention, Division of Adolescent and School Health, *Guidelines for School Health Programs to Prevent Tobacco Use and Addiction* (Atlanta: Centers for Disease Control and Prevention, 2000). Retrieved from the Internet at http://www.cdc.gov/nccdphp/dash/nutptua.htm on November 12, 2000.

65. U.S. Department of Health and Human Services, Substance Abuse and Mental Health Services Administration, *Summary of Findings from the 1999 National Household Survey on Drug Abuse* (Rockville, Md.: U.S. Department of Health and Human Services, 1999): 21. Retrieved from the Internet at http://www.samhsa.gov/oas/NHSDA/1999/titlepage.htm on November 12, 2000.

66. *Supra* note 57, at 52.

67. University of Michigan, *Monitoring the Future Survey, 2000* (Ann Arbor, Mich.: University of Michigan, 2000): Table 4. Retrieved from the Internet at http://www.monitoringthefuture.org/data/00data.html#2000data-cigs on December 14, 2000.

68. *Supra* note 64.

69. *Supra* note 57, at 58.

70. Douglas A. Luke, Katherine A. Stamatakis, Ross C. Brownson, "State Youth-Access Tobacco Control Policies and Youth Smoking Behavior in the United States," *American Journal of Preventive Medicine* 19, no. 3 (2000): 180-7.

71. National Center for Health Statistics, "Births: Final Data for 1998." *National Vital Statistics Reports* 48, No. 3 (March 28, 2000), Tables 4 and 9; and National Center for Health Statistics, "Births: Preliminary Data for 1999," *National Vital Statistics Reports* 48, No. 14 (August 6, 2000), Table 1.

72. *Ibid.* at tables 4 and 9.

73. Centers for Disease Control and Prevention, "HIV/AIDS Surveillance Report, 2000" 12, no. 1 (Atlanta: Centers for Disease Control and Prevention, 2000): 14, 27.

74. Centers for Disease Control and Prevention, "Status of Perinatal HIV Prevention: U.S. Declines Continue, November 1999." Retrieved from the Internet at www.cdc.gov/hiv/pubs/facts/perinatl.pdf on February 8, 2001; Centers for Disease Control and Prevention, "HIV/AIDS Surveillance Report, 1999" 11, no. 2 (Atlanta: Centers for Disease Control and Prevention, 2000): 1, 5.

75. Centers for Disease Control and Prevention, "HIV/AIDS Surveillance Report, 1999" 11, no. 2 (Atlanta: Centers for Disease Control and Prevention, 2000): 31.

76. *Supra* note 73, at 22.

77. *Supra* note 73, at 14.

78. Centers for Disease Control and Prevention, "Youth Risk Behavior Surveillance, United States, 1999," *Morbidity and Mortality Weekly Report* 49, no. SS-5 (June 9, 2000): 78.

79. Advisory Committee on Childhood Lead Poisoning Prevention, "Recommendations for Blood Lead Screening of Young Children Enrolled in Medicaid: Targeting a Group at High Risk," *Morbidity and Mortality Weekly Report* 49, no. RR14 (December 8, 2000): 1-13.

80. Morri Markowitz, "Lead Poisoning," *Pediatrics in Review* 21, no. 10 (October 2000): 327-335.

81. Natural Resources Defense Council, "Lead Paint in Schools," Retrieved from the Internet at www.nrdc.org/health/kids/qleadsch.asp on November 20, 2000. See also Environmental Protection Agency, "EPA Announces Tough New Standards for Lead" (December 26, 2000): Press release.

82. U.S. Department of Housing and Urban Development, "Cuomo Awards Nearly $70 Million to Help Communities Protect Children from Environmental and Safety Hazards" (October 6, 2000): Press release.

83. National Center for Health Statistics, *Current Estimates for the National Health Interview Survey, 1996* (PHS) 99-1528. Series 10, no. 200 (Hyattsville, Md.: National Center for Health Statistics, October 1999): p. 94, Table 62.

84. Edmund J. Graves, Maria F. Owings, "1996 Summary: National Hospital Discharge Survey" *Advance Data from Vital and Health Statistics*, no. 301 (Hyattsville, Md.: National Center for Health Statistics, August 31, 1998): 6. Luz Claudio et al., "Socioeconomic Factors and Asthma Hospitalization Rates in New York City," *Journal of Asthma* 36, no 4 (1999): 343-50. David M. Mannino, David M. Homa, Carol A. Pertowski, et al. "Surveillance for Asthma – United States, 1960-1995," *Morbidity and Mortality Weekly Report* 47, no. SS-1 (April 24, 1998): 1-28.

85. Center for Children's Health and the Environment, Mount Sinai School of Medicine, "Asthma Hospitalization Rates in Poor New York City Neighborhoods Up to 5 Times the City Average" (July 27, 1999): Press release. Retrieved from the Internet at http://146.203.34.27/press/1999-07-27.htm in January 2000.

86. Michael Rich, Steven Lamola, Colum Amory, et al., "Asthma in Life Context: Video Intervention/Prevention Assessment (VIA)," *Pediatrics* 105, no. 3 (March 2000): 469-477.

87. Pew Environmental Health Commission, *America's Environmental Health Gap: Why the Country Needs a Nationwide Health Tracking Network* (Baltimore, Md.: Johns Hopkins School of Public Health, September 2000). Retrieved from the Internet at http://health-track.org/reports/pehc/ on January 17, 2001.

88. U.S. Department of Health and Human Services, *Healthy People 2010* (Washington, D.C.: U.S. Department of Health and Human Services, 2000). Available on the Internet at http://www.health.gov/healthypeople.

89. National Institutes of Health, National Institute for Environmental and Health Sciences, *FY 2000 Congressional Justification* (Research Triangle Park, N.C.: National Institute for Environmental and Health Sciences, 2000): pp. 2, 8. Retrieved from the Internet at www.niehs.nih.gov on January 6, 2001.

90. See National Institutes of Health, National Institute for Environmental Health Sciences, "Health Disparities: Minority Research and Training Opportunities at NIEHS" Retrieved from the Internet at http://www.niehs.nih.gov/oc/factsheets/justice.htm on January 26, 2001. See also, National Institute for Environmental Health Sciences, "Health Disparities (Environmental Justice)." Retrieved from the Internet at http://www.niehs.nih.gov/external/resinits/ri-2.htm#full on January 26, 2001. See also, Harvard Divinity School, "Environmental Ethics and Public Policy Program, Summary Report 1989-99." Retrieved from the Internet at http://www.ecoethics.net on December 10, 2000.

91. David Satcher, U.S. Surgeon General, Remarks at Asthma and Allergy Foundation of America Press Conference, Washington, D.C., September 13, 2000.

92. National Academy of Sciences, Institute of Medicine, *Toward Environmental Justice: Research, Education, and Health Policy Needs* (Washington, D.C.: National Academy Press, 1999).

CHAPTER 3

Child Care

The increasing numbers of parents in the workforce, especially low-income single mothers, and the growing recognition of the need to give children a strong, early start should be moving high quality early care and education and after-school experiences to the top of the nation's agenda. Quality early care and education and after-school activities help families work and children succeed. The first five years of life are particularly critical to children's early learning. Research on the development of children's brains has shown that how children grow and develop depends on the interplay between nature (the child's genetic endowment) and nurture (which includes their nutrition, surroundings, care, and stimulation). Children's experiences in these early years lay the groundwork for future learning and success in school.

Given the importance of the early years, ensuring access to high quality child care and early education experiences must be an essential part of any education reform plan. When former President Bush and the nation's governors developed a national education agenda over a decade ago, their first goal was that by the year 2000, all children in America should start school ready to learn. A primary component of this goal was access to high quality, developmentally appropriate preschool programs that help prepare children for school. While progress has been made over the past decade, the goal has not been reached.

In fact, 46 percent of kindergarten teachers reported that half of their class or more have specific problems with entry into kindergarten, including difficulty following directions, lack of academic skills, disorganized home environments, and/or difficulty working independently.[1]

In quality child care and prekindergarten classes, children have frequent interaction, conversations, and storytelling time with their teachers. Prekindergarten children have opportunities to build their language and literacy skills so they can start school prepared to learn to read. These experiences can help children understand the structure and sound of words, the meaning of words, and the concept that print conveys meaning — all of which are crucial in developing literacy skills.

Research confirms that high quality early care and education experiences have positive effects on the academic performance of all children, especially low-income children and children at risk of school failure. Studies of several state prekindergarten initiatives demonstrate that the benefits include higher math and reading scores, stronger learning skills, increased creativity, better school attendance, improved health, and greater involvement by parents in their children's education.[2] Similarly, studies show that quality after-school programs have a critical impact on children's school achievement and long-term success as well as their safety and well-being.

Stable child care and affordable after-school activities also help parents get and keep a job and make ends meet. For low-income families, safe, stable, affordable child care may make the difference between climbing out of poverty or falling deeper into it. Unfortunately, the cost of quality care is often beyond the reach of low-income families whose children, in many cases, are most in need of these services. Child care assistance can help low-income parents afford quality care. In North Carolina, 83 percent of respondents who received child care subsidies said the assistance improved the quality or reliability of their children's care. Over one-third of all respondents receiving assistance noticed positive changes in their children's behavior after being placed in stable, subsidized care.[3]

Despite the importance of a strong, early start and constructive after-school activities, no state currently ensures that all families have access to quality child care and school-age opportunities. However, over the past several years, a number of states have taken notable steps to ensure that children and families have access to quality care and early education. For example, Georgia uses lottery funds to offer all 4-year-olds, regardless of income, the opportunity to participate in a part-day, part-year prekindergarten program. Ohio contributes state funds to the federal Head Start program to ensure that nearly every eligible 3- and 4-year-old has access to Head Start's comprehensive services. Rhode Island guarantees assistance in paying for child care to all families with incomes below 225 percent of poverty ($31,833 for a family of three). North Carolina's Smart Start program provides nearly $300 million to local communities to help meet the needs of families and children from birth to age five.

Studies Show Increased Need for Expanded Child Care and After-School Resources

New reports in 2000 provide additional evidence of the growing need for more quality child care, early education, and after-school opportunities for America's families. An increasing number of mothers, in both two-parent and single-parent families, are working outside the home. A U.S. Census Bureau report, based on data from 1998, finds that for the first time 51 percent of married-couple families had children and had both parents employed at least part time, compared with 33 percent in 1976.[4] After remaining steady at around 58 percent from 1986 to 1993, the proportion of single mothers with jobs also increased sharply to 71.5 percent in 1999.[5] Census Bureau figures on the employment of welfare recipients show a similar trend. In 1995, about 40 percent of welfare recipients worked at some time during the year, but that proportion had leapt to 58 percent by 1999. This trend was likely related to 1996 changes in the welfare law requiring parents to work, as well as a growing economy. The need to strengthen child care for very young children and family leave opportunities for parents is reflected in the increased number of mothers with infants in the labor force. Fifty-nine percent of women with babies younger than one year were employed in 1998, compared with 31 percent in 1976.[6]

According to another Census Bureau report released in 2000, more affordable child care and after-school opportunities for older children may not be available to the growing number of parents in the workforce. Almost 7 million children ages 5 to 14 cared for themselves on a regular basis without adult supervision.[8] Nearly one in 10

◆ Each day, an estimated 13 million children under age 6 — including children whose mothers work outside the home and those who do not — spend some part of their day being cared for by someone other than their parents.

◆ Full-day child care easily costs $4,000 to $10,000 per year — at least as much as college tuition at a public university. Yet, more than one out of four families with young children earns less than $25,000 a year, and a family with both parents working full time at the minimum wage earns only $21,400 a year.

◆ Nationally, only 12 percent of children eligible for child care assistance receive help.

◆ The average salary of a child care worker is only $15,430 a year, less than yearly salaries for funeral attendants, bellhops, and garbage collectors.

◆ A major study of a high quality early childhood program that continued to support children and their parents into elementary school found that children who participated had a greater chance of completing high school, were less likely to be charged in juvenile court, and were less likely to repeat a grade.

◆ Nearly 7 million children ages 5 to 14 care for themselves on a regular basis without any adult supervision.

The U.S. Military Child Development Program: Model for Success

One of the most significant advances has been made not by a state, but by the U.S. Military. The success of the U.S. Military Child Development Program demonstrates that with a solid vision and a commitment of resources, families and children can be ensured access to quality child care. Just a decade ago, the military faced child care challenges similar to those in communities across the country today. The need for child care had grown because of the large increase in military personnel with children. Tens of thousands of children were on waiting lists for care. Many facilities were not safe or suitable for children. The military lacked both comprehensive standards and a strong inspection system to ensure that programs were safe for children. Caregivers did not have access to adequate training and because compensation was so limited, turnover rates were extraordinary. Congress was concerned that this contributed to problems with recruitment, motivation, productivity, and retention, which in turn placed military readiness at risk.

The military has stepped up to improve families' access to quality child care by:

◆ Establishing uniform certification standards for all centers, determining whether the standards are being met, and enforcing sanctions for failing to meet standards.

◆ Establishing an accreditation system that requires centers to "meet a set of specific criteria in addition to those required for certification, and to have compliance confirmed by an outside validator." The certification process is based on the military's own set of standards, while the accreditation process is based on the National Association for the Education of Young Children (NAEYC) standards. Ninety-five percent of all military child care centers now meet NAEYC accreditation, in contrast to 8 percent of all centers across the country.

◆ Raising caregiver compensation and linking increased wages to training, developing a comprehensive training program, and hiring training and curriculum specialists.

◆ Increasing parental involvement by requiring the establishment of a board in each center composed of parents of children who attend the program.

◆ Ensuring that programs have the necessary resources to maintain high quality care while remaining affordable by providing sufficient funds to help parents pay for child care and establishing a fee scale for parents based on income.

◆ Expanding the availability of care by measuring need and meeting that need by developing facilities, adding slots, expanding the family child care program, using off-base care, and increasing the role of resource and referral agencies.

Unfortunately, the military model has not been replicated in states and communities, leaving far too many families without the high quality care they need.

Source: Nancy Duff Campbell, Judith C. Appelbaum, Karin Martinson, et al., *Be All That We Can Be: Lessons from the Military for Improving Our Nation's Child Care System* (Washington, D.C.: National Women's Law Center, 2000).

children ages 5 to 11 went home to an empty house after school during some part of each week while more than four out of 10 children ages 12 to 14 spent time unsupervised after school.

These are alarming statistics given that:

◆ The rate of juvenile violence is highest in the after-school hours between 3 p.m. and 7 p.m.[8]

◆ Nearly 45 million children ages 14 years and younger are injured in their homes every year.

◆ Most unintentional, injury-related deaths occur when children are out of school and unsupervised.[9]

◆ Being unsupervised after school puts youths at greater risk of truancy, poor academic performance, mental depression, and substance abuse.[10]

The Census Bureau report also reveals disparities in participation in after-school enrichment programs by income and education of parents. Children living in families with a monthly income of $4,500 or higher were more than twice as likely to participate in enrichment activities such as sports, lessons, or clubs as children living in families with a monthly income of under $1,500. Over half (52 percent) of the children living in families at or above 200 percent of the poverty line participated in at least one enrichment activity, compared with only one-quarter (24 percent) of the children living below the poverty line.[11]

Labor Force Participation of Women

Labor Force Participation of Women with Children Under Age Six, Selected Years

	All mothers		Married mothers	
	Number	Percent	Number	Percent
1950	–	–	1,399,000	11.9%
1955	–	–	2,012,000	16.2
1960	–	–	2,474,000	18.6
1965	–	–	3,117,000	23.2
1970	–	–	3,914,000	30.3
1975	–	–	4,518,000	36.7
1980	6,538,000	46.8%	5,227,000	45.1
1985	8,215,000	53.5	6,406,000	53.4
1990	9,397,000	58.2	7,247,000	58.9
1999	10,322,000	64.4	7,246,000	61.8
2000	10,316,000	65.3	7,341,000	62.8

– Data not available

Source: U.S. Department of Labor, Bureau of Labor Statistics.

These discrepancies are troubling since constructive after-school activities can boost low-income children's ability to succeed in school.

The Census data also show that low-income working families use a significant portion of their income to pay for child care. In 1995, poor families with incomes below the poverty level who paid for child care spent 35 percent of their income on child care, compared with 7 percent spent by non-poor families.[12]

Although stable care is important for children's development and reliable care is important to parents' ability to get and keep a job, parents use multiple child care arrangements for both younger and older children. About 44 percent of children under age 5 and 75 percent of children ages 5 to 14 regularly spent time in more than one arrangement per week. Preschool-age children with employed parents or parents in school averaged 2.2 different arrangements per week.

High Quality Care Benefits Children and Families

New research further demonstrates that low-income children benefit from comprehensive, high quality care and after-school activities. Yet it also reveals that the nation has a long way to go in ensuring that quality care is available to children and in guaranteeing the basic health and safety of children in child care settings.

The U.S. Department of Health and Human Services released a preliminary report showing the effectiveness of the federal Early Head Start program, enacted in 1994 to support infants, toddlers, and their families. Two-year-old children enrolled in Early Head Start programs after a year performed better in measures of language, cognitive, and socio-emotional development compared with children who did not participate in the program. In addition, the evaluation indicated that parents involved in the program had more positive parenting behavior, used physical punishment less often, and were more likely to provide help to their children at home. The evaluation found that the services provided by Early Head Start were generally of high quality and the strongest positive findings were found in programs that had fully implemented Head Start performance standards.[13]

A University of Wisconsin study found that low-income children who attended one of Chicago's 24 Child Parent Centers (CPCs) received many expected and unexpected benefits when compared with similar children who did not attend CPCs.[14] Participating children had a greater chance of completing high school, were less likely to be charged in juvenile court, and were less likely to have to repeat a grade. Boys were found to benefit more than girls. Boys who attended the preschool were 40 percent more likely to graduate from high school than similar boys who did not attend. The CPCs offer both academic support to children and opportunities for parents to be involved. The centers provide ongoing services through third grade and bring parents into the schools by offering a resource center where parents can learn more about working with their children at home.

The study, which is the nation's largest longitudinal study of a government-funded preschool, found that for every dollar invested in the CPC preschool program, the benefit to society at large is $4.39. This includes cost reductions for crime and remedial education, and projected increases in tax revenues and higher earnings for participants.

At the same time, researchers expressed concern about the current system of supports for children and families. *From Neurons to Neighborhoods: The Science of Early Childhood,* published by the National Research Council and Institute of Medicine of the National Academies, calls on the country to improve significantly how it cares for its children and families.[15] The authors argue that the extensive scientific findings from the past two decades despite leading to a greater understanding of child development, particularly between birth and age five, the importance of the early years, and how quality intervention programs can increase positive outcomes for children, have not been used to influence public policy. They point to the fact that children need at least one close and dependable relationship and emphasize the roles of both parents and regular caregivers in children's lives. The authors conclude that society must "recognize the significance of out-of-home relationships for young children and significantly rethink the interactions among early childhood science, policy, and practices."[16]

A 2000 U.S. General Accounting Office report raises concern that the nation has yet to address comprehensively a very basic issue — the health and safety of children in child care settings. The report, *State Efforts to En-force Safety and Health Requirements,* examined different state licensing and enforcement activities, including background checks, timing and regularity of monitoring visits, sanctions, training for licensing staff, and caseloads for licensing staff.[17] State policies were compared with recommendations from the National Association for the Education of Young Children and the National Health and Safety Performance Standards — comprehensive standards developed by the American Academy of Pediatrics and the American Public Health Association. The report found that a majority of states met or exceeded recommended monitoring practices in certain respects, but fell short in other areas. For instance, 46 states visited child care centers one or more times per year, and 36 states visited family child care homes at least once every five years. However, the capacity of states to adequately inspect and support child care programs is questionable. Only four states invested in adequate training for licensing staff, and only 11 states reported that their licensing staff had caseloads at or below the recommended level of 75 facilities per person. In one-third of the states, caseloads were twice the recommended level or higher. The study also found that states do not regulate all caregivers, contrary to recommendations. As a result, child care providers who care for large numbers of children can operate legally without being required to meet standards or receive regular inspections to ensure that children are safe. Finally, although unregulated providers that receive public funds must meet the health and safety standards required in the federal Child Care and Development Block Grant (CCDBG) program, many states do not visit these providers to assure that they are providing safe care. Instead, states simply rely on "self-certification," asking providers to verify in writing that they are operating a safe and healthy facility.

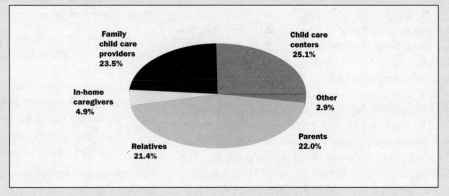

Child Care Arrangements

Child Care Arrangements for Children Younger than Five with Working Mothers, 1995

Family child care providers 23.5%

Child care centers 25.1%

In-home caregivers 4.9%

Other 2.9%

Relatives 21.4%

Parents 22.0%

Source: Kristin Smith, Who's Minding the Kids? Child Care Arrangements, U.S. Department of Commerce, Bureau of the Census, *Current Population Reports,* P70-70 (2000).

Older children also benefit from constructive after-school activities according to several studies released in 2000. In 1998, the Urban School Initiative School Age Child Care (SACC) Project began a $10 million expansion of school-age care in Columbus and Cleveland, Ohio. As of summer 1999, more than 3,000 children had participated in the after-school program at 125 centers in 17 Ohio school districts. According to a 1998-1999 evaluation of the initiative, children, schools, and parents experienced positive outcomes because of the programs.[18] Children who attended the school-age programs missed significantly fewer days of school than they had the previous school year, and they outperformed their peers on statewide fourth- and sixth-grade proficiency tests. Principals and teachers reported an increase in the completion of homework assignments, better school behavior, and better school attendance. Parents were able to work more hours with more flexible schedules.

A three-year study, released in 1999, of four after-school programs that were offered free of charge to children living in targeted, high-crime neighborhoods determined that children in these programs had fewer school absences, better conflict management strategies, and better work habits at school than their classmates who lived in the same neighborhoods but did not attend an after-school program.[19] In addition, children who participated more frequently had better work habits, better interpersonal skills, engaged in less misconduct in their neighborhoods and at school, and missed less school than children who attended for fewer days.

A U.S. Department of Education study of 21st Century Community Learning Centers — the major federal source of support for after-school programs — also finds positive effects of after-school programs on student behavior and academic performance.[20] In Montgomery, Alabama, after-school programs report a 25 percent reduction in violence in the community while in Highland Park, Michigan, the community reports a 40 percent drop in local juvenile crime since inception of the after-school program.

In rural McCormick, South Carolina, 120 students would have been retained in grade without the after-school program, the study reported. At one school in Chattanooga, Tennessee, absentee days dropped from 568 days to 135; at a second school in the city, the number declined from 148 days to 23. Despite the effectiveness of the 21st Century program, many communities are unable to participate because of limited funding. Last year, 2,252 communities applied to establish or expand 21st Century after-school programs, but only 310 grants were awarded. (See the Juvenile Justice and Youth Development chapter for more information on after-school programs.)

Finding Affordable Child Care is a Challenge

Simply finding affordable child care much less high quality care continues to be a challenge faced by the millions of low- and moderate-income families. A 2000 update of a Children's Defense Fund report, *The High Cost of Child Care Puts Quality Care Out of Reach for Many Families*, finds that the average annual cost of child care for a 4-year-old in an urban area child care center is more than the average annual cost of public college tuition in all but one state. In some cities, child care costs twice as much as college tuition.[21] The cost for infant care is even higher. The average cost of center care for a 12-month-old is above $5,750 per year in almost two-thirds of all cities surveyed and more than $6,750 per year in over one-third of the cities surveyed.

However, child care providers cannot lower their prices because they already operate on extremely tight budgets. A large proportion of a child care program's budget is devoted to staff salaries, which are unacceptably low. The average annual salary for a child care worker is only $15,430.[22]

The high costs of care are even more disturbing because many parents simply do not have access to help in paying for child care. A 2000 U.S. Department of Health and Human Services report found that of the nearly 15 million children eligible for child care assistance, only 12 percent are receiving any help.[23] Families without child care assistance spend a large proportion of their meager earnings on child care. A study of families on waiting lists in New York City found that half of those earning $6,000 to $12,000 a year spent one-fifth to half of their earnings on child care.[24] Forty-one percent of all families surveyed said they had to cut back on other essential expenses such as food and children's clothing to help pay for care. In many cases, families may settle for lower quality care because it is less expensive. Seventy-seven percent believed that their current child care arrangements were negatively affecting their children.

Another study, *Choices and Tradeoffs: The Parent Survey on Child Care in Massachusetts*, found that the cost of child care had a dramatic impact on the financial well-being of a large portion of low-income families. More than one-quarter of all low-income families who used child care reported that they have gone on welfare because of child care costs. Low-income parents were also more likely to have quit or lost a job because of problems with child care.

Few employers provide help to these hard-pressed families. While close to one-third of high-income families had employers who offered employer-sponsored child care benefits, only 5.8 percent of low-income families and

Cost of Child Care by State

States Where the Average Annual Cost of Child Care for a 4-year-old in an Urban Area Center Is at Least Twice the Average Annual Cost of Public College Tuition

State	Urban area	Average annual cost of child care for a 4-year-old in a center	Average annual cost of public college tuition
Alaska	Anchorage	$6,019	$2,769
Arizona	Tucson	4,352	2,158
Florida	Orange County	4,255	2,022
Georgia	Atlanta	4,992	2,442
Idaho	Boise	4,814	2,380
Iowa	Urban areas statewide	6,198	2,869
Kansas	Wichita	4,889	2,392
Massachusetts	Boston	8,121	4,012
Nevada	Reno	4,862	1,956
New Mexico	Albuquerque	4,801	2,180
New York	Rockland County	8,060	3,905
North Carolina	Durham	5,876	1,958
Utah	Salt Lake City	4,550	2,174
Washington	King County (Seattle)	6,604	3,151

Source: Karen Schulman, *The High Cost of Child Care Puts Quality Care Out of Reach for Many Families* (Washington, D.C.: Children's Defense Fund, 2000).

10.1 percent of middle-income families had similar benefits available.

Compounding these problems, many low-income families work odd hours, when child care is particularly hard to find and even when available, often more costly. Nationwide, more than 25 percent of low-income working families primarily work evening or overnight shifts, according to a report from the Urban Institute.[25] In contrast, 83 percent of higher-income working families work traditional daytime hours, with only 17 percent primarily working evening or overnight duty.

Polls Show Support for New Investments and Improved Policies

The public recognizes the urgency of addressing these tremendous gaps between what low-income families need and the child care assistance available. New polls in 2000 show strong public support for improving families' access to high quality child care and after-school opportunities and for helping parents stay home during the early months after their child's birth or adoption. "What Grown-Ups Understand About Child Development," a poll sponsored by Zero to Three, Civitas, and Brio Corporation, found that in spite of widespread misconceptions about the emotional and physical development of children, parents and the general public understand the importance of quality care:[26]

◆ Seventy-two percent of parents of young children and 69 percent of all adults surveyed believe that providing a young child with quality child care is critical in promoting the child's intellectual development.

◆ Eighty-eight percent of parents of young children and 80 percent of all adults support paid parental leave, and 89 percent of young parents and 84 percent of all adults support expanding disability or unemployment insurance to fund paid family leave.

◆ Three-quarters (73 percent) of parents of young children and 65 percent of all adults support government financial assistance to help families pay for quality child care.

Waiting Lists

Waiting Lists for Child Care Assistance in Selected States

	Number of Children or Families on the Waiting List
Alabama	6,411 children
Arkansas	5,150 families
Florida	44,055 children
Georgia	15,536 families
Iowa	2,000 children
Maine	2,069 children
Massachusetts	16,398 children
Minnesota	3,069 families
Mississippi	15,208 children
North Carolina	14,510 children
Tennessee	5,100 children
Texas	41,240 children
Virginia	4,255 families

Source: Data provided by state child care administrators, February 2001.

There is similar support for expanding after-school care. A poll released by the Afterschool Alliance found that nine out of 10 voting Americans want after-school programs for children, eight out of 10 voters believe federal and state governments should set aside money for after-school programs, and nine out of 10 agree that there is a need for some type of organized activity or place where children can go after school.[27]

A Fight Crime: Invest in Kids poll found that the public supports new investments in both child care and after-school programs over tax cuts. Two out of three Americans indicate that government should invest in educational child care and after-school programs before cutting taxes, while over 85 percent of those polled say that educational child care and after-school programs will greatly reduce crime.[28] When asked which priorities, if any, are more important than cutting taxes, 68 percent selected "providing access to after-school programs and early childhood development programs like Head Start," and the same percent chose "shoring up Social Security and Medicare."

Policy Developments

In 2000, some positive initiatives at the federal, state, and local levels as well as by the private sector

expanded access to family leave, quality child care, early education, and after-school opportunities. However, more must be done so all communities can ensure that their families can find the quality care that helps them work and their children succeed.

Progress at the federal level

Families and children had something to cheer about as the final budget or appropriations bill for 2001 included historic increases in funding for child care, Head Start, and after-school programs and authorized or created several new early childhood programs.

The Child Care Development Block Grant (CCDBG) was increased by $817 million for a total of $2 billion in discretionary funds. In addition, the mandatory portion of the CCDBG was increased by $200 million bringing total federal CCDBG funding up to $4.567 billion for FY 2001. States must spend at least 4 percent of the CCDBG funds to bolster the quality of child care. Congress also set aside $173 million of the $2 billion in discretionary funds for additional quality-building activities, $100 million (up from $50 million last year) to improve and expand infant and toddler care programs, $10 million for child care research, $18.1 million for school-age care and resource and referral programs, and $1 million for a toll-free child care hotline.

Head Start received its biggest increase in history — $933 million — bringing it to a total of $6.2 billion, which the Department of Health and Human Services estimates will allow a total of 916,500 children to participate in Head Start. In addition, many more children will be able to participate in after-school programs with an almost $400 million increase in the 21st Century Community Learning Centers Program bringing the total amount to $845.6 million. Funding for a number of smaller programs was also increased. Support for students using child care programs on college campuses was increased by $20 million for a total of $25 million. A small program to support national and regional nonprofit organizations, to provide technical assistance to low-income child care providers, and to improve child care quality and supply was authorized and funded at $2.5 million. One million dollars was appropriated for loan forgiveness for individuals with degrees in early childhood education. Ten million dollars was made available for the Early Childhood Education Professional Development Program, which will provide funds for training early childhood educators in low-income communities to strengthen children's language and literacy skills to help prevent reading difficulties once they enter school.

The appropriations bill also authorized a new Early Learning Opportunities Act. Twenty million dollars will be available for demonstration programs for councils in local communities to improve early childhood supports to children and families. Councils can choose to fund new infant and toddler initiatives, home-visiting parent education programs, initiatives to bolster the quality of child care, efforts to expand the hours of part-day Head Start or prekindergarten programs, or other family strengthening activities. The initiative was inspired by North Carolina's Smart Start program. When the program's funding reaches a higher level, funds will go directly to the states to distribute to communities.

More children will also be able to receive nutritious meals through the Child and Adult Care Food Program (CACFP). For-profit child care programs that enroll 25 percent of children who are eligible for free and reduced-price lunch will now be able to receive CACFP funding for meals and snacks. Previously, a program could not participate unless 25 percent of their funding came from the Title XX Social Services Block Grant.

The Children's Day Care Health and Safety Improvement Act enacted in 2000 could also help states better protect children in child care. Although no funds were appropriated in 2000, the bill authorizes $200 million for states to spend on various activities such as: enforcing child care standards, helping providers meet standards, conducting criminal background checks, providing information to parents, improving the transportation of children in child care, training child care providers to prevent illness and injuries, and enforcing child care regulations.

On the regulatory side, the Department of Labor finalized an important rule that will potentially help working parents afford time off when they have or adopt a child. The rule gives states the option of using their unemployment funds to provide unemployment benefits to new parents while on unpaid parental leave. Unfortunately, no state has acted on this option yet. In another step to help parents balance competing demands of work and family, the U.S. Office of Personnel Management finalized a rule that will allow federal employees to use their accrued sick leave, up to the full 12 weeks a year, to care for a seriously ill child or other family member.

In releasing the final rule for the Temporary Assistance for Needy Families (TANF) High Performance Bonus Measures, the Department of Health and Human Services encouraged improvements in state child care policies by including good child care policies as one of the factors determining state bonuses. States that make efforts to help more families pay for child care and to ensure that low-income parents have the ability to choose quality care will be rewarded. Ten million dollars will be available for up to 10 states that choose to compete in the child care category. The performance measure will include three measures on a 10-point scale: accessibility (the percent of children eligible under the Child Care Development Block Grant who are currently served), affordability (co-payments required of families receiving assistance compared to family income), and quality (state reimbursement rates to providers compared to the market rate for care).

Progress at the state level

A number of states made progress in expanding the availability and quality of child care, early education, and after-school programs in 2000. Kentucky took a comprehensive approach while several other states addressed individual issues such as caregiver training and compensation, child care tax credits, and prekindergarten. Three states, New York, Illinois, and California, took small but important steps to address caregiver wages. Massachusetts made a strong commitment to help caregivers who work with low-income children improve their skills and earn higher education degrees. Connecticut made an initial move forward on family leave.

After an exhaustive, Governor-sponsored task force report on early childhood, **Kentucky** approved a $55 million annual investment — representing 25 percent of the state's tobacco settlement money — to support the

Governor's KIDS Now! Initiative. The initiative adopts a comprehensive approach to early childhood by focusing on improving maternal and child health, supporting families, and enhancing early care and education. To help low-income families with their child care costs, the initiative increases the income eligibility cutoff for child care assistance from 160 to 165 percent of the federal poverty level. The initiative also calls for a tiered rating system for child care centers and family child care homes that will trigger higher payments to publicly funded child care providers that meet higher quality standards. In addition, child care centers and family child care homes that reach a higher standard will be offered a one-time cash award. To improve quality, the state will also:

◆ Establish a scholarship fund through the Kentucky Higher Education Assistance Authority to offer tuition assistance and stipends to providers who work at least 20 hours a week and to trainers seeking a specialty trainer's credential.

◆ Appoint a Professional Development Council to establish credentials for early child care and early education with the intent to develop a director's, a teacher's, and a trainer's credential.

◆ Require the Cabinet for Families and Children to set training requirements for all child care providers who receive child care subsidy payments.

◆ Increase licensing personnel so caseloads can be reduced.

◆ Establish local councils to improve the availability of quality child care in their communities.

◆ Make local health department consultants available to child care centers and family child care homes.

A newly appointed Business Council composed of business and community leaders who are interested in early childhood and workplaces that support families will encourage the corporate community and local governments to help address these issues. In addition, funds will support a campaign about the importance of folic acid for pregnant women, universal newborn hearing screenings, an immunization program for underinsured children, eye examinations prior to school entry, and a voluntary home visiting program for first-time parents who are at risk.

New York enacted the Quality Child Care and Protection Act, which included $40 million to provide one-time grants to child care providers for salary enhancements and professional development. Eligible child care providers will have worked full-time for at least 12 months, spent 50 percent or more of their time on direct care or support duties, and made less than the average salary for a kindergarten teacher ($42,000 a year). Six months after applying, and as long as funds are available, eligible ap-

plicants will receive $750 if they hold an Associate degree in child care or a Bachelor's degree or higher in any field; $500 if they do not have these degrees but do have a child development credential, an equivalent certificate in a field related to child care, or an Associate degree in any field; or $300 for meeting certain eligibility criteria. Licensed and registered child care centers, group family child care homes, family child care homes, and school-age child care programs are all eligible for the grants. In order for this program to continue beyond a year, it must be reauthorized by the legislature.

Illinois' Great Start program will provide $3 million to support semi-annual bonuses to licensed family child care providers as well as teachers, assistants, and directors in licensed child care centers. Similar to the North Carolina WAGE$™ program, the amount of the bonus will be based on a provider's level of education. The bonuses will be paid every six months to child care personnel who have been at the same center or home for at least six months. One-time "signing bonuses" and bonuses for staff who have remained with the same program for a number of years may also be available. A commission is working out the program's details.

California passed the CARES bill, which will provide $15 million to increase compensation for staff working in child care centers that receive state contracts for low-income children. The funds will be allocated to local planning councils that will develop a plan to distribute and administer funds.

Massachusetts took an innovative step to help child care providers improve their skills and obtain credentials. The state will offer free tuition to individuals working in child care programs that have a contract with the state where a majority of children in the program are funded by the state. Full tuition will be remitted for students enrolled in four-year institutions of higher learning or a community college and for students enrolled in a continuing education program half of their tuition will be remitted. Although students must still pay for program fees, free tuition is an important incentive for them to earn degrees.

Tennessee made noteworthy improvements in its licensing requirements. The staff-child ratio for infants was increased from one to five to one to four and the ratio for toddlers increased from one to eight to one to seven. Ratios were also improved for older children but these will not be implemented until 2002 or 2003. In addition, all early childhood education staff will have required fingerprinting through the FBI computer system and the state will pay for this process. State licensing fees were also significantly increased and a civil penalty provision was passed with the revenue going into a fund for training. The state will also regulate drop-in care and require fingerprinting of providers. The number of unannounced visits to child care providers was increased substantially. Centers will now have six annual unannounced visits as opposed to one, family child care homes will have four, and unlicensed care receiving public funds will have two. Annual child care center training requirements for both directors and teachers were also increased. Directors' annual training hours were increased from 12 to 18 and teachers' hours were from 6 to 12. To cover the costs of this expanded training, the state provided additional funding for the Tennessee Early Childhood Training Alliance.

Two states made significant improvements in their child care tax credits. **California** became the tenth state with a refundable child care tax credit available to low-income families. The state will invest $200 million in a sliding scale credit to provide more assistance to low-income families. **Colorado's** expanded tax credit will allow parents who currently claim up to one-half of their federal tax credit to claim 70 percent of their federal credit. Family income eligibility for the state credit will be increased from $60,000 to $64,000 annually. In addition, family child care providers will be eligible for a $200 tax credit for their own children under age 13.

A number of states continued to increase their investments in preschool programs. **Michigan** expanded its School Readiness Program by $18.4 million to $84.7 million while **New York** allocated $225 million for the state's universal prekindergarten program, up from $100 million last year. In **New Jersey,** there has been significant debate surrounding the importance of a high quality prekindergarten program. A 1996 settlement in a school finance equity lawsuit *(Abbott v. Burke)* required the state to provide funds for low-income school districts (referred to as the 30 "Abbott districts") to extend part-day kindergarten to full-day for 5-year olds and offer half-day moving to full-day prekindergarten to 3- and 4-year-olds.

In 2000, the New Jersey Supreme Court affirmed the rights of preschool children in the Abbott districts to well-planned, high quality early education by conveying a strong sense of urgency saying "another generation of children will pay the price for each year of delay." The Court's decision supported and acknowledged that using existing community-based child care and Head Start programs was "necessary and appropriate." At the same time, the Court found that existing child care standards were not adequate in providing a well-planned, high quality program, which would enable children to enter kindergarten on a par with their more advantaged peers. The Court also affirmed the need for high quality among programs in both community child care and public school settings.

The Court ordered the state to:

◆ Adopt substantive standards for the educational content of preschool programs.

◆ Require that teachers in every preschool classroom (in both schools and community programs) be certified.

◆ Limit class size to 15 students, with one teacher and an aide.

◆ Require community outreach efforts to inform parents of the availability of preschool programs, with outreach funding provided by the Department of Education.

◆ Handle reasonable requests to provide supplemental funds to programs fairly and quickly.

The Court also directed that:

◆ Teachers currently working in child care programs will have only four years to obtain a college degree and the new early childhood certification.

◆ All new hires must have a Bachelor's degree and will have until September 2001 to obtain certification.

◆ Waivers from these requirements must be based on a clear standard and limited to one year.

◆ Scholarship money be available to help pay for the required college courses.

The Governor's 2000 budget also included $70 million in additional funds for Abbott preschool programs to help make required full-day services possible.

Recognizing that paid family leave is an important issue, **Connecticut's** Office of Policy and Management, the Department of Labor, and the Department of Administrative Services will study the costs and benefits of providing wage replacement to Connecticut workers on family and medical leave.

Innovative approaches at the local level

Several cities and counties are also investing in creative initiatives to help meet families' child care and after-school needs and improve the quality of child care. Their efforts have focused on creating networks of trained family child providers, increasing families' access to accredited providers, expanding part-day programs to full-day, creating and improving child care facilities, and ensuring that after-school opportunities are available to all children who need them.

Chicago: Mayor Richard Daley plans to help meet the city's child care needs through a new initiative. The Early Child Care and Education Plan outlines a series of goals for the next two years and creates a $41.2 million multi-source Children's Capital Fund to renovate and construct licensed facilities.

The goals include:

◆ Doubling the number of available full-day, full-year slots in licensed child care settings. A total of 5,040 slots will be created.

◆ Building and renovating child care centers and family child care homes in high-need communities.

◆ Improving the quality of services for young children in early childhood settings and strengthening the transition from early child care to kindergarten.

◆ Creating and expanding citywide partnerships to support the development of young children.

The plan outlines very specific activities to achieve these goals, such as:

◆ Converting over 2,000 existing Head Start slots from half day to full day.

◆ Enrolling an additional 3,000 children (birth to age five) in licensed, full-day, full-year early childhood settings.

◆ Building and/or renovating 24 child care centers and providing minor renovations for 30 centers.

◆ Supporting the professional development of early childhood staff with a citywide academy, operated through the City Colleges of Chicago and St. Augustine College, to provide credit-based training for the Child Development Associate and Associate of Arts credentials.

◆ Creating two new Family Start Learning Centers in partnership with the University of Illinois Center for Literacy, which promotes family literacy activities in communities serving Latino families.

◆ Assisting child care centers and family child care homes in implementing strategies that create father-friendly environments.

◆ Allowing teen mothers who participate in the Chicago Public Schools' Cradle to Classroom program to use family child care homes as well as child care centers.

◆ Developing a state legislative agenda to address the need for increases in staff salaries and benefits and a capital development and facility improvement fund.

◆ Developing appropriate local legislation along with related policy recommendations in support of improved access to adequate health insurance for all child care staff employed by licensed child care programs.

◆ Initiating a pilot project through the Chicago Park District to support family child care providers in arranging for age-appropriate recreational activities at local park district facilities.

Cuyahoga County, Ohio: This large county, which includes Cleveland, began its Early Childhood Initiative in 1999. It is a three-year, $40 million partnership — $30 million coming from local, state, and federal sources and $8.5 million from 18 local foundations. The initiative serves the county's children and families through health, parenting, and child care support efforts. The child care portion, called Starting Point, seeks to increase the availability of quality child care by recruiting and training family child care providers and linking them to a network that is managed by a local organization. Providers are supported by the network and regional coordinators who will train and certify them, visit regularly to monitor the safety and quality of the homes, promote parent involvement, and coordinate these efforts with other services offered by the initiative. So far, 800 providers have submitted applications for certification. Starting Point is also seeking to expand and improve the availability of quality care for children with special needs.

San Diego has taken a giant step to ensure that children and youths in every elementary and middle school in the city will have a safe and supportive place to go after school. Through a pooling of resources, each of the 194 elementary and middle schools in San Diego will offer a before- and after-school program by next fall. The "6-to-6" program, which began in 1998 serving just 2,000 children, will serve 25,000 by September 2001. Children will be offered a wide variety of activities including help with homework, as well as tutoring and mentoring, arts and crafts, music, drama, sports programs, and other recreational activities.

California's After-School Learning and Safe Neighborhoods Partnership Program, which requires a 50 percent local match, covers a large portion of the costs. Funds for "6-to-6" also come from the city and county share of a state claim against the major tobacco firms, the federal 21st Century Community Learning Centers program, and the city general fund.

Business steps out for child care

In 2000, several employers made investments to support child care organizations. The Chase Manhattan Bank and the Chase Manhattan Foundation have launched the Chase Child Care Initiative, a $1.1 million effort to support child care organizations in New York, New Jersey, and Connecticut. The program includes $500,000 in grants to support the work of eight nonprofit intermediaries in the child care area. The grants will be used to expand child care services and improve the quality of services by providing technical and business skills assistance to child care providers. In addition, Chase is providing $625,000 in recoverable grant support to three nonprofit community development institutions that will use the money to make loans to both center- and home-based child care providers, enabling them to expand and enhance their services. The initiative, which recognizes the critical role child care plays in enabling individuals to find and retain employment, is designed to strengthen Chase's focus on work force development and reflects the interests of senior women executives at Chase who have urged the bank to address issues of concern to women.

In an effort to meet a wide range of work force and community needs, the leadership of the United Auto Workers (UAW), Ford Motor Company, and Visteon Corporation developed the Family Service and Learning Center (FSLC) program, a union-management partnership to support working families, individuals, retirees, and the communities in which they live.

The theme of the 1999 contract negotiations between the UAW and Ford, which sparked the beginning of the FSLC program, was "Bargaining for Families." In that spirit, the FSLC initiative will create an integrated array of programs and services, which will include high quality child care, before- and after-school pre-teen and teen programs, adult and family education classes, and volunteer support networks. Many activities will be intergenerational. The program will open two child care centers in 2001, eight in 2002, and three more by September 2003, for a total of 13. These 13 centers will each care for more than 220 children and operate up to 24 hours a day to offer full-time, part-time, back-up, school-age, and get-well care. In addition, high quality community child care networks will be established in 30 communities where providers will receive assistance in becoming accredited.

After-school programs will be established for youths aged 6 to 18 years. Most of these pre-teen and teen programs will be initiated in partnership with local school districts and community organizations. Programming will address educational, recreational, and volunteering opportunities. Specific offerings will be customized to each FSLC location.

Summer camp, after-school, and school vacation educational programs will focus on special learning projects, computer and Internet-based activities, and science and nature projects. Art studios, sports teams, and creative movement opportunities will also be available.

Middle school and younger high school students (12 to 15 years) will have access to tutoring and test-taking assistance, babysitting training, CPR and First Aid training, as well as teen health and computer classes. Teens may also participate in sports teams; special interest clubs such as book, drama, or nature exploration; art studio; creative movement; and Teen Café and movie nights. They will have the opportunity to volunteer for community service and special events such as benefit walks.

Older teens will be able to participate in programs aimed at preparing them for adulthood. Driver's education, teen health, and tutoring will be supplemented with SAT/ACT preparation classes, college counseling, resume preparation, interview skills courses, and vocational assessment. Sports teams, clubs, art studio, and other recreational activities will also be available to these teens. Community service and similar volunteering opportunities will be encouraged. Older teens may also mentor younger students and assist them with computer skills.

Moving Forward: A 2001 Agenda for Action

With the growing body of research affirming the benefits of high quality early education and after-school experiences, especially for low-income children, it is time to move forward with a strong national agenda.

Advocates and policy makers must work together to ensure that adequate funding is available so child care policies provide:

◆ A solid foundation for young children that allows them to enter school with the early learning skills necessary to become strong readers and good students.

◆ Access to after-school activities for older children that not only offer a safe haven, but also provide them with the academic enrichment they need to stay and succeed in school.

◆ Reliable, affordable child care options that enable parents to work outside the home or give children extra learning opportunities if their parents stay at home.

◆ The opportunity for parents to stay at home during a child's critical first months.

The following outlines a broad-based agenda that will help parents stay home in the initial months after their child's birth, help younger children get a strong start, ensure that families can work, and enable older children to have access to safe and enriching after-school programs.

Advocates should support policies at the federal level to:

◆ Fully fund the Child Care and Development Block Grant (CCDBG) to improve the quality of child care and make child more care affordable for low-income families. Investments in the quality of child care should be substantially increased given the serious gaps in the supply and quality of child care, especially for children under age 3, and targeted funding for infant and toddler care should be expanded. States should be encouraged to improve child care assistance by paying rates that make it possible for parents to choose quality care and establishing responsive administrative systems to ensure that parents can easily apply for and receive child care assistance.

- Improve the Dependent Care Tax Credit by increasing the amount of credit for low- and middle-income families, making it refundable, and providing tax credits for parents who stay at home.

- Fully fund Head Start so all eligible 3- and 4-year-olds can participate and expand Early Head Start so more infants and toddlers can participate.

- Expand funding for the Early Learning Opportunities Act so children from birth to age five and their parents receive the support they need so children have a successful early school experience.

- Expand funding for the 21st Century Community Learning Centers program and strengthen the program to provide more children with safe and supportive after-school activities.

- Increase funding for campus-based child care centers to help parents in school.

- Enact a program to provide funds to states for prekindergarten for 3-,4-, and 5-year olds.

- Support new funding to improve and expand child care facilities to ensure that children are in healthy, safe, and appropriate environments and that programs meet the needs of working parents.

- Support an initiative to improve compensation and training for child care providers.

- Extend the Family and Medical Leave Act to cover all employers with 25 or more employees — a decrease from the current cutoff of 50 employees — bringing this essential benefit (up to 12 weeks of unpaid leave for employees with a new child or a serious illness in the family) to 10 million more Americans. In addition, support a demonstration program to allow states to offer paid leave.

- Amend the Child and Adult Care Food Program to permanently fund meals and snacks at for-profit child care centers serving low-income children and allow youths up to age 19 enrolled in both community- and school-based after-school programs to receive meals and snacks. The program should also be revised to improve access to the program for children enrolled in family child care homes.

- Restore funding for the Social Services Block Grant (Title XX) to $2.4 billion.

Advocates should work for policies at the state level to:

- Invest whatever is necessary to guarantee child care assistance to all low-income working families.

- Transfer 30 percent of TANF funds, when available, to the Child Care and Development Block Grant and use additional TANF funds within the TANF Block Grant for child care, Head Start, after-school, and youth development activities.

- Conduct outreach to inform low-income families that child care assistance is available and explain how to get it — many families are unaware that they may be eligible. States should also streamline their application process so families receiving TANF or working for low wages can more easily access child care assistance. In addition, states should provide parents with counseling and support in choosing reliable, quality child care options.

- Ensure a real choice of child care providers by setting reasonable fees for families and establishing reimbursement rates that are, at a minimum, based on the 100th percentile of current market rates (but higher for programs offering higher quality care, care during non-traditional hours, and special-needs care).

- Provide program grants to assist providers in meeting higher quality standards.

- Offer opportunities and resources to local communities to plan and fund comprehensive early childhood programs for young children and families.

- Expand and improve infant care by creating family child care networks, setting infant care reimbursement rates high enough to ensure access to services, offering specialized training for infant caregivers, and setting strong licensing standards related to infant and toddler care.

- Expand child care opportunities for parents who work irregular hours by providing higher reimbursement rates and special contracts for providers who offer care during early morning hours, evenings, and weekends.

- Ensure that child care is available for children with disabilities and other special needs.

- Provide refundable state dependent care tax credits to help parents afford child care.

- Give parents the option of staying home with their very young children through policies such as paid family leave.

- Offer child care providers opportunities and incentives — including adequate compensation and benefits — to receive training and education and to encourage them to remain in the early childhood field.

- Strengthen state licensing and monitoring standards and support an adequate number of well-trained inspectors so parents can be confident that their children are in safe and supportive settings. States should ensure that all providers receiving public funds are visited at least twice a year. Parents should have easy access to information about how well child care programs and providers are measuring up to state standards.

◆ Ensure that every community has resource and referral programs to help families find child care that meets their needs and to support child care providers, including informal caregivers.

◆ Provide capital and affordable loans through bonds, grants, and other financing mechanisms to ensure a sufficient supply of safe child care facilities suited to children's needs.

◆ Fund high quality, comprehensive prekindergarten programs for all families who wish to participate. Programs should be operated by a range of community child care and Head Start providers as well as public schools, be available on a full-day/full-year basis to meet the needs of working families, and be easily accessible to all families, including those whose children have special needs, speak languages other than English, or lack transportation.

◆ Increase the availability of before- and after-school as well as summer programs that offer academic, recreational, and creative enrichment activities for elementary, middle, and high school students.

Advocates should act at the local level to:

◆ Persuade county and municipal government leaders to invest additional local dollars in improving the quality, affordability, and supply of child care and after-school programs.

◆ Encourage faith-based organizations, schools, and community organizations to support child care and after-school programs by mobilizing funds, volunteers, space, and other resources.

◆ Create partnerships with schools, parks and recreation departments, libraries, community-based organizations, and local public agencies to maximize before- and after-school opportunities for elementary, middle, and high school students.

◆ Enact zoning and land-use policies that make it possible to operate family child care homes by defining them as residential use.

◆ Work with community development corporations to expand child care options, especially in low-income communities.

◆ Work with local housing officials to ensure that public housing projects offer high quality center-based and family child care.

◆ Urge localities to use Community Development Block Grant funds for child care facilities.

Advocates should encourage the private sector to:

◆ Make child care more affordable and available for their employees by supporting on- or near-site programs, offering resource and referral services, and helping families with the cost of child care.

◆ Establish family-friendly policies such as flextime, compressed work weeks, job sharing, and paid family leave.

◆ Invest in their community's quality of life by helping to finance community child care funds that assist families in paying for child care and that bolster the quality of child care.

◆ Support renovation and construction of child care facilities by establishing loan funds or guaranteeing bank loans made to child care programs.

◆ Play a leadership role in raising public awareness about the need for increased investments in child care, early education, and after-school programs and in urging federal, state, and local policymakers to follow suit.

Endnotes

1. S.E. Rimm-Kaufman, R.C. Pianta, and M.J. Cox, Early Childhood Research Quarterly, Vol. 15, No. 2, 2000 cited in Early Education Clearinghouse "Kindergarten Teachers Perceive Difficulty in Transitions to School," *Facts in Action*, Associated Day Care Services, Nov. 2000. Available on the Internet at http://www.factsinaction.org/brief/bmov001.htm.

2. Karen Schulman, Helen Blank, and Danielle Ewen, *Seeds of Success: State Prekindergarten Initiatives 1998-1999* (Washington, D.C.: Children's Defense Fund, 1999).

3. Jeffrey D. Lyons, Susan D. Russell, Christina Gilgor, et al., *Child Care Subsidy: The Costs of Waiting* (Chapel Hill, N.C.: Day Care Services Association, 1998).

4. Amara Bachu, *Fertility of American Women: June 1998 (Current Population Reports, P20-526)* (Washington, D.C.: U.S. Census Bureau, 2000).

5. Robert Pear, "Far More Single Mothers Are Taking Jobs," *The New York Times* (November 5, 2000).

6. *Supra*, note 4.

7. Kristin Smith, *Who's Minding the Kids? Child Care Arrangements: Fall 1995 (Current Population Reports P70-70)* (Washington, D.C.: U.S. Census Bureau, 2000).

8. Howard Snyder and Melissa Sickmund, *Juvenile Offenders and Victims: 1999 National Report* (Washington, D.C.: U.S. Department of Justice, Office of Juvenile Justice and Delinquency Programs, 1999).

9. Sherry Karasik, "Experts: More Latchkey Kids Means More Trouble — High Risk Behavior Increases When Parents Are Gone," *APB News*, April 14, 2000. As cited in Sanford A. Newman, James Alan Fox, Edward A. Flynn, and William Christeson, *American's After-School Choice: The Prime Time for Juvenile Crime, Or Youth Enrichment and Achievement* (Washington, D.C.: Fight Crime: Invest in Kids, 2000).

10. J.L. Richardson, "Relationship Between After-School Care of Adolescents and Substance Use, Risk Taking, Depressed Mood, and Academic Achievement," *Pediatrics*, 92, No.1 (July 1993).

11. *Supra*, note 7.

12. *Ibid.*

13. "Early Head Start Shows Significant Results for Low-Income Children and Families," Administration for Children and Families Press Release, January 11, 2001. Available on the Internet at http://www.acf.dhhs.gov/news.

14. Arthur J. Reynolds, J.A. Temple, D.L. Robertson, et.al., *A 15-Year Follow-up of Low-income Children in Public Schools* (Madison, Wisconsin: Chicago Longitudinal Study, University of Wisconsin, 2000).

15. Jack P. Shonkoff, "From Neurons to Neighborhoods: The Science of Early Childhood Development," (Opening Statement, Public Briefing), October 3, 2000.

16. *Ibid.*

17. U.S. General Accounting Office, *Child Care: State Efforts to Enforce Safety and Health Requirements*, GAO/HEHS-00-28 (Washington, D.C.: U.S. General Accounting Office, January 2000).

18. University of Cincinnati, *Urban School Initiative School Age Child Care Project: 1998-1999 School Year Evaluation Report* (Columbus, Ohio: Ohio Hunger Task Force, September 1999).

19. Deborah Lowe Vandell and K. M. Pierce, "Can After-School Programs Benefit Children Who Live in High-Crime Neighborhoods?" A presentation at the Poster Symposium, Children's Out-of-School Time: The Next Generation of Research (Albuquerque, N.M.: Biennial Meeting of the Society for Research in Child Development, April 1999).

20. U.S. Department of Education, *21st Century Community Learning Centers: Providing Quality Afterschool Learning Opportunities for America's Families* (Washington, D.C.: U.S. Department of Education, September 2000). Available on the Internet at www.ed.gov/21stcclc/.

21. Karen Schulman, *Issue Brief: The High Cost of Child Care Puts Quality Child Care Out of Reach for Many Families* (Washington, D.C.: Children's Defense Fund, 2000).

22. U.S. Bureau of Labor Statistics, "1999 National Occupational Employment and Wage Estimates," Available on the Internet at stats.bls.gov/oes/1999/oes_nat.htm.

23. U.S. Department of Health and Human Services, "New Statistics Show Only Small Percentage of Eligible Families Receive Child Care Help" (December 6, 2000): Press release. Available on the Internet at www.acf.dhhs.gov/news/ccstudy2.htm.

24. P. Coltoff, M. Torres, and N. Lifton, *The Human Cost of Waiting for Child Care: A Study* (New York, N.Y.: The Children's Aid Society, December 1999).

25. Gregory Acs, Katherin Ross Phillips, and Daniel McKenzie, *On the Bottom Rung: A Profile of Americans in Low-Income Working Families* (Washington, D.C.: Urban Institute, October 2000). Available on the Internet at www.urban.org.

26. Zero to Three, *What Grown-ups Understand About Child Development: A National Benchmark Survey* (Research conducted by DYG Inc., October 2000). Available on the Internet at www.zerotothree.org.

27. Afterschool Alliance, "Afterschool Alert: Poll Report," (Washington, D.C.: Afterschool Alliance, July 2000). Retrieved from the Internet at www.afterschoolalliance.org.

28. Fight Crime/Invest in Kids, "Back-to-School Poll Shows Public Wants Investments in Child Care and After-School Programs Far More Than Tax Cuts" (Press Release), September 5, 2000.

CHAPTER

Education

Every child needs a solid education, and our nation needs children who are well-educated. An educated citizenry is the foundation of a democratic society and is essential for America to maintain its leadership in the global marketplace. A good education is the surest way out of poverty for poor children. Making sure all children receive the best quality education should be among our top national priorities.

Ninety percent of the nation's children attend public schools. For more than a decade, the nation has focused on reforming America's public schools. In 1989, then President Bush and the nation's governors developed a series of national educational goals to be attained by 2000.[1] Not one of these goals has been achieved. Although some progress has been made, the nation has a long way to go in ensuring that every child receives a quality education. Student performance in reading, writing, and math has modestly improved in certain grades, but too many students still lag far behind. American students in the early grades perform above the international average, but as they reach higher grades, they fall farther and farther behind their peers in other countries. The U.S. public education system faces many challenges. Schools are overcrowded and school buildings are deteriorating. Increased school enrollments are contributing to a shortage of qualified teachers. Funding inequities contribute to lagging academic achievement for children who are assigned to the poorest school districts.

Comprehensive reform — with the commitment of elected officials, administrators, parents, teachers, community leaders, and students — is needed for all children to achieve at the highest levels. School districts need support in recruiting, training, and hiring teachers, strengthening the workforce, and helping to reduce class size. States must establish clear performance benchmarks for state and local education agencies in order to improve accountability and student achievement. To address glaring achievement gaps, a greater emphasis must be placed on improving the performance of schools with disproportionately high minority and low-income populations. Additional financial resources must be invested in school facilities to address dilapidated and sometimes dangerous school environments. The paramount goal of school reform efforts should be to provide every child with equal access to a world-class education so they can become educated, successful, productive adults.

Reading, Writing, and Mathematics Performance

In order to succeed, children must be able to achieve in reading, writing, and mathematics at high levels. Unfortunately, the overall performance of U.S. students falls woefully short. The National Education Goals Panel set a goal for all students to be reading and writing at the "Proficient" or "Advanced" levels by the year 2000.[2] The Proficient level means achieving a solid understanding of the knowledge and skills required in fourth, eighth, and twelfth grade. The vast majority of students are not performing at Proficient levels, and few are performing at Advanced levels. According to the National Assessment of Educational Progress (NAEP), reading, writing, and mathematics achievement levels have improved in certain grades depending on the subject, but performance levels have not improved across the board and are still unacceptably low.[3] Reading and writing are the areas most in need of improvement. Over a six-year period, from 1992 to 1998, reading performance increased at the eighth-grade level but did not improve at the fourth- and twelfth-grade levels.[4] In fact, twelfth-grade reading scores decreased between 1992 and 1994, but returned to the 1992 level in 1998.[5] In spite of modest improvements, reading achievement levels are remarkably low with only 31 percent of fourth graders, 33 percent of eighth graders, and 40 percent of twelfth graders scoring at or above the Proficient level.[6]

An even lower percentage of students showed satisfactory achievement in writing levels. The majority of fourth-, eighth-, and twelfth-grade students wrote at the Basic level with most students exhibiting only partial mastery of the skills and knowledge tested. Only 22 percent of fourth-grade, 25 percent of eighth-grade, and 21 percent of twelfth-grade students performed at the Proficient level.[7] And only 1 percent of students across the board performed at the Advanced level in writing.[8]

The good news is that students have demonstrated overall improvement in their mathematics performance.[9] The number of students performing above Basic level improved with one-quarter of eighth-grade students and about one-fifth of fourth- and twelfth-grade students performing at or above the Proficient level.[10] However, there are mixed results when comparing the nation's performance in mathematics with the performance of students in other countries around the world. U.S. fourth-grade students performed above the international average in mathematics — above 12 countries and below seven countries.[11] However, of the 41 countries participating at the eighth-grade level, U.S. students were outperformed by students in 20 countries and outperformed their peers in only seven countries.[12] Student performance further declined in the twelfth grade, with 14 out of the 21 participating countries scoring above America's students and only two countries performing below.[13] To maintain America's position as a leader in the world economy, schools must do more to prepare students to compete both nationally and internationally.

Poor and Minority Students Being Left Behind

One of the major factors contributing to poor achievement levels is the dramatic disparity in resources provided to the poorest children. According to a 1997 U.S. Department of Education analysis, the richest school districts spent 56 percent more per student than the poorest did.[14] Schools serving large numbers of poor children tend to have teachers with less training and fewer books and supplies. The report found that more than 70 percent of teachers in schools with a high concentration of

- Ninety percent of the nation's children attend public schools.
- Only 31 percent of fourth graders read at or above the Proficient level.
- The richest school districts spend 56 percent more per student than the poorest do.
- Hispanic students have the lowest high school completion rates at 62 percent, compared with 89 percent for Black Students and 93 percent for White students.
- Children in the poorest families are five times as likely as children in wealthier families to drop out of high school.
- Three-quarters of the nation's public schools are in need of repairs, renovations, and modernization. The average school is more than 40 years old.
- College participation rates for minority students continue to lag behind White students: 29 percent of young White adults hold bachelor degrees compared with only 14.4 percent of young Black adults and 11 percent of young Hispanic adults.

CDF's Ten Point Education Agenda for Every Child

Too often lost amid rhetoric about education reform is this simple fact: education is about one thing only — **our children.** If America's public education system — the pillar of our democracy — is to be revitalized, it must be refocused exclusively on the well-being of **all** students. While appropriately ambitious, the following ten point agenda for education reform is realistic, achievable, and absolutely essential. A deep sense of urgency is necessary to face this challenge of preparing a new generation of children for the future. This agenda puts children first in education by insisting that America:

1. **Operate from the premise that all children can learn and perform at high levels** — and thus focus every action in our education system from school board decisions down to teaching in the classroom on helping all children perform at high levels.

2. **Ensure that every child enters school ready to learn and ready to succeed** — and that requires access to safe, nurturing, quality early child development experiences and preschool education opportunities.

3. **Set measurable and appropriate standards for success** — and hold everyone — administrators, teachers, parents, students, and communities, in that order — accountable for meeting those standards.

4. **Empower teachers and principals** — working with parents — to make as many key education decisions as possible — reduce the size of educational bureaucracies and change their role from one of direction to one of support because decisions made at the level closest to the students will best meet their needs.

5. **Invest in quality teaching** — by ensuring lifelong training and retraining, strengthening and renewing respect for the teaching profession, and compensating teachers commensurate with their ability and essential role in our society.

6. **Provide every child facilities that support learning and state-of-the-art tools** — ranging from up-to-date text books (many school districts still don't have enough) to Internet access.

7. **Ensure adequate resources to make all of the above a reality** — but use those resources wisely and efficiently.

8. **Involve the entire community — especially parents — in this cause, ensuring that students receive the support and services they need to succeed in school** — that requires a coordinated effort by social service agencies, the business community, law enforcement officials, neighborhood groups, faith-based institutions, health care providers, and the full range of voluntary organizations that work with children along with educators.

9. **Engage the public in the school reform debate** — only with full participation by those who elect education decision-makers and pay taxes can child-centered reform succeed.

10. **Address every one of the above elements now** — in its entirety this agenda will succeed. Addressed in pieces, it will not.

low-income students reported lacking some necessary materials for their class. And these students were more likely than students attending more affluent schools to be taught by teachers who did not major in the subject area in which they taught.

A new wave of school finance litigation has emerged in an effort to address the inequitable and inadequate funding available for many low-income children. Parents, students, and school districts have challenged over two dozen states for their failure to provide adequate resources to educate the poorest students. A major cause of the school funding inequalities is that most states rely heavily on local property taxes for education funding. In wealthy districts, property taxes generate ample funds for local schools. But in poor districts, property tax revenues do not come close to meeting the need. Recently, a New York trial court found that New York's funding system deprived New York City students of the "sound, basic education" guaranteed by the state constitution and violated federal civil rights laws because it disproportionately hurt minority students in New York City public schools. The court ordered the state legislature to redesign a new system that adequately addresses and finances the needs of the poorest school districts.[15]

Children of color, concentrated in underfunded urban school districts, disproportionately suffer the consequences of these unequal resources. Nearly five decades after the *Brown v. Board of Education* decision, too many minority children still do not have equal opportunity to succeed in school and their future careers. Achievement gaps between minority and White students continue to persist. In 1999, White students had higher overall reading scores than their Black and Hispanic peers. However, over the past several decades, Black and Hispanic students have demonstrated positive gains in reading. Between 1971 and 1999, the reading gap between White and Black students narrowed in each age group.[16] For Hispanic students, over a similar period, the reading gap narrowed only for twelfth graders.[17]

Math achievement for Black and Hispanic students mirrors national progress. In grades four, eight, and 12, White, Black, and Hispanic students showed mathematics gains. The overall mathematics gap between Black and White students has narrowed; however, the gap has widened for eighth graders since 1986 and for twelfth graders since 1990.[18] For eighth- and twelfth-grade Hispanic students, the gap narrowed since 1973 but widened since 1982 for fourth graders.[19]

Minority students are becoming an increasingly large population in many school systems. The number of students of color in public schools grew from 22 percent in 1974 to 36 percent in 1997.[20] In California, Texas, and New York, the country's largest states, students of color are or soon will be the majority.[21] Urban school districts across the country have a majority of students of color, and increasingly these districts are almost exclusively made up of students of color. Today, White students make up only 10 percent of the school population in 40 percent of all urban schools.[22]

With the demand for a highly skilled labor force, a high school degree is usually a minimum requirement for entry-level jobs and a prerequisite for the additional education or job training necessary for higher paying employment. Although a greater proportion of the population attain a high school education, too many young people still leave high school before they graduate. The percentage of 25- to 29-year-olds who completed high school rose to 88 percent in 1999, compared with 78 percent in 1971.[23] Yet, five out of every 100 students enrolled in high school in October 1998 dropped out of school

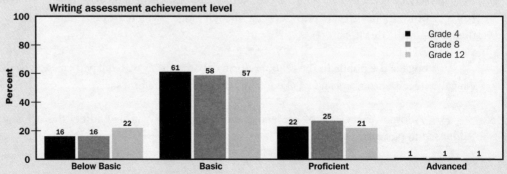

Writing Performance

Percentage distribution of students according to NAEP writing assessment achievement levels, by grade, 1998

Writing assessment achievement level

Legend: ■ Grade 4 ■ Grade 8 ■ Grade 12

	Below Basic	Basic	Proficient	Advanced
Grade 4	16	61	22	1
Grade 8	16	58	25	1
Grade 12	22	57	21	1

Source: U.S. Department of Education, National Center for Education Statistics, *NAEP 1998: Writing: Report Card for the Nation and the States* (September 1999): p. 24.

before October 1999.[24] Hispanic students have the lowest high school completion rates at 62 percent, compared with an 89 percent completion rate for Black students and 93 percent for White students.[25] Family income is also associated with high school completion rates. Children from poor families have a significantly higher risk of dropping out. In 1999, young adults living in the poorest families (in the lowest 20 percent of family incomes) were five times as likely as their peers in wealthier families (in the top 20 percent of family incomes) to have dropped out of high school.[26]

Racial disparities also appear in areas such as use of computers. While schools are narrowing the gap between minority and White students in the use of computers, evidence shows disparities in how students use them. Based on data from the October 1997 Current Population Survey School Enrollment Supplement conducted by the U.S. Census Bureau, 21 percent of White students used computers to access the Internet compared with 15 percent of Black students and 12 percent of Hispanic students.[27] In 1997, Black high school students were slightly more likely to use computers in school than White students, 73 percent compared with 72 percent. Sixty-five percent of Hispanic students used computers in high school.[28] However, in grades one through eight (elementary and middle school), White students were still much more likely to use computers in school than their Hispanic and Black peers.[29]

Changing Public School Population

One of the largest challenges facing an already strained education system is growth. In the 2000 school year, 53 million children entered public and private schools, the highest enrollment in history.[30] In 20 years, this number is expected to increase by 7.2 percent to 55.2 million.[31] The anticipated increase will be dramatic, with a steady rise in the next five years, a small dip, and then a surge in enrollments through 2020.[32] These increasing numbers of children entering school are a result of a continuing "baby boom echo" and include the grandchildren of the "baby boomers," the generation born between 1946 and 1975. The bulk of this growth is in large metropolitan areas, the same areas with the highest concentrations of poor and minority students who are consistently performing at lower levels than their White and suburban peers.

A small number of schools carry the heaviest burden of educating a rapidly growing population in their school districts. These districts are largely comprised of minorities and historically understaffed, underfinanced, and underperforming. In fact, 100 of the largest public school districts, which represents less than 1 percent (.06) of all school districts in the nation, are responsible for educating 22.9 percent of all public school students.[33] Further, 52 percent of students in the 100 largest school districts, compared to 38 percent of students in all reporting states, were eligible for free and reduced-price lunch.[34] In the 100 largest school districts, minority students made up 66.9 percent of the student population compared to 38.8 percent in all other school districts.[35] Three states — Florida, Texas, and California — accounted for about 40 percent of the largest school districts.[36] These same three states are experiencing the strongest influx of immigrants and the need to meet the demands of population changes in their schools.

As a result of a wave of immigration, the greatest growth in the composition of minority public school students will occur among Hispanics. In the next 20 years, the Hispanic school-age population is predicted to increase about 60 percent. In 25 years, it is predicted that one in

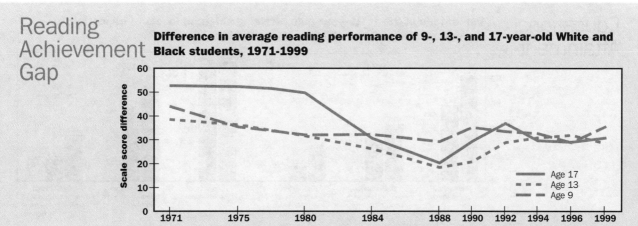

Reading Achievement Gap

Difference in average reading performance of 9-, 13-, and 17-year-old White and Black students, 1971-1999

Source: U.S. Department of Education, National Center for Education Statistics, *NAEP 1999: Trends in Academic Progress: Three Decades of Student Performance* (August 2000), Table B-11.

four school-aged students will be Hispanic.[37] This change in student population will force public school systems to accommodate distinctive needs such as linguistic challenges, fluid immersion into the mainstream curriculum, and a need to recruit more minority teachers.

Teacher Shortage

Teacher quality is a critical element of successful school reform. It is estimated that 2.2 million additional teachers will be needed in the next decade to accommodate increasing student populations, class size reductions, and teacher attrition. Unfortunately, in order to meet these new demands, many states have lowered standards and hired teachers with marginal qualifications. More than 30 percent of newly hired teachers lack full certification when they enter the profession, more than 11 percent enter the classroom without a license, and more than one-quarter of public school teachers are teaching subjects out of their field of study.[38] Ironically, students who have a higher need for quality teachers are less likely to have them. Schools with high minority populations or a high percentage of low-income students are more likely to have teachers without master's degrees than schools with fewer minorities and poor students.[39]

Training and licensing new teachers is not the only challenge. High turnover is also a serious problem. More than 20 percent of newly hired teachers leave the teaching profession within three to four years. In order to retain the quality teachers needed to educate the nation's children, professional development through peer mentoring and continued coursework, higher salaries, and improved working conditions must complement new licensing requirements.

Safe and Quality Learning Environments

Not only does the nation's education system face a challenge to build an adequate number of schools to accommodate the student population growth, the current facilities are seriously in need of renovation and modernization. The average public school was built 42 years ago. About one-third of all public schools were built before 1970 and have not been renovated since 1980.[40] According to a study by the National Center for Educational Statistics, three-quarters of schools reported the need for repairs, renovations, and modernizations to put the school's buildings into good overall condition.[41] The total amount needed for school repair is approximately $127 billion.[42] One in four schools reported that at least one type of building (e.g., original and temporary buildings, permanent additions) was in less than adequate condition.[43] Approximately 11 million students were enrolled in the schools that reported these problems. Schools in central cities and schools with the highest concentrations of poverty were more likely to report at least one of the building features (e.g., roofs, floors, walls, plumbing, heating, ventilation, electric power, light) as less than adequate.[44] Forty-three percent of schools reported at least one of six unsatisfactory environmental conditions (e.g., lighting, heating, ventilation, indoor air quality, noise control, physical security of buildings).[45] One-fifth of schools indicated less than adequate conditions for life safety features (e.g., sprinklers, fire alarms), roofs, and electric power. About one-quarter of schools reported less than adequate conditions for plumbing, exterior walls, finishes, windows, and doors.[46]

Many rural public schools, where one-fourth of all children in America go to school, have serious building

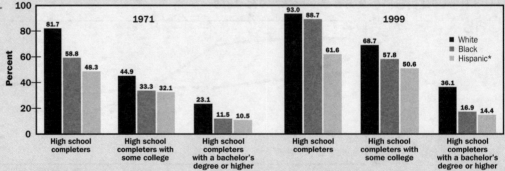

Educational Attainment

Percentage of 25- to 29-year-olds attaining selected levels of education, by race-ethnicity, March 1971 and March 1999

*Persons of Hispanic origin can be of any race.
Note: "High school completers" includes those who have attended college and those who have a bachelor's degree or higher.
Source: U.S. Department of Education, National Center for Education Statistics, *The Condition of Education 2000* (June 2000): Tables 38-1, 38-2, and 38-3, from U.S. Department of Commerce, Bureau of the Census, Current Population Survey, March, various years.

problems. A staggering 78 percent of the schools in rural America report needing to be repaired and modernized.[47] Nearly one-half (47 percent) of rural schools have learning environments that are unsatisfactory. Over 30 percent of rural schools report inadequate heating, ventilation, and air conditioning.[48] With a declining financial base, many rural schools are finding it increasingly more difficult to renovate their public schools.

Some research has found correlations between the quality and age of a school building and student performance. For example, a study in rural Virginia found that achievement scores for students enrolled in schools that need repair were up to 5 percentile points lower than those enrolled in higher quality schools.[49] A study of District of Columbia students found that students in poor condition schools scored 11 percent below students who were in schools that were in excellent condition and 6 percent below students in schools that were in fair condition.[50]

In addition, the U.S. General Accounting Office has found that many classrooms are not prepared to accommodate modern technology: nearly two-thirds lack sufficient modem lines, more than half have inadequate wiring for communications, and less than 15 percent had fiber optic cables available.[51] The nation must substantially invest in the public school infrastructure to ensure that there are enough classrooms to accommodate growing student populations, to reduce the number of students in each class, to achieve safe and conducive learning environments, and to support the technological systems needed to increase student learning.

Early Learning

A child's physical and emotional health is critical to successful transition into kindergarten, performance in the early school grades, and future learning outcomes. A recent study published in the American Sociological Review found that low birthweight affected children's achievement all the way through high school. The researchers used data of families from 1968 to 1992 from the University of Michigan's Panel Study of Income Dynamics.[52] Compared with the general population, babies who weighed less than average (less than 5 pounds 8 ounces) at birth were 34 percent less likely to graduate from high school by age 19. And compared with their normal-birthweight siblings, the low-birthweight children were 74 percent less likely to graduate on time.[53] This research underscores the important link between a child's health and educational achievements and the need to focus on the whole child in order to ensure his or her success. (See the Child Health chapter for more information on the role of early prenatal care in preventing low birthweight).

Early childhood programs help to ensure children are ready to learn and ready to succeed when they enter elementary school. The first of the 1989 national educational goals was that "by the year 2000, all children in America will start school ready to learn." The objectives were to encourage parents to spend time helping their children learn, to make sure that children are physically healthy so they are prepared to learn when they start school, and to provide access to high quality, developmentally appropriate preschool programs.[54] The nation has shown gradual progress in each of these areas. From 1990 to 1997, the percentage of infants born with one or more of four health risks decreased by four percentage points. From 1994 to 1997, the percentage of 2-year-olds who had been fully immunized against preventable childhood diseases increased by three points. From 1993 to 1999, the number of 3-to 5-year-olds whose parents read to them or told them stories regularly increased by three points. But most importantly, from 1991 to 1999, the gap in preschool participation for 3-to 5-year-olds from high- and low-income families decreased by 15 percentage points.[55] According to the National Education Goals Panel, in 1991, 73 percent of 3- to 5-year-olds from families earning over $50,000 a year attended preschool compared to only 45 percent of children from families earning $10,000 a year or less. By 1999, however, participation rates for children from high-income families in center-based preschool or child care programs was 70 percent compared to a rise to 57 percent for children of low-income families.[56] Even though the gap in participation between low- and high-income children has narrowed, it is still too large.

Studies consistently show that the quality of early education a child receives before they enter school will impact their future achievement. The Abecedarian Project, a prominent longitudinal study on the impact of early childhood programs on low-income children from infancy to adulthood, found that those participating in high quality child care were more likely to attend college than those who did not receive quality child care. Another recent study found a link between high quality child care and juvenile arrests. The study of 20 child–parent centers in Chicago serving 3- and 4-year-olds compared juvenile arrest records of 1,000 at-risk 18-year-olds who had been enrolled in early learning at those centers with the arrest records of those similarly at-risk who attended kindergarten but not quality preschool or early education programs. Twenty-six percent of those who had only attended kindergarten compared to 16 percent who attended quality preschool had at least one arrest. Fifteen percent of those who attended kindergarten compared to 8 percent who had attended quality preschool had two or more arrests.[57]

Unfortunately, too many at-risk children still do not get the early start on educational success that they need. More than one-third of children entering kindergarten are unprepared for school challenges.[58] Children in families with higher incomes enter school with a vocabulary of 20,000 words. In contrast, children in low-income families enter first grade with 5,000-word vocabularies.[59] In addition, a study of low-income families found that over half of these households had fewer than 10 children's books, and almost a quarter contained fewer than 10 books.[60] (See the Child Care chapter for more information on the importance of quality child care and early education experiences).

School Reform

School reform efforts span many areas from increased testing and establishing academic standards to class size reductions and measures to enhance teacher quality.

Standards-based reform

The drive to improve academic achievement has precipitated a national debate over "standards-based reform." The standards-based reform movement is based on the following principles:

◆ Establish clear and challenging goals in specific subject areas for each grade

◆ Focus teaching on helping students achieve these goals

◆ Develop accurate measures to determine student progress towards these goals

As part of the 1994 reauthorization of Title I of the Elementary and Secondary Education Act, the federal aid program for schools serving disadvantaged students, Congress launched a standards movement demanding that states set high standards, assess student performance, and hold state and local officials accountable for results. The reforms assume that all students can perform at the highest levels, and schools that consistently produce students with low levels of achievement must raise their expectations.

According to a 50-state survey by *Education Week* on standards and achievement, states have demonstrated notable progress but are still far from achieving the goal of reforming schools to improve student achievement.[61] The survey examined six basic public school indicators as the core elements to successful school reform:

◆ Tests that measure whether students have met state standards

◆ Report cards that summarize the performance of individual schools

◆ Rating systems that determine whether a school's performance is adequate

◆ Targeted assistance to help schools improve

◆ Rewards for schools based on their performance

◆ The authority to close, take over, or reconstitute schools that do not improve over time[62]

Forty-eight states test their students. Thirty-six states publish annual school report cards; unfortunately, only 19 publish the performance of all the schools in the state. Only 16 states have the power of reconstitution — to close, take over, or overhaul consistently failing schools. Only 14 states provide monetary rewards to individual schools for improved performance. Nineteen states require students to pass state tests to graduate from high school. Only two states tie students' achievement to an evaluation of individual teacher's performance.[63] The two states that have come close to putting all of the school reform pieces together, North Carolina and Texas, have demonstrated the greatest gains in NAEP test scores.[64] In 1999, 40 states had standards in all core subjects, up from 38 in 1998. In 1999, 34 states went beyond multiple-choice tests and included performance questions (e.g., essays, projects, open-ended questions, experiments), an increase of 14 states since 1998.[65]

States vary in their reform efforts; however, there are some similarities. For example, in determining rewards and sanctions, most states rely on test scores and focus on schools rather than individual educators. States have not reached consensus on how to fix low-performing schools; few states have used severe penalties for schools that are chronically underperforming.[66]

The standards-based reform movement has also raised concerns over the potential overemphasis and misuse of test results. There is justifiable concern that students will be penalized for their performance when their schools lack sufficient resources to help them. Some proposals have been advanced that would reduce funding to schools that do not perform well enough on the standardized tests, further reducing resources where the need is greatest.

The use of high-stakes testing to determine whether students move on to the next grade or graduate poses other problems. Many decry social promotion, or promoting students to the next grade despite their low academic progress. A high school diploma should not simply represent four years of attendance but rather denote a student's acquisition of knowledge and skills represented by the degree. At the same time it is critical that tests used to determine promotion and graduation be fair, non-discriminatory, and measure what is actually taught in the classroom.

Critics of standards-based reform fear that the focus on testing simply encourages educators to teach to the tests by narrowly focusing on what will be tested rather than a student's mastery of the broader subject matter that tests are intended to gauge. Critics argue that tests should not be the final arbiter in determining grade promotion, graduation, or student achievement because they do not sufficiently measure student comprehension and progress. To address this problem, the U.S. Department of Education encourages alternative ways to assess student learning such as open-ended questions, projects or experiments, and portfolios of a student's work. These strategies require students to demonstrate knowledge and skills that cannot be determined through multiple choice exams.[67]

Despite these concerns, states continue to enact legislation preventing grade promotion until students pass a required examination. Some states have coupled these policies with intensive summer school and remedial attention to encourage student progress. Delaware's Educational Accountability Act of 1998 requires students in grades three, five, eight, and 10 who score below grade level to attend summer school.[68] Other states have begun to moderate strict retention policies. California enacted legislation that requires districts to promote students only if they pass academic-skills tests. However, with written explanations, teachers have the power to override the retention.[69] Under South Carolina's Accountability Act of 1998, third and eighth graders who perform below grade level are put on one-year academic probation. After a year, if a student does not meet standards, they will be held back.[70]

Retention policies can have detrimental effects on many students. A student who has been held back more than once is 90 percent more likely to drop out of school.[71] A recent study by the Consortium on Chicago School Research found that third and sixth graders who were socially promoted did as well, and sometimes better, than students who were retained. In addition, the study found that one-third of students retained in eighth grade eventually dropped out of school.[72] As the standards-based reform movement continues to evolve, an appropriate balance that promotes accountability without undermining the underlying purpose of education reform efforts needs to be achieved. Tests should be used as a tool to help students learn, identify weaknesses, and target resources to improve achievement levels.

When school reform succeeds

Many failing schools serve predominately poor or minority students. However, schools with high concentrations of low-income or minority students can perform well with the right combination of support. According to a recent national study by the RAND Corporation, strategies such as smaller class sizes, resources for teachers, and preschool programs can result in higher overall test scores for students in poor communities.[73]

When high standards are supported by a substantive curriculum, school districts have produced dramatic gains in even the most challenging circumstances. In Philadelphia, a school district with high numbers of poor and minority students and known for its consistently low student performance, school reform efforts resulted in a 21.6 percent increase in tenth graders' scores on standardized tests.[74] When the Baltimore school district, also known for low achievement scores and high numbers of low-income and minority students, implemented an intensive reading program for students in all city schools, they invested in professional development for teachers. Baltimore students' scores on the Comprehensive Test of Basic Skills rose three years in a row with first-grade reading scores jumping 20 points from 1998 to 2000.[75] In an effort to improve scores of Cleveland's low-income and minority students, the district improved professional development for teachers, implemented a new summer school program, and mandated a 90-minute reading block in all elementary grades. Cleveland has demonstrated tremendous gains, with a 44 percent rise in fourth-grade reading scores.[76]

At Public School 187 in Brooklyn, only 39 percent of eighth graders met state standards in 1999. One year later, 57 percent passed the test, a rise of 18 percentage points and the biggest gain of any school in New York City.[77] In order to improve student's scores, any student who scored far below standards was scheduled for double periods of math; students could review classroom work in smaller tutorials comprised of 10 to 12 students; and all students, even those who passed the test, were offered homework help, peer tutoring, and test-taking strategies during lunch and before and after school.[78] Eighty percent of students at Owen School in Detroit are poor, and more than 90 percent are Black. But these students have transcended demographics: 94 percent of fourth graders passed the state math test, 80 percent passed the reading test, and 94 percent of fifth graders passed the science test.[79] The secrets to their success include highly trained, stable teachers and small class sizes of about 17 students per class. The school's success is also attributed to a dedicated principal who works to ensure that parents are involved in their child's learning.[80] Across the nation, there are countless other public schools demonstrating success in raising student achievement in low-income, predominately minority communities. These schools underscore the importance of continuing to focus on strengthening public education, not abandoning it.

Comprehensive School Reform Demonstration

The Comprehensive School Reform Demonstration (CSRD) program, now in its third year, is an effort to promote research-based, whole-school reform where it is most urgently needed so all children receive a first-rate education. Sponsored by Representatives David Obey (D-WI) and John Porter (R-IL) and included in the fiscal year 1998 appropriation for the Department of Education, CSRD uses financial incentives to encourage schools with poor track records in educating children — particularly at-risk students — to forgo incremental change in favor of comprehensive, systemic, research-based reform.

The program is targeted, but not limited, to Title I schools. The Title I Basic Grants formula is used to provide grants to state education agencies over a three-year period—$45 million in FY 1998 and FY 1999, $220 million in FY 2000. State Education Agencies (SEAs) award these grants on a competitive basis, through school districts, to individual schools committed to implementing comprehensive, all-school reform. While the CSRD legislation lists 17 well-established reform programs that schools can adopt, it does not prescribe or endorse any program and explicitly states that other plans meeting the nine criteria described in the legislation are equally acceptable.

For any school, a crucial factor in making reform work is choosing the reform program that will best meet its needs. Before implementing any program, school staff must first systematically assess the school's needs and then "shop" for the most effective program. Once chosen, the reform program must be faithfully implemented. To be eligible for a CSRD grant, a school's plan must include research-based, replicable strategies for learning, teaching, and management; a comprehensive design that addresses all aspects of school life; pre-implementation training and continuous professional development; measurable achievement goals; faculty, administration, and staff commitment and significant parent and community involvement; continuing external support and guidance from a university or comparable school-reform organization; and procedures for evaluating the effectiveness of the plan.

Although CSRD was established just three years ago, the research on whole-school reform is well established. A few of the models — Direct Instruction and Dr. James Comer's School Development Program are notable examples—were introduced more than thirty years ago. Some programs, like Success for All (which was developed by Robert Slavin and associates at Johns Hopkins), date back to the 1980s. Other programs, like Expeditionary Learning/Outward Bound, are more recent. The most recognized programs are similar in certain aspects: they aim to raise achievement levels of all students; they change established assumptions and procedures throughout a school; they require preparatory training and continuing, high quality professional development for teachers; and they use a "facilitator" or "coach" to guide implementa-

tion. In other respects, however, they differ greatly. Programs vary in the degree to which they require a formal "buy-in" by the school staff and in their emphasis on family involvement. Some programs provide underlying principles and leave details for individual schools to decide. Others have specific content and require precisely orchestrated classroom procedures. Some concentrate on reading and math, others include areas such as the arts. Some turn the traditional schedule upside-down, others leave it intact.

CSRD has moved comprehensive school reform forward by establishing a national platform for the implementation and assessment of research-based programs. All fifty states, the District of Columbia, and Puerto Rico have been awarded CSRD funds, and just under 2,000 higher poverty, low-performing schools have received annual grants of about $50,000 to transform long-established habits, attitudes, and practices.

CSRD has already yielded substantial results. It has led to important research, development, and technical assistance projects. Also, it has created a remarkable network for disseminating and exchanging information through the Department of Education's 10 Regional Education Laboratories (RELs); 15 Comprehensive Assistance Centers; the National Clearinghouse on Comprehensive School Reform (NCCSR); the Education Commission of the States; and dozens of university departments, research organizations, and professional associations. It has also encouraged serious and fundamental review at the state level and in schools about effective approaches to teaching.

CSRD schools — at most one or two years into the implementation of whole-school reform — have not yet produced data definitively linking student achievement to specific reform models. There have been some early efforts to assess the effectiveness of some reform plans — including a 1998 RAND study of the eight New American Schools models and an early 1999 study by American Institutes of Research (a nonprofit, nonpartisan research organization) that catalogues, briefly analyzes, and rates 24 different plans. In September, the Department of Education published the first in a series of annual evaluations, *Early Implementation of the Comprehensive School Reform Demonstration (CSRD) Program: Summary Report 2000*, in response to the legislative mandate. The purpose of the report, which covers only the first year of the program, is to assemble baseline data for future evaluations and to identify successes and problems in implementation procedures. The report stresses that "it is too early in the implementation process to draw conclusions on achievement outcomes.... While research has documented the strength of comprehensive rather than piecemeal approaches to reform, more rigorous research is needed to evaluate the effects of particular reform designs being implemented with CSRD funds." The Department of Education has provided grants to six established research organizations to study the effects of comprehensive school reform models on student achievement over three to five years. Evaluation, the next critical phase in the CSRD program, is underway.

Teacher quality

With high-stakes standards-based reform, there is a great need to prepare teachers to meet the challenges of raising student performance. Studies show that a teacher's training and command of a subject affects student performance. A recent study by the Educational Testing Service (ETS) shows a strong link between teachers' education levels, teaching style, and student outcomes.[81] The students of teachers who majored or minored in the subject they taught outperformed their peers by 40 percent in math and science.[82] Students outperformed their peers by more than one grade level when they were taught by teachers who received professional development for working with special populations.[83] For example, students of teachers who used innovated teaching techniques such as hands-on learning experiences outperformed their peers by 70 percent of a grade level in math and by 40 percent of a grade level in science.

State licensing and certification requirements play an important role in ensuring qualified teachers for the classroom. Forty-one states require teachers to pass licensure exams. However, only 14 states administer teaching exams that go beyond multiple choice questions. Twenty-nine states require high school teachers to pass tests in subjects they will teach in the classroom, and 39 states require teachers to have a major or a minor in their subjects.[84] Yet all of the states, except New Jersey, allow these requirements to be waived. Only nine states require all middle school teachers to pass tests in the subjects they will teach.[85] According to an interim report by the Committee on Assessment and Teacher Quality, while licensing tests provide useful information about literacy, mathematical skills, and knowledge of subject matter, important for effective teaching, such tests do not measure whether a teacher has the skills to be an effective educator in the classroom.[86] Evaluation of a teacher's classroom performance should also be used to measure teacher qualifications.

Schools must be able to recruit and retain qualified teachers. State financial incentives can be used to attract talented individuals into the teaching profession. Twenty-seven states have loan-forgiveness or scholarship programs for teachers.[87] But only 10 states encourage these teachers to work in the neediest school districts, which are usually poor, urban, and rural.

Teachers' salaries are also a concern for both recruitment and retention. Teachers ages 22 to 28 earned an average of $7,894 less than their college-educated peers in other professions.[88] For teachers ages 44 to 50, the pay gap is three times wider with teachers earning an average of $22,655 less than their peers.

Class size

Most research shows that smaller class sizes improve learning, particularly in the early grades. Small classes and small schools create a more intimate learning environment with closer relationships between students and teachers, fewer discipline problems, and more opportunity for teachers to provide individual attention to students who need it the most. Also, in smaller classes, teachers spend more time on instruction and less time on classroom management. Unfortunately, the drive to reduce class size comes at a time when there is already a shortage of teachers.

A study on the impact of class size in Tennessee schools found that students who were in class sizes of 13 to 17 showed learning gains that continued even after students returned to larger classes.[89] Poor and Black students within the study achieved the largest learning gains as a result of small classes. In New York City, a study found that students in overcrowded schools scored significantly lower in reading and mathematics than students in less crowded facilities.[90] New York City reduced classroom sizes from an average of 28 students to about 20 students per classroom by adding 950 new classes in kindergarten through third grade. The reduction to about 20 students per classroom resulted in fewer disciplinary measures, improved teacher morale, and higher student participation in classroom exercises.[91] According to a third year evaluation report of Wisconsin's SAGE (Student Achievement Guarantee in Education) program, which reduces classes to a ratio of 15 students to 1 teacher in grades K-2, Wisconsin's elementary students exhibited real improvements in achievement. For example, after class size reduction, Black students made much larger gains than their peers in larger classrooms.[92]

Public School Choice

Charter schools

Charter schools are designed to offer students and their families a broader range of education opportunities within the public school system than traditional public schools provide. Since the first charter school opened in Minnesota in 1992, the movement has expanded nationwide; 36 states, the District of Columbia, and Puerto Rico now have charter-school laws. In the current school year, an estimated 518,000 students are enrolled in approximately 2,000 charter schools. More than half of the schools, and nearly two-thirds of the students, are concentrated in five states: Arizona, California, Florida, Michigan, and Texas.[93] Although charter school enrollment is increasing, it accounts for less than 1 percent of total public school enrollment.

Charters can be entirely new schools or existing schools that were converted to charter status. Nearly three-quarters are new, 18 percent are converted from existing public schools, and about 10 percent were formerly private schools. A charter functions as a contract between the school's organizer — who may be a group of parents, an individual, a university, or some other interested party — and the designated chartering agency, generally a local or state school board. Arizona and California, the states with largest numbers of charter schools and highest student enrollment, are among the handful that allow charters to be granted directly to for-profit companies. Other states, however, permit charter recipients to hire for-profit companies to run the school. A charter school commits to specific goals, objectives, operating procedures, forms of governance, standards, and assessments. In return, it receives public funding, generally on a per-student basis, and a broad exemption from districtwide regulations. Thus it enjoys much greater latitude to set its own course in budgeting, hiring, and purchasing, and in fundamental academic matters such as curriculum, calendar, schedule, even the length of the school day than a traditional public school. Charters are usually in effect for three to five years, and they are renewable. If a school fails to meet the terms of its charter, the charter can be revoked. Roughly 4 percent of charter schools have had to close, often due to lack of funds or financial mismanagement.

States differ in the priorities and flexibility they grant their charter schools. Many, but not all, give preference for charters to schools that are located in low-performing districts or targeted to at-risk students. Some states restrict the number of charters — Illinois is capped at 45 and Massachusetts at 50 — while others, like Pennsylvania and Minnesota, impose no limits. Some provide start-up funds in addition to per-capita funding, others do not. States vary in their teacher-certification guidelines and reporting requirements:

◆ New Jersey requires annual reports to parents and to the local school board, the county superintendent, and the state commissioner of education.

◆ Missouri charter schools submit an annual report card to the school's sponsor, local district, and state.

◆ Wisconsin charter schools must file the standard reports that all public schools file.

◆ Illinois charter school reporting requirements include the local district, the state board of education, the governor, and the legislature.

In some ways, charters are similar to other public schools. The racial/ethnic make-up of the student population tends to mirror the district in which the school is located, both have about the same percentage of students eligible for free or reduced-price lunch, and the student-teacher ratio overall is not much different. Their students are required to take state assessments tests. As public schools, charters may not use selective admissions policies, but they appear consistently to enroll relatively lower percentages of special education students.

Still, certain distinct patterns seem to be emerging.[94] A substantial majority of charter schools were explicitly created to realize an "alternative vision" of education,[95] and a significant number of schools were designed to serve a special population. A major factor in public school conversions was the desire for greater autonomy, while private schools converted for a variety of reasons, often financial. Charter schools tend to be small, with a median enrollment of 137, compared to 475 for other public schools; only one charter school in 12 has more than 600 students, compared to one in three public schools. Charters are less likely to adhere to the elementary/middle/high school model and span grades K-8 or even K-12 in their schools. Nationwide, a higher proportion of Hispanic and especially Black students are enrolled in charter schools, particularly in Massachusetts, Michigan, Minnesota, New Jersey, Pennsylvania, and Texas. Most charter schools face common financial problems. While public funding on a per-student basis covers a substantial part of operating expenses, state and federal start-up support is minimal where it exists at all.

The long-term prospects for charter schools remain uncertain. Although these schools are intended to strengthen public education and raise student achievement levels, sufficient data to assess their effectiveness or determine which charter-school innovations can serve as viable models for broader school reform is not yet available. In the short term, however, with the number of charter schools increasing, they are sure to occupy a significant place in the debate over education reform.

Vouchers

The debate surrounding the use of public funds for school vouchers, which are used to help pay for private school education, continued in 2000. Two very different arguments are made on behalf of school vouchers. The first, put forward nearly half a century ago by Milton Friedman,[96] contends that school vouchers would stimulate a competitive, free-market system, resulting in better schools for all children by forcing the closure of low-performing

Violence in Schools

Overall school crime rates are declining. According to the 2000 Annual Report on School Safety, in 1998, all nonfatal crimes — including theft, rape, sexual assault, robbery, aggravated assault, and simple assault — declined from 3.4 million in 1992 to 2.7 million in 1998. Thefts at school have dramatically declined — from 95 thefts per 1,000 students in 1992 to 58 per 1,000 student in 1998. Unfortunately, the rate of serious violent crime (including rape, sexual assault, robbery, and aggravated assault) has remained constant since 1992; in 1998, 252,700 incidents were reported committed at school or going to and from school. However, more victimizations happen away from school than at school. In 1998, students were two times more likely to be victims of serious violent crime away from school than at school. Most student incidents involve thefts. This is the same for teachers who are victims of crime.

The number of students who report carrying a weapon to school on one or more days during the previous month also declined from 12 percent in 1993 to 7 percent in 1999. In addition, the percentage of students who reported being involved in a physical fight declined from 16 percent to 14 percent. While overall indicators show declines in school crimes, students still feel unsafe at school. All ethnic groups reported a decreasing fear of attack or harm from 1995 to 1999, but larger percentages of Hispanic and Black students reported fear of attacks at schools. Student reports of gang presence in schools dropped from 29 percent in 1995 to 17 percent in 1999. The National Association of Secondary School Principals recommends reducing school size to a maximum of 600 or creating schools within schools as ways of reducing violence in schools because smaller environments allow students to feel less alienated and more connected to their peers and teachers. (See Juvenile Justice and Youth Development chapter for more information on reducing violence against children and teens.)

Sources: P. Kaufman, X. Chen, S.P. Choy et al., *Indicators of School Crime and Safety, 2000* NCES 2001-017/NCJ-184176 (Washington, D.C.: U.S. Departments of Education and Justice, 2000); Kenneth Cooper, "Education Chief Prescribes Smaller Schools to Curb Violence," *The Washington Post* (September 6, 1999).

schools. The second argues that vouchers can guarantee better educational opportunities to children from low-income families who cannot afford private school or cannot move to neighborhoods with better public schools.

These differing perspectives were reflected in school-voucher ballot initiatives in California and Michigan last November. California's sweeping Proposition 38 proposed to make every family, regardless of income, eligible for vouchers of $4,000 per child. It encompassed the state's 6.6 million students including families with children already in private schools and covered religious schools. Michigan's Proposition 1 targeted vouchers worth about $3,300 only to students in districts that failed to meet minimum high-school graduation rates — a standard by which students in seven Michigan districts were eligible. But Proposition 1 also authorized school boards and voters to adopt voucher programs in their own districts.

Although both proposals were defeated by more than 2-1, the voucher debate is far from over. Privately funded voucher or scholarship programs operate in a number of cities,[97] and some members of Congress, along with the Bush administration, continue to promote various publicly funded voucher proposals. Limited, publicly financed voucher programs already exist in Milwaukee, Cleveland, and Florida. The Milwaukee Parental Choice Program, introduced in 1990, is targeted to low-income families and capped at 15 percent of the district's public school population; about 10,000 students currently receive vouchers of more than $5,000. A 1995 decision to include religious schools in the program was contested in court; in 1998, the Wisconsin Supreme Court found the program constitutional, and the U.S. Supreme Court subsequently declined to review the case. The Cleveland program awards vouchers of up to $2,250 to about 3,500 students primarily in grades K-3 and also includes religious schools. Almost from the moment it was introduced in 1995, it has been the subject of litigation in both state and federal court. In December 2000, a federal court of appeals upheld a lower court's decision that the inclusion of religious schools made the program unconstitutional. Florida's Opportunity Scholarship Program, introduced in 1999 as part of a comprehensive state education reform plan that grades public schools on the basis of students' test scores, offers vouchers worth about $4,000 to students in failing schools. Litigation over the constitutionality of the Florida program is ongoing in the state courts. Meanwhile, the program remains very small. In the first year, only a limited number of students in two schools received vouchers. No more vouchers were issued in the second year because test scores rose so markedly that no additional schools received a failing grade.

Publicly funded voucher programs that include religious schools, as the three existing programs do, inevitably raise the constitutional issue of church–state separation. But vouchers also raise other serious issues. They drain tax dollars from public schools at a time when those resources are most needed to cover the costs of school reform. Also, the choice that vouchers offer is often misleading. Most private schools have limited enrollments and selective admissions policies, and private-school tuition often exceeds the value of the voucher. Furthermore, private schools can expel students at their discretion for poor academic performance, learning disabilities, behavioral problems, or other reasons. And because private schools are generally exempt from public oversight and their students rarely, if ever, take state-mandated assessment tests, it is difficult to track the progress of students who transfer from failing public schools. Despite abundant data and numerous studies, evidence on the effectiveness of vouchers in raising student achievement levels remains inconclusive.[98]

Fundamentally, voucher proposals divert attention from the challenge of improving all public schools at just the time when public education is being rethought, redirected, and reformed. They siphon off resources and obscure the movement toward public school choice, which includes varied forms such as charter schools, pilot schools, model schools, magnet schools, and districtwide controlled choice. When the overarching objective must be to strengthen public schools, which serve 90 percent of the children, publicly funded vouchers move in the wrong direction.

Higher Education

Attainment

In today's economy, a college degree is one of the greatest factors determining potential job opportunities and higher earnings. Those who have not completed a college education are likely to be unprepared to compete in a highly skilled job market. The good news is that in 1999, college completion rates continued to show steady increases. The percentage of 25- to 29-year-olds who completed at least some college increased from 44 percent in 1971 to 66 percent in 1999, and the percentage who obtained a bachelor's degree or higher rose from 22 percent to 32 percent.[99]

Unfortunately, too many poor and minority students face tremendous obstacles in getting a college education. Compared with higher-income peers, high school graduates from low-income families enter four-year, post-secondary institutions at lower rates.[100] One of the reasons for lower enrollment is that lower-income students are often less qualified for college because the public school system has failed to prepare these students with the basic education needed to succeed in college. The National Center for Education Statistics reports that 86 percent of students from higher-income families (with annual incomes of $75,000 or more) were at least minimally academically qualified for admission to a four-year college compared with 68 percent from middle-income families ($25,000-$74,999) and 53 percent from low-income families (less than $25,000).[101]

The high financial costs of gaining a college degree also makes it exceedingly difficult for many low-income students to enroll in higher education. The Hope and Opportunity for Post-secondary Education Act (HOPE), passed in 1997, expanded the Pell Grant program, which helps low-income students pay for college costs, and provided tax incentives to help families pay tuition. This past year, the 106th Congress increased the maximum Pell Grant up to $3,750. These proposals, however, provided only modest assistance in alleviating the rising costs of tuition. Tuition and fees at public and private colleges and universities have increased fivefold since the 1976-1977 academic year, exceeding all rates of inflation.[102] For the 2000-2001 academic year, the average tuition of public four-year colleges and universities is $3,510, up 4.4 percent from $3,362 in 1999-2000.[103] Private four-year college tuition increased by 5.2 percent, from $15,518 to $16,332. Room and board increased between 4.2 percent and 5.1 percent since last year.[104] Room and board averages $6,209 at four-year private colleges and $4,960 at four-year public colleges.

The increased costs make financial aid more important than ever. But while financial aid has grown significantly, it remains inadequate to meet the needs of many families and the shift from grant aid to loans has increased the debt that many students incur in acquiring a college degree. Available student aid reached $68 billion in 1999-2000, an increase of 4 percent, adjusting for inflation.[105] Over the past 10 years, total aid has increased by 90 percent. Loans increased by 125 percent, accounting for two-thirds of the total increase, while grant aid increased by only by 55 percent. Federal loans accounted for 51.4 percent of total student aid, institutional and other grants accounted for 19.4 percent, and federal Pell Grants accounted for 10.7 percent.[106] While state aid accounts for only 6 percent of total student aid, it has increased by 58 percent over the past 10 years.

A state-by-state survey conducted by the National Center for Public Policy and Higher Education graded states on how well they prepare students for college, whether a higher education is affordable, and how many students earn their degrees in a timely manner. The survey found wide disparities in accessibility and affordability in college completion rates for states:[107]

◆ Alabama and Louisiana both received F's in how well they prepare their students for college.

◆ Alaska, Connecticut, Illinois, Massachusetts, Nebraska, New Jersey, Utah, and Wisconsin all received A's in their preparation.

◆ California, Illinois, Minnesota, North Carolina, and Utah received A's in making higher education affordable.

◆ Maine, New Hampshire, and Rhode Island received F's in the affordability category.

◆ Alaska and Nevada received F's and Iowa, Massachusetts, New Hampshire, New York, Pennsylvania, Rhode Island, and Vermont all received A's in the category of whether students earn degrees in a timely manner.

While the percentage of minorities enrolled in higher education rose slightly in the past year, the college participation rate for minorities still lagged behind their White peers with 29 percent of White adults between the ages of 25 and 29 holding a bachelor's degree, 14.4 percent of Black adults, and only 11 percent of Hispanic adults.[108] However, minorities experienced enrollment gains in all post-secondary levels in 1997 with the largest gain, 8.9 percent, in professional schools, followed by a 5.6 percent gain in graduate schools, and a 3.5 percent gain at the undergraduate level.

Legislative Action in 2000

The 106th Congress failed to reauthorize the Elementary and Secondary Education Act of 1965, the largest federal elementary and secondary education program. Funds from Title I of the act provide supplementary education services to low-achieving students attending schools with relatively high concentrations of low-income students. It is expected to be one of the first measures considered in the 107th Congress.

The Labor, Health and Human Services, Education Appropriations package, negotiated at the end of the 106th Congress, includes a $6.5 billion increase in education and raises total federal education spending to $44.5 billion. Class size reduction initiatives were funded at $1.6 billion, which continues the Clinton administration's plan to put 100,000 additional teachers in the classroom over a seven-year period. While legislation to authorize school modernization bonds was not enacted, $1.2 billion was provided for school construction and modernization grants. Special education was funded at $6.3 billion, over $1 billion more than the Clinton administration requested.

State legislatures acted on numerous education-related measures, but most noteworthy was the record number of education initiatives placed on the November 2000 election ballots. As discussed earlier, voucher initiatives in California and Michigan both failed. Arizona's ballot initiative to ban bilingual education and substitute one year of immersion in English passed, and Colorado's ballot initiative to increase funding for kindergarten through twelfth grade by at least 1 percent more than the inflation rate for every year for a decade also passed. One Oregon initiative that would have mandated performance-based teacher pay raises beyond the cost-of-living increase was rejected. Another Oregon measure that requires the state legislature provide sufficient funding to meet its quality education goals or explain why funds are unavailable was approved by the voters. Finally, Washington state voted down a proposal authorizing the state's first charter school, but approved ballot initiatives that mandated cost-of-living raises to teachers and allocated state lottery revenue to reduce class sizes and construct schools.

Moving Forward:
A 2001 Agenda for Action

If America's education system is to be revitalized, it must strive to succeed in helping all children achieve at high levels. This requires a commitment to common sense steps intended to change our educational system so that it is singularly focused on excellence for every child.

Setting high standards for students

All students must be encouraged to excel.

◆ Clear, comprehensive, and rigorous standards should apply to all schools and all students.

◆ Everyone — school administrators, teachers, parents, and students as well as policy makers and communities — must be held accountable for whether these standards are met.

◆ Instructional support and services that will enable students to master the subjects they need to know to progress successfully through the education system must be provided.

◆ After-school programs, summer programs, mentoring, or other extra support must be provided to students who need help.

Setting high standards for all educators

Few students will excel when their teachers do not. Before students are held accountable, the people responsible for their learning must be.

◆ All teachers must have strong knowledge of their subject areas and training in how children learn.

◆ Teacher preparation at colleges and universities must be improved.

◆ Continuing professional development for the nation's teaching corps must be provided so classroom teachers are up-to-date on the most effective approaches and techniques.

◆ Student loan-forgiveness programs should be improved to help recruit aspiring teachers.

◆ New teachers should be mentored by more experienced, successful teachers, and struggling teachers should be coached to improve or be counseled out of the profession.

◆ Teachers must be adequately prepared and compensated and held accountable for the progress of the children they are hired to teach.

Setting high standards for all schools

Those responsible for the state of schools, including state superintendents, boards of education, local superintendents, school boards, and principals, also must be held accountable. If they do not create an environment optimally conducive to learning, educational success will be difficult to achieve.

◆ Schools must be held accountable for student progress.

◆ State and local education agencies should be required to produce annual report cards that include such factors as student performance, attendance, graduation rates, professional qualifications of teachers, average class size, school safety, and parental involvement.

◆ States must establish specific goals and performance benchmarks for improving the performance of all students within a prescribed period of time.

◆ Schools should be recognized and rewarded when they have helped children succeed.

◆ Aggressive, but constructive, intervention must take place when schools fail to make progress in reaching their goals.

◆ Schools should be given the resources they need to help children succeed and empowered to make decisions that will help them reach that goal.

Setting high standards for parents and communities

Education does not occur in a vacuum. Whether students are prepared to succeed in school is very dependent on their parents, as their children's first and most important teachers, and on whether communities address the full range of children's developmental needs, including health care, child care, after-school activities, and support for families in poverty.

◆ Parents and advocates must be actively involved in monitoring school performance, staying informed about what is happening in the schools in their communities, and demanding accountability from their schools.

◆ All parents must accept responsibility for helping children learn, reading to them, and providing them with the support they need to succeed.

◆ The entire community needs to make sure that every student has the support and services he or she needs to succeed in school. This requires the coordinated efforts of health care providers, police, social service agencies, neighborhood groups, faith organizations, and the full range of volunteer organizations that work with children.

◆ The general public should be engaged in the school reform debate. The public needs to demand real leadership from elected officials and solid results from education reform efforts.

Setting high standards for elected officials, as well as all citizens

Elected officials largely determine the amount of funding provided to schools and how it is allocated, as well as the regulations under which schools operate. They, and the citizens who elect them, must be held accountable for whether public schools have the resources and the ability to ensure that every child achieves at a high level.

◆ Government, at all levels, needs to invest adequate resources in education and treat it like the priority it is if our democracy and economy are to remain vibrant in the 21st century.

◆ The federal government must maintain a commitment to leadership and an allocation of funds to help states and local school districts meet the needs of children, particularly those in low-income communities where resources are scarce and needs are greatest.

◆ State and local officials must make sure that all public school systems have the necessary resources to help children achieve.

◆ Inequalities in school financing must end.

◆ Officials must invest in funding to help school districts recruit, train, and hire additional teachers to reduce class size in grades one through three to an average of 18 students per class.

◆ All children should have access to the high quality early education opportunities that will enable them to enter school ready to learn and ready to succeed.

◆ Resources must be made available so all children who want to get a college education can do so, regardless of income.

◆ Resources should be made available for school construction, renovation, and modernization, so all students have the opportunity to learn in safe environments that are conducive to learning.

◆ All schools should have access to technology and resources so students can learn through computers and use the Internet.

Endnotes

1. National Education Goals Panel, *The National Education Goals Report: Building a Nation of Learners 1999* (Washington D.C.: U.S. Government Printing Office, 1999).

2. *Ibid.* at 77.

3. For nearly 30 years, the progress of student achievement in a number of areas has been tracked by the National Assessment of Educational Progress (NAEP). NAEP data show relatively few students achieve at high levels of proficiency across subject areas. The NAEP scores students at five levels of proficiency in various subject areas from reading to science. The National Education Goals Panel has set its performance standards at the two highest levels of achievement (Proficient or Advanced) on the NAEP tests.

4. U.S. Department of Education, National Center for Education Statistics, *The Condition of Education 2000.* (Washington, D.C.: U.S. Government Printing Office, 2000): 23

5. *Ibid.*

6. U.S. Department of Education, *NAEP 1998 Reading, A Report Card for the Nation and the States,* Executive Summary, NCES 1999-500 (Washington, D.C.: U.S. Government Printing Office, 1999).

7. *Supra* note 4 at 24.

8. *Ibid.*

9. *Ibid.* at 25.

10. *Ibid.* at 25.

11. *Ibid.* at 28.

12. *Ibid.*

13. *Ibid.*

14. U.S. Department of Education, National Center for Education Statistics, *The Condition of Education 1997: The Social Context of Education* (Washington, D.C.: U.S. Government Printing Office, 1997).

15. Abby Goodnough, "The Ruling in the Schools: The Overview; State Judge Rules School Aid Is Unfair to City," *The New York Times* (January 11, 2001): A1.

16. U.S. Department of Education, *The Nation's Report Card, NAEP 1999 Trends in Academic Progress: Three Decades of Student Performance,* Executive Summary (Washington, D.C.: U.S. Government Printing Office, August 2000).

17. *Ibid.*

18. *Ibid.*

19. *Ibid.*

20. Applied Research Council, *Still Separate, Still Unequal* (May 2000): 2, *citing* U.S. Department of Education, Office of Civil Rights, *1997 Elementary and Secondary School Civil Rights Compliance Reports.*

21. *Ibid.*

22. *Ibid.* at 3, *citing* U.S. Department of Education, National Center for Education Statistics, *Common Core of Data, 1995.*

23. *Supra* note 4 at 56.

24. U.S. Department of Education, National Center for Education Statistics, "Dropout Rates in the United States: 1999." Available on the Internet at http://nces.ed.gov/pubs2001/dropout.

25. *Supra* note 4 at 56.

26. *Supra* note 24.

27. Mary Ann Zehr, "Study Finds Disparity in Internet Use," *Education Week on the Web* (May 24, 2000). Available on the Internet at www.edweek.org *citing* a study by Alan B. Krueger, Princeton University, *The Digital Divide in Educating African-American Students.*

28. *Ibid.*

29. *Ibid.*

30. "Children of Change: Overview," *Education Week on the Web* (September 27, 2000). Available on the Internet at www.edweek.org.

31. "School-Age 'Millenni-Boom' Predicted for Next 100 Years," *Education Week on the Web* (September 27, 2000). Available on the Internet at www.edweek.org.

32. *Ibid.*

33. U.S. Department of Education, National Center on Education Statistics, "Characteristics of the 100 Largest Public Elementary and Secondary Districts in the United States: 1998-1999." Available on the Internet at_http://nces.ed.gov/pubs2000/100largest.highlights.

34. *Ibid.*

35. *Ibid.*

36. *Ibid.*

37. "Minority Groups To Emerge As a Majority in U.S. Schools," *Education Week on the Web* (September 27, 2000). Available on the Internet at www.edweek.org.

38. U.S. Department of Education, "Statement by the U.S. Secretary of Education Richard W. Riley on the National Board for Professional Teaching Standards' Study that Teachers with National Board Certification Outperform Others" (October 18, 2000): Press release.

39. *Supra* note 4 at 73, *citing* U.S. Department of Education, National Center for Education Statistics, *Teacher Quality: A Report on the Preparation and Qualifications of Public School Teachers,* NCES 1999-080 (Washington, D.C.: U.S. Government Printing Office, 1999).

40. Supra note 4 at 75, *citing* U.S. Department of Education, National Center for Education Statistics, *How Old are America's Public Schools?* NCES 1999-048 (Washington, D.C.: U.S. Government Printing Office, 1999).

41. U.S. Department of Education, National Center for Education Statistics, *Condition of America's Public School Facilities: 1999,* NCES 2000-032 (Washington D.C.: U.S. Government Printing Office, 2000): iii.

42. *Ibid.* at iv.

43. *Ibid.*

44. *Ibid.* at v.

45. *Ibid.*

46. *Ibid.*

47. U.S. Department of Education, "Growing Pains, The Challenge of Overcrowded Schools is Here to Stay." In *A Back to School Report on the Baby Boom Echo* (August 21, 2000). Available on the Internet at http://www.ed.gov/pubs/bbecho00/part2.

48. *Ibid.*

49. U.S. Department of Education, "The Urgent National Need for School Construction and Modernization," (June 27, 2000). Available on the Internet at www.ed.gov/inits/construction/urgentneed.html.

50. *Ibid.*

51. U.S. General Accounting Office, *School Facilities, Profiles of School Conditions by State,* GAO/HEHS-96-148 (Washington, D.C.: U.S. General Accounting Office, June 1996):78.

52. Debra Viadero, "Low Birthweight Found To Affect Children Through High School," *Education Week on the Web,* (July 12, 2000). Available on the Internet at www.edweek.org.

53. *Ibid.*

54. National Education Goals Panel, *Data Volume for the National Education Goals Report* (Washington, D.C.: U.S. Government Printing Office, 1999): v.

55. *Ibid.* at 9.

56. National Education Goals Panel, "Gap Narrows in Preschool Participation

Rates" (August 28, 2000): Press release. Available on the Internet at www.negp.gov.

57. "High-Quality Child Care Again Linked to Fewer Juvenile Arrests," *Education Week on the Web* (May 10, 2000). Available on the Internet at www.edweek.org.

58. Children's Defense Fund, "Quality Child Care is Key to School Readiness." Available on the Internet at www.childrensdefense.org/childcare citing Carnegie Corporation of New York, *Years of Promise: A Comprehensive Learning Strategy for America's Children*, (1996).

59. *Ibid. citing* Betty Hart, Ph.D. and Todd R. Risley, Ph.D., *Meaningful Differences in the Everyday Experience of Young American Children* (Baltimore, Md.: Paul H. Brookes Publishing Co., 1995).

60. *Ibid. citing* Urban Institute and Child Trends, *Snapshots of America's Families: Children's Environment and Behavior, Reading and Telling Stories to Young Children* (Washington, D.C.: Urban Institute, 1997).

61. "Quality Counts '99," *Education Week on the Web* (January 1999). Available on the Internet at www.edweek.org.

62. *Ibid.* at "Shining a Spotlight on Results."

63. *Ibid.* at "Demanding Results."

64. *Ibid.*

65. *Ibid.*

66. *Ibid.*

67. U.S. Department of Education, "What Are Promising Ways to Assess Student Learning," *Improving America's Schools: A Newsletter on Issues in School Reform* (September 1996). Available on the Internet at http://www.ed.gov/ pubs/ IASA/newsletters.

68. *Supra* note 61 at "Turning Up the Heat."

69. *Ibid.*

70. *Ibid.*

71. Center for Law and Education, "Tests Scores, Retention Get Dubious Results," *Connection* 3, no. 5 (September/October 1999): 3.

72. "Chicago Study Questions Results of Retention," *Education Week on the Web* (September 20, 2000). Available on the Internet at www.edweek.org.

73. American Federation of Teachers, "Doing What Works: Improving Big City School Districts," *Educational Policy Issues Policy Brief* No. 12 (October 2000) citing David Grissmer et al., *Improving Student Achievement: What NAEP Test Scores Tell Us* (Santa Monica, Calif.: RAND Corporation, 2000).

74. *Ibid.*

75. *Ibid.*

76. *Ibid.*

77. Anemona Hartocollis, "Brooklyn School Finds a Way to Break From the Pack," *The New York Times* (October 19, 2000): A28.

78. *Ibid.*

79. Kenneth J. Cooper, "School Defies its Demographics, Low-Income Students Meet Principal's High Expectations in Urban Detroit," *The Washington Post* (June 7, 2000) A3.

80. *Ibid.*

81. Harold Wenglinsky, *How Teaching Matters: Bringing the Classroom Back into Discussions of Teacher Quality* (Princeton, N.J.: Milken Family Foundation and Educational Testing Service, October 2000). Available on the Internet at www.ets.org/research/pic.

82. *Ibid.*

83. *Ibid.*

84. "Quality Counts 2000, Who Should Teach? The States Decide, Executive Summary," *Education Week on theWeb* (January 2000). Available on the Internet at www.edweek.org.

85. *Ibid.*

86. National Research Council, Committee on Assessment and Teacher Quality, *Tests and Teaching Quality, Interim Report* (Washington, D.C.: National Academy Press, 2000).

87. *Supra* note 84.

88. *Ibid.*

89. "Class Size," *Education Week on the Web* (September 28, 2000) citing Frederick Mosteller, Ph.D., "The Tennessee Study of Class Size in the Early Grades," *The Future of Children* 5, no. 4 (Summer/Fall 1995).

90. *Supra* note 49.

91. U.S. Department of Education, *The Class Size Reduction Program: Boosting Student Achievement in Schools Across the Nation, A First Year Report* (Washington, D.C.: U.S. Government Printing Office, September 2000).

92. *Ibid. citing* Alex Molnar et al., "Wisconsin's Student Achievement Guarantee in Education (SAGE) Class Size Reduction Program: Achievement Effects, Teaching and Classroom Implementation." *The CEIC Review* 9, No. 2, (March 2000).

93. "Charter School Highlights and Statistics," *Center for Education Reform* (November 28, 2000). Available on the Internet at http://www.edreform. com/pubs/chglance.htm.

94. U.S. Department of Education, "The State of Charter Schools 2000," Executive Summary and passim (January 2000). Available on the Internet at http://www.ed.gov/pubs/charter4th/es.html.

95. *Ibid.*

96. For a recent statement of the argument, see Milton Friedman, "Why America Needs School Vouchers," *Wall Street Journal* (September 28, 2000).

97. David A. DeSchryver, "Private Scholarship Programs: A Matter of Priority" (August 1999). Available on the Internet at http://www.edreform.com/ pubs/privprog/htm.

98. For example, in the first five years of the Milwaukee program, before it was expanded to include religious schools and annual evaluations were discontinued, John Witte of the University of Wisconsin-Madison was the official evaluator. Witte has concluded that although parents' satisfaction with their children's schools was relatively high, overall, "achievement was no different than the achievement of Milwaukee public school students." His conclusions have been challenged, largely on methodological grounds, by a research team led by Jay Greene of the Manhattan Institute and Paul Peterson of the Program on Education Policy and Governance at the John F. Kennedy School of Government at Harvard University, who found significant improvement over time in both math and reading. Cecilia Rouse of Princeton has conducted a third study in an effort to resolve the methodological issues; she concluded that voucher students' scores in reading did not differ from their public-school counterparts, but were higher in math. Still, fundamental questions remain about the appropriate sample to use for comparison purposes and especially about the characteristics of families choosing to enter the voucher program in the first place. One strikingly consistent characteristic is the relatively higher level of mothers' education. For a summary comparison, see CERAI at http://www.uwm.edu/Dept/CERAI/EdVouchers/educationalvouchers.html and http://www.aft.org/research/vouchers/mil/rouse2/rouse2.html. See also John F. Witte, Jr., *The Market Approach to Education* (Princeton, N.J.: Princeton University Press, 1999); Jay P. Greene, Paul E. Peterson, and Jiangtao Du, "Effectiveness of School Choice: The Milwaukee Experiment," Occasional paper 97-1 (March 1997). Available on the Internet at http://www.ksg.harvard.edu/ pepg/mil.htm; and Cecilia Rouse, "Private School Vouchers and Student Achievement: An Evaluation of the Milwaukee Parental Choice Program," *The Quarterly Journal of Economics* 113, No. 2 (1998).

99. *Supra* note 4 at 56, "Completions, Education Attainment 2000."

100. *Ibid.* at 47, "Transitions to College, Who is Prepared for College."

101. *Ibid.*

102. The Institute for Higher Education Policy, *The Tuition Puzzle: Putting the Pieces Back Together* (Washington, D.C.: The Institute for Higher Education Policy, February 1999). Available on the Internet at http://www.ihep.com/ PUB.htm.

103. The College Board, "Trends in College Pricing 2000." Available on the Internet at http://www.collegeboard.org/policy/html/pafa.html.

104. *Ibid.*

105. The College Board, "Trends in Student Aid 2000." Available on the Internet at http://www.collegeboard.org/policy/html/pafa.html.

106. *Ibid.* at 4.

107. Jacques Steinberg, "Looking at Higher Education, Report Finds Vast Differences Among States," *The New York Times* (December 1, 2000).

108. American Council on Education, "Students of Color Make Gains in Higher Education, ACE Report Shows," *Higher Education and National Affairs* 49, no. 3 (February 14, 2000). Available on the Internet at http://www.acenet.edu/ hena/issues/2000/02_14_00/status_report.html citing American Council on Education, *The Seventeenth Annual Status Report on Minorities in Higher Education* (Washington, D.C.: American Council on Education, 2000).

CHAPTER 5

Children and Families in Crisis

We enter the new millennium at an important crossroads in securing safety, permanence, and well-being for children and families in crisis. We know more than ever about the needs of these children and families. We know more about what we must do to make sure that they have basic supports. We know more about how to prevent and treat child abuse and neglect, domestic violence, substance abuse, and mental health problems. Some communities and states are using this knowledge to craft new approaches to service delivery with the help of multiple service systems, informal support networks, and new community partners. Most importantly, there is an increasing understanding that it takes all of us to protect children. Policy makers, service providers of all types, community leaders, young people, and family members must all be engaged to ensure that as a society, we make better choices for children and families and help them make better choices for themselves.

However, serious challenges remain. Children continue to be abused and neglected as their parents struggle with substance abuse, domestic violence, and poverty.

Child welfare systems are overloaded, and children linger in foster care without the assurance of permanent families. The special services these children and families need are scarce. Kin who provide a vital safety net for families in crisis are struggling to support the children they raise. Troubled families continue to depend on troubled systems — agencies, courts, and service providers that face a lack of resources, staff, and links to communities.

Keeping every child safe in a nurturing family and community requires attention to increasing the capacity of public and private agencies, communities, families, and individuals to identify and implement the best available solutions for families in crisis. To accomplish this goal, the use of existing supports must be maximized, new resources and partnerships must be created, and new ways of doing business must be established. At the same time, the quality and availability of health care, child care, education, housing, income supports, youth violence prevention, and other basic supports that are essential for all children and families, especially for those carrying added burdens, must continue to be improved.

Children and Families in Crisis: The Needs Continue

Child abuse and neglect continue at high levels

According to the Department of Health and Human Services (HHS), 2.9 million children were reported as abused or neglected and referred to public child protection agencies for investigation or assessment in 1998. Nationally, approximately 903,000 children were determined to be victims of maltreatment. More than half the children who were maltreated suffered neglect, while just over one-third suffered physical or sexual abuse. One-quarter of the children were victims of more than one type of maltreatment. Only about half of the victims of child abuse and/or neglect received services after the investigation was completed. As in past years, infants and toddlers had the highest abuse and neglect rates. Preschool children under five accounted for 78 percent of the 1,100 children who died of abuse and neglect in 1998.[1]

At first glance, these figures indicate a decline in child abuse and neglect that started in 1994 when 1,011,628 children were reported as abused and neglected. Although there seems to be a real decline in some states, in others the reductions are more likely due to changes in the way states are responding to reports of abuse and neglect and other administrative anomalies than to actual reductions in maltreatment.

Some states, such as Arizona, Missouri, New Jersey, Ohio, North Dakota, and South Dakota, have instituted alternative response systems to provide assessments and services to families who are reported to child protection agencies but do not appear to present problems that warrant investigation. These cases are diverted from the child protection agency and never turn up as investigations. In other states, such as Kansas, between 1997 and 1998 the large decreases in reports, investigations, and substantiated cases of child abuse and neglect were attributed to the conversion of the state's data collection system. In Maine, one-third of the reports were not assigned for investigation because staff resources were not available, a problem that likely occurred in other states as well. All of these changes would affect counts from one year to the next.[2]

Gaps remain in substance abuse treatment

The 1999 National Household Survey reported that 14.8 million Americans were current users[3] of illicit drugs in 1999, and 3.6 million were identified as dependent[4] on illicit drugs. A total of 11.8 million people were dependent on alcohol and/or illicit drugs.[5]

Approximately 8.3 million children lived in households where one or more parents were dependent on alcohol or in need of treatment for illicit drug use.[6] Children whose parents abuse alcohol and drugs are almost three times more likely to be abused and more than four times more likely to be neglected than children of parents who do not abuse alcohol and drugs.[7] State child protection agencies report that as many as 40 to 80 percent of the children referred to them are from families with alcohol or drug problems.[8] Nationally, only about 20 to 25 percent of those persons in need of treatment for alcoholism and/or drugs receive it. While there is a shortage in all types of publicly funded substance abuse treatment services, treatment that is specially tailored to meet the needs of women and parents is in chronically short supply. Parents with substance abuse problems who are in the child welfare system face multiple and especially complex problems such as mental illness, domestic violence, health

- An estimated 2.9 million children were reported as suspected victims of child abuse and neglect and referred for investigation or assessment in 1998; 903,000 of them were confirmed as victims of child maltreatment.

- Young children are most at risk for being abused and neglected. They also enter foster care in greater numbers than any other age group and remain in care longer than other children.

- Child abuse and domestic violence co-occur in an estimated 30 to 60 percent of the families where there is some form of family violence.

- A record 568,000 children were reported to be in foster family homes, group homes, or child care institutions as of September 1999 — a 48 percent increase over the past decade. Almost one-third of them are in foster homes with relatives.

- 5.4 million children lived in households headed by a relative other than a parent in 1998. 2.13 million of these children lived with relatives, most often grandparents, with no parent present.

problems like HIV/AIDS, and abuse or neglect as a child.[9] These all pose special challenges for alcohol and drug treatment and recovery.

Domestic violence threatens both children and adults

Domestic violence is one of the most insidious forms of violence that children may experience. It is often chronic, physically and emotionally intense, and children often have no refuge from it. Domestic violence also teaches children that violence is an acceptable behavior — even between those they love and trust the most.

The Bureau of Justice Statistics in the U. S. Department of Justice estimates that about four out of 10 victims of domestic violence live in homes with children under 12.[10] It is estimated that between 3.3[11] and 10 million[12] children witness domestic violence in their homes each year. The overlap between domestic violence and child abuse and neglect is also significant. Child maltreatment and domestic violence co-occur in an estimated 30 to 60 percent of families where there is some form of family violence.[13] Some experts argue that domestic violence is the single most significant precursor to child abuse and neglect fatalities in this country.[14]

Children who witness violence in the home may display a range of emotional and behavioral disturbances, physical disorders, and academic problems.[15] In addition, numerous studies have shown that children who have been exposed to domestic violence are more likely to perpetuate the cycle of violence in their own families and communities.[16] Yet, children have shown remarkable resilience in the face of domestic violence, despite its potential for harm. Studies have shown that the consequences of domestic violence vary, depending on the nature and extent of the violence and the personality of each child.[17] A recent review of current research by the David and Lucile Packard Foundation concluded that "the most important protective resource to enable a child to cope with exposure to violence is a strong relationship with a competent, caring, positive adult, most often a parent."[18]

Mental health problems continue to plague children of all ages

It is estimated that in the United States, one in 10 children and adolescents suffer from mental illness severe enough to cause some level of impairment. Yet, in any given year, only about one in five children receives mental health services — the same as it was 20 years ago.[19] In some cases, the lack of available, appropriate services for children leaves parents with no alternative but to place their children in the custody of the public child welfare system in order to get them the treatment they need.

Study findings reported in February 2000 in the The Journal of the American Medical Association indicated that the number of preschool-age children taking psychotropic medications increased dramatically between 1991 to 1995, when specific treatment settings were examined. The reported increase for the use of Ritalin alone, which carries a warning against use for children under six, was more than 150 percent, and the use of some antidepressants increased by more than 200 percent.[20] In response to the study findings, then-First Lady Hillary Clinton convened a meeting of national organizations representing family members, treatment providers, professionals of various types, and advocates working on behalf of children with mental health problems. The discussion revealed how little is known about the behavioral and emotional needs of these young children and the efficacy of medication and other treatment approaches for them. More effective help is needed for parents, early childhood teachers, child care providers, physicians, and others to address the needs of these children and get them back on track developmentally as quickly as possible.

Foster care caseload at record high

As of September 30, 1999, 568,000 children were in foster care,[21] about three-quarters of them clustered in fewer than one-third of the states. This record number represents an increase of 48.3 percent over the past 10 years.[22] While the numbers of children entering care has decreased, the total number of children in care has increased because fewer children are leaving foster care. The Chapin Hall Center for Children, which operates the Multistate Foster Care Data Archive, reports that in every state in the Archive, infants continue to be the largest group of children entering foster care and they stay in care the longest.[23] In urban areas in Illinois, Maryland, New York, and Ohio, for example, an estimated five of every 100 children between birth to three months in the general population enter foster care shortly after birth.[24]

In fall 1999, 60 percent of the children in care were children of color.[25] Forty-two percent of them were Black, almost three times the percent of Black children in the total child population.[26] On average, a child in foster care was 10 years old, had been in care for almost three years, and was likely to have a plan to return to parents or relatives. Almost one out of five of the children in foster care had no case plan goal. For 46,000 children, their parents' rights had been terminated and those children had been waiting an average of two years for a permanent home. Of the children who left foster care during a six-month period in 1999, 68 percent of the children were reunited with their parents or placed with kin; 16 percent were adopted. Those who left had been in foster care an average of about two years. Half of the children leaving care had been in care less than a year; 21 percent had been in care less than a month.[27]

More than 100,000 children continue to wait for adoptive families

Despite important recent gains in the number of children adopted (see Promoting Adoption discussion), an estimated 118,000 children in foster care who had a goal of adoption continued to wait for permanent families as of September 30, 1999. On average, these children were 4-years-old when they entered care and had been in care for close to four years. Seventy-four percent of the children were in foster family homes, and more than one-third of these were living with relatives.[28]

Staff of the Children's Bureau in HHS reported that of the children adopted between FY 1996 and FY 1999, almost four out of five were age 10 or younger. Almost nine out of 10 of the children received adoption subsidies. About two-thirds of the adoptive parents had been the child's foster parents.[29] Recent research from the Multistate Foster Care Data Archive on adoption of children in foster care demonstrates that the likelihood of adoption declines sharply as the child gets older. Children who enter care as infants are the most likely to exit to adoptive families.[30]

Children raised by kin also have unmet needs

An increasing number of grandparents and other relatives (kinship caregivers) are raising children whose parents are not available due to substance abuse, incarceration, illness, and other crises. Nationally, 5.4 million children live in homes headed by a grandparent or other relative; 2.13 million of these children are being raised by grandparents and other relatives with no parent present

in the home — a 51.5 percent increase since 1990.[31] Studies have reported that grandparents and other relative caregivers are 60 percent more likely to live in poverty than grandparents who do not have the same full-time caregiving responsibilities.[32]

While the vast majority of children in kinship care families live in informal arrangements, some are in the formal foster care system. States typically place 20 to 40 percent of foster children with their relatives.[33] Several of the largest states (California, Florida, Illinois, and New York) account for about half of all the children in public kinship care arrangements.[34]

Inside and outside of the child welfare system, kinship care families have a broad range of needs:

◆ Kinship caregivers sometimes have difficulty enrolling children in school, obtaining medical care and public benefits, staying in public housing, and accessing other important services on behalf of the children they are raising because, even though they are full-time caregivers, kin may not have legal custody or guardianship of the children. Children raised by kinship caregivers may also have difficulty accessing public health insurance through Medicaid and the Children's Health Insurance Program (CHIP). (For a copy of CDF's report on Medicaid and CHIP enrollment of children in kinship care families, and supplemental materials for kinship care families, log on to www.childrensdefense.org.)

◆ Kinship caregivers caring for children in formal foster care settings may have difficulty securing the same support services available to non-related foster families. They may receive little, if any, advance preparation for assuming their roles, less information from child welfare caseworkers, and fewer services for themselves and for the children in their care than their non-kin counterparts.[35]

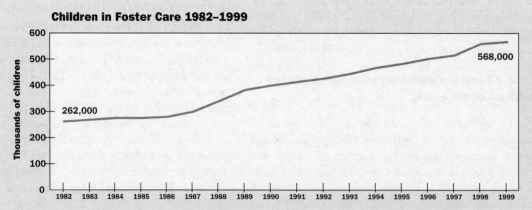

Foster Care

Children in Foster Care 1982–1999

Thousands of children

262,000

568,000

1982 1983 1984 1985 1986 1987 1988 1989 1990 1991 1992 1993 1994 1995 1996 1997 1998 1999

Source: Voluntary Cooperative Information System (VCIS) of the American Public Human Services Association (APHSA) for data through 1996, and Adoption and Foster Care Analysis and Reporting System (AFCARS) for data for 1997-1999. The data reflect the number of children in care on a single date of each year.

◆ Kinship care families often need a variety of personal and family support services (e.g., counseling and access to peer support groups). In the recent Stuart Foundation Kinship Care Study conducted by the Edgewood Center for Children and Families in San Francisco, kinship caregivers participating in the center's Kinship Care Support Network reported a significant need for respite care that would provide them with a break from their daily caregiving responsibilities. Caregivers in that study also reported that they frequently rely on community and faith-based organizations. Generally, these are organizations with which they already have an established relationship of trust, to help them cope with their caregiving responsibilities.[36]

◆ Many kinship caregivers, especially those with lower incomes or living on fixed incomes, have a vital need for financial support. The majority of kinship care families receive no financial help from public programs to assist with their caregiving demands. In some families, children (and sometimes the caregivers) receive financial assistance through the Temporary Assistance for Needy Families (TANF) program. Relatives may be able to receive higher assistance payments if they are caring for children in the foster care system, but stringent licensing requirements may keep them from qualifying as foster parents.

Increase in children with parents who are incarcerated

A growing number of children who end up with kinship caregivers or in foster care are children of incarcerated parents, mostly mothers. Close to 1.5 million children had a parent in state or federal prison in 1999, and 22 percent of them were under five. Since 1991, that number has grown by 59 percent or more than 500,000 children. Black children were nine times and Hispanic children were three times more likely than White children to have a parent in prison.

During that same period, the number of children with a mother in prison (126,100) nearly doubled. Mothers were more likely than fathers to be living with their children prior to the arrest. More than three-quarters of the mothers said their children were living with relatives. Of mothers in state and federal prisons, 9.6 and 3.2 percent, respectively, said their children were in foster care.

Thirty-one percent of the mothers in prison had been living alone with their children before they were detained. Although most parents reported some contact with their children since admission, more than half of both mothers and fathers in state prison reported never having a personal visit. This is not surprising given that fewer than 20 percent of the inmates who were parents were less than 50 miles from their last place of residence.

More than half of the mothers in state and federal prisons reported sentences in excess of five years. More than one-third of the mothers in state prison were sentenced for drug offenses; 11 percent were sentenced for fraud. In federal prison, 74 percent of the mothers were convicted of drug offenses.

The mothers in prison reported more serious drug use histories than fathers and were about twice as likely to have committed their crimes while under the influence of cocaine-based drugs. Twenty-nine percent reported they had committed their crimes while drinking. Mothers were more likely than fathers to have been homeless in the year prior to admission, especially those in state prisons. Half of the mothers in state prisons were also unemployed in the month before their arrest.[37]

Multi-problem families involved in multiple service systems

Too often families have more than one of the needs discussed above. Families in which there is child abuse may be struggling with substance abuse, mental health problems, or domestic violence. For example, families facing these multiple problems or other barriers comprise increasing portions of states' decreasing Temporary Assistance for Needy Families (TANF) caseloads. In a recent report, the National Center for Children in Poverty documented the need to help parents and their young children who are affected by these problems in the context of welfare reform.[38]

Snapshots of America's Families II, the Urban Institute's first look at the well-being of children and adults in the first few years following federal welfare reform, also noted pressures on families. In 1997 and 1999, children in families with incomes below 200 percent of poverty and those living with single parents were more than twice as likely to have a parent reporting symptoms of poor mental health as children in families with incomes over 200 percent of poverty or children living with two parents.[39] The survey also found that public health insurance coverage of low-income parents with children has eroded since passage of the 1996 welfare law. Lack of access to health insurance to help cover the costs of mental health services can exacerbate or help explain the prevalence of mental health problems like these.

Families facing such barriers are also likely to be overrepresented among those families who have been sanctioned and have lost TANF benefits. In *Families Struggling to Make It in the Workforce: A Post Welfare Report*, a report on families who had left welfare since 1996, the Children's Defense Fund noted that many families were pushed off welfare despite serious barriers to employment. These parents were more likely to have mental health problems or face other barriers to employment than any other group of former recipients.[40] The Center on Budget and Policy Priorities, in its analysis of state sanction policies and practices, cited several state studies that found a high prevalence of health and behavioral health barriers to employment in sanctioned families.[41] Families facing such barriers are also more likely to end up in the child welfare system if TANF benefits end and parents have not found employment. But that system already struggles with these problems. Available treatment for such problems far outweighs available resources. Frequently, the comprehensive, coordinated approach to services that these families need is not available, and parents who enter the system, either directly or from the welfare system, are at increased risk of losing their children.

Investments in out-of-home care far exceed preventive investments

Current child welfare spending patterns make it difficult to address adequately the unmet needs described above. Investments in out-of-home care continue to exceed investments in prevention or other services. Expenditure data collected by the Urban Institute from state child welfare agencies indicate that in 1998, states spent more than three times as much on out-of-home placements than on adoption and other services. In the 17 states that were able to categorize all of their spending, 63 percent of the total was spent for out-of-home care, 9 percent for adoption, 17 percent for other services, and 11 percent for administration. The vast majority of federal funds ($4.5 billion of the $7.1 billion spent) went for out-of-home care, most of it funded under the Title IV-E Foster Care Program.[42] Services to address the complex, multiple needs of the children and families in the child welfare system and to adequately support children with kin remain in short supply.

Inadequate care challenged

The crises and overwhelming demands facing child welfare systems across the country have been repeatedly documented throughout the year. In about half the states, consent decrees are in place or lawsuits are pending that address inadequate, sometimes abusive, conditions for children in the care of public child welfare agencies and some of the private agencies with which they contract. The District of Columbia continues to operate under a 7-year-old court order requiring the District's child welfare agency to improve its care and services for abused and neglected children. In 2000, new lawsuits challenging child welfare system failures were filed in Tennessee and Florida by Children's Rights, Inc. The Tennessee suit, *Brian A., et al. v. Sundquist*, charges that the state failed to provide the safety and permanence to children, which they have a right to under both federal and state laws. *Foster Chil-*

dren Bonnie L., et al. v. Bush, filed in Florida, challenged the failure of the state's Department of Children and Family Services to provide appropriate services and support for children in foster care. The suit highlights overcrowding, inadequate supervision, threats to children's safety, and the lack of medical care and education for foster children. It also addresses the state's failure to move these children to permanent homes in a timely and proper way. In some states, such litigation has prompted important system improvements and has been a catalyst for broader reforms. In others, it has stimulated increased resources that have helped officials undertake necessary innovations.

Opportunities to Increase Capacity in Service Delivery Systems, Communities, and Families

Promoting adoption

In December 1996, former President Clinton committed to at least doubling the number of foster child adoptions and other permanent placements by 2002. In FY 1999, states were more than halfway toward that goal. Forty-six thousand children who had been waiting in foster care or in pre-adoptive families were adopted that year, a 64 percent increase since FY 1996, when only 28,000 children were adopted from foster care.[43]

The expedited timelines for decision-making in the Adoption and Safe Families Act (ASFA) and the new fiscal incentives in ASFA helped to prompt the adoption increases. ASFA was enacted in 1997 with the goal of promoting safety and permanence for children. Among other things, it authorized adoption incentive payments to states that increased their adoptions of children from foster care over an established baseline. States are eligible to receive incentive payments for each child adopted over the baseline and higher payments for children with special needs who were in the federal adoption assistance program. The increasing number of adoptions represented a positive development for children who were in the limbo of foster care or placed with adoptive families but never formally adopted.

Forty-two states were eligible for adoption incentive payments in FY 1999. In the two years in which the incentive payments have been made available, every state plus the District of Columbia and Puerto Rico have qualified for the bonuses for at least one year. The National Association of State Adoption Programs surveyed the 35 states that were awarded adoption incentive payments for FY 1998 and found that the funds were being invested in adoptive parent recruitment, pre- and post-adoption services, increased hiring and training of adoption staff, and other adoption activities.[44] A challenge remains, however, to ensure that Congress appropriates sufficient funds to reward fully those states that qualify for the incentive payments. Efforts to expand funding by $15 million for FY 2001 were not successful.

In response to the increased emphasis on adoption, more is being done to identify children who are ready for adoption and parents who want to adopt, to expedite the agency and court processes involved in finalizing adoptions, and to provide post-adoption services to families to ensure permanent adoptive placements.[45] In 2000, Congress authorized funding, but did not provide it, for a national public awareness campaign and project grants focused on the adoption of children with special needs. The grants would focus on the children waiting in foster care for adoptive families; support groups for adoptive parents, adopted children, and siblings of adopted children; and research to identify the reasons for adoption disruptions.[46] As adoptions have increased, there are growing concerns that the push for adoption could result in children being moved prematurely into adoptive families before the children or families are ready. As a result, potential adoptions may be disrupted before they are finalized or dissolved after finalization, although no data are available yet to determine whether there is real cause for concern.

Some of the adoption activities underway are creative collaborations between agencies, courts, attorneys, and adoption advocates. Many have focused on eliminating the backlog of children who were in the system at the time ASFA was enacted and are still waiting for permanent adoptive homes.

◆ **First Mondays.** In the Salt Lake City Juvenile Court, at least one judge holds adoption reviews on the first Monday of every month for all children whose parents' rights were terminated in her court and who are awaiting finalization of adoption. These group reviews help to prevent the creation of "legal orphans" — children whose parents' rights have been terminated but who continue to wait for new parents. Caseworkers must prepare monthly reports for the judge in advance. The goal of the group meeting is to identify ways of removing barriers that prevent children from finding permanent homes. All parties are held accountable for making reasonable efforts to find permanent homes for the children for whom they are responsible.[47]

◆ **Adoption Saturdays.** In Los Angeles County, four Adoption Saturdays were held in 2000, and each event finalized an average of about 300 adoptions. The Alliance for Children's Rights in Los Angeles coordinates a network of pro bono and staff attorneys who can help expedite the paperwork for children whose parents' rights have already been terminated but still wait for long periods for their adoptions to be finalized. Since April 1998, this approach for handling uncontested adoptions has been expanded to other California counties, and in November 2000, National Adoption Days were held in major cities in five other states and in the District of Columbia.[48]

Court initiatives to promote permanency will be enhanced by the Strengthening Abuse and Neglect Courts Act (SANCA), once it is funded.[49] SANCA, which was enacted in 2000, authorizes funding for courts to improve their systems of tracking children through the child welfare system, eliminate backlogs of children waiting to be adopted, and expand the Court Appointed Special Advocates (CASA) Program.

Other states and organizations are focused on enhancing post-adoption services, recognizing that adoption is a lifelong process and families may need ongoing support at different times as the child grows up. These

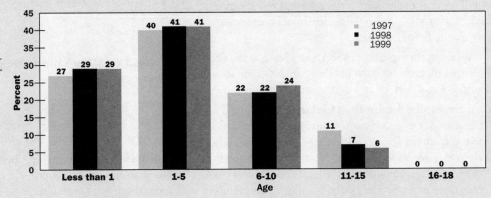

Children Waiting for Permanent Homes

Age of Waiting Children at Time of Removal, FY 1997–FY 1999

Source: Penelope L. Maza, The Latest from AFCARS on Adoptions and Waiting Children, Children's Bureau, Sixth National Child Welfare Conference, March 2000.

New Jersey Took the Adoption and Safe Families Act Mandates Seriously

I n its Adoption and Safe Families Act (ASFA) review, New Jersey found that almost 4,000 of the 6,500 children in foster care were in the queue for adoption. Adoption officials and advocates, working closely with legislators, were able to quantify what resources it would take to get these children adopted or into other permanent homes. They also had a vision of how the system should work for waiting children. As a result, the Governor approved $6 million to assist with a state permanency project. The funds became available in July 2000. Since then, staffing in the regional adoption centers has been increased by more than 100 staff. A new office also has been established to focus exclusively on children being adopted by parents other than their foster parents. It will pursue expedited and specialized placements for the children, explore legal options other than adoption when appropriate, and help promote intensive casework to help prepare children and families for adoption or other permanency options.

services are important to prevent adoptions from dissolving and children returning to foster care.

◆ **Maine Adoption Guides.** The Maine Adoption Guides Program offers ongoing support to help families who have adopted children with special needs. These services are in addition to the adoption assistance payments and Medicaid that all parents who adopt children with special needs in the state receive. Casey Family Services' Post-Adoption Services Program trains the social workers who serve as Adoption Guides to support the adoptions by helping the families get ongoing respite care, short- or long-term therapy, access to an adoptive support group, crisis services, and advocacy with schools, health and mental health service providers, and others. The Maine Department of Human Services uses federal Title IV-E dollars through a Waiver Demonstration Program and Medicaid dollars to pay for the services. An extensive evaluation is underway.[50]

Services like these can help communities reduce the backlog of children waiting for adoptive families and ensure permanent families are maintained. As a result, the overall number of children in the system is reduced, and children who enter care in the future should be more likely to get the help they need.

While states implement ASFA, Congress has focused on other groups of adopted children. In 2000, substantial attention was given to intercountry adoptions:

◆ **Citizenship for Foreign-Born Children.** The Child Citizenship Act of 2000[51] confers automatic and retroactive U.S. citizenship on all foreign-born children who are under 18, admitted to the United States as lawful permanent residents, and in the legal and physical custody of at least one parent who is a U.S. citizen. These children include those adopted from abroad and other foreign-born children of American parents. The act

addresses the unintended consequences of a 1996 immigration law that makes noncitizens, including foreign-born children of American parents, who commit certain crimes subject to mandatory deportation even if they have lived in the United States since infancy and have no ties to the country where they were born.

◆ **Hague Convention on Intercountry Adoption.** The Intercountry Adoption Act of 2000[52] ratifies and implements the Hague Convention on Intercountry Adoption, which the United States signed in 1994. The act establishes the State Department as the central authority to oversee and coordinate international adoptions with other countries. It also requires special accreditation standards for international adoptions to help ensure quality care for children and to prevent illegal trafficking and fraud involving children.

Supporting kin

In response to the growing numbers of children raised by grandparents and other relatives inside and outside of the child welfare system, policy makers, government agencies, and community and faith-based organizations are using a variety of strategies to build service capacity and empower kinship care families.

Expansion of state laws to help kinship care families

In the past year, several states have passed laws that eliminate legal barriers and create new financial and family supports for kinship care families.

◆ **Subsidized guardianship programs.** Subsidized guardianship programs provide continuing public financial support for children who exit the child welfare system under the guardianship of grandparents and other relative caregivers who cared for them in foster care and agree to look after them permanently. States use several different types of financing mechanisms to fund these programs. This year, California implemented a subsidized guardianship program funded by TANF funds,[53] bringing the total number of TANF-funded subsidized guardianship programs to five states and one county. In addition, seven states have been granted waivers to use federal funds from the Title IV-E Foster Care Program to establish subsidized guardianship programs under the Child Welfare Waiver Demonstration Program. Several additional states have established state-funded subsidized guardianship programs financed by a combination of sources that provide maintenance subsidies for children living with kin inside and outside of the child welfare system.[54] These include Louisiana's Grandparent Subsidy Program, which became effective in March 2000.[55]

◆ **Standby guardianship laws.** Providing a less adversarial alternative to traditional custody and guardianship laws, standby guardianship laws allow parents to designate a grandparent or other relative to assume legal responsibility for a child if the parent dies or become incapacitated. In 2000, Minnesota[56] became the 18th state to enact a standby guardianship law.[57]

Increasing support services for kinship care families

National and community-based organizations are also mobilizing to expand the supportive services available to kinship care families. Examples of these efforts in the past year include:

◆ **Comprehensive kinship care support programs.** The Tennessee Department of Children's Services (DCS) is building support for kinship families outside the foster care system. Using TANF funding, DCS is contracting with community-based agencies in three pilot regions to create coordinated Kinship Support Networks that deliver basic services to kinship care families, including respite care, parenting classes, homemaker services, and transportation.[58] Generations United, a national organization that focuses on the needs of kinship care families, as well as other issues, also received a grant from HHS to work with The Brookdale Foundation to create the Kin Net Project, a network of 20 support groups across the country that will be specifically designed to help kin raising children in the child welfare system.

◆ **Creating specialized mental health services.** Generations United is also working with the Center for Mental Health Services in HHS and The Brookdale Foundation to establish support groups for grand-

parents and other relative caregivers in four mental health centers across the country.

Federal recognition of kinship caregivers' commitment

Congress passed the National Family Caregiver Support Act in 2000, recognizing the needs of grandparents and other relative caregivers.[59] The act, which is part of the Older Americans Act, authorizes grants to states to provide supportive services for grandparents and other relative caregivers, including information about available services, counseling, support groups, and respite care.

The Kinship Care Advisory Panel, established by ASFA, made recommendations for the HHS report to Congress on children in kinship foster care placements. The report emphasized the need to maintain policies that adequately ensure the safety of all children in the child welfare system, including those living in relative placements.[60] Expressing concern about children's safety, in January 2000, HHS also issued child welfare regulations that require states to use one set of licensing standards in approving kin and non-kin foster parents for federal foster care reimbursement.[61] While this change was intended to enhance safety, some are concerned that it will deter relative caregivers who cannot meet some of the non-safety related measures included in licensing standards from applying to be foster parents.

Assisting older youths transitioning from foster care

In the first year since it was enacted, the Foster Care Independence Act, and the John H. Chafee Foster Care Independence Program that it established (Chafee Foster Care Program), has raised awareness of the needs of the estimated 20,000 young people who leave foster care each year without having been adopted or reunited with their families.

The Chafee Foster Care Program is designed to promote practice-level and system-level changes aimed at improving and expanding services for young people transitioning from foster care, strengthening partnerships to expand the continuum of support for them, and giving youths and others more voice in deciding how services are delivered. The long-term goal is to make independent living an integrated part of the whole child welfare services continuum for young people in foster care.[62] All states have received their funding for the first year of the Chafee Foster Care Program and are in different stages of preparation of the required four-year plan they must submit to HHS.[63]

Four states, Arizona, California, New Jersey, and Wyoming, have already taken advantage of another provision in the Foster Care Independence Act that allows states to extend Medicaid to young people ages 18 to 21 who are transitioning from foster care. When states take full advantage of the Medicaid option, all young people who were in foster care and under the responsibility of the state on their 18th birthday and who are not yet 21, can be automatically eligible for Medicaid, regardless of their income.[64] In December 2000, the Administration on Children, Youth and Families and the Center for Medicaid and State Operations in the Health Care Financing Administration in HHS encouraged state Child Welfare and Medicaid directors to work together to extend the new Medicaid health benefit and ensure that children transitioning from foster care get the physical and mental health care they need.[65]

In 2000, Congress also took another step to help young people aging out of foster care. It expanded eligibility for the Family Unification Program to youths aging out of foster care at age 18. Prior to the change, the U.S. Department of Housing and Urban Development awarded Section 8 vouchers under the Family Unification Program to communities so the child welfare and local housing authorities could offer housing assistance only to families whose children were at risk of placement in foster care or to assist children of any age who were preparing to return to their families from foster care.

Young people who have "aged out" of foster care and other graduates of the child welfare system played an important role in getting the Foster Care Independence Act enacted. It is also critically important that they be actively involved in states as the Chafee Foster Care Program and related independent living activities are being implemented. Participants in the California Youth Connection, an organization of current and former foster care youths, worked hard to get California to extend Medicaid to young people leaving care. It had done a special report on the need for mental health services for youths in and transitioning from foster care.[66] Another of the California Youth Connection members explored the opinions of a large group of young people who were or had been in foster care to learn about the types of services that might have been helpful to their families when they first entered care.[67]

A similar leadership movement of young people is beginning in the mental health system. Young people, both current and former consumers of mental health services, are becoming actively engaged in mental health systems reform in some states. Allowing youths to have a voice in efforts to reform service delivery systems can not only improve programs and outcomes for them but also build their leadership skills, self-confidence, and a sense of direction. Some have gotten involved through participation as youth mentors, in youth advisory boards to agencies and programs, or through community service so they can give back to the communities that have helped them.[68] Several young people delivered a message about the importance of recognizing them and their need for appropriate treatment at the Surgeon General's First National Conference on Children's Mental Health.[69]

Such involvement by young people who have been in the child welfare and mental health systems builds on the principles of youth development being implemented in education and other areas. For too long it was assumed that the young people in these two systems could not make any decisions for themselves, made bad decisions when they did, and could not assume leadership. The leadership initiatives are not without their trouble spots and challenges, and it is important to train adults partnering with the young people as well as the teens themselves, but such activities can enrich the efforts in which partnerships are sought and add value to all involved.

Helping children exposed to domestic violence

Building on the importance of supportive adult relationships for children who have witnessed domestic violence, several promising initiatives are underway across the country to forge new relationships within communities to help children:

◆ **Now focus on multi-disciplinary partnerships to improve service responses for child and adult victims of domestic violence.** The David and Lucile Packard Foundation, in its publication *Domestic Violence and Children,* brought together advocates for women who are victims of domestic violence and advocates for children as well as representatives from the health, education, child care, and law enforcement fields to create a blueprint for multi-disciplinary partnerships that better serve the needs of children who experience domestic violence.[70] Among other strategies, the authors recommend that professionals who have regular contact with families and children, including teachers, child care workers, health and mental health care providers, law enforcement officers, child welfare workers, and court personnel, should receive training on domestic violence and its impact on children. They also emphasize the importance of educating the public and engaging public support of programs that address the impact of domestic violence on children.

◆ **A strategic public response to the impact of domestic violence on children.** In a recent report by The Open Society Institute's Center on Crime, Communities and Culture, *Domestic Violence and Children: Creating a Public Response,* a team of domestic violence experts and children's advocates recommended strategies for crafting a more effective public policy response to the impact of domestic violence on children. It is based on the premise that the well-being of children who experience domestic violence can be restored if their parents get the help they need to restore safety and stability in their lives. The report also emphasized that because of the harm created by repeated and ongoing exposure to violence, interventions must be designed to reach children at the earliest possible moment.[71]

◆ **Improved coordination between child welfare and domestic violence agencies and the courts.** The National Council of Juvenile and Family Court Judges' (NCJFCJ) guidelines for better coordination between domestic violence and child maltreatment agencies and the courts is drawing attention to the overlap between domestic violence and child maltreatment.[72] In working together, these organizations commit to developing policies and procedures to enhance the safety and well-being of women and children. A number of agencies within the U.S. Departments of Justice and Health and Human Services also collaborated to fund comprehensive service sites in six communities—San Francisco, California; Santa Clara County, California; El Paso County, Colorado; St. Louis County, Missouri; Grafton County, New Hampshire; and Lane County, Oregon—to implement the NCJFCJ's guidelines. These sites will, among other things, train domestic violence and child welfare workers and court staff on the relationship between domestic violence and child maltreatment and the broader impact of domestic violence on children and involve a broader range of community organizations in their activities. The NCJFCJ, Family Violence Prevention Fund, and American Public Human Services Association will provide technical assistance to the communities.

◆ **Legislation and guidelines to help women and children victimized by domestic violence.** Helping battered women find shelter and support services helps their children. In September 2000, Congress reauthorized the Violence Against Women Act, which renewed funding for prevention, education, treatment services, and support programs that address the needs of battered women. In a provision aimed specifically at child victims of domestic violence, the law authorized a pilot program awarding grants to states for establishing "safe havens" for children where they can interact safely with the battering parent.[73] In addition, the Children's Health Act of 2000 authorized funding for programs in local communities to assist children in dealing with the psychological effects of violence, including domestic violence.[74] On another front, the National Advisory Council on Violence Against Women issued in 2000, *Ending Violence Against Women: An Agenda for the Nation*, a blueprint for government agencies to work together to end domestic violence, sexual assault, and stalking.[75]

While partnerships and strategies are being developed to protect children who witness domestic violence, there is concern that in the haste to protect children, some jurisdictions are instituting new rules that may exacerbate the harm to the child as well as the adult victim of the battering. Even though most child abuse and neglect laws already provide grounds for pursuing parents who allow their child to be abused without trying to protect the child, some states have explicitly amended their child abuse laws to make witnessing domestic violence per se abuse. There is also an increasing trend in other jurisdictions towards prosecuting the non-battering parent for failure to protect a child from witnessing abuse or from being abused by the violent parent. This may result in removing the child from the non-battering parent on whom the child most depends. Too frequently neither of these approaches considers the nature of the harm experienced by the child, the efforts of the non-battering parent to protect the child, or other vital protective factors.

Meeting the Mental Health Needs of Young People

A collaborative effort between the Departments of Health and Human Services, Justice, and Education, the first Surgeon General's Conference on Children's Mental Health was held in 2000. Building on the recommendations in the 1999 *Surgeon General's First Report on Mental Health*, the meeting was convened to develop the National Action Agenda for Children's Mental Health. The conference highlighted innovative activities and made a strong case for the necessity to do more to appropriately identify children's mental health needs early, to recognize and address disparities in the quality and availability of services, to increase funding for services, and to ensure the effectiveness of services for children with differing needs. There was emphasis on the need to help very young children and older youths with serious emotional disturbances and on the extent to which the stigma attached to mental health problems prevents children from getting the help they need. Later in the year, the National Institute of Mental Heath and the Food and Drug Administration also convened a meeting to consider the research needs in the field of psychopharmaceuticals for young children and the efficacy of such treatment.

Released in January 2001, the Surgeon's General's National Action Agenda for Children's Mental Health has as its vision a commitment to:

◆ Recognizing mental health as an essential part of child health

◆ Integrating family, child, and youth-centered mental health services in all child-serving systems

◆ Engaging families and the perspectives of children and youths in all mental health care planning

◆ Developing and enhancing a public–private health infrastructure to support this vision[76]

Such a vision is in place, at least in part, in a number of the 43 "systems of care" sites underway in 37 states. These activities, funded under the Comprehensive Community Mental Health Services for Children and Their Families Program, engage parents as well as multiple child-serving systems in broadening the range of individually tailored services for young people and their families. In the systems of care, services must include at least diagnosis and evaluation, outpatient, emergency, intensive home-based and day treatment, transitional and case management, and respite care. Initial findings of evaluations from various sites conducted for the Center for Mental Health Services in the Department of Health and Human Services show some positive impact on school performance and reduced involvement in the juvenile justice system. There have also been some positive reductions in out-of-home care and the length of stay when out-of-home placements are necessary. In some cases, the sites also promote broader system reforms. In Kansas, for example, two sites were instrumental in helping the state get a Home and Community Medicaid Waiver, which allowed the state to open up community-based treatment opportunities for many more children with serious emotional disturbances. Maine now uses the systems of care approach, developed in one of its sites, across the state.[77]

In 2000, Congress authorized new funding for programs that integrate child welfare and mental health services for children and youths at risk of entering the child welfare system as part of the Children's Health Act of 2000. Forty million dollars was also authorized in the same bill to treat individuals with a co-occurring mental health and substance abuse disorders, although efforts to allow states to use both mental health and substance abuse block grant dollars for funding these integrated treatment programs were not successful.[78]

Responding to parental substance abuse and child safety

While substance abuse did not have the same visibility as mental health issues in 2000, some important activities are underway. According to a public opinion poll conducted for Drug Strategies, three in five Americans say that drug use is a public health problem better handled by prevention and treatment programs than by the criminal justice system. Three years ago, slightly more than half of the respondents categorized drug use as a public health problem.[79]

In 2000, the National Treatment Plan Initiative for Improving Substance Abuse Treatment issued *Changing the Conversation.*[80] It describes the consensus among a broad range of consumers and other experts about what needs to be done to make effective substance abuse treatment available to all who need it. Some communities and states are using themes similar to those in the National Treatment Plan to address the alcohol and drug problems of families who come to the attention of the child welfare system. These emerging programs and activities recognize alcoholism and drug dependence as treatable illnesses; the importance of individualized high quality treatment that is timely, affordable, and sufficiently intensive; and the benefits of treatment for not only the client but for the client's children and family and the broader community:

◆ In 2000, Arizona and Maryland passed legislation that increases resources for comprehensive services to treat parents whose substance abuse is a barrier to preserving or reunifying their families. Arizona uses TANF funding for services to assist families with alcohol and drug problems in both the child welfare and TANF systems. The Maryland legislation first requires that the state Departments of Human Resources and Health and Mental Hygiene develop and administer a protocol for integrating their services; funding will then be provided in 2001.[81] The Maryland and Arizona initiatives both include some similarities to the proposed bipartisan Child Protection Alcohol and Drug Partnership Act that was introduced in Congress in 2000 and again in early 2001.[82] The proposed legislation would provide funds to states where the child welfare and alcohol and drug agencies jointly undertake activities to address comprehensively the needs of children and families with substance abuse problems who come to the attention of the child welfare agency.

◆ A cluster of states, including Delaware, New Hampshire, Illinois, Maryland, and Massachusetts, have promoted staff partnerships by outstationing alcohol and drug staff in child protection offices to assist child welfare workers who are helping families with substance abuse problems. Some are involving parents in recovery as mentors for parents who are in treatment and working their way through the child welfare system.

In studying the effectiveness of substance abuse treatment, experts report that drug addiction treatment works as well as treatment of other chronic illnesses.[83] HHS reports that nearly one-third of those in treatment achieve permanent abstinence in their first attempt at recovery. An additional one-third have periods of relapse but eventually achieve long-term abstinence, and one-third have chronic relapses that result in premature death from substance abuse and related consequences.[84] Treatment also improves physical and mental health, increases rates of employment, and reduces the incidence of criminal behavior. Numerous studies also show that longer lengths of stay and treatment completion are linked with better outcomes.

Although research on treatment of women with children is scarce, reports from a cross-site evaluation of 34 residential programs for women, which serve pregnant women or women and children, show promising results despite very complex problems faced by the families. Eighty percent of the more than 1,800 women in the sample had been investigated at least once by child protective services, and 57 percent had one or more children removed from their custody temporarily or permanently. Many women reported histories of abuse or neglect as children. Most of them had been abused at some point in their lives. Those who successfully completed their planned treatment showed reductions in alcohol and drug use and arrests and increases in employment. Those who left treatment early also showed improvement on these same indicators but not to the same degree. For the almost 600 pregnant women in residential treatment, rates of adverse birth outcomes were lower than would be expected for substance abusing women and also lower than in the general population. Only 5.9 percent of the babies born while in treatment with their mothers had low birthweight, and the infant mortality rate was 0.3 percent, below the national average of 0.7 percent.[85]

Reaching across systems and into communities

Several communities across the country are forming progressive new partnerships that will better protect children and support families. In Jacksonville, Florida, for example, the Community Partnership for Protecting Children has built new relationships among service providers, developed a network of community supports for residents, and engaged family members and community representatives in developing individualized supports.[86] At the Governor's urging, the Florida legislature has allocated about $3 million to expand the partnerships to 11 additional sites in the state, five of them in the Jacksonville area.

The connections formed in partnership sites, like those in Jacksonville, also educate parents about the Adoption and Safe Families Act. ASFA is discussed at community meetings and family group conferences. The St. Louis Neighborhood Network, together with the local child protective services agency and the family court, made a video that educates families about ASFA while they are

waiting at the courthouse. Some partnership sites also make special arrangements to facilitate visitation, which is key to helping families meet the ASFA timelines. In Louisville, Kentucky, Neighborhood Partners help facilitate visits between parents and children. In St. Louis, the Family Resource Center (one of the community partners) trains its workers to help child protective service workers facilitate visitation by transporting children and monitoring the visits.

Other types of partnerships are also enhancing ASFA's goals of promoting safety and permanence for children. Courts and agencies in many communities are now using family group decision-making, a unique process that involves the bringing together, in some individual cases, of relatives, friends, and others to plan how to protect the child and support the family. Many advocates of family group decision-making say that convening an informal support network to develop a plan for the child naturally supports ASFA's goals. Parents are generally more willing to accept services and follow through when they have been involved in developing the service plan. "Families come up with things workers never would have thought of," said one staff member. In Louisville, Kentucky, where the Community Partnership for Protecting Children is doing family group decision-making, 93 percent of the children had been placed according to the plan developed by the group and over three-fourths of them were in the same placement six months later. There had been no new reports to child protective services.

The real challenge in activities like these is to educate communities about their responsibility in keeping children safe. Parents, community residents, and neighborhood leaders must be committed and engaged from the beginning in making a community safe for children. Public and private agency staff must build on families' strengths. Funding must be available to support the comprehensive array of formal and informal supports that community members and staff need to support children and their families. In 2000, legislation protecting parents who abandon their babies at hospitals, police stations, and some other "safe havens" from prosecution was passed in 15 states. The bills have focused on the worthy goal of saving the lives of these infants. Unfortunately, most of these states did not take the crucial step of determining why parents felt they had no options but to abandon their children and then expand community supports for these families and others within their state. More must be done.

Increasing accountability

Important groundwork was laid in 2000 for increased accountability for child safety and permanence. More was done to assess the impact of state child welfare policies and practices on children and families including birth, foster, adoptive, and kinship care families. HHS issued *Child Welfare Outcomes 1998,* a publication mandated by ASFA that included data to establish a baseline for measuring states' performance on seven specified outcomes for children and families.[87] States are required to report annually on these outcomes and to address outcomes in their annual Child and Family Service Reviews, which will be conducted by HHS. While not all of the states have yet been able to report data on all of the outcome measures, *Child Welfare Outcomes 1998* provides an opportunity for advocates and providers to meet with child welfare staff and agree on what additional data are needed, how to get them, and what needs to be done to ensure safety and permanence for children.

HHS also announced an important new initiative for reviewing states' performance in the delivery of services to children and families who come to the attention of the child welfare system. The goal of the new Child and Family Service Review process is to assess the state's actual results for children and families and to determine states' conformity with requirements in federal law. The new review process, described in federal regulations issued in January 2000,[88] involves a more comprehensive, hands-on process than was required in the past. The reviews will be conducted in 17 states in 2001 (with the remaining states reviewed over the next two years).[89]

The reviews should provide a comprehensive look at state agency performance. First, states, together with a broad group of stakeholders they designate, must conduct a self-assessment of various factors to measure the state's ability to deliver services that lead to improved outcomes for children and families. After the statewide assessment, an on-site review that focuses on program areas identified as requiring improvement or further examination will be conducted by the state and an external review team, including staff from the federal Administration for Children and Families (ACF). This part of the review process includes a review of up to 50 cases of children in the child welfare system, involving case records and interviews with children and families, caseworkers, foster parents and service providers, and other key stakeholders involved with the children and families.

After both parts of the review are complete, ACF will decide, based on the recommendation of the review team, whether a state conforms to the protections required for children and families in federal law. States that are approved will be reviewed again in five years, unless problems are identified earlier. States that are not operating in conformity with federal law can develop a program improvement plan to address the problem areas and will have up to two years to address them before any fiscal penalties will be imposed for non-conformity. Those

states that are in conformity may also choose to implement a program improvement plan process to increase the effectiveness of its services for children and families.

The Child and Family Service Review process is unique in its comprehensiveness, its inclusiveness, and its opportunities for corrective action that could benefit children and families. It has great potential to increase states' accountability for ensuring the safety and permanence of children in the child welfare system. State officials and advocates can also use the reviews to educate communities about the problems facing the child welfare system and the children and families it serves and how various stakeholders can work together to address these problems.

Moving Forward: A 2001 Agenda for Action

The goal must be to keep all children safe in nurturing, permanent families and communities. We must build upon what we know about the needs of children and families in crisis and how to prevent and treat the child abuse and neglect, domestic violence, substance abuse, and mental health problems that threaten children's safety and well-being. New partnerships are needed among multiple service systems and agencies, those providing informal support, and new community partners. Parents, grandparents and other relatives, young people, foster and adoptive families, public and private agencies, community and business leaders, faith-based organizations, educators, and other child and family advocates all must be engaged to ensure that communities offer young people and their families the supports they need. This requires building on the strengths of families and communities and changing the way that formal child protection agencies, courts, and other service providers do business.

All partners should take action to:

Move children in foster care who are waiting for permanent families into permanent homes. More than 100,000 children in foster care are waiting for permanent families, and many of these children have been there for years. States will need help from multiple partners to move these waiting children to permanent families. Extra help with permanency efforts will benefit the children involved, reduce the number of children in care, and increase the likelihood that children still in care or entering care in the future will be ensured safety and permanence as the Adoption and Safe Families Act (ASFA) intended. Together the partners should:

◆ Identify and describe the children in care who were there when ASFA was passed. What other steps have also been taken to get them into permanent homes? Are they already with foster parents or relatives who want to adopt them? If adoption is the plan, have their parents' rights been terminated, and if not, what are the barriers preventing the termination of their parents' rights? What steps have already been taken to move them to permanent homes?

◆ Quantify what it would take to move these waiting children to appropriate permanent homes and ensure that they will remain there. What strategies would be most effective? What additional resources would be needed to put such strategies in place?

◆ Mobilize support from Congress, the Department of Health and Human Services, state legislatures, foundations, and other private sources to get the extra financial assistance and technical help states need to move these children to permanent homes in the next two years.

Support grandparents and other relatives who are caring for children and empower them to take action. More than 2 million children who cannot be raised by their parents are fortunate enough to have a relative willing and able to safely care for them, but their caregivers need help to do so. Federal, state, and community partners should:

◆ Encourage teachers, child care and health care providers, faith-based organizations, and other community-based groups to identify what kin caregivers need most to protect and nurture the children in their care and to join with others to help expand kinship care families' access to appropriate education, special education, health and mental health care, respite services, and peer support.

◆ Increase state and federal support for subsidized guardianships for kin who agree to care permanently for children they have cared for in the foster care system. Ensure that ongoing supports, in addition to cash assistance, will be provided after the caregiver obtains guardianship of the child.

◆ Make sure kinship caregivers in all states know that they can apply for Medicaid or CHIP on behalf of the children they are raising. Inform caregivers that legal custody or guardianship generally is not required and their income will not be counted in determining a child's eligibility for health care coverage.

Expand assistance to young people transitioning from foster care. Build on the new Foster Care Independence Act and John H. Chafee Foster Care Independence Program to assist young people leaving foster care at ages 18 and 19. Help expand new supports for these young people to address their unmet needs for health care, housing, education, employment, and personal support and connections. Join with partners in states and communities to:

◆ Use the development of the Multi-Year State Plan required by the John H. Chafee Foster Care Independence Program to engage a range of partners, including young people, to ensure that quality services with positive results are offered to youths leaving foster care at ages 18 or older.

◆ Develop opportunities for young people who are or have been in the foster care system or who have had experience with the mental health system to get involved in improving how these systems respond to the needs of young people.

◆ Ensure that every state takes advantage of the new federal option to extend Medicaid to youths up to age 21 who were in foster care on their 18th birthday.

◆ Explore state opportunities to extend free tuition at all state-operated colleges, universities, and vocational schools to youths aging out of foster care as Texas, Florida, Maine, and several other states have already done.

◆ Encourage the U.S. Departments of Education and Health and Human Services and their state counterparts to assess the proportion of young people who leave foster care at ages 18 or 19 with a high school diploma. Make recommendations for agencies to provide incentives for greater attention to these young peoples' educational needs.

Educate the public, policy leaders, children's services and domestic violence providers, the courts, and representatives of law enforcement about the impact of domestic violence on children. If children are to be safe, attention must be focused on the multiple victims of domestic violence. Making adult victims safer and stopping batterers' assaults will help remove the risk to children and keep them safe. Take steps with other partners in the community to:

◆ Bring together child welfare agencies, domestic violence programs, courts, and community organizations, building on the guidelines of the National Council of Juvenile and Family Court Judges, to establish responses to domestic violence and child maltreatment — when they occur concurrently. These must protect all victims from physical harm, offer adequate social and economic supports for families, and offer services that are responsive to the individual needs of the child and adult victims. Batterers must also be held responsible for their abusive behavior.

◆ Expand services and supports provided by domestic violence programs for adult victims of domestic violence and their children who witness the violence but are not victims of child maltreatment.

◆ Educate those service providers who have regular contact with children about domestic violence and its impact on children and effective strategies for appropriately addressing this impact, working closely with domestic violence advocates in communities and states.

Promote partnerships among alcohol and drug prevention and treatment and child welfare agencies. Child welfare agencies and alcohol and drug prevention and treatment agencies must work together at the federal, state, and local levels with other service providers, the courts, community leaders, and family members to keep children safe and address the alcohol and drug treatment needs of families who come to the attention of the child welfare system. Federal support should be provided to these partnerships to help:

◆ Implement a range of comprehensive, individualized alcohol and drug prevention and treatment services for parents, children, and other family members.

◆ Improve screening and assessment procedures.

◆ Eliminate barriers to treatment.

◆ Develop effective engagement and retention strategies to keep families in treatment.

◆ Provide cross-system training for staff from child welfare and alcohol and drug agencies and the courts.

◆ Improve data collection within and across these systems.

◆ Evaluate states' progress in achieving the above goals and in improving outcomes for children and families.

Build on the steps in the National Action Agenda from the Surgeon General's Conference on Children's Mental Health. Make quality mental health services a central part of all child-serving systems. Children need help early on in coping with trauma and other negative happenings in their lives to stay on track developmentally. Communities and states should take action to:

◆ Reduce the stigma about mental illness that prevents too many children and their families from getting the help they need.

◆ Ensure that the mental health systems in states specifically address and respond to the special needs of children and adolescents with mental health problems.

◆ Educate family members, early childhood providers, pediatricians, teachers, and others about the importance of identifying and responding to children's mental health needs early by increasing access to and coordination with quality mental health services and by routinely providing mental health consultation for children, families, and staff.

◆ Continue to assess the effectiveness of different prevention and treatment services for children of different ages and with differing needs.

◆ Work to increase children's and parents' access to appropriate health care and ensure that such care includes a comprehensive array of services to address children's mental health needs.

Promote community child protection strategies to keep children safe. Systemic changes are necessary to help children, families, and communities better interact to meet children's needs and prevent child abuse and neglect. Keeping children safe must be everybody's business. Child protection agencies should use new strategies to partner with families and communities. To encourage community partnerships to protect children:

◆ Federal, state, and local governments, in partnership with foundations, should provide incentives to states and communities that are using family and community engagement strategies in the areas of child protection, family support, family group decision-making, family to family foster care, adoption or independent living to expand these strategies in other areas of the state or for other purposes. Communities should be encouraged to implement multiple strategies so the full potential of each can be realized.

◆ Child welfare administrators, judges handling abuse and neglect cases, child advocates, and state legislators should all promote new ways of doing business to get community child protection strategies in place. For example, child welfare agencies should assign staff geographically and deploy staff to neighborhood settings, implement family team meetings, and help to organize neighborhood networks of formal and informal service providers.

◆ Faith-based communities can promote community child protection strategies by opening their facilities to services for children and their parents, pairing members of their congregations (young and old) with children and families in need of assistance, sponsoring scholarships for children to participate in special recreation activities, and surveying their members about talents they have to offer children and families in their community.

Increase accountability measures for positive outcomes for children and families. As states and communities identify a vision for reform that will keep children safe and in nurturing families and communities, it is important to establish child and family outcomes to measure progress in achieving the vision. This is an important time to ensure that states are taking full advantage of opportunities to monitor state outcomes and assess their efforts in serving children and families who are at risk of entering or are already in the child welfare system. Child advocates and community partners should:

◆ Monitor state child welfare agencies' progress in meeting the performance outcomes related to child abuse and neglect and permanence that were established by HHS pursuant to the Adoption and Safe Families Act as well as other activities that will improve state performance. Meet with state child welfare staff and discuss *Child Welfare Outcomes 1998* to see what data the state currently has available to assess progress on outcomes. Work with others to improve the available data and to use them effectively on behalf of children.

◆ Seventeen states will have their activities reviewed this year, in 2001, as part of the Child and Family Service

Reviews, conducted by HHS, and the remainder will be reviewed over the next two years. This process requires states to include community partners in its assessment activities. It must first assess itself and then engage with federal representatives and others in a more careful case-by-case analysis of what children and families in the state are actually receiving. Make sure community representatives are involved and that the review recognizes connections between child welfare, domestic violence, substance abuse, mental health, and other problems and related service systems.

Endnotes

1. U.S. Department of Health and Human Services, Administration on Children, Youth and Families, *Child Maltreatment 1998: Reports From the States to the National Child Abuse and Neglect Data System* (Washington, DC: U.S. Government Printing Office, 2000).

2. *Ibid.*

3. "Current users" were defined as those who had used an illicit drug in the month prior to the interview.

4. "Dependence" was estimated based on responses to a series of questions about health, emotional problems, attempts to reduce use, tolerance, withdrawal, and other symptoms related to criteria for drug dependence in the Diagnostic and Statistical Manual of Mental Disorders, Fourth Edition (DSM-IV).

5. U.S. Department of Health and Human Services, Substance Abuse and Mental Health Services Administration, *Summary of Findings from the 1999 National Household Survey on Drug Abuse* (Washington, DC: U.S. Department of Health and Human Services, August 2000).

6. U. S. Department of Health and Human Services, Substance Abuse and Mental Health Services Administration, *National Household Survey on Drug Abuse, Main Findings, 1996* (Washington, DC: U. S. Department of Health and Human Services, 1998).

7. P. Jaudes and J. Voohis, "Association of Drug and Child Abuse," *Child Abuse and Neglect* 19(9) (1995): 1065-1075.

8. Nancy K. Young and Sidney L. Gardner, *Responding to Alcohol and Other Drug Problems in Child Welfare: Weaving Together Practice and Policy* (Washington, DC: Child Welfare League of America Press, 1998).

9. U. S. Department of Health and Human Services, Administration for Children and Families, Substance Abuse and Mental Health Services Administration, Office of the Assistant Secretary for Planning and Evaluation, *Blending Perspectives and Building Common Ground: A Report to Congress on Substance Abuse and Child Protection* (Washington, DC: U.S. Government Printing Office, April 1999).

10. Callie Marie Rennison and Sarah Welchans, *Intimate Partner Violence* (Washington, DC: U.S. Department of Justice, Bureau of Justice Statistics Special Report, May 2000).

11. Bonnie E. Carlson, "Children's Observations of Interparental Violence" in A.R. Roberts (Ed.), *Battered Women and Their Families* (New York: Springer Publishing, 1984): 147-167.

12. Murray A. Straus, Richard J. Gelles, and Susanne K. Steinmetz, *Behind Closed Doors: Violence in the American Family* (Garden City, NY: Doubleday, 1980); Murray A. Straus, "Children as Witnesses to Marital Violence: A Risk Factor for Lifelong Problems Among a Nationally Representative Sample of American Men and Women" in D.F. Schwartz (Ed.), *Children and Violence: Report of Twenty-third Ross Roundtable on Critical Approaches to Common Pediatric Problems* (Columbus, Ohio: Ross Laboratories, 1992): 98-109.

13. Jeffrey L. Edelson, "The Overlap Between Child Maltreatment and Woman Battering," *Violence Against Women* 5(2) (February 1999):134-154.

14. U.S. Department of Health and Human Services, U.S. Advisory Board on Child Abuse and Neglect, *A Nation's Shame: Fatal Child Abuse and Neglect in the United States: Fifth Report* (Washington, DC: U.S. Department of Health and Human Services, April 1995).

15. Einat Peled, Peter G. Jaffe, and Jeffrey L. Edelson, (Eds.), *Ending the Cycle of Violence: Community Responses to Children of Battered Women* (Thousand Oaks, Calif.: Sage Publications, 1995).

16. *Ibid.*

17. The David and Lucile Packard Foundation, "Domestic Violence and Children," *The Future of Children* 9(3) (Winter 1999).

18. *Ibid.*

19. U.S. Department of Health and Human Services, Office of the Surgeon General, *Report of the Surgeon General's Conference on Children's Mental Health: A National Action Agenda* (Washington DC: Office of the Surgeon General, January 2001). The Virtual Office of the Surgeon General, http://www.surgeongeneral.gov/cmh/childreport.htm.

20. Julie Magno Zito, Daniel J. Safer, Susan dos Reis, et al, "Trends in the Prescribing of Psychotropic Medication to Preschoolers," *The Journal of the American Medical Association* 283(8) (February 23, 2000):1025-1030; Joseph T. Coyle, "Psychotropic Drug Use in Very Young Children," *The Journal of the American Medical Association* 283(8) (February 23, 2000):1059-1060.

21. U.S. Department of Health and Human Services, Administration on Children, Youth and Families, Children's Bureau, *The AFCARS Report, Current Estimates as of October 2000.* Retrieved from the Internet at www.acf.dhhs.gov/programs/cb on March 9, 2001.

22. 383,000 children were in foster care in 1989. Toshio Tatara, *Characteristics of Children in Substitute and Adoptive Care: A Statistical Summary of the VCIS National Child Welfare Data Base* (Washington, DC: American Public Welfare Association, May 1993).

23. Chapin Hall Center for Children at the University of Chicago, *Foster Care Dynamics: An Update from the Multistate Foster Care Data Archive, 1983-1997* (Chicago: Chapin Hall Center for Children, 1999).

24. Chapin Hall Center for Children at the University of Chicago, *Foster Care Data Archive* (Chicago: Chapin Hall Center for Children, 1999).

25. *Supra* note 21.

26. U.S. Bureau of the Census, Population Estimates Program, Population Division, *Estimates of the Population of the States by Age, Sex, Race, and Hispanic Origin: July 1, 1999.* Internet release date: August 30, 2000. Calculation by CDF.

27. *Supra* note 21.

28. *Supra* note 21.

29. Penelope L. Maza, "The Latest from AFCARS on Adoptions and Waiting Children," Presentation at Children's Bureau's Sixth National Child Welfare Conference, Arlington, Va., March 28-31, 2000.

30. Fred Wulczyn, Kristen Brunner Bishop, and Robert Goerge, *Foster Care Dynamics: An Update from the Multistate Foster Care Data Archive: 1988-1998* (Chicago: Chapin Hall Center on Children at the University of Chicago, 2001).

31. U.S. Census Bureau, Current Population Reports (P-20-450), *Marital Status and Living Arrangements: March 1990* (Washington, DC: U.S. Census Bureau, May 1991); U.S. Census Bureau, Current Population Survey, *Marital Status and Living Arrangements: March 1999 Update* (Washington, DC: U.S. Census Bureau, October 1999); Lynne M. Casper and Ken Bryson, *Coresident Grandparents and Their Grandchildren*, Special Studies P 23-198 (Washington, DC: U.S. Census Bureau, May 1999).

32. D. Fuller-Thompson and Meredith Minkler, "A Profile of Grandparents Raising Grandchildren in the United States," *The Gerontologist* 37(3) (1997).

33. Rob Geen, Rebecca Clark, and Jennifer Ehrle, *A Detailed Look at Kinship Caregiving*, Paper prepared for the 21st Annual Association for Public Policy Analysis and Management Research Conference (Washington, DC: Urban Institute, November 5, 1999).

34. *Supra* note 21.

35. *Supra* note 33.

36. Don Cohon, L. Itines, B. Cooper, et al, *Stuart Foundation Kinship Care Study:Final Report* (San Francisco: Edgewood Center for Children and Families, Institute for the Study of Community-based Services, July 2000).

37. Christopher J. Mumola, *Incarcerated Parents and Their Children.* (Washington, DC: U.S. Department of Justice, Bureau of Justice Statistics Special Report, August 2000).

38. Jane Knitzer, *Promoting Resilience: Helping Young Children and Parents Affected by Substance Abuse, Domestic Violence, and Depression in the Context of Welfare Reform* (New York: National Center on Children in Poverty, 2000).

39. Urban Institute and Child Trends, *Snapshots of America's Families II, Children's Family Environment: Findings from the National Survey of America's Families, 1997-1999* (Washington, DC: Urban Institute, 2000).

40. Children's Defense Fund, *Families Struggling to Make It in the Workforce: A Post Welfare Report* (Washington, DC: Childrens Defense Fund, 2000).

41. Heidi Goldberg and Liz Schott, *A Compliance-Oriented Approach to Sanctions in State and County TANF Programs* (Washington, DC: Center on Budget and Policy Priorities, October 1, 2000).

42. Roseana Bess, Jacob Leos-Urbel, and Rob Geen. *The Cost of Protecting Vulnerable Children II: What Has Changed Since 1996* (Washington, D.C.: Urban Institute, 2000).

43. *Supra* note 21.

44. Kathy Ledesma, "Incentive Payments Reinvested in Program Improvement," *The Roundtable*, 14(1) (2000.) [Newsletter of the National Resource Center for Special Needs Adoption].

45. See, for example, Kate Welte, *Shortening Children's Stay in Temporary Care: Innovative Programs* (Baltimore: Annie E. Casey Foundation and North American Council on Adoptable Children, 1999), and Steve Christian and Lisa Elkman, *A Place to Call Home: Adoption and Guardianship for Children in Foster Care* (Denver: National Conference of State Legislatures, March 2000).

46. P.L. 106-310 (Title XII, Subtitle B), The Children's Health Act, enacted October 17, 2000.)

47. Presentation by The Honorable Sharon P. McCully, Third District Juvenile Court, Salt Lake City, Utah, June 2000, and conversations with and materials from staff of the Permanency Planning for Children Department, National Council of Juvenile and Family Court Judges, Reno, Nev.

48. Conversations with and materials from staff of the Permanency Planning for Children Department, National Council of Juvenile and Family Court Judges, Reno, Nev.

49. P.L. 106-314, enacted October 17, 2000. No funding was appropriated for the programs for FY2001.

50. For more information on the Maine Adoption Guides, contact Loren Coleman, Project Manager, at 202-772-0245 or MaineAdoptionGuides@lorencoleman.com.

51. P.L. No. 106-365, enacted October 30, 2000.

52. P.L. No. 106-279, enacted October 6, 2000.

53. Calif. Welfare and Institutions Code, sections 11360-11370.

54. Steve Christian and Lisa Elkman, *A Place to Call Home: Adoption and Guardianship for Children in Foster Care* (Denver: National Conference of State Legislatures, March 2000). See also, Anna Beltran, *Fact Sheet: Grandparents and Other Relatives Raising Children: Subsidized Guardianship Program* (Washington, DC: Generations United, August 2000).

55. La. Revised Statutes, section 46:237.

56. Senate File 3018; codified in Minn. Stat., Chapter 257B.

57. AARP and Generations United, "State Laws and Regulations Affecting Grandparents and Other Relative-Headed Families"(Washington, DC: AARP and Generations United, 2000).

58. Tenn. Public Chapter Number 989.

59. P.L. 106-501, enacted November 13, 2000.

60. U.S. Department of Health and Human Services, Administration for Children and Families, *Report to the Congress on Kinship Foster Care* (Washington, DC: U.S. Department of Health and Human Services, June 2000). See also, Jacob Leos-Urbel, Roseana Bess, and Rob Geen, *State Policies for Assessing and Supporting Kinship Foster Parents* (Washington, DC, Urban Institute, May 2000).

61. *Federal Register*, 65 (16) (January 25, 2000): 4020-4093.

62. MaryLee Allen and Robin Nixon, "The Foster Care Independence Act and John H. Chafee Foster Care Independence Program: New Catalysts for Reform for Young People Aging Out of Foster Care," *Clearinghouse Review Journal of Poverty Law and Policy* 34 (July-August 2000): 196-216.

63. For information on how to promote implementation of the program in states, see: National Foster Care Awareness Project, *Frequently Asked Questions About the Foster Care Independence Act of 1999 and the John H. Chafee Foster Care Independence Program* (Seattle: Casey Family Programs, February 2000) and National Foster Care Awareness Project, *Frequently Asked Questions II About the Foster Care Independence Act of 1999 and the John H. Chafee Foster Care Independence Program* (Seattle: Casey Family Programs, December 2000).

64. Abigail English and Kathi Grasso, "The Foster Care Independence Act of 1999: Enhancing Youth Access to Health Care," *Clearinghouse Review Journal of Poverty Law and Policy* 34 (July-August 2000): 217-232.

65. Letter to State Child Welfare and State Medicaid Directors from Patricia Montoya, Commissioner, Administration on Children, Youth and Families, and Timothy M. Westmoreland, Director, Center for Medicaid and State Operations, Health Care Financing Administration, U.S. Department of Health and Human Services, December 2000. [Reproduced as Appendix G in *Frequently Asked Questions II About the Foster Care Independence Act of 1999 and the John H. Chafee Foster Care Independence Program.* See note 63 above.]

66. California Youth Connection, *Foster Youth Proposals to Improve Mental Health Services: The Consumer's Perspective* (San Francisco: California Youth Connection, 2000).

67. Alfred G. Pérez, *Family Preservation Initiatives: Foster Youth Share Their Perspectives for Change* (San Francisco: California Youth Connection, 2000).

68. Research and Training Center on Family Support and Children's Mental Health, "Roles for Youth in Systems of Care," *Focal Point: A National Bulletin on Family Support and Children's Mental Health* 14(2) (Fall 2000).

69. *Ibid.*

70. *Supra* note 17.

71. Susan Schechter and Jeffrey L. Edelson, *Domestic Violence and Children: Creating a Public Response* (New York: The Open Society Institute Center on Crime, Communities & Culture, 2000).

72. National Council of Juvenile and Family Court Judges, *Effective Intervention in Domestic Violence & Child Maltreatment Cases: Guidelines for Policy and Practice* (Reno, Nev.: National Council of Juvenile and Family Court Judges,1999).

73. P.L. 106-386, enacted October 28, 2000.

74. P.L. 106-310, Title XXXI, Sec. 3101, enacted October 17, 2000.

75. U.S. Department of Justice, National Advisory Council on Violence Against Women, *Ending Violence Against Women: An Agenda for the Nation* (Washington, DC: U.S. Department of Justice, October 2000).

76. *Supra* note 19.

77. For additional information about the systems of care supported by the Comprehensive Community Mental Health Services for Children and their Families Program, see the Center for Mental Health Services website at http://www.samhsa.gov/centers/cmhs/cmhs.html.

78. P.L. No. 106-310, Title XXXII, Sec. 3211, enacted October 17, 2000.

79. Drug Strategies, "America's Failing Public Health Approach to Controlling Drugs, Poll Finds." [News Release] (Washington, DC: Drug Strategies, July 19, 2000.)

80. *Changing the Conversation: The National Treatment Plan Initiative to Improve Substance Abuse Treatment* (Washington, DC: U.S. Department of Health and Human Services, Substance Abuse and Mental Health Services Administration, Center for Substance Abuse Treatment, November 2000).

81. Steve Christian and Karen Edwards, *Linking Child Welfare and Substance Abuse Treatment: A Guide for Legislators* (Denver: National Conference of State Legislatures, August 2000).

82. S. 484, The Child Protection and Alcohol and Drug Partnership Act was introduced in the the the Senate on March 7, 2001 by Senators Olympia Snowe (R-Me.), John D. Rockefeller, IV (D-W.V.), Mike DeWine (R-Ohio), Christopher Dodd (D-Conn.), Susan Collins (R-Me.), Blanche Lambert Lincoln (D-Ark.), and John Breaux (D-La.).

83. Physician Leadership on National Drug Policy, "Major Study Finds Drug Treatment as Good as Treatment for Diabetes, Asthma, etc. And Better and Cheaper than Prison (Washington, DC: Physician Leadership on National Drug Policy, March 17, 1998)." [Press release from website at http://center.butler.brown.edu/plndp.]

84. *Supra* note 9.

85. Discussions with staff in the Center for Substance Abuse Treatment in the Substance Abuse and Mental Health Services Administration in the U.S. Department of Health and Human Services, about the finding of the cross-site evaluation, July 2001.

86. Andrew White, *Citizen Power for Stronger Families: Community Partnerships for Protecting Children, Jacksonville* (New York: The Edna McConnell Clark Foundation, 2000). This booklet is available free from the Edna McConnell Clark Foundation, 250 Park Avenue, New York, NY 10177, 212-551-9100.

87. U.S. Department of Health and Human Services, Administration on Children, Youth and Families, Children's Bureau, *Child Welfare Outcomes 1998: Annual Report* (Washington, DC: U.S. Department of Health and Human Services, 2000). Copies of the report may be obtained from the National Clearinghouse on Child Abuse and Neglect Information at 1-800-394-3366 or from the Children's Bureau web site at http://www.acf.dhhs.gov/programs/cb.

88. *Supra* note 61.

89. The 17 states to be reviewed in 2001 include: Delaware, North Carolina [March]; Vermont [April]; Minnesota [May]; New York, Oregon [June]; Arkansas, District of Columbia, Georgia, Massachusetts [July]; Florida, Indiana, Kansas, New Mexico [August]; Arizona, North Dakota, South Dakota [September]. For the tentative schedule of additional reviews in FY2002-FY2004, see the Child Welfare Review Project's website at http://www.childwelfarereview.com/.

CHAPTER

Juvenile Justice and Youth Development

E very child deserves to grow up in a safe, nurturing environment that promotes positive development from childhood through adolescence and into adulthood. After a decade of record economic growth and, for the sixth consecutive year, decreasing crime rates, America now has the opportunity to invest aggressively in proven violence prevention and youth development activities to ensure that children and families are able to thrive in the next century. Targeted investment in prevention efforts that give children and teens what they need to stay on track works. Appropriate education services, mental health treatment, and consistency in their lives are key to a child's healthy development. In order to have a sense of value and purpose, children must feel connected to parents and adults. Providing parents with the skills and treatment they need to be better parents is equally critical. A comprehensive prevention approach that looks at the entire family and identifies the specific needs of the child within that family can reduce the incidence of aggressive and risky behavior that often leads to delinquency.

Most children who behave violently have already encountered violence in their lives to one degree or another. Families, schools, and communities must work together to protect children and ensure their healthy development. Communities need to provide more opportunities for young people to develop the competencies and character to become productive adults and citizens.

The debate about how to treat juvenile offenders must focus on investment and rehabilitation, not punishment and fear. Otherwise, these children may be lost forever. When children get into trouble, they need a second chance to turn their lives around. Instead of capitalizing on the opportunity to rehabilitate these youths and help them make better choices, treating juveniles as adults allows adult criminals to become their mentors, their role models. Unsurprisingly, youths placed in adult jails are more likely to re-offend. The prevalence of mental health and substance abuse problems among the juvenile delinquent population also underscores the need for treatment — not punishment — for these young people. Proper screening of both violent and nonviolent juvenile offenders is necessary to provide appropriate intervention and treatment services. Finally, in order to prevent juvenile offenders from re-offending and to ensure that the efforts to rehabilitate them are effective, these young people need help once they return home. Juveniles are unlikely to re-enter their community successfully without support services to help address the problems that brought them in contact with the juvenile system in the first place.

No one can ever be completely safe until something is done about the gun violence that plagues neighborhoods, playgrounds, schools, and workplaces. To protect children instead of guns, national, state, and local leaders should be called upon to support a comprehensive gun safety policy that requires licensing and registration, trigger locks and safe storage devices, consumer safety standards, and background checks for all firearms. America must change the way firearms are regarded and regulated if this epidemic of violence is to be stopped.

Youth, Violence, and Crime

Children victimized by violence

Children are more secure today than they have been in recent years. Overall, violent crime rates have declined, and communities are safer for everyone. The national crime rate has dropped by 8 percent and is the lowest it has been since 1973, according to the most recent Federal Bureau of Investigation (FBI) reports.[1] Serious violent crime is also down 8 percent from 1998 and 23 percent from 1995. The number of murders in 1999 declined 9 percent from 1998 and 30 percent from 1995. In 1999, the murder rate dropped to its lowest level in almost 35 years.

Although the number of children hurt by violent crime has declined significantly, 22 percent of violent crime victims in the United States are juveniles. According to a new reporting system developed by the FBI to detail information about juvenile victims of crime, simple assault is the most commonly reported crime against juveniles, constituting 41 percent of all victimizations reported to police. Of those who harm children, 80 percent are family members, friends, or acquaintances; only 11 percent are strangers.[2] The data suggest that while campaigns cautioning children to be wary of strangers are important, more needs to be done to protect children from being victimized by someone they know and trust. Sex offenses

against children also remain a serious problem. Juveniles make up 12 percent of all crime victims reported to police, including 71 percent of all sex crime victims. Although boys are more likely overall to be victimized than girls, girls far outnumber boys as victims of sexual assault (82 percent and 18 percent, respectively). The youngest children are particularly vulnerable. One out of every 18 victims of violent crime and one of every three victims of sexual assault is under age 12.[3] Children under age 12 make up approximately one-quarter of all juvenile victims known to police and at least one-half of juvenile victims of kidnapping and sex offenses.[4]

In addition to reports of single incidents of violent crime against children, many children experience routine violence in their homes. Too many children suffer from abuse and neglect, and the needs of these children and their families are often left unmet. In 1998, an estimated 2.9 million children were reported as suspected child abuse or neglect cases, and more than 903,000 of them were confirmed as victims of maltreatment.[5] Domestic violence also has serious implications for healthy youth development because children are taught to accept and use violence in their interactions with others. (See the Children and Families in Crisis chapter for more information.)

Research indicates that children who experience some form of violence in their homes are more likely to behave violently throughout adolescence and into adulthood. One survey of studies conducted in three regions of the country found that children who were abused and neglected were almost twice as likely to be arrested as a juvenile for a violent crime as a child who had not suffered maltreatment.[6] A study of a group of incarcerated adult males found that violent offenders reported more childhood abuse and neglect (20 percent) than nonviolent offenders (6 percent).[7] It is estimated that millions

◆ 10 children and teens die each day from gunfire in America — one child every two and a half hours.

◆ More children died in 1998 from gunfire than from cancer, pneumonia, influenza, asthma, and HIV/AIDS combined.

◆ Juvenile arrests for violent crime have declined 23 percent since 1995.

◆ Between 50 to 75 percent of incarcerated youths have a diagnosable mental health disorder.

◆ The United States accounts for one-third of the world total of persons sentenced to death for crimes committed while under age 18.

◆ The average America child watches 28 hours of television a week and by age 18 will have seen 16,000 simulated murders and 200,000 acts of violence.

◆ The unemployment rate for teens is more than four times the adult rate.

of children experience violence in the home and come to see violence as acceptable behavior. Any comprehensive approach to curb juvenile delinquency and promote positive youth development must consider the impact of domestic violence, abuse, and neglect on a child's development and respond to the interplay between these factors.

Juvenile offenders

Juveniles accounted for 17 percent of all criminal arrests and 16 percent of arrests for serious violent crime in 1999, a decrease of 8 percent from 1998.[8] The arrest rate for violent crime by juveniles had dropped 23 percent since 1995, notwithstanding steady growth in the number of children in America over the past decade.[9] The juvenile murder arrest rate has declined even more rapidly, dropping over 55 percent over the past 10 years.[10]

Contrary to popular perception, the vast majority of children involved in the juvenile justice system are non-violent offenders. Less than 10 percent of young people who come in contact with the juvenile justice system are serious, habitual, violent offenders. The majority of juvenile crime involves property offenses: arson, burglary, car theft, and larceny. According to one study, more than half of the males and nearly three-quarters of the females who enter the juvenile justice system never return.[11]

Criminalization of youth

Although most juvenile offenders are not violent and do not re-offend, the trend among policy makers at the national and state levels has been to advance broad policies in response to a small number of serious, violent offenders. Highly publicized events involving teens and unfounded reports on the emergence of the youthful "superpredator" continue to be used by lawmakers to justify a shift away from rehabilitative approaches towards more punitive remedies for juveniles. Since 1992, 47 states and the District of Columbia have made their juvenile justice systems more punitive. Nearly all have passed laws that make it easier to transfer young offenders from the juvenile justice system to adult court, which subjects juveniles to adult sentences and adult prison.[12] Although transfer of juveniles to adult court is commonly believed to be a response to serious violent crime, 21 states either require or allow adult prosecution of juveniles for certain property offenses, and 19 states authorize or mandate prosecution of juveniles who are accused of drug offenses in criminal court.[13] As a result, trying children in adult court, where the primary goal is punishment and deterrence rather than rehabilitation, has become increasingly easy.

Is the move towards harsher treatment and away from rehabilitation working? Early evidence says no. Treating children as adults and subjecting them to the severity of the adult criminal justice system mainly teaches children to be better criminals. Recent research indicates that transfer to adult court does not reduce recidivism. In fact, youths who are transferred to criminal court are more likely to re-offend, and to re-offend more quickly and more often, than those retained in the juvenile justice system.[14] In adult prison, youths are more likely to learn social rules and norms that validate domination, exploitation, and retaliation. Additionally, the threat of adult court does not appear to deter juveniles from criminal behavior. A comparison of Idaho, Montana, and Wyoming found that when Idaho passed legislation requiring transfer of all violent youthful offenders ages 14 and above to adult court, the state's juvenile crime rate increased. In neighboring states Montana and Wyoming, where the juvenile courts retained jurisdiction of most violent juvenile offenders, the violent juvenile crime rate decreased.[15]

Juvenile Arrests for Violent Crimes

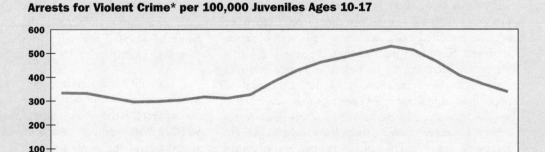

Arrests for Violent Crime* per 100,000 Juveniles Ages 10-17

*Murder, rape, robbery, and aggravated assault.

Source: U.S. Department of Justice, Office of Juvenile Justice and Delinquency Prevention, OJJDP Statistical Briefing Book, at http://www.ojjdp.ncjrs.org/ojstatbb/qa256.html.

Mental Health: An Unmet Challenge

The ability to assess adolescent competency for adult court is complicated by the prevalence of mental health disorders among juvenile delinquents. Recent estimates indicate that between 50 to 75 percent of incarcerated youths have a diagnosable mental health disorder, and many youths with mental illness in the juvenile justice system also have a co-occurring substance abuse disorder. Suicide in juvenile detention and correctional facilities is more than four times greater than youth suicide overall. Additionally, among those suffering from mental health problems, minority, female, and homosexual youths are most vulnerable to mistreatment in the system. The problem of mental illness and the multiple issues surrounding the treatment of these youths stands out as one of the most significant challenges facing juvenile justice officials. Treating juvenile delinquents with mental health disorders requires a comprehensive effort that collaborates across youth serving systems, adequately screens youths who come in contact with the juvenile system, implements community-based alternatives whenever possible, and diverts youths from the juvenile system to more appropriate systems of care.

The National Mental Health Association (NMHA) conducted a survey of 11 states to assess the mental health needs of youths in the juvenile justice system. The study affirmed the tremendous need for mental health and substance abuse treatment among the juvenile delinquent population and articulated a number of commonly cited barriers to serving these youths, including scarcity of resources, inadequacies of health care insurance policies, and lack of coordination between agencies. The NMHA recommends that advocates address the shortcomings of the juvenile justice and other support systems in serving youths mental health needs by:

◆ working to change attitudes about juvenile delinquency

◆ challenging systems to work together

◆ expanding resources

◆ helping the justice system identify children with needs earlier

◆ encouraging treatment and justices systems to involve families more effectively

◆ addressing service gaps

◆ educating stakeholders

Sources: *Youth With Mental Health Disorders: Issues and Emerging Responses* (Office of Juvenile Justice and Delinquency Prevention, April 2000); *Community Perspectives on the Mental Health and Substance Abuse Treatment Needs of Youth Involved in the Juvenile Justice System* (National Mental Health Association and Office of Juvenile Justice and Delinquency Prevention, October 2000); and *Handle with Care: Serving the Mental Health Needs of Young Offenders* (Coalition for Juvenile Justice, December 2000).

Youths are also more likely to be victimized in the adult system. Children who are held in adult prisons are eight times more likely than young people in juvenile facilities to commit suicide, five times more likely to be sexually assaulted, twice as likely to be beaten by prison staff, and 50 percent more likely to be attacked with a weapon.[16] According to the Bureau of Justice Statistics Annual Survey of Jails, a one-day count of the total jail population at midyear 1999 estimates that nearly 9,500 youths under age 18 were held in adult jails. This represents a 17 percent increase since 1998 and a 21 percent increase since 1995. The majority (91 percent) of youths under age 18 held in adult jails were held as adults (they had been charged or convicted in an adult court), while a relatively small number of those in adult jails were held as juveniles (under the jurisdiction of the juvenile court). Although the number of juveniles tried as juveniles but

held in adult jails has declined 65 percent from 1997 to 1999 the decline is more than offset by the number of juveniles held in adult jails as adults.[17] Overall, more juveniles are ending up in adult jails simply because they are being adjudicated through the adult, rather than the juvenile, system.

The shift towards trying more children as adults raises basic concerns about fairness. As more youthful offenders are subject to the adult system, questions arise as to whether these youths are capable of fully appreciating their situation and the implications of being tried in adult court. Developmental research indicates that many of the decision-making skills required of a defendant in adult criminal court emerge at different stages of adolescence, from ages 12 through 17.[18] Children grow and mature at different rates, a reality that served as the founding principle in the creation of a separate justice system for juveniles over 100 years ago. Children and adolescents are not adults. The justice system must be able to assess each young offender's competency to make the long-term decisions involved in an adult adjudication process.

Serious and violent juvenile offenders

As more young offenders are transferred to adult court, the fundamental tenet of the juvenile system that all juveniles, even violent offenders, have the capacity to change and should be afforded rehabilitative opportunities is being lost. In fashioning appropriate responses to the small percent of juveniles engaged in serious, violent offending, it is critical to understand the factors that contribute to this type of behavior. The majority of serious, violent juvenile offenders are boys who display minor behavior problems as early as age 7. These problems tend to escalate gradually and do not come to the attention of the police, the court system, or other authorities until the boy reaches age 14, which allows more than seven years to elapse between the earliest indication of problem behavior and the first court appearance. Not surprisingly, most serious, violent juvenile offenders have multiple difficulties such as substance abuse and mental health problems and are disproportionately victims of violence.[19]

Serious youth violence usually occurs in groups. Much of the violent behavior exhibited by children and teens can be directly attributed to peer pressure and a strong desire to achieve group status. Association with deviant peers in early adolescence is a strong predictor of later criminal activity.[20] According to National Crime Victimization Survey data, one in every two violent crimes by juveniles involved multiple offenders, while just one in five violent crimes by adults involved more than one offender.[21] Much of this group activity falls under the category of gang violence; however, stereotypes of youth gang members as predominately urban, minority males may be missing the mark. Recent research has found that modern youth gangs are less territorial, increasingly active in rural and suburban areas, more prevalent in schools and detention facilities than ever before, and more likely to include females.[22] To help communities address gang violence, the Office of Juvenile Justice and Delinquency Prevention (OJJDP) organizes model programs into three components: prevention, early intervention, and graduated sanctions. Several successful models in these areas are being implemented across the country to reduce gang violence.[23] For example:

◆ The Gang Resistance and Education Training Program (G.R.E.A.T.) involves use of a school-based curriculum for middle school students, which is administered by uniformed law enforcement officers. Follow-up surveys reported that participants in the program had lower levels of gang involvement, drug use, and delinquency than those in the control group. Program participants also reported more positive attitudes toward the police, fewer delinquent friends, and high levels of self-esteem.

◆ Minnesota HEALS (Hope, Education, Law and Safety) is a public–private partnership, modeled after Boston's successful Operation Night Light intervention program, which targets gang members who possess weapons and are multiple offenders. Decreases in gang-related violence in Minneapolis have been attributed to the successful efforts of the HEALS task force.

Minorities in the juvenile justice system

The injustice faced by minority youths in the American juvenile justice system has been well documented. At every stage of the process (arrest, detention, prosecution, adjudication, and transfer to adult court), racial and ethnic minority children are represented disproportionately when compared with their numbers in the community. Nearly seven out of 10 youths in secure confinement facilities are members of minority groups, and more than 75 percent of youths newly admitted into state prisons are minorities.[24] Black youths are more likely than White youths to be held in a detention facility, formally charged in juvenile court, or transferred to adult criminal court for similar offenses.[25] When compared with White youths, Black youths are committed to detention facilities an average of two weeks longer for the same offenses.[26] In California, a study of juvenile delinquents in Los Angeles County found that minority youths arrested for violent crime were transferred to adult court two and a half times more often than White youths arrested for violent offenses. The study also found that in adult court, minority youths, when compared with White youths, receive harsher sentences for similar offenses.[27]

A 1988 amendment to the federal Juvenile Justice and Delinquency Prevention Act (JJDPA) addressed the disproportionate confinement of minority youths by requiring states to determine whether the percentage of minorities in confinement exceeds their percentage in the general population and, if so, implement efforts to achieve equitable treatment. However, as indicated earlier, minority over-representation is not limited to confinement in secure facilities; it appears at every major decision point in the juvenile justice system. Many attribute this over-representation to "selection bias," a process where the justice system deals more severely with minority juveniles than White juveniles. Recent research has shown that although bias can occur at all stages of processing within the juvenile justice system, the most pronounced disparity occurs primarily at the arrest and detention decision points.[28] Because racial bias continues to permeate all aspects of the judicial process, it is critical that states continue to be pushed to address this serious problem.

Unfortunately, while the pervasiveness of the problem has become more evident, the U.S. Senate has tried to take a step back. In its 1999 juvenile crime bill, the Senate passed an amendment that would have undermined the disproportionate minority confinement (DMC) provision of the JJDPA. The new provision would have eliminated any reference to "race" and instead only required states to examine how their juvenile systems treated certain "segments of the population." The change failed to acknowledge the distinctly racial issue the DMC requirement was designed to address. Weakening the provision, particularly in light of evidence of continued racial bias within most state juvenile systems, would have effectively sanctioned discriminatory practices. Fortunately, these provisions were not enacted in the 106th Congress.

Girls in the juvenile justice system

Although girls are far less likely than boys to become involved in the juvenile justice system, the arrest rate for females ages 17 and under increased over 30 percent between 1990 and 1999. By contrast, arrest rates for males ages 17 and under rose just 5 percent during that same period.[29] Today, just over one-fourth of all juvenile arrests involve females. Also, disproportionate minority representation is not limited to boys; approximately two-thirds of females in the juvenile justice system are minorities.[30]

In response to the growing population of girls being arrested and detained in the Philadelphia area, the Juvenile Unit of the Philadelphia Defender Association conducted a survey in an effort to understand what was behind this disturbing trend. Based on data compiled from females housed in Philadelphia's Youth Study Center, the typical female juvenile offender was Black, had experienced five or more foster care transitions, had at least one parent with a drug or alcohol problem, had experienced some type of abuse, had likely attempted suicide at least once, and had a drug or alcohol problem.[31] According to the study, 81 percent of the girls had experienced some form of past trauma or abuse, 77 percent had used drugs or alcohol, and 54 percent had been hospitalized for psychiatric reasons. One of the largest problems facing girls in the juvenile justice system was the misdiagnosis of mental health issues.

Although girls represent the fastest growing segment of the juvenile justice population, their unique needs are not being served. The National Girls' Caucus, formed in 1993, focuses attention on girls in the juvenile system and helps advocates at the federal, state, and local levels identify programs and strategies geared toward girls in the juvenile justice system.[32] Promising initiatives involve a strong emphasis on family-based programs that recognize the prevalence of abuse and domestic violence and include training for law enforcement and juvenile court officials on the characteristics and needs of female offenders. Targeted investment is necessary if the nation is going to be successful in stopping and reversing the trend of increasing crime and delinquency among young women.

Juvenile Justice and Delinquency Prevention Act of 1974

For the past 25 years, federal law has protected America's children from the dangers of adult jails. A generation ago, children — including those picked up for running away and truancy — were routinely housed in adult jails. Studies in the early 1970s including the Children Defense Fund's 1976 report, *Children in Adult Jails,* found that the problem of children in adult jails was widespread. Some of these children were committing suicide and were victims of sexual and physical assaults by adult inmates. Congress enacted the Juvenile Justice and Delinquency Prevention Act (JJDPA) to provide states with incentives to improve their juvenile justice systems. Under the act (and subsequent renewals), states can receive funds under a formula grant as long as they meet the following four protections: (1) children must be removed from adult facilities, with some narrow exceptions such as in rural areas where alternatives are limited, (2) children who are placed in adult facilities must be separated from adult inmates by both "sight and sound," (3) children who are arrested for running away, skipping school, or other non-criminal (status) offenses are to be placed in community facilities, not jails or prisons, and never in adult jails or prisons, (4) if disproportionate confinement of minority children is found, states must address this problem.

For the past five years, Congress has attempted, unsuccessfully, to reauthorize the act, which expired in September 1996.[33] In June 1999, the House of Representatives approved reauthorizing legislation that would have weakened current law, turned the clock back 25 years, and again placed children at risk of assault and abuse in adult jails. The measure lacked adequate investments in prevention programs, failed to address the problem of gun violence, and would have done little to reduce juvenile crime. In May 1999, the Senate passed a juvenile crime bill that would have preserved most of the core mandates of the JJDPA, established a 25 percent funding set-aside for prevention programs, and included several basic gun safety provisions (see following discussion on Gun Violence). Despite these positive measures, the Senate bill also contained provisions that would have weakened other protections for children by undercutting the core protection against disproportionate minority confinement and allowing children to be placed in adult jails for unacceptably long periods of time with parental consent.

Juvenile Death Penalty: The U.S. Stands Alone

Since 1973, the United States has sentenced 196 people to death for crimes committed while they were juveniles — 17 have been executed, 105 have had their convictions reversed, and 74 remain on death row in 16 states. Currently, 38 states have legalized capital punishment. Of these jurisdictions, 23 allow persons convicted of a capital offense committed while under age 18 to receive a sentence of death.

Detailed information about the circumstances of these cases is limited, but several studies present a disturbing picture. Of the cases reviewed, the majority of juvenile offenders sentenced to death had a previous head injury, a history of psychotic disorders and psychiatric disturbances, a very low IQ, or severe past abuse — physical, sexual, or both. Inadequate legal defense compounds the tragic personal histories of these defendants. Although the jury is required to look at mitigating factors when determining a sentence of death, this is impossible without background information. In most cases, the juvenile offenders were represented by public defenders or other appointed counsel who often did not have the time or resources to adequately investigate possible mitigating factors.

Of the 154 members of the United Nations, the United States and Somalia are the only two that have failed to ratify the U.N. Convention on the Rights of the Child, which contains a provision outlawing the death penalty for juvenile offenders. The United States accounts for one-third of the world totals of persons put to death for crimes committed while under age 18. In the last five years, only four other countries (in addition to the United States) have actually executed anyone for crimes committed while a juvenile — Iran, Pakistan, Nigeria, and the Democratic Republic of Congo. In July 2000, Pakistan took steps to abolish such executions. The almost universal acceptance of the U.N. Convention demonstrates that such executions run counter to contemporary standards and humane treatment in every corner of the world.

Sources: U.S. Department of Justice, Office of Juvenile Justice and Delinquency Prevention, *Juveniles and the Death Penalty* (Washington D.C.: Coordinating Council on Juvenile Justice and Delinquency Prevention, November 2000). Mark Hansen, "Death Knell for Death Row?," *ABA Journal* (June 2000): 40-48.

At the close of the 106th Congress, a House–Senate Conference Committee was unable to reconcile the differences between the two bills. Although both bills represented improvements over previous measures that would have severely gutted even more core protections, neither the House nor the Senate bill maintained the level of protection for children provided by current law or provided adequate resources for prevention programs.

Despite the deadlock over authorization legislation, Congress maintained funding in Fiscal Year 2001 for the JJDPA at $279.1 million, including $95 million for local delinquency prevention programs. Congress also appropriated $250 million for the Juvenile Accountability Incentive block grant program, which provides funds for states to use in 12 juvenile justice law enforcement areas including construction of juvenile detention facilities, training programs for prosecutors, and establishment of gun and drug courts for juveniles.

The challenge with all juvenile offenders — both violent and nonviolent — is to determine what leads children to make bad choices, to identify those children at high risk for serious delinquent or risky behavior, and to provide appropriate interventions. Most juvenile offend-

ers have multiple problems and often struggle with social, educational, or economic hardships beyond their control. In addition to the prevalence of mental health and substance abuse disorders among youths in the juvenile justice system, family disruption and frequent family transitions such as divorce, separation, remarriage, and cohabitation are also considered risk factors for delinquency. Prevention strategies that address these risks before they translate into criminal behavior are essential to reduce delinquency and promote positive youth development. Appropriate interventions that help children handle their emotions and better manage their reactions to others can reduce recidivism for those who have already strayed. After-care programs, which involve close supervision and counseling services to help youths successfully re-enter their communities, have also been found to be essential in keeping these children from falling back into patterns of dangerous behavior.[34] This comprehensive array of services and programs helps give at-risk and delinquent children what they need to become peaceful, productive members of the community. The alternative is a waste of human capital and economic resources. A 1998 study suggests that the lifetime cost of allowing one child to drop out of high school and into a future of crime can total anywhere from $1.3 to $1.5 million.[35]

Substance Abuse: Tracking the Trends

Adolescent drug use has declined from its peak in 1997. According to the Partnership for a Drug-Free America, the number of teenagers who have tried an illicit drug in their lifetime declined from 53 percent in 1997 to 48 percent in 2000. Although the use of some illicit drugs, like heroin, cocaine, and LSD, has remained constant in recent years, the use of marijuana has declined. In 1997, 44 percent of teens reported using marijuana at least once, a rate that dropped to 40 percent in 2000.

While most illicit drug use among youths has declined, certain types of drug use have increased. Ecstasy, also known as a "club drug," has surged in popularity; the number of teens who have used the drug in their lifetime has doubled from 5 percent in 1995 to 10 percent in 2000. Thirteen percent of teens said they had used inhalants in the past year, an increase from 11 percent in 1999. And, teen use of methamphetamines (meth) appears to have rebounded after declining steadily from 1996 to 1999. The percentage of teens who have reported using meth in the past month increased from 3 percent in 1999 to 5 percent in 2000.

While smoking has declined statistically, 39 percent of teens have smoked within the last 30 days. Alcohol consumption continues to be extremely high; 31 percent of teens reported binge drinking within the last two weeks. In addition to the legal penalties involved in drug and alcohol use by youths, juvenile substance abuse is often accompanied by an array of other heavy consequences. Academic disinterest and difficulty, health-related problems, poor peer relationships, mental health issues, involvement in the juvenile justice system, and death are all possible effects of teen substance abuse.

Connections between juvenile substance abuse and juvenile delinquency cannot be ignored. When compared with their non-offending counterparts, delinquent youths use drugs at a higher rate and at an earlier age. Studies have shown that delinquents who use drugs are responsible for disproportionately higher rates of offending, face greater risk of re-offending, and are violent compared with delinquents who do not use drugs. Researchers have also shown that drug and alcohol abuse contribute to gun violence. In the world of drug dealing, guns are considered "tools of the trade" and are often used in crimes to support a drug habit.

In efforts to combat child substance abuse and delinquency, comprehensive community-based prevention and intervention programs that reinforce positive adolescent behavior have been shown to be effective. Project STAR, a comprehensive drug abuse program, includes a school-based component, mass media efforts, parental involvement, and community organization. Research has shown positive, long-term effects on high school seniors who started the program in junior high school. Project STAR students were 30 percent less likely to use marijuana, 25 percent less likely to smoke cigarettes, and 20 percent less likely to consume alcohol.

Sources: *Partnership Attitude Tracking Study: Spring 2000 Teens in Grades 7 through 12* (Partnership for a Drug-Free America, November 2000); *Juvenile Delinquency and Substance Abuse Fact Sheet* (Washington, D.C.: Office of Juvenile Justice and Delinquency Prevention, December 1997); *Enabling Prosecutors to Address Gang and Youth Violence* (Washington, D.C.: Office of Juvenile Justice and Delinquency Prevention, December 1999); *Research Reveals Links Between Substance Abuse and Gun Violence* (Join Together Online, March 1999); and *Preventing Drug Use Among Children and Adolescents: A Research-Based Guide* (Washington, D.C.: U.S. Department of Health and Human Services, National Institute on Drug Abuse, April 1997).

Youth Trends in Drug Use

Trends in Drug Use Among 8th, 10th, and 12th Graders, 1991-2000

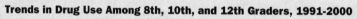
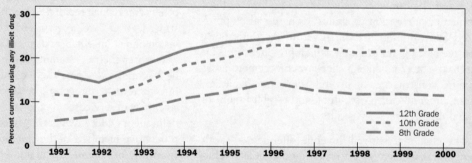

Source: University of Michigan, The Monitoring the Future Study, 2000, Table 2, at http://www.monitoringthefuture.org.

Gun Violence

In 1998, 3,761 children and teens were killed by gunfire in the United States,[36] which is one child every two and a half hours, 10 children every day, more than 70 children every week. Gun violence was responsible for 609 children not reaching high-school age (15 years old), 179 children not getting to celebrate their tenth birthday, and 83 children not even reaching age five. Nearly three times as many children under 10 died from gunfire as the number of law enforcement officers killed in the line of duty.[37] More children and teens died in 1998 from gunfire than from cancer, pneumonia, influenza, asthma, and HIV/AIDS *combined.*[38]

After peaking in 1994 at 5,793 young lives, youth firearm deaths dropped 35 percent between 1994 and 1998. Since 1994, the number of Black children and teens killed by guns has decreased 45 percent, and the number of White children and teens has dropped 28 percent.[39] Although the number of child gun deaths per year has dropped below 4,000 for the first time since 1988, the number remains disturbingly high. Too many children are dying. When compared to other industrialized countries, the numbers are even more staggering. According to the Centers for Disease Control and Prevention, the rate of firearm deaths among children under age 15 is almost 12 times higher in the United States than in 25 other industrialized countries combined. American children are 16 times more likely to be murdered with a gun, 11 times more likely to commit suicide with a gun, and nine times more likely to die in a firearm accident than children in these other countries.[40] The impact of gun violence on children is, in many ways, a distinct and shameful American phenomenon.

Fifty-eight percent of young people killed by gunfire are victims of homicide. In 1998, homicide accounted for 2,184 deaths among children age 19 and younger.[41] Although the decrease in firearm homicides accounted for most of the decrease in child firearm deaths from 1997 to 1998, not all communities are experiencing the decline. While many large cities, such as New York, Miami, and Boston, have experienced a decline in homicide rates over the last several years, Baltimore's murder rate has only recently dropped and despite the decline, there is evidence that gun violence victims in Baltimore are getting younger. In 1999, Johns Hopkins Hospital treated 390 gunshot wounds, more than one a day, and almost two-thirds of the patients were between 15 and 20 years old.[42]

Although a majority of child gun deaths are homicides, two out of every five young firearms deaths are the result of suicide or an accidental shooting. Thirty-three percent of young people killed by guns take their own lives. In 1998, suicide accounted for 1,241 child and teen gun deaths — an average of more than three every day.[43] Guns are used in two out of three youth suicides and unlike other attempted methods are more than 90 percent likely to be fatal.[44] This is particularly notable when considering that federal law requires individuals to be at least 21 years old to purchase a handgun, and more than 20 states have some minimum age requirement for the possession of rifles and long guns.[45] Where are children getting these guns? Unfortunately, in most cases, the weapons come from their own homes or from someone they know. More than two-thirds of firearms involved in self-inflicted firearm injuries and deaths come from either the victim's home or the home of a friend or relative.[46]

Accidental shootings accounted for about 7 percent of child firearm deaths in 1998; 262 children and teens lost their lives in accidental shootings.[47] One-third of all victims of fatal, unintentional shootings in the United States are age 19 or younger, and nearly 60 percent are under age 30.[48] America loses the equivalent of 25 youth basketball teams each year to accidents because a gun was left unlocked, loaded, and too easy for the wrong hands to reach. As with adolescent suicide, a vast majority of firearms used in unintentional shootings of children and teens come from the victim's home or the home of a relative, friend, or parent of a friend of the victim. A study reported in the *American Journal of Public Health* found that 1.4 million homes with 2.6 million children had firearms that were stored unlocked and loaded or unlocked and unloaded but stored with ammunition.[49] A recent survey found that most gun-owning parents store their firearms loaded or unlocked in the belief that their child can properly handle a gun and can tell the difference between a toy gun and a real gun.[50]

Protect children instead of guns

To stop our children from dying and being injured by guns, whether in a homicide, suicide, or accidental shooting, guns must be kept out of the hands of children and people who would harm children. There are nearly 200 million firearms in the hands of private citizens across America, and approximately 40 percent of all U.S. households have a gun.[51] Of the households with firearms, nearly half (43 percent) are home to one or more children.[52] In response to accidental deaths resulting from children who found unsecured firearms in their homes, the National Crime Prevention Council (NCPC) launched a three-year public awareness campaign in 2000, urging Americans to store their firearms securely in order to reduce the threat of injury and death to children and adults. A firearm in the home is an undeniable risk for firearm accidents and suicide. And although an oft-cited reason for a firearm in the home is protection against intruders, according to the National Crime Victimization Survey, the use of guns in self-defense is extremely rare. One study of this data found that as little as 3 percent of

Firearm Deaths

Firearm deaths, by manner, persons under age 20, 1979-1998
(excludes legal intervention)

	Total	Homicide	Suicide	Accident	Unknown
1979	3,710	1,651	1,220	726	113
1980	3,749	1,743	1,214	689	103
1981	3,589	1,660	1,213	604	112
1982	3,332	1,498	1,207	550	77
1983	2,962	1,238	1,150	504	70
1984	3,030	1,289	1,114	552	75
1985	3,169	1,322	1,256	519	72
1986	3,349	1,513	1,293	472	71
1987	3,400	1,573	1,281	467	79
1988	3,974	1,953	1,387	543	91
1989	4,384	2,367	1,380	567	70
1990	4,935	2,852	1,476	541	66
1991	5,329	3,247	1,436	551	95
1992	5,353	3,336	1,426	501	90
1993	5,715	3,625	1,460	526	104
1994	5,793	3,579	1,565	512	137
1995	5,254	3,249	1,450	440	115
1996	4,613	2,836	1,309	376	92
1997	4,205	2,562	1,262	306	75
1998	3,761	2,184	1,241	262	74
Total	83,606	45,277	26,340	10,208	1,781

Source: National Center for Health Statistics, Division of Vital Statistics, Table 292 (unpublished). Calculations by Children's Defense Fund.

victims were able to use their gun against someone who broke in or attempted to break into their home.[53]

In response to growing concern about the epidemic of firearm violence in homes and communities, health care professionals have become increasingly involved in educating health practitioners and the public about the public health risks posed by the presence of firearms in the home. Last spring, the American Academy of Pediatrics, in collaboration with PAX: The Movement to End Gun Violence, launched the Asking Saves Kids (ASK) campaign to help educate the public about the risk posed by a firearm in the home. The campaign encourages parents to ask the adults in a home where their child may visit if there is a gun in the home and gives parents tips on how to broach the potential awkwardness of asking such questions. Additionally, Physicians for Social Responsibility has published a *Physician's Pocket Guide to Counseling Patients on Gun Violence Prevention* to encourage health care professionals to spread the word about the dangers of allowing children and adolescents access to firearms.

Federal response

On Mother's Day 2000, hundreds of thousands of mothers, grandmothers, daughters, sisters, and others gathered on the National Mall in Washington, D.C. as part of the Million Mom March to urge the country to reform gun policies. Hundreds of women shared personal stories of tragedies related to gun violence at the largest public rally against gun violence in the nation's history. These women and their families called on national leaders to do more to protect children — not only through greater enforcement of gun crime, but through a comprehensive, national policy to ensure every child's right to a safe, gun-free environment. Unfortunately, Congress has done little to further gun safety. The march was held almost one year after the Senate passed several modest gun safety measures as part of a larger juvenile crime bill (see previous discussion) that were never approved by the full Congress. These gun safety provisions would have closed the gun show loophole by requiring background checks for all firearm sales at gun shows; requiring trigger locks be sold with all new handgun purchases; banning juvenile possession of semi-automatic weapons; banning importation of large capacity ammunition clips; and making the transfer of a handgun, semi-automatic weapon, or high capacity clip to a juvenile a felony punishable by up to five years in prison.

The House of Representatives took up its own gun safety legislation, but failed to address the gun show loophole or any other aspect of the gun safety issue in a meaningful way. In fact, during debate on the House bill, an amendment was adopted that would actually weaken current law at gun shows by reducing the time allowed to conduct a background check. More than 90 percent of background checks clear within a few hours,[54] but the remaining checks require additional follow-up with official state or local offices that are generally open only during business hours, Monday through Friday. Since most gun shows are held on Saturday, a one-day background check requirement would enable many potentially prohibited purchasers to walk away with a gun.

To fill the void left by Congress, the Clinton administration announced that Smith & Wesson, the nation's largest gun manufacturer, had agreed to include internal locking devices in all new handguns by 2002, to devote revenues to developing smart gun technology (which limits a gun's use to its adult owner or other authorized users), and to sell only to authorized dealers and distributors who agree to a code of conduct. Additionally, in its Fiscal Year 2001 budget, the administration called for a $280 million increase in investments for a series of gun crime enforcement initiatives, including funding to help law enforcement crack down on violent gun criminals and illegal gun traffickers. Congress approved the administration's funding request.

State and local response

Despite Congress' failure to enact any gun safety measures during the 106th Congress, several state legislatures have passed gun safety laws. For example:

◆ In California, the state legislature has passed a one-gun-a-month policy, which limits gun buyers to one gun purchase in a 30-day period. The legislation is designed to combat the practice of "gun-running," where an individual purchases an unrestricted quantity of firearms in a state with weak gun laws and transports them for sale illegally in a state with stricter gun laws.

◆ In Maryland, the state legislature has approved legislation that requires all guns in Maryland to have built-in trigger locks by 2003, increases enforcement of gun-related laws, and increases investment in smart gun technology and research.

◆ In Massachusetts, the state's Attorney General implemented standards to regulate firearms as consumer products. Among other things, the plan calls for all guns sold in Massachusetts to have a trigger pull that requires 10 pounds of pressure to be fired.

Where state governments have balked, citizens have taken action. After the Governor of Colorado vetoed legislation to close the gun show loophole in the state, citizens got the measure included on the ballot. In November 2000, Colorado voters joined the citizens of Oregon in overwhelmingly approving referendums to close the gun show loophole in their states.

Localities have also begun to use the court system as a way to effect change. A total of 32 municipalities have filed lawsuits against the firearms industry to recover damages for the creation of a public nuisance, for the negligent distribution of their products, and for producing products with inadequate safety systems. In June of last year, New York became the first state to file suit against the gun industry.[55] These efforts are necessary to hold the firearms industry accountable for the products it manufactures. Currently, the firearms industry is completely exempt from any national consumer safety regulation.

Violence in Schools

The safety of our schools continues to be a major concern as evidenced by a recent CNN/USA Today/Gallup poll in which 43 percent of parents said they fear for their child's safety at school. One in three parents believes that it is "very likely" that a Columbine-type shooting could happen in their community.[56] Yet, the reality is that schools remain one of the safest places for children. In fact, school crime has declined for the third year in a row. There is a less than 1 percent chance that a student will be murdered at school (or while travelling to and from school). And, although theft remains the most prevalent school crime, the percentage of students who reported property stolen has also decreased. Incidents of students engaging in physical fights have declined, and fewer students are carrying weapons on school property.[57]

Overall, students are feeling increasingly safe at school. According to *Indicators of School Crime and Safety, 2000*, a joint report by the U.S. Departments of Education and Justice, the number of students who fear attack at school has declined from 9 percent in 1995 to 5 percent in 1999. The number of students who reported avoiding certain areas at school out of fear has also declined, down from 9 percent in 1995 to 5 percent in 1999. However, 5 percent, which represents 1.1 million children, is still a significant number of students who are reporting concern for their safety. An even larger number of Black and Hispanic students report fear of attack. While 4 percent of White students feared harm at school, 9 percent of Black students and 8 percent of Hispanic students reported fearing for their safety.[58]

Gangs, a common perpetrator of student victimization, play a significant role in increased tensions at school. By definition, gangs are often actively involved in drug crimes and weapons trafficking — activities closely linked to violence. While the number of students reporting the presence of gangs in their schools has decreased from 29 percent in 1995 to 17 percent in 1999,[59] gangs remain prevalent in schools. In schools where gangs were present, 12 percent of the students reported seeing a student with a gun, compared to 3 percent of students when gangs were not present. Students who reported that drugs were readily available at their school were more likely to report gangs at their school as well, compared to those who said no drugs were available. The presence of gangs more than doubles the likelihood of violent victimization at school, nearly 8 percent compared with 3 percent.[60]

In reaction to school violence concerns, some officials have responded with increased school security measures. High-tech hardware such as metal detectors, security surveillance cameras, and photo-ID systems linked to a school computer database have been installed in schools across America with the intention of making them safer. Some students are required to carry belongings in transparent book-bags and subjected to locker checks and locked doors during the school day. The effect is often a heightened safety concern, with students feeling less safe and more distrusted because the school feels more like a correctional facility than a place of learning.[61]

Concentrating efforts on technologies and other measures to secure schools should not replace investments in personnel. According to *An Interim Report on the Prevention of Targeted Violence in Schools,* a collaboration of the Secret Service and the Department of Education, students involved in the most violent behavior exhibited warnings prior to their attack. The majority of these youths told someone about the idea prior to the attack, previously engaged in behavior that indicated a need for help, and caused concern to an adult.[62] Counselors, mental health professionals, and administrators trained in identifying early problem warning signs are critical in responding to troubled students who need assistance and must be a component of any school's effective security plan.

Seattle Public Schools have implemented a comprehensive safety plan in an effort to prevent violence in its schools. Starting with the priority of maximizing student academic achievement, the school district ties school safety to academic success. The district recognizes that schools will not have optimum security without socially and emotionally fit students, trained school leadership, and instructional excellence. Using a four-tiered management model, the school system offers an all-inclusive safety plan.

◆ **Prevention:** Create an environment that provides effective limit–setting on what is and is not considered appropriate behavior for its students. Administrators are encouraged to identify at-risk youths early, and schools emphasize self-management and pro-social skills training.

◆ **Preparedness:** Train staff in crisis/emergency management, de-escalation, and threat analysis and educate

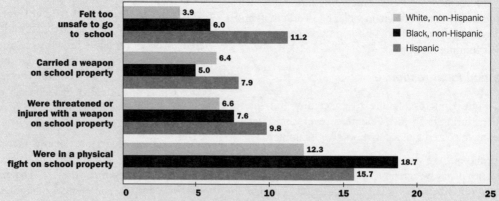

School Safety

Percentage of high school students who:

Felt too unsafe to go to school
- White, non-Hispanic: 3.9
- Black, non-Hispanic: 6.0
- Hispanic: 11.2

Carried a weapon on school property
- White, non-Hispanic: 6.4
- Black, non-Hispanic: 5.0
- Hispanic: 7.9

Were threatened or injured with a weapon on school property
- White, non-Hispanic: 6.6
- Black, non-Hispanic: 7.6
- Hispanic: 9.8

Were in a physical fight on school property
- White, non-Hispanic: 12.3
- Black, non-Hispanic: 18.7
- Hispanic: 15.7

Legend:
- White, non-Hispanic
- Black, non-Hispanic
- Hispanic

Source: U.S. Department of Health and Human Services, Centers for Disease Control and Prevention, "Youth Risk Behavior Surveillance — United States, 1999," *MMWR,* Vol. 49, Number SS-5 (June 9, 2000), Table 10.

Violence in the Media: The Impact of Images

The typical American child watches 28 hours of television a week and by age 18 will have seen 16,000 simulated murders and 200,000 acts of violence. The American Psychological Association reports that 80.3 percent of all television programs contain acts of violence, and commercial television for children is 50 to 60 times more violent than prime time programs for adults. Some cartoons average more than 80 violent acts per hour. Watching violence in the media has been linked to higher levels of anti-social behavior, which range from trivial to serious violence, increased hostility, and acceptance of violence as a solution to problems. Viewing violence also leads to desensitization, which is exhibited by reduced arousal and emotional disturbance to regular exposure to violence, reduced tendency to intervene to stop a fight, and less sympathy for victims of violence.

In addition to the concern about violent content in media programming, the marketing and advertising practices of the media industry have also come under scrutiny. Last fall, the Federal Trade Commission (FTC) released a report detailing the results of a year-long investigation on the marketing practices of the entertainment industry. According to the report, the motion picture, music recording, and electronic games industries routinely targeted children under age 17 when marketing products that their own rating systems had deemed as inappropriate for children or had cautioned parents about for violent content. It also found that advertisements for violent video games, movies, and music were aired during television shows for younger audiences and printed in teen magazines. Congress held several hearings on the report and called on the industry to tighten up its standards for marketing products with violent content to children. Leading media executives agreed to follow a set of 12 guidelines established by the Motion Picture Association of America (MPAA) to regulate marketing practices. It remains to be seen whether these self-regulatory measures will lead to more responsible marketing practices.

Addressing the problem of violence in the media requires everyone's involvement. Parents should limit the amount of television and types of programs their children watch, and parents should learn about the movies, videos, and electronic games available for rent or purchase. Citizens should demand responsible marketing and production by the media industry. Government should use its regulatory authorities to promote the elimination of violence from children's programming.

Sources: APA Online, "Psychiatric Effects of Media Violence," Public Information: APA Fact Sheet Series (Washington D.C.: American Psychological Association). Retrieved from the Internet at www.psych.org/psych/htdocs/ pulic_info/media_violence.html on April 5, 2000; Joanne Cantor, "Media Violence," *Journal of Adolescent Health* 27S, no. 2 (2000): 30-34; Federal Trade Commission, *Marketing Violent Entertainment to Children: A Review of Self-Regulation and Industry Practices in the Motion Picture, Music Recording & Electronic Game Industries* (Washington, D.C.: Federal Trade Commission, · September 2000).

staff on the district's discipline policies while providing necessary resources.

◆ **Response:** Appropriate strategies exist to handle a full spectrum of safety issues including child abuse, harassment, school–police relations, weapons, and drugs. Any incident that could compromise the school's safety is met with an established command structure that delegates team responsibilities to each authority at the school.

◆ **Recovery:** In the aftermath of a critical incident, the district offers stress debriefing and defusing as well as long-term counseling to the students. To assist parents and the community, the district will also host a forum where concerns may be expressed.

In recent years, many school systems have adopted zero-tolerance policies in response to crime and violence. An overwhelming majority of schools have zero-tolerance

policies for offenses such as acts of violence and possession of weapons and drugs. Unfortunately, overzealous enforcement of zero-tolerance policies have only served to distort their original intent. Too frequently, administrators have used zero-tolerance policies to suspend and expel children based on relatively minor infractions. In the sweeping application of these policies, aspirin and Tylenol have been treated as drugs and nail clippers have been classified as weapons. During the 1998 school year, more than 3 million students were suspended, and 87,000 were expelled. Overwhelmingly, the victims of these school disciplinary policies have been minorities, particularly Black students. A disproportionate number of Black students are being suspended and expelled when compared to their White classmates. While Black students represent only 17 percent of public school enrollment nationally, they constitute 32 percent of out-of-school suspensions. On the other hand, White students make up 63 percent of enrollment and represent 50 percent of suspensions and 50 percent of expulsions. The disparate application of punishment has been linked to administrators who punish Black students more severely for similar and even less disruptive behavior.[63]

Consequently, an increased number of children are being shunned by the educational system. Only 26 states require alternative education assignments for students suspended and expelled,[64] and many children are being expelled without adult supervision or educational guidance. These youths suffer academically and are at risk for delinquency and contact with the juvenile justice system. Furthermore, students who are suspended are more likely to drop out of school, and students who drop out are more likely to be arrested. Future examination of the success or failure of these all-or-nothing disciplinary approaches will be necessary to be sure that zero-tolerance of behavior does not become zero-tolerance of children.

Investing in Our Youth

Although official indicators, such as arrest rates, victimization data, and hospital emergency room records, show that youth violence has declined significantly over the past several years, there is disturbing evidence that a serious problem remains. In January, the U.S. Surgeon General released a comprehensive report on youth violence, which found that youths' confidential self-reports about their behavior revealed very little change over the past decade in the proportion of young people who have engaged in potentially dangerous acts. However, the report also concludes that youth violence is not an intractable problem.[65] The key is to minimize the risk factors that contribute to aggressive and violent behavior and maximize those protective factors that diminish the likelihood of violent activity by youth.

Who's most at risk and why?

In general, the strongest demographic predictors of violent activity are age and gender. Boys in late adolescence and young men are more likely to be violent. Studies show that most youth violence is perpetrated by males whose violent behavior begins by age 15. Race is also an indicator — data have consistently found that prevalence rates of violent activity are higher among Black youths than among White youths. Additionally, research has shown other factors that make children and adolescents more likely to behave violently. These factors can be grouped into three general areas: individual, family, and community. Individual risk factors include social or cognitive problems, a history of aggressive behavior, beliefs that support use of violence, and drug or alcohol abuse. Family factors include lack of parental supervision; spousal

or child abuse; access to firearms; a parent's use of drugs or alcohol; and divorce, relocation, or other family disruption. External or community risk factors include problems at school, isolation from peers or association with peers who are violent, and lack of positive interaction with non-familial adults.[66]

Prevention strategies that work

Although more comprehensive research and evaluation must continue, several strategies have emerged as promising approaches in preventing youth violence. The Centers for Disease Control and Prevention recently released a comprehensive report outlining the four basic youth violence prevention strategies with examples of best practices in each area:[67]

◆ **Parent and Family-Based** — These strategies are designed to improve family relations by combining parenting skills training, child development education, and communication and conflict resolution skills training. This approach has been most successful for families with young children or at-risk parents expecting a child. One of the most successful examples of this approach is Multisystemic Therapy (MST), which focuses on the interconnectedness of families. A study of the approach in Simpsonville, North Carolina, found that adjudicated youths who received the therapy had fewer arrests and were incarcerated less frequently than those receiving other services.

◆ **Home-visiting** — These strategies bring community resources to at-risk families in their homes. Intervention staff provide information, health care, counseling, and other support services to families in their homes. On average, these interventions last at least one year and are most effective with expectant families and parents with newborns.

◆ **Social-cognitive** — These strategies attempt to equip children with the skills they need to deal effectively with others in social situations. It teaches children how to handle being teased or being isolated by another group of children. The approach is based on the theory that children learn social skills from interaction with the adults in their lives, relationships with their peers, and role models in the media. Role-playing, conflict resolution exercises, and nonviolence curriculum are all elements of this violence prevention strategy. PATHS (Promoting Alternative Thinking Strategies) is an example of a school curriculum program designed to help students in kindergarten through grade five develop problem-solving and emotional management skills. PATHS trials conducted in four sites over the past 15 years have shown improvements in social competencies and reductions in aggression and other risk factors for violence.

◆ **Mentoring** — This approach pairs a young person with an adult who serves as a supportive, nonjudgmental role model. Mentoring has been shown to work with all age groups with significant improvements in school attendance and performance and reductions in substance abuse and violent behavior. Big Brothers/Big Sisters continues to be the best-known and most successful mentoring program in the country, but others are emerging. The SAGE (Supporting Adolescents with Guidance and Employment) is a community-based program in North Carolina that works to prevent violence and other risky behaviors among young Black males. The program brings together successful Black businessmen and civic leaders to create an entrepreneurial experience for Black youths. Results suggest that the program is working — SAGE participants report decreases in weapon carrying, drug trafficking, heavy drinking, and violent activity.

Beyond Preventing Violence to Promoting Positive Youth Development

Investing in activities that engage children in positive ways reaps multiple benefits. According to the U.S. Census Bureau, nearly 7 million children are left home alone after school each week. It has been well-documented that after-school programs help to curb delinquent behavior when it most frequently occurs — between the hours of 3 p.m. and 6 p.m. However, these programs do more than just make communities safer, they also help to ensure positive youth development. Youths who participate in after-school and youth development programs are less likely to use drugs, drink alcohol, become sexually active, or smoke and are more likely to have stronger interpersonal skills, higher academic achievement, and healthier relationships with others.[68] Quality after-school programs also have a lasting impact on children's attitudes, values, and skills.

The primary source of federal funding for after-school activities flows through the 21st Century Community Learning Centers (CCLC) program, which provides expanded learning opportunities for children and youths in a positive, supervised environment. The program provides grants to community-based organizations to stay open longer and provide a safe place for activities such as academic enrichment, mentoring, tutoring, drug and violence prevention, and recreation. Congress has increased funding from $453.4 million in Fiscal Year 2000 to $845.6 million in Fiscal Year 2001 for this important program, which has served more than 650,000 youths nationwide.

Investing in positive youth development does not begin with school-age children. Ensuring that all children have what they need to become productive, healthy adults requires investment in quality child care, health care, and other life essentials. It involves addressing the needs of the child and that child's family. To prevent a child from making a bad choice, attention must be paid to all the factors that lead to the behavior rather than on the behavior alone. By focusing on the child and not the act, violence prevention becomes one of the many positive consequences of a comprehensive youth development strategy.

Youth employment and preparing young people for life

Despite prosperous economic times and low levels of unemployment, many young people, particularly those who are at-risk, struggle to find jobs with wages that allow them to be self-sufficient. In 2000, the unemployment rate for teens ages 16 to 19 was 13.1 percent compared to just 3.4 percent for adults 20 and older. These statistics are particularly troubling for Black teens between the ages of 16 and 19 who were unemployed at a rate of 24.7 percent in 2000.[69] In an increasingly high-tech economy, many youths do not have the computer and technology skills necessary to compete for jobs that pay adequately, relegating these young people to work in low-paying jobs with no benefits and no opportunity for advancement.

Many of the youths in dead-end jobs are the most vulnerable — often they are low-income, school dropouts, young parents, juvenile offenders, or homeless. Until the enactment of the 1998 Workforce Investment Act (WIA), little was done to improve employment opportunities for these at-risk youth. The WIA, the successor to the former Job Training Partnership Act (JTPA), was designed to provide a more comprehensive method of delivering job skills, training, and opportunities to young people in local communities. In accordance with the legislation, funding streams are combined, and summer employment opportunities are included as part of a year-round academic and occupational plan for youths.[70] In addition, 30 percent of all local youth program funding under the WIA is set aside for out-of-school youths.[71]

The WIA has also created local youth employment policy boards called Youth Councils. Local Workforce Investment Boards (WIB), which oversee employment plans and job training providers, are responsible for establishing Youth Councils to advise the WIB on local youth employment concerns.[72] The Youth Councils bring together experts in each community who are knowledgeable about their youths' employment needs to help address the specific needs of their communities. The WIA also provides funding for the Youth Activities formula grants, which support local summer and year-round youth employment activities, and the Youth Opportunity grants, a five-year investment in youths who live in the poorest areas of the country.

The Department of Labor (DOL) has launched its Youth Opportunity Movement, which is a variety of efforts to ensure that all youths, particularly those who are out of school, have the skills and training to transition successfully to employment and adulthood. Several of these programs are encompassed in the WIA, but additional sources of DOL funding under the Youth Opportunity Movement are available to assist the most vulnerable youths. In addition to WIA funding, DOL supports other initiatives that help at-risk youths find jobs, complete high school, or enroll in college. For example, the Responsible Reintegration for Young Offenders incorporates job training and education into programs to help young offenders and youths between ages 14 and 21 who are at risk of getting in trouble.[73]

While the WIA and several of the new DOL Youth Opportunity Movement initiatives are in their beginning stages, several new challenges and opportunities have already emerged. Some communities were not able to serve as many youths under the new funding schemes as they had in previous years. Because the WIA now requires local communities to provide more services, more resources are needed for the Youth Activities formula grant program so more youths who are in danger of falling through the cracks have the opportunity to succeed. Young people and youth service providers need to take advantage of the opportunities that the WIA's new Youth Councils provide to shape local youth employment policy. Participating youths can develop leadership skills and influence community employment issues. Youth service providers can ensure, through advocacy, that young people's employment and job training needs are being met.

The National Youth Employment Coalition highlights several promising youth employment and development programs with their annual Promising and Effective Practices Network (PEPNet) awards. Last year's PEPNet awardees include:

◆ **Baltimore City Fire Cadet Program: Baltimore City Office of Employment Development** — This program is a three-phase initiative that begins during the summer between the junior and senior year of high school. The first phase includes driver education training followed by eight weeks of fire fighter training, including emergency medical technician training and physical fitness activities. During the school year, cadets attend their home schools for academic classes in the morning and are then transported to the Department's Fire Academy to continue fire cadet classes. Phase three occurs the summer after graduation from high school. The cadet is employed by the Fire Department and assigned to one of five departments while continuing to be involved in community service activities.

◆ **Casa Verde Builders Program: American Youth-Works** — In Austin, Texas, the Casa Verde Builders Program specializes in building energy efficient homes using environmentally friendly products. Participants commit at least six months to the program, spending half their time in on-site construction training activities and the other half of their time at educational activities at American Youth Work's Charter High School.

◆ **Diploma Plus: Center for Youth Development and Education Corporation for Business, Work, and Learning** — In Boston, the nine Diploma Plus sites include those operated by community-based organizations that function as satellites to the public schools. Diploma Plus is divided into two stages. The first features preparation in core academic competencies and other foundation skills while exposing students to a variety of career pathways as preparation for college and the program's second stage. The second stage, the Plus Year, prepares students to transition to life after high school with a combination of small group seminar work, community college attendance, and work-based learning.

Moving Forward:
A 2001 Agenda for Action

The declines in violent crime and the juvenile crime rate are good signs for everyone. But far too many young people end up in a juvenile justice system that has become increasingly punitive, and too many children are hurt by violence in society, particularly gun violence. At all levels, advocates should:

◆ **Fight for increased investment in prevention programs.** Prevention works. We need to invest more money in keeping children out of trouble rather than continuing to pour dollars into building new prisons.

◆ **Develop after-school and summer programs to give children productive activities in their out-of-school hours.** After-school and summer programs — at schools, churches, YMCAs, and other community-based organizations — provide positive opportunities for children during the hours when they are not in school and their parents are at work. Programs such as the 21st Century Community Learning Centers need to be developed and expanded so more children can participate.

◆ **Provide positive youth development activities such as mentoring to help youths explore and develop healthy relationships.** Communities need to provide more opportunities for young people to develop solid relationships with caring adults. If young people feel connected, they are more likely to make good choices for themselves and contribute to a healthy, safe community. Enactment of the Younger Americans

Act could help communities mobilize and implement youth development programs.

◆ **Provide youth employment opportunities so young people can gain confidence and hope for the future.** Job training programs help our youths get a foothold in the job market and this, in turn, reduces the odds of involvement in crime and other risky behaviors. Programs like YouthBuild can help provide job training opportunities for young people while strengthening communities. Funding for these programs needs to be expanded so more youths can participate.

◆ **Oppose efforts to pass regressive legislation.** Advocates and community leaders from all sectors need to tell Congress not to weaken laws that protect children from confinement in adult jails. Troubled children

need positive role models as mentors, not the hardened adult criminals who would be their fellow inmates. Runaways and truants do not belong behind prison bars. Juvenile justice systems need sufficient resources to provide appropriate services and treatment for children who commit crimes.

◆ **Support common sense legislation to keep children safe from guns.** Laws to keep children safe from guns are urgently needed. No child should be able to get their hands on a gun at home or in the community. Policy makers must understand the connection between the availability of guns and violence by and against children. Our homes and communities need to be protected from gun violence.

Endnotes

1. U.S. Department of Justice, Federal Bureau of Investigation, *Crime Reports in the United States, 1999: Uniform Crime Reports* (Washington, D.C.: U.S. Government Printing Office, October 2000): 6.

2. David Finkelhor and Richard Ormrod, *Characteristics of Crimes Against Juveniles* (Washington, D.C.: U.S. Department of Justice, Office of Juvenile Justice and Delinquency Prevention, June 2000).

3. U.S. Department of Justice, Office of Juvenile Justice and Delinquency Prevention, "Children as Victims," *1999 National Report Series, Juvenile Justice Bulletin* (Washington, D.C.: U.S. Department of Justice, Office of Juvenile Justice and Delinquency Prevention, May 2000).

4. *Supra* note 2.

5. U.S. Department of Health and Human Services, Administration on Children, Youth, and Families, *Child Maltreatment 1998: Reports From the States to National Child Abuse and Neglect Data System* (Washington, D.C.: U.S. Government Printing Office, 2000).

6. Cathy Spatz Widom, "Child Victims: In Search of Opportunities for Breaking the Cycle of Violence," *Perspectives on Crime and Justice: 1996-1997 Lecture Series* (Washington, D.C.: U.S. Department of Justice, National Institute of Justice, November 1997).

7. Robin Weeks and Cathy Spatz Widom, *Early Childhood Victimization Among Incarcerated Adult Male Felons* (Washington, D.C.: U.S. Department of Justice, National Institute of Justice, April 1998).

8. Howard N. Snyder, "Juvenile Arrests 1999," *Juvenile Justice Bulletin* (Washington, D.C.: U.S. Department of Justice, Office of Juvenile Justice and Delinquency Prevention, December 2000).

9. U.S. Census Bureau, "Resident Population Estimates of the United States by Age and Sex: April 1, 1990 to July 1, 1999, with Short-Term Projection to November 1, 2000" (Washington, D.C.: U.S. Department of Commerce, 2001).

10. *Supra* note 1, at 216.

11. Howard N. Snyder and Melissa Sickmund, Juvenile Offenders and Victims: *1999 National Report* (Washington, D.C.: U.S. Department of Justice, Office of Juvenile Justice and Delinquency Prevention, September 1999): 80-81.

12. *Ibid.* at 89.

13. U.S. Department of Justice, Office of Juvenile Justice and Delinquency Prevention, *Trying Juveniles as Adults in Criminal Court: An Analysis of State Transfer Provisions* (Washington, D.C.: U.S. Department of Justice, Office of Juvenile Justice and Delinquency Prevention, December 1998): 13.

14. Jeffrey Fagan and Franklin Zimring, *The Changing Borders of Juvenile Justice: Transfer of Adolescents to the Criminal Court* (Chicago: The University of Chicago Press, 2000): 261.

15. Richard Mendel, *Less Hype, More Help: Reducing Juvenile Crime, What Works — and What Doesn't* (Washington, D.C.: American Youth Policy Forum, 2000): 41. Available on the Internet at www.aypf.org.

16. Martin Forst, Jeffrey Fagan, and T. Vivona, "Youth in Prisons and Training Schools: Perceptions and Consequences of the Treatment-Custody Dichotomy," *Juvenile and Family Court Journal* 40 (1989): 1-14.

17. Allen J. Beck, *Prison and Jail Inmates at Midyear 1999*, (Washington, D.C.: U.S. Department of Justice, Bureau of Justice Statistics, April 2000).

18. Thomas Grisso and Robert Schwartz, *Youth on Trial: A Developmental Perspective* (Chicago: The University of Chicago Press, 2000): 22-23.

19. U.S. Department of Justice, Office of Juvenile Justice and Delinquency Prevention, *Serious and Violent Juvenile Offenders*, (Washington, D.C.: U.S. Department of Justice, Office of Juvenile Justice and Delinquency Prevention, May 1998).

20. *Supra* note 18, at 47.

21. *Supra* note 11, at 63.

22. John C. Howell, *Youth Gang Programs and Strategies* (Washington, D.C.: U.S. Department of Justice, Office of Juvenile Justice and Delinquency Prevention, August 2000): 50. Available on the Internet at www.ojjdp.ncjrs.org.

23. *Ibid.* at 11, 32, 34.

24. U.S. Department of Justice, Office of Juvenile Justice and Delinquency Prevention, "Minorities in the Juvenile Justice System," *Juvenile Justice Bulletin* (Washington, D.C.: U.S. Department of Justice, Office of Juvenile Justice and Delinquency Prevention, December 1999).

25. Eileen Poe-Yamagata and Michael A. Jones, *And Justice For Some* (Washington, D.C.: Youth Law Center, Justice Policy Institute, Building Blocks for Youth, April 2000).

26. *Supra* note 11, at 202.

27. Mike Males and Dan Macallair, *The Color of Justice: An Analysis of Juvenile Adult Court Transfers in California* (Washington, D.C.: Youth Law Center, Justice Policy Institute, Building Blocks for Youth, January 2000).

28. *Supra* note 11, at 192-193.

29. *Supra* note 1, at 217.

30. Leslie Acoca, "Investing in Girls: A 21st Century Strategy," *Juvenile Justice* VI, no. 1 (Washington, D.C: U.S. Department of Justice, Office of Juvenile Justice and Delinquency Prevention, October 1999): 3-13.

31. Anne Marie Ambrose and Sandra Simpkins, *Improving Conditions for Girls in the Justice System: The Female Detention Project* (Philadelphia: Philadelphia Defender Association, December 1999). Retrieved from the Internet at http://www.abanet.org/crimjust/juvjus/gji.html on September 20, 2000.

32. LaWanda Ravoira, "National Girls' Caucus," *Juvenile Justice* VI, no. 1 (Washington, D.C: U.S. Department of Justice, Office of Juvenile Justice and Delinquency Prevention, October 1999): 21-28.

33. The Juvenile Justice and Delinquency Prevention Act of 1974 is subject to Congressional reauthorization every four years. The law expired on September 30, 1996 and has not been reauthorized. However, the programs created by the JJDPA have remained intact as Congress has continued to appropriate funds for

the Office of Juvenile Justice and Delinquency Prevention and for the Juvenile Accountability Block Grant since 1996.

34. Rolf Loeber and David P. Farrington, eds., *Serious and Violent Juvenile Offenders: Risk Factors and Successful Interventions* (Thousand Oaks, Calif.: Sage Publications, 1998): 356-66.

35. *Supra* note 11, at 82.

36. Children's Defense Fund (CDF). Calculations based on unpublished data from National Center for Health Statistics, *National Vital Statistics System, 1979-1998*.

37. U.S. Department of Justice, Bureau of Justice Statistics, *Sourcebook of Criminal Justice Statistics – 1999*, (Washington, D.C.: U.S. Department of Justice, 2000): 318.

38. U.S. Department of Health and Human Services, Centers for Disease Control and Prevention, "Deaths Final Data for 1998," *National Vital Statistics Reports* 48, no. 11 (Washington, D.C.: U.S. Department of Health and Human Services, Centers for Disease Control and Prevention, July 24, 2000).

39. *Supra* note 36.

40. U.S. Department of Health and Human Services, Centers for Disease Control and Prevention, "Rates of Homicide, Suicide, and Firearm-Related Death Among Children — 26 Industrialized Countries," *Morbidity and Mortality Weekly Report* 46, no. 5 (Washington, D.C.: U.S. Department of Health and Human Services, Centers for Disease Control and Prevention, February 7, 1997): 101.

41. *Supra* note 36.

42. Mike Adams, "The Trauma of Gun Violence," *The Baltimore Sun* (March 12, 2000): 1C.

43. *Supra* note 36.

44. American Academy of Pediatrics, "Firearm-Related Injuries Affecting the Pediatric Population," *Pediatrics* 105, no. 4 (April, 2000): 888-895.

45. Open Society Institute, Center on Crime, Communities & Culture and the Funders' Collaborative for Gun Violence Prevention, *Gun Control in the United States: A Comparative Survey of State Firearm Laws* (April 2000). Available on the Internet at http://www.soros.org/crime/guncontrol.htm.

46. David Grossman, Donald T. Reay, and Stephanie A. Baker, "Self-Inflicted and Unintentional Firearm Injuries Among Children and Adolescents," *Archives of Pediatric Adolescent Medicine* 153 (August 1999): 875-878. Available on the Internet at www.ama-assn.org/peds.

47. *Supra* note 36.

48. Philip J. Cook and Jens Ludwig, *Gun Violence: The Real Costs* (New York: Oxford University Press, 2000): 27.

49. Mark A. Schuster, et al., "Firearm Storage Patterns in U.S. Homes with Children," *American Journal of Public Health* 90, no. 4 (April 2000): 588-594.

50. Mirna M. Farah, et al., "Firearms in the Home: Parental Perceptions," *Pediatrics* 104, no. 5 (November 1999): 1059-1063.

51. Tom W. Smith, "1999 National Gun Policy Survey of the National Opinion Research Center: Research Findings," *National Opinion Research Center* (Chicago: The University of Chicago Press, 2000): 15. Available on the Internet at www.norc.uchicago.edu/online/gunrpt.htm.

52. Peter D. Hart Associates, Center to Prevent Handgun Violence, "Parents, Kids, & Guns: A Nationwide Survey" (October 31, 1998). Retrieved from the Internet at http://www.handguncontrol.org/press/1998/98archive/oct31-98c.htm on November 21, 2000.

53. *Supra* note 48, at 37.

54. U.S. Department of Justice, Federal Bureau of Investigation, *National Instant Criminal Background Check System (NICS), Operations Report (November 30, 1998 – December 31, 1999)* (Washington, D.C.: U.S. Department of Justice, Federal Bureau of Investigation, March 2000). Available on the Internet at http://www.fbi.gov/programs/nics/nic1year.pdf.

55. Educational Fund to End Handgun Violence, "Firearms Litigation Update," *Stop Gun Violence News* 25 (September 2000): 2.

56. Mark Gillespie, "One in Three Say It Is Very Likely That Columbine-Type Shootings Could Happen in Their Community," *Gallup News Service* (April 20, 2000). Retrieved from the Internet at http://www.gallup.com//poll/releases/pr00420.asp on November 29, 2000.

57. U.S. Department of Education, U.S. Department of Justice, *2000 Annual Report on School Safety* (Washington, D.C.: U.S. Department of Education, U.S. Department of Justice, 2000). Available on the Internet at http://www.ed.gov/offices/OESE/SDFS/annrept00.pdf.

58. U.S. Department of Education, U.S. Department of Justice, *Indicators of School Crime and Safety 2000* (Washington, D.C.: National Center for Education Statistics, Bureau of Justice Statistics, October 2000): 30 - 31.

59. *Ibid.* at 35.

60. John C. Howell and James P. Lynch, "Youth Gangs in Schools," *Juvenile Justice Bulletin* (Washington, D.C.: U.S. Department of Health and Human Services, Centers for Disease Control and Prevention, August 2000). Available on the Internet at www.ojjdp.ncjrs.org.

61. Kim Brooks, Vincent Schiraldi, and Jason Ziedenberg, *School House Hype: Two Years Later* (Washington, D.C.: Justice Policy Institute and Children's Law Center, April 2000). Retrieved from the Internet at http://www.cjcj.org/schoolhousehype/shh2.html on April 12, 2000.

62. U.S. Secret Service National Threat Assessment Center, *Safe School Initiative: An Interim Report on the Prevention of Targeted Violence in School* (Washington, D.C.: U.S. Department of Education, National Institute of Justice, October 2000).

63. Penda Hair, Christopher Edley, Jr., et al., *Opportunities Suspended: The Devastating Consequences of Zero Tolerance and School Discipline* (Cambridge, Mass.: Advancement Project and The Civil Rights Project at Harvard University, June 2000).

64. *Ibid.* at vi.

65. Office of the U.S. Surgeon General, *Youth Violence: A Report of the Surgeon General* (Washington, D.C.: U.S. Department of Health and Human Services, Office of Public Health and Science, January 2001).

66. U.S. Department of Justice, Office of Juvenile Justice and Delinquency Prevention, *Report to Congress on Juvenile Violence Research* (Washington, D.C.: U.S. Department of Justice, Office of Juvenile Justice and Delinquency Prevention, July 1999).

67. Timothy N. Thornton, Carole A. Craft, and Linda L. Dahlberg, et al., *Best Practices of Youth Violence Prevention: A Sourcebook for Community Action*, (Atlanta: U.S. Department of Health and Human Services, Centers for Disease Control and Prevention, September 2000).

68. Sanford Newman, James Alan Fox, Edward A. Flynn, et al., *America's After-School Choice: The Prime Time for Juvenile Crime Or Youth Enrichment and Achievement* (Washington, D.C.: Fight Crime: Invest in Kids, 2000).

69. U.S. Department of Labor, Bureau of Labor Statistics, *Labor Force Statistics from Current Population ages 16-19* (Washington, D.C.: U.S. Department of Labor, January 2001).

70. Linda Schade, *Getting Good Jobs: An Organizer's Guide To Job Training* (Washington, D.C.: Center for Community Change, 1999): 18.

71. MaryAnn Amore, *Bringing Youth Into the Workforce Investment System* (New Brunswick, N.J.: The John J. Heldrich Center for Workforce Development Rutgers University, 1999).

72. *Supra* note 70, at 10.

73. U.S. Department of Labor, Employment and Training Administration, Office of Youth Services, *Youth Activities at the United States Department of Labor* (Washington, D.C.; U.S. Department of Labor, September 2000).

Poverty Among Children

Year	Number of Children Under 18 Who Are Poor	Child Poverty Rate	Number of Children* Under 6 Who Are Poor	Poverty Rate for Children* Under 6
1959	17,552,000	27.3%	n/a	n/a
1960	17,634,000	26.9	n/a	n/a
1961	16,909,000	25.6	n/a	n/a
1962	16,963,000	25.0	n/a	n/a
1963	16,005,000	23.1	n/a	n/a
1964	16,051,000	23.0	n/a	n/a
1965	14,676,000	21.0	n/a	n/a
1966	12,389,000	17.6	n/a	n/a
1967	11,656,000	16.6	n/a	n/a
1968	10,954,000	15.6	n/a	n/a
1969	9,691,000	14.0	3,298,000	15.3%
1970	10,440,000	15.1	3,561,000	16.6
1971	10,551,000	15.3	3,499,000	16.9
1972	10,284,000	15.1	3,276,000	16.1
1973	9,642,000	14.4	3,097,000	15.7
1974	10,156,000	15.4	3,294,000	16.9
1975	11,104,000	17.1	3,460,000	18.2
1976	10,273,000	16.0	3,270,000	17.7
1977	10,288,000	16.2	3,326,000	18.1
1978	9,931,000	15.9	3,184,000	17.2
1979	10,377,000	16.4	3,415,000	17.8
1980	11,543,000	18.3	4,030,000	20.5
1981	12,505,000	20.0	4,422,000	22.0
1982	13,647,000	21.9	4,821,000	23.3
1983	13,911,000	22.3	5,122,000	24.6
1984	13,420,000	21.5	4,938,000	23.4
1985	13,010,000	20.7	4,832,000	22.6
1986	12,876,000	20.5	4,619,000	21.6
1987	12,843,000	20.3	4,852,000	22.4
1988	12,455,000	19.5	5,032,000	22.6
1989	12,590,000	19.6	5,071,000	22.5
1990	13,431,000	20.6	5,198,000	23.0
1991	14,341,000	21.8	5,483,000	24.0
1992	15,294,000	22.3	5,781,000	25.0
1993	15,727,000	22.7	6,097,000	25.6
1994	15,289,000	21.8	5,878,000	24.5
1995	14,665,000	20.8	5,670,000	23.7
1996	14,463,000	20.5	5,333,000	22.7
1997	14,113,000	19.9	5,049,000	21.6
1998	13,467,000	18.9	4,775,000	20.6
1999	12,109,000	16.9	4,170,000	18.0

*Related children in families.

Source: U.S. Department of Commerce, Bureau of the Census.

TABLE A2

Maternal and Infant Health

Year	Infant Mortality Rates*				Low Birth-weight**	Percent of Babies Born to Mothers Who Received Late*** or No Prenatal Care		
	Total	White	Black	Black-White Ratio		Total	White	Black
1940	47.0	43.2	72.9	1.69	n/a	n/a	n/a	n/a
1950	29.2	26.8	43.9	1.64	n/a	n/a	n/a	n/a
1959	26.4	23.2	44.8	1.93	n/a	n/a	n/a	n/a
1960	26.0	22.9	44.3	1.93	7.7%	n/a	n/a	n/a
1961	25.3	22.4	41.8	1.87	7.8	n/a	n/a	n/a
1962	25.3	22.3	42.6	1.91	8.0	n/a	n/a	n/a
1963	25.2	22.2	42.8	1.93	8.2	n/a	n/a	n/a
1964	24.8	21.6	42.3	1.96	8.2	n/a	n/a	n/a
1965	24.7	21.5	41.7	1.94	8.3	n/a	n/a	n/a
1966	23.7	20.6	40.2	1.95	8.3	n/a	n/a	n/a
1967	22.4	19.7	37.5	1.90	8.2	n/a	n/a	n/a
1968	21.8	19.2	36.2	1.89	8.2	n/a	n/a	n/a
1969	20.9	18.4	34.8	1.89	8.1	8.1%	6.3%	18.2%
1970	20.0	17.8	32.6	1.83	7.9	7.9	6.2	16.6
1971	19.1	17.1	30.3	1.77	7.7	7.2	5.8	14.6
1972	18.5	16.4	29.6	1.80	7.7	7.0	5.5	13.2
1973	17.7	15.8	28.1	1.78	7.6	6.7	5.4	12.4
1974	16.7	14.8	26.8	1.81	7.4	6.2	5.0	11.4
1975	16.1	14.2	26.2	1.85	7.4	6.0	5.0	10.5
1976	15.2	13.3	25.5	1.92	7.3	5.7	4.8	9.9
1977	14.1	12.3	23.6	1.92	7.1	5.6	4.7	9.6
1978	13.8	12.0	23.1	1.93	7.1	5.4	4.5	9.3
1979	13.1	11.4	21.8	1.91	6.9	5.1	4.3	8.9
1980	12.6	10.9	22.2	2.04	6.8	5.1	4.3	8.8
1981	11.9	10.3	20.8	2.02	6.8	5.2	4.3	9.1
1982	11.5	9.9	20.5	2.07	6.8	5.5	4.5	9.6
1983	11.2	9.6	20.0	2.08	6.8	5.6	4.6	9.7
1984	10.8	9.3	19.2	2.06	6.7	5.6	4.7	9.6
1985	10.6	9.2	19.0	2.07	6.8	5.7	4.7	10.0
1986	10.4	8.8	18.9	2.15	6.8	6.0	5.0	10.6
1987	10.1	8.5	18.8	2.21	6.9	6.1	5.0	11.1
1988	10.0	8.4	18.5	2.20	6.9	6.1	5.0	10.9
1989	9.8	8.1	18.6	2.30	7.0	6.4	5.2	11.9
1990	9.2	7.6	18.0	2.37	7.0	6.1	4.9	11.3
1991	8.9	7.3	17.6	2.41	7.1	5.8	4.7	10.7
1992	8.5	6.9	16.8	2.43	7.1	5.2	4.2	9.9
1993	8.4	6.8	16.5	2.43	7.2	4.8	3.9	9.0
1994	8.0	6.6	15.8	2.39	7.3	4.4	3.6	8.2
1995	7.6	6.3	15.1	2.40	7.3	4.2	3.5	7.6
1996	7.3	6.1	14.7	2.41	7.4	4.0	3.3	7.3
1997	7.2	6.0	14.2	2.37	7.5	3.9	3.2	7.3
1998	7.2	6.0	14.3	2.38	7.6	3.9	3.3	7.0

*Infant deaths before the first birthday per 1,000 live births.

**Birthweight less than 2,500 grams (5 lbs., 8 oz.).

***Prenatal care begun in the last three months of pregnancy.

Source: U.S. Department of Health and Human Services, National Center for Health Statistics. Calculations by Children's Defense Fund.

TABLE A3

Adolescent Childbearing

Year	Total Fertility Rate*	Total Unmarried Birth Rate**	Teen Fertility Rate***	Teen Unmarried Birth Rate****
1959	118.8	21.9	89.1	15.5
1960	118.0	21.6	89.1	15.3
1961	117.1	22.7	88.6	16.0
1962	112.0	21.9	81.4	14.8
1963	108.3	22.5	76.7	15.3
1964	104.7	23.0	73.1	15.9
1965	96.3	23.5	70.5	16.7
1966	90.8	23.4	70.3	17.5
1967	87.2	23.9	67.5	18.5
1968	85.2	24.4	65.6	19.7
1969	86.1	25.0	65.5	20.4
1970	87.9	26.4	68.3	22.4
1971	81.6	25.5	64.5	22.3
1972	73.1	24.8	61.7	22.8
1973	68.8	24.3	59.3	22.7
1974	67.8	23.9	57.5	23.0
1975	66.0	24.5	55.6	23.9
1976	65.0	24.3	52.8	23.7
1977	66.8	25.6	52.8	25.1
1978	65.5	25.7	51.5	24.9
1979	67.2	27.2	52.3	26.4
1980	68.4	29.4	53.0	27.6
1981	67.4	29.5	52.2	27.9
1982	67.3	30.0	52.4	28.7
1983	65.8	30.3	51.4	29.5
1984	65.4	31.0	50.6	30.0
1985	66.2	32.8	51.0	31.4
1986	65.4	34.2	50.2	32.3
1987	65.7	36.0	50.6	33.8
1988	67.2	38.5	53.0	36.4
1989	69.2	41.6	57.3	40.1
1990	70.9	43.8	59.9	42.5
1991	69.6	45.2	62.1	44.8
1992	68.9	45.2	60.7	44.6
1993	67.6	45.3	59.6	44.5
1994	66.7	46.9	58.9	46.4
1995	65.6	45.1	56.8	44.4
1996	65.3	44.8	54.4	42.9
1997	65.0	44.0	52.3	42.2
1998	65.6	44.3	51.1	41.5

*Births per 1,000 females ages 15-44.
**Births per 1,000 unmarried females ages 15-44.
***Births per 1,000 females ages 15-19.
****Births per 1,000 unmarried females ages 15-19.
Source: U.S. Department of Health and Human Services, National Center for Health Statistics.

TABLE A4

Youth Unemployment

Year	Total Unemployment Rates			Unemployment Rates, Youths Not Enrolled in School		
				Level of Education		
	All Ages	Age 16-19	Age 20-24	Less than Four Years of High School	High School Graduate Only	Four Years or More of College
1959	5.5%	14.6%	8.5%	n/a	n/a	n/a
1960	5.5	14.7	8.7	n/a	n/a	n/a
1961	6.7	16.8	10.4	n/a	n/a	n/a
1962	5.5	14.7	9.0	n/a	n/a	n/a
1963	5.7	17.2	8.8	n/a	n/a	n/a
1964	5.2	16.2	8.3	n/a	n/a	n/a
1965	4.5	14.8	6.7	n/a	n/a	n/a
1966	3.8	12.8	5.3	n/a	n/a	n/a
1967	3.8	12.9	5.7	n/a	n/a	n/a
1968	3.6	12.7	5.8	n/a	n/a	n/a
1969	3.5	12.2	5.7	n/a	n/a	n/a
1970	4.9	15.3	8.2	17.2%	9.9%	6.5%
1971	5.9	16.9	10.0	18.0	9.6	6.6
1972	5.6	16.2	9.3	16.8	9.5	7.2
1973	4.9	14.5	7.8	14.9	7.2	4.9
1974	5.6	16.0	9.1	19.2	9.8	5.0
1975	8.5	19.9	13.6	25.3	13.6	8.2
1976	7.7	19.0	12.0	24.7	12.1	7.1
1977	7.1	17.8	11.0	20.6	10.5	8.0
1978	6.1	16.4	9.6	18.8	8.8	6.3
1979	5.8	16.1	9.1	19.2	9.9	5.0
1980	7.1	17.8	11.5	25.3	12.5	5.9
1981	7.6	19.6	12.3	26.9	13.8	5.3
1982	9.7	23.2	14.9	31.8	17.3	9.2
1983	9.6	22.4	14.5	27.3	15.2	7.0
1984	7.5	18.9	11.5	25.8	11.8	5.9
1985	7.2	18.6	11.1	25.9	12.7	5.4
1986	7.0	18.3	10.7	24.3	11.5	4.8
1987	6.2	16.9	9.7	21.8	10.7	5.5
1988	5.5	15.3	8.7	20.0	10.1	4.8
1989	5.3	15.0	8.6	19.9	10.1	5.0
1990	5.5	15.5	8.8	20.0	10.4	5.2
1991	6.7	18.6	10.8	23.1	12.7	6.9
1992	7.4	20.0	11.3	24.9	13.9	6.5
1993	6.8	19.0	10.5	22.8	13.1	6.1
1994	6.1	17.6	9.7	23.1	11.9	5.5
1995	5.6	17.3	9.1	21.5	12.2	5.6
1996	5.4	16.7	9.3	22.1	12.1	5.4
1997	4.9	16.0	8.5	n/a	n/a	n/a
1998	4.5	14.6	7.9	n/a	n/a	n/a
1999	4.2	13.9	7.5	n/a	n/a	n/a
2000	4.0	13.1	7.1	n/a	n/a	n/a

n/a — Data not available.

Source: U.S. Department of Labor, Bureau of Labor Statistics.

Appendix B
Children in the States

TABLE B1

Population and Poverty

	All children, 1999		Poor children, 1997				
	Number	Percentage of state population	Number	Percentage of children in the state	Rank	County with highest child poverty rate	Rate in county
Alabama	1,066,177	24.4%	260,970	23.8%	43	Perry County	45.2%
Alaska	196,825	31.8	31,968	16.2	20	Wade Hampton Census Area	48.3
Arizona	1,334,564	27.9	305,109	23.2	40	Apache County	45.4
Arkansas	660,224	25.9	169,089	25.0	48	Phillips County	45.8
California	8,923,423	26.9	2,223,674	24.6	45	Imperial County	43.8
Colorado	1,065,510	26.3	155,960	14.6	8	Costilla County	46.8
Connecticut	828,260	25.2	121,256	14.7	9	New Haven County	18.0
Delaware	182,450	24.2	28,193	15.4	16	Sussex County	21.5
District of Columbia	95,290	18.4	33,503	33.7	51	District of Columbia	33.7
Florida	3,569,878	23.6	775,812	21.8	36	Hardee County	38.6
Georgia	2,056,885	26.4	470,440	22.8	37	Clay County	47.2
Hawaii	289,340	24.4	48,849	16.2	20	Hawaii County	23.4
Idaho	350,464	28.0	61,496	17.3	27	Shoshone County	29.5
Illinois	3,181,338	26.2	564,675	17.5	29	Alexander County	43.9
Indiana	1,528,991	25.7	228,246	14.8	10	Crawford County	23.4
Iowa	719,685	25.1	100,262	13.7	6	Decatur County	25.6
Kansas	698,637	26.3	109,324	15.4	16	Elk County	31.0
Kentucky	965,528	24.4	229,043	23.1	39	Owsley County	50.0
Louisiana	1,190,001	27.2	316,991	26.0	49	East Carroll Parish	52.9
Maine	290,439	23.2	44,122	14.9	12	Washington County	24.5
Maryland	1,309,432	25.3	194,703	14.9	12	Baltimore city	34.4
Massachusetts	1,468,554	23.8	250,244	17.0	25	Suffolk County	35.4
Michigan	2,561,139	26.0	468,947	18.0	31	Lake County	34.5
Minnesota	1,271,850	26.6	167,853	13.1	5	Mahnomen County	30.4
Mississippi	752,866	27.2	188,272	24.5	44	Sharkey County	43.7
Missouri	1,399,492	25.6	252,485	17.7	30	St. Louis city	38.4
Montana	223,819	25.4	49,055	21.3	35	Glacier County	40.2
Nebraska	443,800	26.6	57,013	12.6	3	Thurston County	27.5
Nevada	491,476	27.2	74,006	15.4	16	Mineral County	23.1
New Hampshire	304,436	25.3	30,356	10.0	1	Coos County	17.2
New Jersey	2,003,204	24.6	302,459	14.8	10	Hudson County	28.6
New Mexico	495,612	28.5	139,854	27.5	50	McKinley County	45.4
New York	4,440,924	24.4	1,121,585	24.7	46	Bronx County	41.9
North Carolina	1,940,947	25.4	361,170	18.6	32	Tyrrell County	33.9
North Dakota	160,092	25.3	27,807	16.8	24	Sioux County	40.8
Ohio	2,844,071	25.3	465,752	16.0	19	Lawrence County	29.2
Oklahoma	882,062	26.3	210,470	23.7	42	Harmon County	43.8
Oregon	827,501	25.0	134,932	16.3	22	Josephine County	28.5
Pennsylvania	2,852,520	23.8	482,596	16.6	23	Philadelphia County	32.8
Rhode Island	241,180	24.3	41,893	17.3	27	Providence County	22.5
South Carolina	955,930	24.6	224,380	23.0	38	Allendale County	44.4
South Dakota	198,037	27.0	38,270	19.0	34	Todd County	49.7
Tennessee	1,340,930	24.5	258,288	18.9	33	Hancock County	36.4
Texas	5,719,234	28.5	1,350,837	23.6	41	Starr County	56.4
Utah	707,366	33.2	89,867	12.5	2	San Juan County	32.0
Vermont	139,346	23.5	18,244	12.7	4	Essex County	21.1
Virginia	1,664,810	24.2	286,182	17.0	25	Petersburg city	39.6
Washington	1,486,340	25.8	227,904	15.2	14	Pend Oreille County	27.8
West Virginia	403,481	22.3	102,253	24.7	46	McDowell County	39.3
Wisconsin	1,348,268	25.7	196,327	14.3	7	Menominee County	32.9
Wyoming	126,807	26.4	20,080	15.3	15	Fremont County	24.1
United States	70,199,435	25.7	14,113,067	19.9		East Carroll Parish, LA	52.9

Source: U.S. Department of Commerce, Bureau of the Census, at http://www.census.gov/population/estimates/state/st-99-09.txt and http://www.census.gov/housing/saipe/estmod97/ . Calculations by Children's Defense Fund.

TABLE B2

Number and Percentage of Children Under 18 Who Are Poor, Based on 1989 Income

	All Races		White		Black		Hispanic*	
	Number	Percent	Number	Percent	Number	Percent	Number	Percent
Alabama	253,636	24.2%	89,959	12.9%	160,510	47.5%	1,829	23.4%
Alaska	19,284	11.4	8,864	7.4	1,086	14.5	809	12.2
Arizona	212,001	22.0	104,283	14.9	12,813	35.7	89,883	34.9
Arkansas	155,399	25.3	82,932	17.7	70,023	52.0	2,290	31.9
California	1,380,275	18.2	591,097	12.7	195,563	30.7	713,980	27.2
Colorado	129,565	15.3	88,222	12.2	13,677	33.8	48,497	32.7
Connecticut	79,020	10.7	36,963	6.1	23,591	28.9	30,002	41.2
Delaware	19,256	12.0	7,543	6.3	10,600	30.8	1,297	25.0
District of Columbia	28,610	25.5	799	4.9	26,339	29.1	1,677	26.3
Florida	525,446	18.7	252,793	12.0	243,435	41.0	93,288	24.6
Georgia	343,068	20.1	108,825	9.9	227,207	40.0	7,163	24.0
Hawaii	31,944	11.6	8,306	9.9	969	11.7	5,296	17.8
Idaho	49,159	16.2	41,528	14.7	281	22.5	7,705	35.4
Illinois	495,505	17.0	204,276	9.7	233,506	43.3	80,047	25.0
Indiana	203,791	14.2	141,319	11.2	55,984	40.1	7,627	21.8
Iowa	101,661	14.3	89,059	13.1	8,241	50.6	3,253	26.7
Kansas	93,066	14.3	65,528	11.5	18,665	40.3	8,233	23.5
Kentucky	234,012	24.8	193,614	22.7	38,193	47.0	1,803	26.2
Louisiana	380,942	31.4	112,404	15.4	259,228	56.5	5,908	23.3
Maine	41,897	13.8	40,429	13.6	440	25.9	435	16.2
Maryland	128,523	11.3	46,164	6.1	77,002	23.2	4,165	12.3
Massachusetts	176,221	13.2	105,129	9.2	29,547	33.3	49,645	49.1
Michigan	450,426	18.6	239,263	12.4	188,405	46.2	22,103	30.2
Minnesota	146,386	12.7	102,624	9.7	17,394	49.5	6,486	30.7
Mississippi	248,705	33.6	59,138	14.9	186,212	55.6	1,471	30.9
Missouri	230,058	17.7	152,757	13.9	71,928	41.5	4,246	20.3
Montana	44,706	20.5	33,458	17.1	221	31.1	1,874	36.0
Nebraska	58,474	13.8	44,420	11.4	8,761	43.2	3,861	27.9
Nevada	38,232	13.3	22,893	9.9	8,358	33.5	8,491	21.5
New Hampshire	20,440	7.4	19,295	7.2	351	15.3	705	16.4
New Jersey	200,726	11.3	84,110	6.4	81,788	27.8	59,531	27.8
New Mexico	122,260	27.8	67,615	22.1	3,542	35.0	70,158	35.0
New York	799,531	19.1	342,541	11.9	274,947	34.1	269,703	41.9
North Carolina	272,923	17.2	102,034	9.3	158,007	35.9	5,047	24.2
North Dakota	29,732	17.1	23,031	14.4	204	15.1	623	27.5
Ohio	493,206	17.8	315,714	13.4	163,131	45.4	15,910	32.0
Oklahoma	179,283	21.7	105,173	16.6	34,475	44.5	11,950	35.8
Oregon	111,629	15.8	91,249	14.2	5,489	36.3	14,285	33.8
Pennsylvania	432,227	15.7	270,941	11.5	124,859	40.6	38,374	46.7
Rhode Island	30,842	13.8	20,274	10.4	4,425	35.9	6,356	41.3
South Carolina	190,873	21.0	52,430	9.5	136,563	39.6	1,635	19.0
South Dakota	39,896	20.4	25,008	14.7	327	26.7	663	27.8
Tennessee	251,529	21.0	142,418	15.2	106,024	43.0	2,400	24.1
Texas	1,159,710	24.3	612,724	18.3	254,287	39.3	638,905	40.2
Utah	78,041	12.5	64,755	11.1	1,290	34.7	9,213	26.8
Vermont	17,020	12.0	16,435	11.9	211	24.9	143	11.8
Virginia	197,382	13.3	88,370	8.1	102,862	30.9	5,147	11.9
Washington	179,272	14.5	124,632	11.9	14,548	30.5	27,381	34.0
West Virginia	115,073	26.2	106,458	25.4	7,887	50.2	814	34.3
Wisconsin	188,863	14.9	110,939	9.9	53,392	55.8	12,435	33.7
Wyoming	19,190	14.4	15,532	12.6	340	31.5	2,724	28.1
United States	11,428,916	18.3	5,876,267	12.5	3,717,128	39.8	2,407,466	32.2

Note: New data on child poverty by race for the states will be produced from the 2000 Census; these data will probably be available in 2002.

*Persons of Hispanic origin can be of any race.

	Native American		Asian/Pacific Islander		Other	
	Number	Percent	Number	Percent	Number	Percent
Alabama	1,519	24.6%	1,166	19.0%	482	28.0%
Alaska	8,621	25.7	500	8.3	213	12.6
Arizona	44,607	53.1	2,204	14.9	48,094	38.2
Arkansas	1,053	26.1	648	17.5	743	34.7
California	17,982	26.5	155,493	19.6	420,140	30.2
Colorado	3,008	35.4	3,130	17.6	21,528	36.8
Connecticut	313	21.4	917	6.6	17,236	47.1
Delaware	80	21.5	149	6.6	884	30.0
District of Columbia	55	35.7	232	16.0	1,185	31.6
Florida	2,541	26.1	5,194	12.9	21,483	31.5
Georgia	938	25.0	2,465	11.5	3,633	29.7
Hawaii	408	25.2	21,327	12.1	934	16.5
Idaho	2,056	40.5	567	20.6	4,727	40.9
Illinois	1,422	23.9	7,640	9.4	48,661	27.8
Indiana	1,132	30.2	1,124	11.6	4,232	27.8
Iowa	1,160	43.4	1,898	23.5	1,303	28.4
Kansas	1,932	26.8	2,203	22.2	4,738	26.6
Kentucky	681	41.8	867	16.5	657	26.2
Louisiana	3,166	46.9	4,414	34.0	1,730	30.3
Maine	583	28.3	326	13.6	119	19.0
Maryland	661	18.5	2,820	7.6	1,876	14.3
Massachusetts	1,309	35.3	9,330	24.1	30,906	51.9
Michigan	6,147	32.5	4,891	14.6	11,720	35.9
Minnesota	10,459	54.8	12,638	37.1	3,271	37.5
Mississippi	1,429	45.6	1,657	39.7	269	32.5
Missouri	1,483	26.2	1,984	17.7	1,906	25.0
Montana	10,238	53.4	224	17.6	565	43.3
Nebraska	2,795	57.0	724	17.9	1,774	31.8
Nevada	1,745	29.8	1,040	10.9	4,196	25.0
New Hampshire	119	25.6	370	13.4	305	22.6
New Jersey	886	26.2	4,622	5.9	29,320	33.0
New Mexico	26,643	50.1	797	18.4	23,663	36.0
New York	4,800	29.6	25,021	14.9	152,222	47.6
North Carolina	7,820	29.9	2,344	16.4	2,718	31.2
North Dakota	6,179	58.3	148	16.8	170	22.6
Ohio	1,588	30.4	3,557	14.1	9,216	39.3
Oklahoma	31,977	34.8	1,427	15.8	6,231	40.4
Oregon	4,288	32.3	3,752	19.2	6,851	37.2
Pennsylvania	1,128	31.1	8,354	20.7	26,945	54.7
Rhode Island	440	39.5	2,043	34.0	3,660	42.5
South Carolina	599	27.4	715	12.1	566	21.6
South Dakota	14,160	63.3	195	17.0	206	26.2
Tennessee	906	30.8	1,438	15.7	743	25.8
Texas	4,501	25.6	14,518	15.6	273,680	40.6
Utah	4,893	47.3	2,281	19.8	4,822	33.5
Vermont	251	36.3	70	7.3	53	20.2
Virginia	666	19.0	3,377	7.8	2,107	13.5
Washington	10,228	37.7	12,594	20.0	17,270	39.8
West Virginia	337	44.6	193	8.5	198	32.1
Wisconsin	6,505	46.1	10,819	48.8	7,208	42.5
Wyoming	1,966	49.0	84	10.0	1,268	35.2
United States	260,403	38.8	346,491	17.1	1,228,627	35.5

Source: U.S. Department of Commerce, Bureau of the Census, 1990 Census of Population and Housing, Summary Tape File 3.
Calculations by Children's Defense Fund.

TABLE B3

Cash Assistance (AFDC/TANF) Benefit Levels and Participation

| | Maximum monthly benefit for a three-person family* | | | | | | Number of welfare (AFDC/TANF) recipients | | |
| | July 1970 | | January 2000 | | | | | | |
	Actual dollars	Inflation-adjusted value in 2000**	Actual dollars	As % of 1999 poverty guideline	State rank	Percent change, 1970 to 2000	August 1996	June 2000***	Percent change***
Alabama	$ 65	$ 281	$164	14.2%	51	-41.7%	100,662	55,168	-45.2%
Alaska	328	1,419	923	63.8	1	-34.9	35,544	24,389	-31.4
Arizona	138	597	347	30.0	33	-41.9	169,442	82,851	-51.1
Arkansas	89	385	204	17.6	45	-47.0	56,343	28,113	-50.1
California	186	805	626	54.1	6	-22.2	2,581,948	1,272,468	-50.7
Colorado	193	835	356	30.8	30	-57.4	95,788	27,699	-71.1
Connecticut	283	1,224	636	55.0	4	-48.0	159,246	63,589	-60.1
Delaware	160	692	338	29.2	35	-51.2	23,654	17,262	-27.0
District of Columbia	195	843	379	32.8	26	-55.1	69,292	44,487	-35.8
Florida	114	493	303	26.2	37	-38.6	533,801	135,903	-74.5
Georgia	107	463	280	24.2	42	-39.5	330,302	135,381	-59.0
Hawaii	226	978	712	53.5	2	-27.2	66,482	42,824	-35.6
Idaho	211	913	293	25.3	38	-67.9	21,780	1,382	-93.7
Illinois	232	1,004	377	32.6	27	-62.4	642,644	259,242	-59.7
Indiana	120	519	288	24.9	41	-44.5	142,604	96,854	-32.1
Iowa	201	869	426	36.8	22	-51.0	86,146	52,293	-39.3
Kansas	222	960	429	37.1	21	-55.3	63,783	36,557	-42.7
Kentucky	147	636	262	22.7	44	-58.8	172,193	85,696	-50.2
Louisiana	88	381	190	16.4	48	-50.1	228,115	79,745	-65.0
Maine	135	584	461	39.9	14	-21.1	53,873	14,813	-72.5
Maryland	162	701	417	36.1	25	-40.5	194,127	70,910	-63.5
Massachusetts	268	1,159	579	50.1	7	-50.1	226,030	93,890	-58.5
Michigan	219	947	459	39.7	16	-51.5	502,354	195,101	-61.2
Minnesota	256	1,107	532	46.0	12	-52.0	169,744	116,589	-31.3
Mississippi	56	242	170	14.7	50	-29.8	123,828	33,781	-72.7
Missouri	104	450	292	25.2	39	-35.1	222,820	122,930	-44.8
Montana	202	874	469	40.5	13	-46.3	29,130	14,001	-51.9
Nebraska	171	740	364	31.5	29	-50.8	38,592	26,841	-30.4
Nevada	121	523	348	30.1	32	-33.5	34,261	16,478	-51.9
New Hampshire	262	1,133	575	49.7	9	-49.3	22,937	13,862	-39.6
New Jersey	302	1,306	424	36.7	23	-67.5	275,637	125,258	-54.6
New Mexico	149	645	439	38.0	19	-31.9	99,661	67,950	-31.8
New York City	279	1,207	577	49.9	8	-52.2	1,143,962	693,012	-39.4
North Carolina	145	627	272	23.5	43	-56.6	267,326	97,171	-63.7
North Dakota	213	921	457	39.5	17	-50.4	13,146	7,734	-41.2
Ohio	161	696	373	32.2	28	-46.4	549,312	238,351	-56.6
Oklahoma	152	657	292	25.2	39	-55.6	96,201	13,606	-85.9
Oregon	184	796	460	39.8	15	-42.2	78,419	42,374	-46.0
Pennsylvania	265	1,146	421	36.4	24	-63.3	531,059	232,976	-56.1
Rhode Island	229	991	554	47.9	10	-44.1	56,560	44,826	-20.7
South Carolina	85	368	204	17.6	45	-44.5	114,273	35,721	-68.7
South Dakota	264	1,142	430	37.2	20	-62.3	15,896	6,702	-57.8
Tennessee	112	484	185	16.0	49	-61.8	254,818	143,823	-43.6
Texas	148	640	201	17.4	47	-68.6	649,018	343,464	-47.1
Utah	175	757	451	39.0	18	-40.4	39,073	24,101	-38.3
Vermont	267	1,155	708	61.2	3	-38.7	24,331	15,528	-36.2
Virginia	225	973	354	30.6	31	-63.6	152,845	67,388	-55.9
Washington	258	1,116	546	47.2	11	-51.1	268,927	146,375	-45.6
West Virginia	114	493	328	28.4	36	-33.5	89,039	31,500	-64.6
Wisconsin	184	796	628	54.3	5	-21.1	148,888	37,381	-74.9
Wyoming	213	921	340	29.4	34	-63.1	11,398	1,103	-90.3
United States****	$184	$796	$379	32.8		-52.4	12,077,254	5,677,443	-53.0

* Where benefits vary by program status (in Hawaii, Massachusetts, and Wisconsin), the highest is used. Michigan benefit level is for Wayne County (Detroit); New York benefit level is for New York City; California benefits are for region 1.

** The Consumer Price Index for All Urban Consumers inflation adjustment used for converting July 1970 dollars to January 2000 dollars was 4.3256.

*** Several states made changes in the definitions of their caseloads: California removed two-parent families, Texas added families enrolled during a month, and Wisconsin added child-only cases.

**** Benefits are medians; enrollment figures are totals.

Source: U.S. House of Representatives, Committee on Ways & Means, 2000 Green Book, Table 7-10, at http://aspe.hhs.gov/2000gb/sec7.txt ,downloaded March 7, 2001; and U.S. Department of Health and Human Services, Office of Family Assistance, at http://www.acf.dhhs.gov/news/stats/aug-dec.htm , downloaded March 8, 2001. Calculations by Children's Defense Fund.

TABLE B4

Number of Children Receiving Food Stamps, FY 1989-99

	FY 1989	FY 1990	FY 1991	FY 1992	FY 1993	FY 1994	FY 1995	FY 1996	FY 1997	FY 1998	FY 1999
Alabama	203,627	233,235	262,315	270,687	287,848	280,653	280,624	272,852	240,164	213,856	216,200
Alaska	13,852	13,718	15,248	19,669	23,974	24,710	24,014	27,040	25,818	21,174	20,743
Arizona	142,460	167,762	217,238	256,159	268,442	280,587	283,945	232,584	219,511	172,725	150,380
Arkansas	103,406	110,277	125,340	133,326	141,257	134,327	133,214	136,400	124,699	122,532	130,021
California	1,130,068	1,241,125	1,481,548	1,699,067	1,931,912	2,206,228	2,034,964	2,042,452	1,808,206	1,632,732	1,336,701
Colorado	108,030	112,473	132,190	149,987	147,542	142,831	126,410	124,324	111,697	91,549	84,579
Connecticut	62,617	74,757	97,769	109,609	117,334	123,647	128,200	106,599	106,247	99,040	86,894
Delaware	15,639	17,504	22,295	27,143	31,113	28,661	28,332	29,055	27,687	22,470	19,432
District of Columbia	29,772	34,682	40,214	47,998	48,102	52,408	52,046	48,037	49,659	42,636	42,400
Florida	319,164	389,332	534,866	743,403	789,136	748,014	720,299	715,204	599,745	488,252	425,329
Georgia	247,169	248,064	349,291	394,684	417,471	415,623	420,557	421,552	367,958	359,535	328,559
Hawaii	39,780	38,188	41,156	43,304	49,655	56,673	61,288	53,460	62,782	62,500	61,446
Idaho	29,783	27,704	33,547	37,316	42,125	43,834	41,338	40,204	36,438	32,829	29,799
Illinois	480,701	489,525	571,382	536,341	612,143	546,825	580,765	545,320	527,842	483,494	397,268
Indiana	139,258	149,436	200,686	246,967	256,511	254,607	219,319	187,689	160,436	156,017	159,095
Iowa	80,704	83,162	89,240	100,367	96,760	96,003	93,444	83,807	78,263	64,964	60,457
Kansas	60,856	64,773	82,603	89,736	92,965	89,723	99,333	87,377	76,244	52,906	56,731
Kentucky	190,408	202,494	238,812	250,845	240,572	228,424	224,438	212,572	203,339	177,054	167,608
Louisiana	356,575	355,061	404,590	444,442	410,456	403,454	384,383	361,890	298,224	287,417	280,474
Maine	38,077	40,194	55,340	61,159	61,468	59,146	53,185	50,452	51,194	42,956	41,572
Maryland	127,879	138,195	159,357	187,701	197,531	206,048	205,898	200,308	185,917	170,221	142,036
Massachusetts	153,172	166,908	206,493	239,137	229,016	240,069	231,599	189,908	180,825	166,369	131,011
Michigan	445,279	463,569	498,853	506,478	513,005	539,922	490,394	459,916	426,683	403,802	343,440
Minnesota	120,559	118,285	141,010	158,632	171,796	175,763	162,594	151,678	121,036	108,118	95,861
Mississippi	224,555	229,689	249,470	256,369	273,355	252,405	250,003	219,635	188,372	173,749	152,968
Missouri	192,188	198,896	246,979	286,819	291,197	295,224	292,320	276,270	241,018	208,711	197,603
Montana	26,322	26,735	28,465	30,836	33,600	35,654	34,659	36,525	32,588	29,656	28,819
Nebraska	45,161	44,604	50,647	54,874	61,100	62,558	53,612	52,190	50,751	47,383	45,471
Nevada	19,408	23,733	32,997	46,163	54,651	45,887	56,256	51,706	44,357	37,374	28,936
New Hampshire	9,273	12,723	20,306	25,910	29,209	30,016	27,939	26,533	21,528	20,897	19,239
New Jersey	191,648	215,221	244,014	263,472	267,689	290,707	283,908	282,080	249,283	217,987	193,346
New Mexico	75,537	80,341	90,280	119,115	131,698	126,461	125,955	124,878	109,901	95,344	92,563
New York	722,389	776,078	887,010	915,006	964,858	1,094,408	950,229	964,670	892,519	815,697	718,290
North Carolina	177,509	195,549	245,744	300,372	323,552	313,632	300,695	304,069	276,226	264,079	258,261
North Dakota	18,890	19,305	22,503	22,445	23,694	22,968	19,014	17,127	18,987	16,183	16,147
Ohio	492,247	526,888	606,867	642,334	611,112	598,321	575,344	488,346	403,912	336,209	305,001
Oklahoma	123,659	122,202	151,905	167,524	179,726	190,671	186,490	163,297	156,927	140,944	131,670
Oregon	90,838	87,647	112,716	126,057	137,388	134,838	139,942	130,552	111,515	101,037	103,126
Pennsylvania	441,560	448,201	500,527	555,539	556,377	544,571	536,023	512,940	470,616	420,440	395,157
Rhode Island	29,370	33,514	41,574	46,181	49,045	51,496	50,195	47,928	45,531	41,638	41,458
South Carolina	137,577	155,603	171,328	186,473	213,828	205,812	198,663	190,077	181,325	175,631	157,901
South Dakota	25,213	26,144	28,813	27,999	31,562	24,734	28,243	24,439	24,783	24,592	22,140
Tennessee	230,158	238,858	286,479	321,614	364,193	347,335	315,220	283,747	272,011	261,115	217,141
Texas	846,306	984,543	1,144,204	1,301,887	1,421,597	1,406,259	1,406,181	1,319,826	1,191,255	924,283	800,811
Utah	52,402	54,943	64,696	69,740	74,253	68,105	64,602	57,942	55,329	52,885	53,059
Vermont	14,362	16,567	19,982	29,196	25,386	29,579	29,262	27,325	21,276	19,418	18,208
Virginia	148,798	166,735	195,617	230,539	261,125	275,223	276,811	260,750	231,941	206,730	168,992
Washington	153,771	175,628	202,310	219,280	229,855	231,318	248,692	246,788	206,101	178,875	152,780
West Virginia	111,043	106,862	117,673	142,017	207,751	135,908	123,361	123,220	114,398	110,049	96,025
Wisconsin	175,538	165,499	171,155	188,910	181,409	181,645	186,263	158,857	129,698	110,175	96,597
Wyoming	14,572	13,996	16,302	17,938	18,512	16,868	18,739	17,260	14,746	12,749	12,554
United States	9,429,127	10,127,129	11,951,940	13,348,769	14,195,859	14,390,783	13,859,204	13,189,657	11,847,508	10,518,978	9,332,299

Source: U.S. Department of Agriculture, Food and Consumer Service, unpublished tabulations from Fiscal Year QC Databases.

TABLE B5

Number of Children Participating in Child Nutrition Programs, FY 2000

	Supplemental Food Program for Women, Infants, and Children (WIC)				School Lunch Program*	School Breakfast Program	Child and Adult Care Food Program (CACFP)	Summer Food Program
	Women	Infants	Children	Total				
Alabama	25,755	33,735	44,440	103,930	537,693	137,876	36,356	40,293
Alaska	5,329	7,095	11,971	24,395	49,508	9,094	7,780	519
Arizona	36,309	39,654	69,429	145,391	445,239	133,226	41,935	22,170
Arkansas	22,614	23,049	36,468	82,131	309,907	122,499	23,604	8,235
California	293,040	280,245	646,145	1,219,430	2,547,989	826,271	281,507	176,816
Colorado	18,709	20,424	32,834	71,967	310,700	55,176	38,706	15,164
Connecticut	11,345	15,728	29,448	56,522	264,603	48,281	20,165	33,205
Delaware	3,449	4,674	7,671	15,794	71,446	17,011	11,169	10,463
District of Columbia	3,730	4,434	6,892	15,056	47,195	18,528	4,420	20,264
Florida	67,060	86,919	142,158	296,138	1,320,708	415,148	106,828	187,797
Georgia	60,209	61,921	93,662	215,792	1,065,549	367,646	107,901	94,049
Hawaii	7,530	7,883	16,667	32,080	143,046	37,967	8,541	7,183
Idaho	7,539	7,108	16,638	31,286	142,648	26,386	7,291	3,893
Illinois	55,954	74,578	113,124	243,655	1,043,029	197,725	99,978	106,115
Indiana	31,168	36,663	52,768	120,599	615,115	107,582	48,026	17,218
Iowa	14,302	14,287	32,204	60,793	383,307	64,612	27,920	4,572
Kansas	12,739	13,581	26,627	52,948	305,293	67,537	50,700	7,755
Kentucky	26,814	29,680	55,657	112,150	499,459	184,204	48,376	25,253
Louisiana	34,254	40,646	55,141	130,042	647,122	240,226	52,176	48,875
Maine	5,050	5,173	11,600	21,822	106,881	26,352	14,379	5,995
Maryland	24,873	27,844	41,525	94,242	391,905	98,178	49,990	38,471
Massachusetts	27,006	27,133	59,961	114,100	521,939	105,754	57,575	52,448
Michigan	49,511	52,057	111,094	212,661	803,158	173,714	63,826	34,771
Minnesota	20,414	22,813	46,865	90,092	560,397	110,232	113,754	30,754
Mississippi	23,726	31,213	40,898	95,836	397,115	171,910	27,602	27,834
Missouri	32,752	33,527	57,459	123,738	586,808	159,631	45,014	27,949
Montana	4,856	4,385	12,040	21,281	79,314	15,068	14,214	5,223
Nebraska	8,003	8,466	16,372	32,841	219,223	36,555	37,090	5,151
Nevada	9,942	10,540	18,272	38,754	114,041	34,611	6,270	5,215
New Hampshire	4,030	4,262	8,757	17,049	103,940	16,449	6,593	2,308
New Jersey	31,705	34,806	60,501	127,012	585,506	87,220	53,618	58,968
New Mexico	13,555	14,290	29,958	57,804	191,195	76,906	41,371	42,327
New York	109,488	119,734	237,562	466,784	1,780,239	461,348	186,997	326,449
North Carolina	50,738	54,450	85,082	190,271	823,038	268,555	110,980	43,098
North Dakota	3,222	3,156	7,926	14,303	80,374	12,733	16,485	1,936
Ohio	57,119	73,688	111,860	242,667	998,503	186,895	77,900	42,055
Oklahoma	27,011	29,097	52,390	108,498	373,728	145,040	42,051	12,103
Oregon	21,148	17,036	47,930	86,113	260,723	95,773	31,651	18,588
Pennsylvania	52,224	55,339	124,079	231,642	1,013,561	187,994	70,767	99,672
Rhode Island	4,664	5,192	11,430	21,287	63,568	12,271	9,172	10,985
South Carolina	29,958	31,467	46,779	108,204	470,915	167,173	29,738	64,137
South Dakota	4,631	4,911	10,882	20,425	105,539	18,039	10,701	4,566
Tennessee	39,286	43,440	65,936	148,662	618,023	190,724	41,305	42,671
Texas	185,086	191,953	360,168	737,206	2,444,986	942,814	175,620	83,818
Utah	15,140	14,999	27,321	57,460	269,662	32,379	33,704	19,005
Vermont	3,646	3,128	9,627	16,401	51,329	13,904	7,718	2,280
Virginia	32,065	34,773	61,646	128,484	662,869	171,665	46,073	36,224
Washington	34,852	37,166	73,844	145,862	467,916	112,540	59,899	30,698
West Virginia	12,275	12,562	26,056	50,893	201,197	85,595	16,573	16,013
Wisconsin	23,076	24,811	52,540	100,427	532,216	54,696	57,800	28,758
Wyoming	2,760	2,429	5,718	10,907	51,623	8,332	7,826	590
United States	1,701,659	1,838,142	3,424,020	6,963,822	26,680,989	7,358,046	2,587,628	2,050,899

*All children receiving a subsidy for lunch, including children receiving free, reduced-price, and full-price lunches.
Source: U.S. Department of Agriculture, Food and Consumer Service. Calculations by Children's Defense Fund.

TABLE B6

Child Support Enforcement, 1998

	Cases	Court order	Percent with court order	Collection	Percent with collection	Rank
Alabama	365,914	227,642	62.2%	78,473	21.4%	31
Alaska	59,272	48,588	82.0	14,552	24.6	23
Arizona	328,944	187,430	57.0	70,435	21.4	31
Arkansas	173,200	114,700	66.2	51,610	29.8	13
California	2,092,732	1,319,177	63.0	588,349	28.1	16
Colorado	216,428	158,801	73.4	43,953	20.3	33
Connecticut	253,977	166,060	65.4	48,271	19.0	39
Delaware	60,634	45,422	74.9	16,962	28.0	17
District of Columbia	106,887	53,246	49.8	14,966	14.0	47
Florida	982,996	432,562	44.0	168,475	17.1	44
Georgia	531,016	318,701	60.0	173,284	32.6	9
Hawaii	68,103	32,689	48.0	15,592	22.9	28
Idaho	87,218	62,508	71.7	16,213	18.6	42
Illinois	746,331	226,967	30.4	88,899	11.9	49
Indiana	343,960	164,696	47.9	51,915	15.1	46
Iowa	207,751	178,757	86.0	47,824	23.0	27
Kansas	144,806	87,643	60.5	54,090	37.4	6
Kentucky	314,518	206,323	65.6	61,037	19.4	35
Louisiana	332,741	147,627	44.4	60,445	18.2	43
Maine	69,981	60,346	86.2	30,770	44.0	2
Maryland	320,357	207,674	64.8	92,071	28.7	14
Massachusetts	239,446	197,262	82.4	68,392	28.6	15
Michigan	1,720,920	794,709	46.2	331,308	19.3	37
Minnesota	268,437	201,766	75.2	107,235	39.9	4
Mississippi	289,339	144,490	49.9	39,921	13.8	48
Missouri	405,522	306,242	75.5	90,367	22.3	30
Montana	41,342	30,827	74.6	12,780	30.9	12
Nebraska	121,421	90,480	74.5	23,827	19.6	34
Nevada	84,116	53,396	63.5	21,311	25.3	21
New Hampshire	51,352	40,617	79.1	20,729	40.4	3
New Jersey	482,752	372,069	77.1	134,857	27.9	18
New Mexico	77,894	18,714	24.0	8,362	10.7	50
New York	1,295,109	866,226	66.9	251,735	19.4	35
North Carolina	520,191	308,052	59.2	3,594	–	–
North Dakota	40,783	29,398	72.1	10,896	26.7	20
Ohio	939,155	700,456	74.6	324,078	34.5	8
Oklahoma	134,461	72,640	54.0	25,220	18.8	40
Oregon	267,783	152,720	57.0	62,186	23.2	25
Pennsylvania	875,637	568,975	65.0	216,697	24.7	22
Rhode Island	72,458	42,954	59.3	12,003	16.6	45
South Carolina	218,833	119,945	54.8	70,748	32.3	10
South Dakota	33,479	31,496	94.1	12,090	36.1	7
Tennessee	497,627	197,440	39.7	93,611	18.8	40
Texas	1,071,067	475,657	44.4	242,375	22.6	29
Utah	109,262	82,885	75.9	33,890	31.0	11
Vermont	27,022	24,010	88.9	12,123	44.9	1
Virginia	414,861	269,272	64.9	96,124	23.2	25
Washington	404,163	361,391	89.4	160,393	39.7	5
West Virginia	124,188	62,485	50.3	29,651	23.9	24
Wisconsin	475,363	278,228	58.5	130,065	27.4	19
Wyoming	59,122	41,111	69.5	11,439	19.3	37
United States	19,170,871	11,383,472	59.4	4,446,193	23.2	

– The figure reported by North Carolina to the Office of Child Support Enforcement for number of cases with collection appears to be wrong; the 1997 figure was 88,163. We have not calculated a rate because of this.

Source: U.S. Department of Health and Human Services, Office of Child Support Enforcement, 23rd Annual Report to Congress, Tables 26-28. Calculations by Children's Defense Fund.

TABLE B7

Fair Market Rent and the Minimum Wage, 2001

	Lowest monthly rent	Minimum wage	Lowest rent as a percentage of minimum wage	Rank
Alabama	$ 312	$ 5.15	36.3%	3
Alaska	599	5.65	63.6	46
Arizona	438	5.15	51.0	41
Arkansas	341	5.15	39.7	10
California	393	6.25	37.7	6
Colorado	427	5.15	49.7	38
Connecticut	552	6.40	51.8	43
Delaware	547	6.15	53.4	44
District of Columbia	773	6.15	75.4	50
Florida	433	5.15	50.4	40
Georgia	361	5.15	42.1	18
Hawaii	713	5.25	81.5	51
Idaho	329	5.15	38.3	7
Illinois	357	5.15	41.6	17
Indiana	338	5.15	39.4	9
Iowa	363	5.15	42.3	21
Kansas	389	5.15	45.3	31
Kentucky	315	5.15	36.7	4
Louisiana	315	5.15	36.7	4
Maine	393	5.15	45.8	34
Maryland	409	5.15	47.7	37
Massachusetts	464	6.75	41.2	16
Michigan	388	5.15	45.2	30
Minnesota	367	5.15	42.8	23
Mississippi	349	5.15	40.7	12
Missouri	300	5.15	35.0	1
Montana	387	5.15	45.1	29
Nebraska	408	5.15	47.5	36
Nevada	570	5.15	66.4	47
New Hampshire	585	5.15	68.2	49
New Jersey	582	5.15	67.8	48
New Mexico	372	5.15	43.3	25
New York	403	5.15	47.0	35
North Carolina	361	5.15	42.1	18
North Dakota	392	5.15	45.7	33
Ohio	344	5.15	40.1	11
Oklahoma	304	5.15	35.4	2
Oregon	456	6.50	42.1	18
Pennsylvania	365	5.15	42.5	22
Rhode Island	523	6.15	51.0	41
South Carolina	370	5.15	43.1	24
South Dakota	431	5.15	50.2	39
Tennessee	353	5.15	41.1	15
Texas	352	5.15	41.0	14
Utah	391	5.15	45.6	32
Vermont	590	6.25	56.6	45
Virginia	373	5.15	43.5	27
Washington	436	6.72	38.9	8
West Virginia	349	5.15	40.7	12
Wisconsin	372	5.15	43.3	25
Wyoming	381	5.15	44.4	28
United States		5.15		

Source: U.S. Department of Labor, Employment Standards Administration, Wage and Hour Division, Minimum Wage and Overtime Premium Pay Standards Applicable to Nonsupervisory NONFARM Private Sector Employment, updated/corrected January 24, 2001; and U.S. Department of Housing and Urban Development, 2001 Final Fair Market Rents, File FMR2001F.EXE, Effective January 2, 2001, posted January 30, 2001. Calculations by Children's Defense Fund.

TABLE B8

Prenatal Care and Low Birthweight, 1998

| | Incidence of early prenatal care, by race, ethnicity of mother* | | | | | | | | Incidence of low-birthweight births, by race, ethnicity of mother** | | | | | | | |
| | All races | | White | | Black | | Hispanic*** | | All races | | White | | Black | | Hispanic*** | |
	Rate	Rank	Rate	Rank	Rate	Rank	Rate	Rank	Rate	Rank	Rate	Rank	Rate	Rank	Rate	Rank
Alabama	82.4%	30	88.3%	12	70.1%	37	62.9%	48	9.3%	47	7.3%	44	13.3%	22	5.9%	7
Alaska	81.4	37	83.5	38	82.3	3	81.3	8	6.0	7	5.6	4	10.5	4	6.4	17
Arizona	75.1	48	76.0	49	73.5	25	64.7	45	6.8	16	6.6	25	12.2	11	6.6	22
Arkansas	77.8	47	80.7	44	67.6	41	61.6	50	8.9	44	7.5	45	13.9	34	6.6	22
California	82.4	30	82.4	41	79.5	6	78.1	14	6.2	9	5.7	6	11.6	9	5.6	2
Colorado	82.2	33	82.7	40	75.9	17	68.3	37	8.6	41	8.3	50	13.3	22	8.4	41
Connecticut	88.0	5	89.3	8	79.0	10	78.2	12	7.8	28	7.0	37	13.3	22	9.7	43
Delaware	83.4	26	86.4	29	74.2	24	69.7	33	8.4	39	6.2	12	14.8	41	7.7	35
District of Columbia	72.0	50	84.8	33	66.9	44	69.5	34	13.1	51	5.9	10	15.8	43	5.9	7
Florida	83.6	25	86.9	26	72.8	27	81.9	7	8.1	37	6.8	34	12.2	11	6.5	18
Georgia	86.4	9	90.0	5	79.4	7	78.2	12	8.5	40	6.4	16	12.7	16	5.3	1
Hawaii	85.4	15	90.2	4	91.5	1	83.5	4	7.5	22	6.2	12	10.7	5	7.7	35
Idaho	78.7	45	79.1	48	69.1	40	61.5	51	6.0	7	6.0	11	–	–	6.8	27
Illinois	82.7	28	85.7	30	70.1	37	73.7	21	8.0	34	6.4	16	14.2	38	6.3	14
Indiana	79.9	43	81.6	43	65.3	47	64.7	45	7.9	32	7.2	42	13.5	28	6.9	28
Iowa	87.3	8	87.9	15	74.8	21	73.0	24	6.4	10	6.2	12	12.8	18	6.1	11
Kansas	85.8	12	86.7	27	76.1	16	68.1	39	7.0	18	6.5	21	13.0	19	5.9	7
Kentucky	86.4	9	87.3	18	78.0	12	73.8	19	8.1	37	7.6	46	13.5	28	6.9	28
Louisiana	82.2	33	89.4	7	72.1	29	85.3	1	10.1	49	7.0	37	14.6	40	7.3	31
Maine	88.9	4	89.1	10	85.6	2	77.9	15	5.8	4	5.8	9	–	–	–	–
Maryland	87.8	6	91.5	1	80.3	4	82.3	6	8.7	42	6.4	16	13.0	19	6.1	11
Massachusetts	89.5	3	90.9	2	80.1	5	79.2	9	6.9	17	6.5	21	10.2	3	7.8	38
Michigan	84.3	20	87.1	23	71.1	30	72.8	25	7.8	28	6.4	16	13.8	33	6.6	22
Minnesota	84.5	18	87.1	23	66.7	45	63.8	47	5.8	4	5.4	2	11.0	6	5.7	3
Mississippi	80.6	41	89.3	8	70.2	35	73.8	19	10.1	49	7.2	42	13.7	32	–	–
Missouri	86.1	11	88.2	13	74.5	22	77.7	16	7.8	28	6.7	29	14.0	36	6.3	14
Montana	82.3	32	84.8	33	77.3	13	78.6	10	7.0	18	6.9	35	–	–	–	–
Nebraska	83.9	23	84.9	32	71.0	31	68.8	35	6.5	11	6.2	12	12.2	11	6.6	22
Nevada	74.6	49	75.3	50	66.3	46	62.2	49	7.6	23	6.9	35	13.3	22	6.3	14
New Hampshire	89.7	1	89.8	6	76.9	15	78.4	11	5.7	2	5.6	4	–	–	–	–
New Jersey	81.6	36	85.5	31	65.1	48	71.0	30	8.0	34	6.7	29	13.3	22	7.4	32
New Mexico	67.6	51	69.1	51	58.5	50	64.8	43	7.6	23	7.7	48	11.4	7	7.5	33
New York	81.2	40	84.4	35	70.8	33	72.1	28	7.8	28	6.7	29	11.9	10	7.8	38
North Carolina	84.5	18	88.1	14	75.2	20	68.5	36	8.8	43	7.0	37	13.9	34	6.2	13
North Dakota	85.6	13	87.3	18	78.8	11	73.6	22	6.5	11	6.5	21	–	–	–	–
Ohio	85.5	14	87.6	16	73.3	26	77.4	17	7.7	27	6.7	29	13.2	21	7.7	35
Oklahoma	78.6	46	80.7	44	69.7	39	68.3	37	7.2	20	6.6	25	12.5	14	6.0	10
Oregon	80.2	42	80.4	46	79.4	7	67.2	40	5.4	1	5.2	1	9.8	1	5.8	5
Pennsylvania	84.8	17	87.3	18	70.8	33	72.4	27	7.6	23	6.6	25	13.5	28	9.4	42
Rhode Island	89.7	1	90.9	2	79.3	9	82.4	5	7.6	23	7.1	40	11.4	7	7.9	40
South Carolina	81.4	37	87.2	22	71.0	31	65.9	41	9.5	48	7.1	40	14.0	36	5.8	5
South Dakota	82.7	28	86.6	28	75.3	19	74.3	18	5.8	4	5.7	6	–	–	–	–
Tennessee	84.1	22	87.3	18	72.7	28	64.8	43	9.1	46	7.6	46	14.3	39	6.5	18
Texas	79.3	44	79.6	47	75.7	18	72.7	26	7.4	21	6.7	29	12.6	15	6.7	26
Utah	82.1	35	82.9	39	64.7	49	64.9	42	6.7	15	6.6	25	14.9	42	7.2	30
Vermont	87.4	7	87.5	17	–		85.3	1	6.5	11	6.5	21	–	–	–	–
Virginia	85.2	16	88.8	11	74.4	23	73.2	23	7.9	32	6.4	16	12.7	16	6.5	18
Washington	83.0	27	83.6	37	77.1	14	71.0	30	5.7	2	5.4	2	10.1	2	5.7	3
West Virginia	83.7	24	84.2	36	70.2	35	84.0	3	8.0	34	7.8	49	13.4	27	–	–
Wisconsin	84.3	20	87.0	25	67.5	42	71.9	29	6.5	11	5.7	6	13.6	31	6.5	18
Wyoming	81.3	39	82.2	42	67.3	43	70.2	32	8.9	44	8.8	51	–	–	7.5	33
United States	82.8		84.8		73.3		74.3		7.6		6.5		13.0		6.4	

*Births to mothers who received care in the first trimester (first three months) of pregnancy, as a percentage of all births among base group.

**Newborns weighing less than 2,500 grams (5 lbs., 8 oz.), as a percentage of all births among base group.

***Persons of Hispanic origin can be of any race.

— Number too small to calculate a reliable rate.

Source: U.S. Department of Health and Human Services, National Center for Health Statistics, National Vital Statistics Report, Vol. 48, No. 3 (March 28, 2000), Tables 34 and 46. Calculations by Children's Defense Fund.

TABLE B9

Teen Birth Rates,* 1990-1998

	1990	1991	1992	1993	1994	1995	1996	1997	1998
Alabama	71.0	73.9	72.5	70.5	72.2	70.3	69.2	66.6	65.5
Alaska	65.3	65.4	63.9	56.8	55.5	50.2	46.4	44.6	42.4
Arizona	75.5	80.7	81.7	79.8	78.7	75.7	73.9	69.7	70.5
Arkansas	80.1	79.8	75.5	73.9	76.3	73.5	75.4	72.9	70.8
California	70.6	74.7	74.0	72.7	71.3	68.2	62.6	57.3	53.5
Colorado	54.5	58.2	58.4	55.2	54.3	51.3	49.5	48.2	48.7
Connecticut	38.8	40.4	39.4	39.2	40.3	39.3	37.4	36.1	35.8
Delaware	54.5	61.1	59.6	59.7	60.2	57.0	56.9	55.8	53.9
District of Columbia	93.1	114.4	116.1	128.8	114.7	106.8	102.1	91.0	86.7
Florida	69.1	68.8	66.3	64.8	64.4	61.7	58.9	57.7	55.5
Georgia	75.5	76.3	74.5	73.0	71.7	71.1	68.2	67.2	65.4
Hawaii	61.2	58.7	53.5	53.0	53.5	47.9	48.1	43.8	45.7
Idaho	50.6	53.9	51.7	50.7	46.6	49.0	47.2	43.3	44.8
Illinois	62.9	64.8	63.6	63.0	62.8	59.9	57.1	54.7	53.2
Indiana	58.6	60.5	58.7	58.6	57.9	57.5	56.1	54.2	53.3
Iowa	40.5	42.6	40.8	41.1	39.7	38.6	37.8	35.7	35.2
Kansas	56.1	55.4	55.7	55.7	53.5	52.2	49.6	48.5	47.0
Kentucky	67.6	68.9	64.7	64.0	64.5	62.5	61.5	59.6	57.0
Louisiana	74.2	76.1	76.5	76.1	74.7	69.9	66.7	66.3	65.4
Maine	43.0	43.5	39.8	37.1	35.5	33.6	31.4	32.0	30.4
Maryland	53.2	54.3	50.7	50.1	49.7	47.7	46.1	43.9	43.1
Massachusetts	35.1	37.8	38.0	37.9	37.2	34.3	32.2	31.7	30.8
Michigan	59.0	59.0	56.5	53.2	52.1	49.2	46.5	43.9	42.6
Minnesota	36.3	37.3	36.0	35.0	34.4	32.4	32.1	32.0	30.6
Mississippi	81.0	85.6	84.2	83.3	83.0	80.6	75.5	73.7	73.0
Missouri	62.8	64.5	63.2	59.8	59.0	55.5	53.7	51.5	51.2
Montana	48.4	46.7	46.2	45.7	41.2	41.8	38.6	37.6	37.1
Nebraska	42.3	42.4	41.1	40.5	42.8	37.6	38.7	37.2	37.0
Nevada	73.3	75.3	71.4	73.4	73.6	73.3	69.6	67.7	65.7
New Hampshire	33.0	33.3	31.3	30.7	30.1	30.5	28.6	28.6	27.1
New Jersey	40.5	41.6	39.2	38.1	39.3	38.0	35.4	35.0	34.6
New Mexico	78.2	79.8	80.3	81.1	77.4	74.5	70.9	68.4	69.0
New York	43.6	46.0	45.3	45.7	45.8	44.0	41.8	38.8	38.5
North Carolina	67.6	70.5	69.5	66.8	66.3	64.1	63.5	61.3	61.0
North Dakota	35.4	35.6	37.3	36.8	34.6	33.5	32.3	30.1	30.4
Ohio	57.9	60.5	58.0	56.8	55.0	53.4	50.4	49.8	48.1
Oklahoma	66.8	72.1	69.9	68.6	65.9	64.0	63.4	64.3	61.6
Oregon	54.6	54.9	53.2	51.2	50.7	50.7	50.8	46.9	47.4
Pennsylvania	44.9	46.9	45.2	44.3	43.8	41.7	39.3	37.3	36.9
Rhode Island	43.9	45.4	47.5	49.8	47.7	43.1	42.5	42.7	41.0
South Carolina	71.3	72.9	70.3	66.0	66.5	65.1	62.9	61.4	60.4
South Dakota	46.8	47.5	48.3	44.3	42.8	40.5	39.5	39.7	38.5
Tennessee	72.3	75.2	71.4	70.2	71.0	67.9	66.1	64.5	64.3
Texas	75.3	78.9	78.9	78.1	77.6	76.1	73.5	71.7	70.9
Utah	48.5	48.2	46.3	44.5	42.7	42.4	42.8	42.6	40.9
Vermont	34.0	39.2	35.6	35.2	33.0	28.6	30.1	26.9	24.4
Virginia	52.9	53.5	51.8	49.8	50.7	48.7	45.5	44.2	43.5
Washington	53.1	53.7	50.9	50.2	48.2	47.6	45.0	42.5	41.7
West Virginia	57.3	57.8	56.0	55.6	54.3	52.7	50.3	49.1	49.2
Wisconsin	42.6	43.7	42.1	41.1	38.8	37.8	36.8	35.9	34.8
Wyoming	56.3	54.2	49.6	49.6	48.2	47.2	44.0	43.3	47.8
United States	59.9	62.1	60.7	59.6	58.9	56.8	54.4	52.3	51.1

*Number of births to women ages 15-19 per 1,000 females in that age group.

Source: U.S. Department of Health and Human Services, National Center for Health Statistics.

TABLE B10

Infant Mortality, by Race of Mother, 1998*

	All races			White			Black		
	Number	Rate	Rank	Number	Rate	Rank	Number	Rate	Rank
Alabama	633	10.2	50	318	7.7	46	311	15.5	20
Alaska	59	5.9	7	31	4.7	2	6	–	–
Arizona	590	7.5	29	469	6.9	37	53	20.0	33
Arkansas	329	8.9	43	215	7.6	45	112	14.0	11
California	3,007	5.8	6	2,239	5.3	8	505	13.7	10
Colorado	399	6.7	14	346	6.4	29	46	16.0	22
Connecticut	307	7.0	16	208	5.6	11	95	17.4	29
Delaware	102	9.6	47	53	6.9	37	49	18.7	31
District of Columbia	96	12.5	51	8	–	–	85	15.5	20
Florida	1,417	7.2	22	857	5.9	18	548	12.3	4
Georgia	1,035	8.5	39	470	6.0	19	553	13.4	6
Hawaii	121	6.9	15	22	–	–	5	–	–
Idaho	140	7.2	22	134	7.1	42	2	–	–
Illinois	1,539	8.4	38	901	6.4	29	614	17.2	26
Indiana	649	7.6	31	482	6.5	32	160	17.3	27
Iowa	246	6.6	13	218	6.2	24	20	–	–
Kansas	270	7.0	16	240	7.0	40	28	–	–
Kentucky	409	7.5	29	332	6.8	35	75	15.4	18
Louisiana	609	9.1	44	219	5.7	12	385	14.0	11
Maine	87	6.3	9	85	6.4	29	2	–	–
Maryland	616	8.6	41	233	5.2	6	367	15.3	17
Massachusetts	416	5.1	2	341	4.9	3	65	8.3	1
Michigan	1,098	8.2	36	668	6.3	26	407	16.8	24
Minnesota	386	5.9	7	294	5.1	5	49	13.4	6
Mississippi	435	10.1	49	145	6.3	26	286	14.8	14
Missouri	577	7.7	32	382	6.1	23	191	16.8	24
Montana	80	7.4	28	68	7.2	43	1	–	–
Nebraska	172	7.3	27	143	6.7	34	24		–
Nevada	200	7.0	16	146	6.0	19	39	17.3	27
New Hampshire	63	4.4	1	60	4.3	1	2	–	–
New Jersey	734	6.4	11	428	5.0	4	274	12.8	5
New Mexico	197	7.2	22	159	6.9	37	9	–	–
New York	1,623	6.3	9	980	5.3	8	591	10.9	2
North Carolina	1,038	9.3	46	514	6.5	32	497	17.6	30
North Dakota	68	8.6	41	58	8.2	49	0	–	–
Ohio	1,221	8.0	34	888	7.0	40	323	14.2	13
Oklahoma	420	8.5	39	316	8.1	48	65	13.5	8
Oregon	245	5.4	3	221	5.3	8	13	–	–
Pennsylvania	1,043	7.1	21	710	5.8	15	320	15.4	18
Rhode Island	88	7.0	16	68	6.2	24	17	–	–
South Carolina	515	9.6	47	206	6.0	19	306	16.2	23
South Dakota	94	9.1	44	63	7.5	44	2	–	–
Tennessee	635	8.2	36	375	6.3	26	253	15.0	16
Texas	2,185	6.4	11	1,678	5.8	15	466	11.6	3
Utah	255	5.6	4	243	5.7	12	2	–	–
Vermont	46	7.0	16	44	6.8	35	1	–	–
Virginia	722	7.7	32	386	5.7	12	328	14.9	15
Washington	455	5.7	5	358	5.2	6	42	13.5	8
West Virginia	166	8.0	34	158	8.0	47	8	–	–
Wisconsin	489	7.2	22	347	6.0	19	122	18.7	31
Wyoming	45	7.2	22	34	5.8	15	2	–	–
United States	28,371	7.2		18,561	6.0		8,726	14.3	

*Infant deaths (before age 1) per 1,000 live births.

– Number too small to calculate a reliable rate.

Source: U.S. Department of Health and Human Services, National Center for Health Statistics, *National Vital Statistics Reports,* Vol. 48, No. 11 (July 24 2000), Table 31. Calculations by Children's Defense Fund.

TABLE B11

Children's Health Insurance Program, Federal Fiscal Year 2000

	Program Type	Implementation Date	Total enrollment in FY 2000	Federal allotment for FY 1998	Percent of allotment spent thru FY 2000	Amount of FY 1998 funds left unspent after 3 years
Alabama	Combination	02/01/98	37,587	$ 85,975,213	66.7%	$ 28,664,175
Alaska	Medicaid	03/01/99	13,413	6,889,296	100.0	0
Arizona	Separate	11/01/98	60,803	116,797,799	32.7	78,555,410
Arkansas	Medicaid	10/01/98	1,892	47,907,958	4.6	45,705,195
California	Combination	03/01/98	477,615	854,644,807	30.1	597,632,857
Colorado	Separate	04/22/98	34,889	41,790,546	57.3	17,847,811
Connecticut	Combination	07/01/98	18,804	34,959,075	71.7	9,896,500
Delaware	Separate	02/01/99	4,474	8,053,463	28.4	5,763,608
District of Columbia	Medicaid	10/01/98	2,264	12,076,002	51.9	5,813,787
Florida	Combination	04/01/98	227,463	270,214,724	67.7	87,168,359
Georgia	Separate	11/01/98	120,626	124,660,136	45.1	68,482,124
Hawaii	Medicaid	07/01/00	2,256	8,945,304	4.7	8,525,008
Idaho	Medicaid	10/01/97	12,449	15,879,707	80.5	3,104,075
Illinois	Combination	01/05/98	62,507	122,528,573	43.6	69,056,371
Indiana	Combination	10/01/97	44,373	70,512,432	100.0	0
Iowa	Combination	07/01/98	19,958	32,460,463	81.1	6,128,334
Kansas	Separate	01/01/99	26,306	30,656,520	70.3	9,094,628
Kentucky	Combination	07/01/98	55,593	49,932,527	100.0	0
Louisiana	Medicaid	11/01/98	49,995	101,736,840	35.0	66,081,692
Maine	Combination	07/01/98	22,742	12,486,977	100.0	0
Maryland*	Medicaid	07/01/98	93,081	61,627,358	100.0	0
Massachusetts	Combination	10/01/97	113,034	42,836,231	100.0	0
Michigan	Combination	05/01/98	37,148	91,585,508	56.5	39,858,760
Minnesota*	Medicaid	10/01/98	n/a	28,395,980	0.1	28,380,759
Mississippi	Combination	07/01/98	20,451	56,017,103	52.1	26,838,680
Missouri	Medicaid	09/01/98	73,825	51,673,123	100.0	0
Montana	Separate	01/01/99	8,317	11,740,395	41.6	6,853,037
Nebraska	Medicaid	05/01/98	11,400	14,862,926	66.5	4,981,680
Nevada	Separate	10/01/98	15,946	30,407,067	43.0	17,343,203
New Hampshire	Combination	05/01/98	4,272	11,458,404	22.2	8,919,154
New Jersey	Combination	03/01/98	89,034	88,417,899	79.2	18,409,571
New Mexico	Medicaid	03/31/99	6,106	62,972,705	6.7	58,762,477
New York	Combination	04/15/98	769,457	255,626,409	100.0	0
North Carolina	Separate	10/01/98	103,567	79,508,462	100.0	0
North Dakota	Combination	10/01/98	2,573	5,040,741	36.9	3,181,416
Ohio	Medicaid	01/01/98	111,436	115,734,364	84.3	18,154,799
Oklahoma	Medicaid	12/01/97	57,719	85,699,060	59.8	34,441,817
Oregon	Separate	07/01/98	37,092	39,121,663	51.5	18,973,767
Pennsylvania	Separate	05/28/98	119,710	117,456,520	100.0	0
Rhode Island	Medicaid	10/01/97	11,539	10,684,422	100.0	0
South Carolina	Medicaid	10/01/97	59,853	63,557,819	100.0	0
South Dakota	Combination	07/01/98	5,888	8,541,224	54.5	3,885,949
Tennessee	Medicaid	10/01/97	14,861	66,153,082	63.0	24,447,949
Texas	Combination	07/01/98	130,519	561,331,521	14.5	480,069,849
Utah	Separate	08/03/98	25,294	24,241,159	86.0	3,405,253
Vermont	Separate	10/01/98	4,081	3,535,445	55.3	1,580,333
Virginia	Separate	10/22/98	37,681	68,314,914	34.5	44,765,003
Washington	Separate	02/01/00	2,616	46,661,213	1.3	46,056,934
West Virginia*	Combination	07/01/98	21,659	23,606,744	45.6	12,835,638
Wisconsin	Medicaid	04/01/99	47,140	40,633,039	57.7	17,171,678
Wyoming	Separate	12/01/99	2,547	7,711,638	13.5	6,670,656
United States			3,333,879	4,224,262,500	51.9	2,033,508,296

* Maryland received approval on November 7, 2000 for a state plan amendment to implement a separate child health program on July 1, 2001. Numbers for Minnesota are misleading because a state program prior to CHIP with eligibility levels far higher than CHIP in other states limits CHIP eligibility to children younger than 2 with family incomes from 275% to 280% of the federal poverty level. West Virginia folded its Medicaid expansion program into its separate child health program so that, effective October 1, 2000, it has a separate child health program and is no longer a combination program.

Notes:

1. Enrollment includes all children enrolled in CHIP from October 1, 1999 through September 30, 2000 and does not include title XIX Medicaid enrollment.

2. States are allowed 3 years to use each year's fiscal allotment; therefore this is the first year we have figures of how much is left from the original FY 1998 allotment. However, through Congressional action, states with unspent FY 1998 funds will receive a portion of those funds back. The remaining unspent funds will be distributed among the states that spent their entire FY 1998 allotment.

3. National totals do not include data from U.S. territories.

Sources: U.S. Department of Health and Human Services, Health Care Financing Administration, "State Children's Health Insurance Program (SCHIP) Aggregate Enrollment Statistics for the 50 States and the District of Columbia for Federal Fiscal Year (FFY) 2000" at http://www.hcfa.gov/init/fy2000.pdf , and "SCHIP Federal Allotments and Application of Expenditures FFY 1998; Status @ 9/30/00; Preliminary," File ST011701.xls, sheet all98. Unspent funds calculated by Children's Defense Fund.

TABLE B12

Health Insurance Coverage of Children

Children under age 19 lacking health insurance throughout the year, 1997-1999*

	Estimated number	Percent	Rank	Medicaid enrollment, FY 1998
Alabama	177,000	15.0%	34	364,832
Alaska	32,000	15.2	35	52,428
Arizona	367,000	25.4	51	412,367
Arkansas	144,000	19.9	46	236,727
California	1,896,000	19.4	45	3,438,056
Colorado	166,000	14.3	31	200,408
Connecticut	93,000	10.6	17	213,695
Delaware	26,000	13.2	27	58,513
District of Columbia	18,000	16.5	38	76,525
Florida	732,000	18.8	41	1,137,381
Georgia	365,000	16.2	37	746,845
Hawaii	28,000	8.8	9	87,249
Idaho	74,000	19.1	42	74,589
Illinois	435,000	12.7	24	1,045,873
Indiana	202,000	12.3	22	371,973
Iowa	68,000	8.8	9	172,238
Kansas	77,000	10.3	14	144,723
Kentucky	147,000	13.8	29	335,619
Louisiana	290,000	21.9	47	430,065
Maine	34,000	10.8	18	95,689
Maryland	186,000	13.0	26	338,566
Massachusetts	136,000	8.7	7	564,560
Michigan	270,000	9.8	13	781,009
Minnesota	113,000	8.3	4	333,186
Mississippi	152,000	18.2	40	298,274
Missouri	141,000	9.4	11	467,499
Montana	48,000	19.3	44	51,466
Nebraska	39,000	8.1	3	132,063
Nevada	116,000	22.0	49	80,747
New Hampshire	28,000	8.6	6	58,861
New Jersey	285,000	13.3	28	460,440
New Mexico	119,000	21.9	47	231,378
New York	672,000	14.0	30	1,621,869
North Carolina	312,000	14.8	33	674,006
North Dakota	26,000	14.7	32	32,657
Ohio	297,000	9.7	12	796,056
Oklahoma	186,000	19.2	43	n.a.
Oregon	111,000	12.3	22	255,894
Pennsylvania	257,000	8.4	5	882,877
Rhode Island	19,000	7.5	2	77,751
South Carolina	189,000	17.9	39	369,983
South Dakota	25,000	11.5	19	52,925
Tennessee	154,000	10.5	16	669,063
Texas	1,582,000	25.2	50	1,689,961
Utah	91,000	11.9	20	126,290
Vermont	11,000	7.2	1	62,282
Virginia	234,000	12.8	25	412,235
Washington	167,000	10.3	14	572,927
West Virginia	54,000	12.2	21	209,341
Wisconsin	126,000	8.7	7	299,364
Wyoming	22,000	15.3	36	31,697
United States	10.8 million	14.1		22,331,022

*The U.S. percentage and number of uninsured are from the March 2000 Current Population Survey. Beginning with the March 1998 CPS, the uninsured includes those whose health coverage is only through the Indian Health Service. The estimated percentage of uninsured children in each state is the average of the percentages of children uninsured during the years 1997-1999. Three-year averages are used because of small sample size in some states. The estimated number of uninsured children in each state is calculated by applying that average percentage to the most recent Census estimates of the number of children under age 19 in each state. The state estimates will not add to the most recent national number of uninsured children.

n.a. - Data not available.

Source: U.S. Department of Commerce, Bureau of the Census, Current Population Survey, March 1998, 1999, and 2000, and July 1, 1999 state population estimates adjusted for the undercount; and U.S. Department of Health and Human Services, Health Care Financing Administration, HCFA 2082 Tables for FFY 1998, unpublished. Calculations by Children's Defense Fund.

TABLE B13

Immunization Status*, by Race/Ethnicity, 1999

Percent of two-year-olds** who received all recommended immunizations in the series

	Total	Non-Hispanic White	Non-Hispanic Black	Hispanic	American Indian or Alaska Native	Asian or Pacific Islander
Alabama	78.4%	80.1%	77.4%	NA	NA	NA
Alaska	80.1	80.9	NA	NA	86.9%	NA
Arizona	72.4	75.6	NA	68.4%	NA	NA
Arkansas	77.1	78.4	NA	NA	NA	NA
California	75.3	79.7	NA	75.2	NA	NA
Colorado	75.8	77.5	NA	NA	NA	NA
Connecticut	85.9	88.1	NA	NA	NA	NA
Delaware	78.2	85.1	NA	NA	NA	NA
District of Columbia	77.5	91.0	75.0	NA	NA	NA
Florida	80.3	79.0	NA	79.3	NA	NA
Georgia	81.9	84.6	79.5	NA	NA	NA
Hawaii	81.6	NA	NA	NA	NA	85.3%
Idaho	69.4	70.9	NA	NA	NA	NA
Illinois	77.4	82.3	NA	NA	NA	NA
Indiana	74.3	77.0	NA	NA	NA	NA
Iowa	83.4	84.3	NA	NA	NA	NA
Kansas	78.9	80.6	NA	NA	NA	NA
Kentucky	87.6	87.9	NA	NA	NA	NA
Louisiana	76.8	75.3	79.4	NA	NA	NA
Maine	82.9	82.5	NA	NA	NA	NA
Maryland	79.4	84.6	74.0	NA	NA	NA
Massachusetts	85.2	86.5	NA	NA	NA	NA
Michigan	74.4	76.7	NA	NA	NA	NA
Minnesota	85.2	85.9	NA	NA	NA	NA
Mississippi	81.7	83.5	78.4	NA	NA	NA
Missouri	75.0	74.8	NA	NA	NA	NA
Montana	82.5	83.4	NA	NA	NA	NA
Nebraska	81.8	82.2	NA	NA	NA	NA
Nevada	73.1	70.7	NA	76.2	NA	NA
New Hampshire	84.5	84.9	NA	NA	NA	NA
New Jersey	80.8	87.4	NA	81.6	NA	NA
New Mexico	73.0	NA	NA	73.4	NA	NA
New York	81.0	81.1	80.3	78.9	NA	NA
North Carolina	81.8	83.0	NA	NA	NA	NA
North Dakota	80.4	81.2	NA	NA	NA	NA
Ohio	78.1	78.4	78.1	NA	NA	NA
Oklahoma	72.9	71.4	NA	NA	NA	NA
Oregon	72.3	74.2	NA	NA	NA	NA
Pennsylvania	86.0	86.6	89.9	NA	NA	NA
Rhode Island	87.4	92.0	NA	NA	NA	NA
South Carolina	80.6	83.6	75.8	NA	NA	NA
South Dakota	81.7	83.3	NA	NA	NA	NA
Tennessee	77.7	79.6	76.4	NA	NA	NA
Texas	72.4	79.8	NA	68.4	NA	NA
Utah	80.2	81.3	NA	NA	NA	NA
Vermont	90.5	89.9	NA	NA	NA	NA
Virginia	80.3	83.9	NA	NA	NA	NA
Washington	74.9	74.6	NA	80.5	NA	NA
West Virginia	81.0	81.2	NA	NA	NA	NA
Wisconsin	84.5	86.9	NA	NA	NA	NA
Wyoming	82.8	84.1	NA	NA	NA	NA
United States	78.4	81.0	73.8	74.9	75.0	77.4

*4:3:1:3 includes four or more doses of diphtheria, tetanus, and pertussis vaccine (DTP/DT); three or more doses of poliovirus vaccine, one or more doses of measles-containing vaccine, and three or more doses of Haemophilus influenzae type b (Hib) vaccine. For comparability with earlier years, the recently recommended immunization series, which includes three doses of the vaccine for hepatitis B, was not used.
** Children born between February 1996 and May 1998. Children of Hispanic origin are excluded from the other racial and ethnic categories.
NA — Data do not meet CDC standard of reliability or precision, so no rate is available.
Source: U.S. Department of Health and Human Services, Centers for Disease Control and Prevention, 1999 National Immunization Survey, at http://www.cdc.gov/nip/coverage/tables/99/4313_race_iap.xls .

TABLE B14

Head Start Enrollment and Race and Ethnicity of Enrollees, 2000

	Total enrollment**	White	Black, African American	Hispanic, Latino	Asian	Hawaiian, Pacific Islander	Native American, Alaskan	Other
			Race of enrollees (percentage distribution)*					
Alabama	15,832	20.3%	76.7%	2.3%	0.3%	0.0%	0.3%	0.0%
Alaska	1,297	20.9	5.3	4.6	2.1	1.1	64.0	1.9
Arizona	11,882	15.1	4.8	47.3	0.5	0.1	32.2	0.0
Arkansas	10,316	45.0	47.0	6.9	0.4	0.1	0.6	0.0
California	95,280	13.6	14.6	64.2	6.0	0.5	1.1	0.0
Colorado	9,333	31.0	10.1	53.5	1.5	0.2	3.3	0.3
Connecticut	6,857	21.6	40.3	36.5	1.4	0.0	0.3	0.0
Delaware	2,119	17.3	60.3	20.5	1.1	0.0	0.0	0.8
District of Columbia	3,345	0.2	80.8	17.7	1.3	0.0	0.0	0.0
Florida	32,389	18.3	59.0	21.6	0.8	0.1	0.2	0.0
Georgia	21,580	17.8	72.1	9.1	0.6	0.5	0.1	0.0
Hawaii	2,916	14.1	4.9	7.4	20.3	52.0	0.8	0.5
Idaho	2,387	54.3	1.3	34.8	0.8	0.2	8.6	0.0
Illinois	37,767	23.9	51.0	23.6	1.1	0.0	0.1	0.2
Indiana	13,323	60.5	31.8	7.0	0.6	0.0	0.2	0.0
Iowa	7,235	71.5	16.7	9.7	1.4	0.1	0.6	0.0
Kansas	7,447	49.8	25.7	21.3	1.3	0.2	1.7	0.0
Kentucky	15,701	74.9	22.6	1.8	0.6	0.1	0.1	0.0
Louisiana	20,975	15.2	83.1	0.8	0.7	0.1	0.2	0.0
Maine	3,631	90.2	2.8	2.6	1.7	0.1	2.6	0.0
Maryland	9,968	19.6	69.7	7.8	1.6	0.3	0.2	0.9
Massachusetts	12,250	36.1	20.8	34.7	6.3	1.6	0.5	0.0
Michigan	33,769	47.2	39.5	9.9	1.0	0.2	2.3	0.0
Minnesota	9,715	49.4	18.3	17.4	7.6	0.0	6.9	0.5
Mississippi	25,455	11.9	85.8	0.6	0.4	0.0	1.3	0.0
Missouri	16,574	57.2	36.4	3.6	0.9	0.3	1.4	0.2
Montana	2,703	54.6	1.8	3.1	0.6	0.1	39.9	0.0
Nebraska	4,571	52.0	18.8	20.6	1.0	0.1	7.0	0.4
Nevada	2,035	20.5	25.1	39.8	1.6	0.9	12.0	0.0
New Hampshire	1,425	83.4	5.8	8.1	1.9	0.2	0.6	0.0
New Jersey	14,567	12.3	52.3	32.4	2.1	0.2	0.3	0.6
New Mexico	7,135	14.2	3.0	61.6	0.3	0.2	20.7	0.0
New York	46,805	29.3	33.8	32.6	3.5	0.1	0.7	0.0
North Carolina	17,808	22.1	63.1	11.3	0.9	0.0	2.6	0.0
North Dakota	2,042	59.0	2.4	2.8	0.7	0.3	34.8	0.0
Ohio	38,261	50.1	44.6	4.2	0.8	0.1	0.2	0.1
Oklahoma	12,655	46.2	20.8	8.7	0.7	0.4	23.2	0.0
Oregon	5,771	46.4	5.6	39.6	1.7	0.2	4.5	2.0
Pennsylvania	29,650	49.7	37.7	10.5	1.6	0.1	0.2	0.2
Rhode Island	2,952	52.6	15.7	23.5	2.4	0.1	1.5	4.2
South Carolina	11,604	7.1	88.7	3.6	0.1	0.0	0.5	0.0
South Dakota	2,587	47.8	3.0	3.0	0.6	0.2	45.4	0.0
Tennessee	15,747	52.3	42.8	3.8	0.8	0.1	0.2	0.0
Texas	63,171	12.0	22.4	64.6	0.7	0.1	0.3	0.0
Utah	5,079	48.5	2.5	37.7	1.8	2.7	6.7	0.0
Vermont	1,438	94.3	2.7	1.2	1.2	0.0	0.5	0.0
Virginia	12,652	33.9	49.8	14.5	1.6	0.2	0.1	0.0
Washington	10,287	35.4	11.1	38.3	5.2	1.1	8.3	0.7
West Virginia	7,144	86.9	12.2	0.5	0.2	0.0	0.1	0.0
Wisconsin	12,953	44.7	28.2	15.0	5.8	0.1	6.2	0.0
Wyoming	1,468	52.5	2.9	23.7	0.6	0.3	19.2	0.9
United States**	761,853							

*Percentages include AIPB, Migrant, and EHS Research Grant Programs.
**Totals do not include Puerto Rico, Virgin Islands, Outer Pacific, Migrant, or American Indian Programs.
Source: U.S. Department of Health and Human Services, Head Start Bureau

TABLE B15

Children Served by the Child Care and Development Block Grant

	Number of low-income children eligible for child care assistance (family income <85% of state median income)	Average monthly enrollment in CCDBG (1998)	Average monthly enrollment in CCDBG (1999)	Percent of eligible children served (1999)
Alabama	233,300	20,530	24,500	10.5%
Alaska	46,700	5,080	6,260	13.4
Arizona	283,800	33,060	36,590	12.9
Arkansas	180,600	9,240	11,250	6.2
California	1,732,500	100,640	226,750	13.1
Colorado	226,300	20,170	23,790	10.5
Connecticut	187,700	11,910	9,790	5.2
Delaware	50,700	6,140	5,920	11.7
District of Columbia	31,500	3,850	1,040	3.3
Florida	705,300	46,640	58,630	8.3
Georgia	485,200	47,210	38,170	7.9
Hawaii	81,200	6,670	7,110	8.8
Idaho	68,200	6,550	7,560	11.1
Illinois	676,000	88,330	92,030	13.6
Indiana	299,800	12,670	20,230	6.7
Iowa	199,200	11,810	15,720	7.9
Kansas	172,800	10,240	11,570	6.7
Kentucky	170,200	25,010	26,220	15.4
Louisiana	219,700	35,180	38,980	17.7
Maine	60,900	N/A	8,890	14.6
Maryland	259,900	21,380	22,070	8.5
Massachusetts	301,700	46,010	40,200	13.3
Michigan	545,100	92,060	101,890	18.7
Minnesota	297,400	25,530	17,200	5.8
Mississippi	185,500	7,870	17,870	9.6
Missouri	305,600	42,600	58,390	19.1
Montana	60,800	5,530	6,430	10.6
Nebraska	115,000	9,350	12,140	10.6
Nevada	97,000	4,830	5,900	6.1
New Hampshire	71,600	6,390	6,790	9.5
New Jersey	350,500	32,500	34,000	9.7
New Mexico	126,900	14,980	16,610	13.1
New York	880,900	158,610	164,200	18.6
North Carolina	411,400	74,250	67,100	16.3
North Dakota	37,700	4,160	4,450	11.8
Ohio	577,300	59,360	58,440	10.1
Oklahoma	191,100	39,930	30,820	16.1
Oregon	188,500	15,210	20,490	10.9
Pennsylvania	533,900	72,680	82,750	15.5
Rhode Island	42,500	6,330	6,390	15.0
South Carolina	231,000	21,730	17,840	7.7
South Dakota	46,200	3,530	3,680	8.0
Tennessee	346,000	54,820	63,090	18.2
Texas	1,161,700	78,960	96,640	8.3
Utah	130,400	12,250	13,260	10.2
Vermont	33,400	4,740	4,980	14.9
Virginia	348,100	23,880	27,120	7.8
Washington	310,500	41,850	46,130	14.9
West Virginia	52,700	12,900	13,310	25.3
Wisconsin	365,800	23,870	24,940	6.8
Wyoming	31,600	3,200	3,330	10.5

Estimates for number of eligible children were generated from the Urban Institute's TRIM3 model. N/A - data not available.

Sources: 1998 enrollment data from U.S. Department of Health and Human Services, Administration for Children and Families, Access to Child Care for Low-Income Working Families (October 1999); 1999 data from U.S. Department of Health and Human Services, "New Statistics Show Only Small Percentage of Eligible Families Receive Child Care Help" (Press Release), at http://www.acf.dhhs.gov/news/ccstudy2.htm .

Tsble B16

State Prekindergarten Initiatives: State Funding and Number of Children Served, in 1998-99

	Program	State spending	Number of children served
Alabama	Preschool Collaboration Project	$ 690,000	1,000
Alaska	Alaska Head Start Program (State-Funded Head Start Model)	5,489,951	725
Arizona	Early Childhood State Block Grant (Prekindergarten Component)	10,013,423	3,482
Arkansas	Arkansas Better Chance	10,000,000	9,048
California	State Preschool Program	127,000,000	145,719
Colorado	Colorado Preschool Program	21,640,000	8,350
Connecticut	School Readiness and Child Care Initiative	39,000,000	5,000
	State-Funded Head Start Model	5,100,000	N/A
Delaware	Early Childhood Assistance Program (State-Funded Head Start Model)	3,600,000	843
District of Columbia	Public School Preschool Program	14,591,000	3,381
	District-Funded Head Start Model	2,570,000	1,450
Florida	Prekindergarten Early Intervention Program	97,000,328	29,639
	State Migrant Prekindergarten Program	3,295,172	7,552
Georgia	Prekindergarten Program for Four-Year-Olds	217,000,000	61,000
Hawaii	Preschool Open Doors	2,700,000	780
	State-Funded Head Start Model	387,387	229
Idaho	No state prekindergarten initiative		
Illinois	Early Childhood Block Grant (Prekindergarten Component)	136,000,000	50,000
Indiana	No state prekindergarten initiative		
Iowa	Comprehensive Child Development Program "Shared Visions"	7,633,087	2,466
Kansas	Four-Year-Old At-Risk Children Preschool Program	3,000,000	1,350
	State-Funded Head Start Model	2,500,000	N/A
Kentucky	Kentucky Preschool Program	39,700,000	15,433
Louisiana	Preschool Block Grant	6,650,000	3,200
Maine	Two-Year Kindergarten	1,300,000	654
	State-Funded Head Start Model	2,329,000	424
Maryland	Extended Elementary Education Program (EEEP)	19,263,000	9,880
Massachusetts	Community Partnerships for Children	78,500,000	18,100
	State-Funded Head Start Model	6,900,000	450
Michigan	Michigan School Readiness Program	67,083,000	21,638
Minnesota	Learning Readiness	10,300,000	44,889
	State-Funded Head Start Model	18,750,000	3,135
Mississippi	No state prekindergarten initiative		
Missouri	Missouri Preschool Project	N/A	N/A
Montana	No state prekindergarten initiative		
Nebraska	Early Childhood Projects	500,000	275
Nevada	No state prekindergarten initiative		
New Hampshire	NH Head Start - State Collaboration (State-Funded Head Start Model)	230,000	N/A
New Jersey	Early Childhood Program Aid (Prekindergarten Component)	70,000,000	8,197
	State-Funded Head Start Model	1,400,000	500
New Mexico	Child Development Program	1,300,000	1,333
	State-Funded Head Start Model	5,000,000	1,300
New York	Universal Prekindergarten	67,000,000	18,906
	Experimental Prekindergarten	50,200,000	19,458
North Carolina	Smart Start	N/A	N/A
North Dakota	No state prekindergarten initiative		
Ohio	Public School Preschool	17,900,000	7,773
	State-Funded Head Start Model	92,562,977	22,072
Oklahoma	Early Childhood Four-Year-Old Program	36,500,708	16,678
	Head Start State-Appropriated Funds (State-Funded Head Start Model)	3,316,918	N/A
Oregon	Oregon Head Start Prekindergarten (State-Funded Head Start Model)	16,272,167	3,064
Pennsylvania	Education Aid for Kindergarten for Four-Year-Olds	5,700,000	2,979
Rhode Island	Early Childhood Investment Fund	–	–
	State-Funded Head Start Model	1,965,000	400
South Carolina	Early Childhood Program (Half-Day Child Development Program)	22,356,688	16,000
South Dakota	No state prekindergarten initiative		
Tennessee	Tennessee Early Childhood Education Pilot Program	3,100,000	600
Texas	Public School Prekindergarten	235,000,000	123,859
Utah	No state prekindergarten initiative		
Vermont	Early Education Initiative	1,315,000	1,097
Virginia	Virginia Preschool Initiative	23,500,000	5,811
Washington	Early Childhood Education & Assistance Program	28,897,592	8,098
	Head Start State Match Program (State-Funded Head Start Model)	470,000	N/A
West Virginia	Public School Early Childhood Education	6,232,702	5,656
Wisconsin	Four-Year-Old Kindergarten	19,800,000	9,550
	State-Funded Head Start Model	4,950,000	1,187
Wyoming	No state prekindergarten initiative		
Total	Number of Initiatives: 58	1,675,455,100	724,610

Data were provided as reported by the states. Some figures may be rounded or estimated.

For some states, the data may not be not comparable because the most recent available figures were from 1997-98, the enrollment counts included some duplication or children were only receiving supplementary services through the prekindergarten initiative or for other reasons. See original source for further details.

Source: K. Schulman, H. Blank, and D. Ewen, Seeds of Success: State Prekindergarten Initiatives 1998-99. (Washington, DC: Children's Defense Fund, September 1999).

TABLE B17

Maximum Number of Children Allowed Per Caretaker
and Maximum Group Size in Child Care Centers, Selected Ages, 2000

	Children per Caretaker			Group Size		
	9 Months	27 Months	4 Years	9 Months	27 Months	4 Years
Alabama	6:1	8:1	20:1	6	8	20
Alaska	5:1	6:1	10:1	NR	NR	NR
Arizona	5:1/11:2	8:1	15:1	NR	NR	NR
Arkansas	6:1	12:1	15:1	NR	NR	NR
California	4:1	6:1	12:1	NR	12	NR
Colorado	5:1	7:1	12:1	10	14	24
Connecticut	4:1	4:1	10:1	8	8	20
Delaware	4:1	10:1	15:1	NR	NR	NR
District of Columbia	4:1	4:1	10:1	8	8	20
Florida	4:1	11:1	20:1	NR	NR	NR
Georgia	6:1	10:1	18:1	12	20	36
Hawaii	4:1	8:1	16:1	8	NR	NR
Idaho	6:1	12:1	12:1	NR	NR	NR
Illinois	4:1	8:1	10:1	12	16	20
Indiana	4:1	5:1	12:1	8	15	NR
Iowa	4:1	6:1	12:1	NR	NR	NR
Kansas	3:1	7:1	12:1	9	14	24
Kentucky	5:1	10:1	14:1	10	20	28
Louisiana	6:1	12:1	16:1	12	12	16
Maine	4:1	5:1	10:1	12	15	30
Maryland	3:1	6:1	10:1	6	12	20
Massachusetts	3:1/7:2	4:1/9:2	10:1	7	9	20
Michigan	4:1	4:1	12:1	NR	NR	NR
Minnesota	4:1	7:1	10:1	8	14	20
Mississippi	5:1	12:1	16:1	10	14	20
Missouri	4:1	8:1	10:1	8	16	NR
Montana	4:1	8:1	10:1	NR	NR	NR
Nebraska	4:1	6:1	12:1	NR	NR	NR
Nevada	6:1	10:1	13:1	NR	NR	NR
New Hampshire	4:1	6:1	12:1	12	18	24
New Jersey	4:1	7:1	15:1	20	20	20
New Mexico	6:1	10:1	12:1	NR	NR	NR
New York	4:1	5:1	8:1	8	10	16
North Carolina	5:1	10:1	20:1	10	20	25
North Dakota	4:1	5:1	10:1	8	10	20
Ohio	5:1	7:1	12:1	12	14	28
Oklahoma	4:1	8:1	15:1	8	16	30
Oregon	4:1	4:1	10:1	8	8	20
Pennsylvania	4:1	6:1	6:1	8	12	20
Rhode Island	4:1	6:1	10:1	8	12	20
South Carolina	6:1	10:1	18:1	NR	NR	NR
South Dakota	5:1	5:1	10:1	20	20	20
Tennessee	5:1	8:1	15:1	10	16	20
Texas	4:1/10:2	13:1	20:1	10	26	35
Utah	4:1	7:1	15:1	8	14	30
Vermont	4:1	5:1	10:1	8	10	20
Virginia	4:1	10:1	12:1	NR	NR	NR
Washington	4:1	7:1	10:1	8	14	20
West Virginia	4:1	8:1	12:1	NR	NR	NR
Wisconsin	4:1	6:1	13:1	8	12	24
Wyoming	5:1	8:1	15:1	NR	NR	NR
Maximum Recommended Level	3:1 to 4:1	4:1 to 6:1	8:1 to 10:1	8	12	20

NR — Not regulated.

Maximum Recommended Level: As recommended in the accreditation guidelines developed by the National Association for the Education of Young Children and in the National Health and Safety Performance Standards developed by the American Public Health Association and the American Academy of Pediatrics.

There may be some exceptions to these ratio and group size requirements in some states under certain circumstances. For example, some states have different requirements for small centers, classes with mixed-age groups, or different levels of licensing. See original source for details.

Source: The Center for Career Development in Early Care and Education at Wheelock College, *Child Care Centers: Child/Staff Ratio and Group Size Requirements* (Boston, MA: 2000).

TABLE B18

Participants in Federal Education and Disability Programs

	Title I 1997-1998	Individuals with Disabilities Education Act (IDEA) 1998-1999 school year					Supplemental Security Income (SSI) child recipients December 2000
		Total	Ages 3-5	Ages 6-11	Ages 12-17	Ages 18-21	
Alabama	262,235	99,813	7,499	44,384	42,337	5,593	22,860
Alaska	19,446	17,712	1,754	8,341	6,896	721	910
Arizona	256,286	88,598	8,876	41,662	34,343	3,717	11,990
Arkansas	156,143	59,110	8,677	23,458	24,310	2,665	14,180
California	2,091,562	623,651	56,837	288,947	253,221	24,646	81,740
Colorado	75,535	75,134	7,814	32,763	31,280	3,277	6,500
Connecticut	79,276	76,740	7,443	32,881	32,893	3,523	5,680
Delaware	5,508	16,233	1,664	7,884	6,060	625	2,900
District of Columbia	52,605	8,162	409	3,440	3,710	603	3,320
Florida	616,848	345,171	28,233	165,705	137,265	13,968	64,660
Georgia	331,140	155,754	15,134	78,449	57,399	4,772	26,660
Hawaii	68,001	20,551	1,646	9,199	9,023	683	1,380
Idaho	40,154	27,553	3,466	12,849	10,276	962	3,020
Illinois	495,487	283,698	27,524	131,192	113,748	11,234	38,890
Indiana	107,997	146,559	13,778	70,759	55,605	6,417	16,640
Iowa	49,084	70,958	5,578	30,188	31,617	3,575	5,500
Kansas	79,675	58,425	6,933	25,703	23,283	2,506	5,680
Kentucky	281,445	87,973	15,161	39,292	30,144	3,376	22,380
Louisiana	342,401	95,245	9,495	40,199	40,349	5,202	26,590
Maine	23,805	34,294	3,690	14,787	14,246	1,571	2,890
Maryland	122,772	111,688	9,714	51,569	46,251	4,154	13,380
Massachusetts	223,532	168,964	15,382	72,753	72,240	8,589	15,630
Michigan	476,604	208,403	18,983	94,387	84,509	10,524	33,440
Minnesota	119,492	106,194	11,327	45,649	44,841	4,377	7,970
Mississippi	284,544	61,778	6,046	27,755	25,059	2,918	18,260
Missouri	167,807	131,565	9,698	59,844	56,002	6,021	16,040
Montana	32,532	18,797	1,688	8,323	7,948	838	1,830
Nebraska	42,745	43,400	3,656	19,614	17,675	2,455	3,300
Nevada	32,507	33,319	3,531	15,585	13,187	1,016	3,660
New Hampshire	14,781	27,502	2,190	11,411	12,467	1,434	1,630
New Jersey	145,775	210,114	15,998	100,989	83,228	9,899	18,960
New Mexico	95,840	52,113	5,133	21,755	22,958	2,267	5,530
New York	719,822	432,119	50,616	176,431	181,245	23,827	66,010
North Carolina	291,133	165,333	16,880	82,127	61,134	5,192	29,940
North Dakota	20,274	13,181	1,197	5,840	5,472	672	990
Ohio	334,555	230,155	18,572	101,583	96,411	13,589	38,890
Oklahoma	194,019	80,289	5,805	36,309	34,182	3,993	10,190
Oregon	104,759	69,919	6,128	33,373	27,599	2,819	5,860
Pennsylvania	358,396	226,378	19,652	97,583	96,789	12,354	39,800
Rhode Island	16,275	27,911	2,510	13,004	11,127	1,270	3,300
South Carolina	207,675	99,033	10,937	50,216	34,435	3,445	16,580
South Dakota	21,901	15,702	2,164	7,546	5,309	683	1,940
Tennessee	231,925	128,273	10,291	57,538	53,477	6,967	21,060
Texas	1,791,323	486,749	34,846	210,056	216,191	25,656	47,550
Utah	54,628	55,252	5,710	25,627	21,451	2,464	3,240
Vermont	16,748	12,709	1,226	5,021	5,813	649	1,220
Virginia	115,610	153,716	13,713	69,200	64,064	6,739	19,500
Washington	171,273	114,144	11,799	53,276	44,165	4,904	10,900
West Virginia	83,534	49,934	5,301	22,775	19,367	2,491	7,110
Wisconsin	167,602	116,328	13,708	49,269	47,789	5,562	13,730
Wyoming	12,541	13,333	1,616	5,544	5,439	734	970
United States	12,107,557	6,055,629	567,628	2,734,034	2,475,829	278,138	842,780

Sources: U.S. Department of Education, Office of Elementary and Secondary Education, Compensatory Education Programs, Title I, unpublished tabulations; U.S. Department of Education, *To Assure the Free Appropriate Public Education of all Children with Disabilities: Twenty-second Annual Report to Congress on the Implementation of the Individuals with Disabilities Education Act (2000)*, Table A1; and U.S. Social Security Administration, Office of Policy, Office of Research, Evaluation, and Statistics, *Children Receiving SSI: December 2000* (2001).

TABLE B19

Public School Education

	Percentage of reading classes with fewer than 20 students (1998)	Percentage of fourth graders reading below proficient level (1998)	Pupil/ teacher ratio (1998)	Percentage of public school teachers lacking major or minor degrees in the field			High school completion rate (percent) (1997-99)	Expenditures per pupil	
				Science (1993-94)	Math (1993-94)	English (1993-94)		Dollars (1997-98)	Rank (1997-98)
Alabama	27%	76%	15.7	19.8%	13.5%	18.4%	83.1%	$ 4,849	45
Alaska	N/A	N/A	16.7	24.4	42.6	25.4	90.8	8,271	5
Arizona	14	78	20.0	24.1	39.2	27.7	75.0	4,595	49
Arkansas	31	77	16.2	21.3	19.9	10.1	82.9	4,708	47
California	7	80	21.0	25.1	39.3	23.2	81.5	5,644	32
Colorado	17	66	17.7	15.0	30.3	13.5	83.3	5,656	30
Connecticut	31	54	14.0	5.3	12.0	12.6	90.1	8,904	2
Delaware	21	75	16.0	27.7	N/A	31.1	89.1	7,420	8
District of Columbia	36	90	13.9	N/A	17.8	10.5	87.2	8,393	4
Florida	19	77	18.4	43.0	16.8	12.3	84.8	5,552	34
Georgia	27	76	15.8	30.8	18.7	34.6	83.7	5,647	31
Hawaii	10	83	17.7	22.9	38.3	9.9	90.7	5,858	27
Idaho	N/A	N/A	18.2	15.7	38.3	21.3	85.5	4,721	46
Illinois	N/A	N/A	16.5	14.8	11.5	18.7	86.2	6,242	19
Indiana	N/A	N/A	17.0	17.1	9.5	16.5	88.6	6,318	18
Iowa	28	65	15.2	13.8	8.4	23.0	88.2	5,998	25
Kansas	36	66	14.8	17.3	19.3	19.0	91.6	5,727	28
Kentucky	25	71	16.1	42.1	20.9	40.0	86.6	5,213	39
Louisiana	23	81	16.6	42.4	34.4	20.2	82.1	5,188	40
Maine	58	64	13.2	34.0	29.0	12.4	92.9	6,742	14
Maryland	17	71	16.9	12.9	23.3	20.3	90.1	7,034	13
Massachusetts	30	63	13.8	11.2	24.6	10.6	90.1	7,778	7
Michigan	11	72	18.5	19.8	21.3	17.6	90.1	7,050	12
Minnesota	17	64	16.9	6.2	6.6	14.9	90.4	6,388	16
Mississippi	17	82	16.1	22.6	18.5	26.4	82.1	4,288	50
Missouri	24	71	14.7	25.3	5.4	13.8	91.6	5,565	33
Montana	33	63	15.7	21.9	10.2	17.3	91.0	5,724	29
Nebraska	N/A	N/A	14.3	24.2	13.1	19.0	91.5	5,958	26
Nevada	13	79	18.9	13.2	19.5	12.7	74.5	5,295	37
New Hampshire	33	62	15.4	13.0	18.0	14.9	87.3	6,156	22
New Jersey	N/A	N/A	13.8	21.5	25.6	11.7	90.2	9,643	1
New Mexico	40	78	16.5	16.6	18.6	12.0	82.7	5,005	43
New York	20	71	14.6	13.5	10.9	10.4	85.2	8,852	3
North Carolina	19	72	15.8	29.3	20.8	13.7	86.1	5,257	38
North Dakota	N/A	N/A	14.4	11.3	8.3	12.9	93.6	5,056	41
Ohio	N/A	N/A	16.2	22.2	24.0	16.1	89.3	6,198	21
Oklahoma	49	70	15.4	30.8	12.1	15.7	85.4	5,033	42
Oregon	16	72	20.0	9.3	40.6	37.3	78.5	6,419	15
Pennsylvania	N/A	N/A	16.4	12.4	1.5	24.6	87.6	7,209	9
Rhode Island	26	68	13.9	11.0	10.4	0.0	86.7	7,928	6
South Carolina	25	78	15.2	23.2	28.7	23.1	86.9	5,320	36
South Dakota	N/A	N/A	14.3	25.3	16.4	29.2	91.5	4,669	48
Tennessee	29	75	15.3	40.4	30.7	30.7	89.5	4,937	44
Texas	60	71	15.2	17.8	13.4	16.7	79.2	5,444	35
Utah	14	72	22.4	23.7	25.7	17.4	89.7	3,969	51
Vermont	N/A	N/A	12.8	23.7	22.8	11.1	95.3	7,075	11
Virginia	33	70	14.2	25.6	23.6	16.2	87.0	6,067	23
Washington	18	71	20.1	16.5	43.6	34.1	87.0	6,040	24
West Virginia	42	71	14.2	22.1	11.3	13.6	89.2	6,323	17
Wisconsin	24	66	14.4	28.9	17.1	22.5	90.6	7,123	10
Wyoming	44	70	14.2	17.0	11.8	18.7	87.8	6,218	20
United States	22	71	16.5	21.8	20.3	19.3	85.5	6,189	

N/A — data not available.

Sources: U.S. Department of Education, National Center for Education Statistics, NAEP 1998 Reading, Summary Data Tables, Table T068101, in XSR1TCH.PDF, available at http://nces.ed.gov/ ; U.S. Department of Education, National Center for Education Statistics, NAEP 1998 Reading: Report Card for the Nation and the States (March 1999), Table 5.3; U.S. Department of Education, National Center for Education Statistics, Digest of Education Statistics 2000 (2001), Tables 67 and 169; U.S. Department of Education, National Center for Education Statistics, SASS by State: 1993-94 Schools and Staffing Survey: Selected Results (1996), Tables 3.4, 3.5, and 3.6; and U.S. Department of Education, National Center for Education Statistics, Dropout Rates in the United States: 1999 (2000), Table 5. Calculations by Children's Defense Fund.

TABLE B20

Child Abuse and Neglect

	Child victims of abuse and neglect*		Type of abuse or neglect, 1998 (percentage distribution)					
	1990	1998	Physical abuse	Neglect	Medical neglect	Sexual abuse	Psycho-logical abuse	Other and unknown
Alabama	16,508	16,668	34.9%	40.7%	0.0%	18.8%	5.7%	0.0%
Alaska	5,217	7,138	25.5	60.9	0.0	10.8	2.6	0.2
Arizona	24,244	8,983	23.9	60.8	9.0	4.4	1.8	0.1
Arkansas	7,922	8,578	21.6	52.7	3.5	21.4	0.8	0.0
California	78,512	157,683	26.2	51.9	0.0	13.4	8.1	0.4
Colorado	7,906	7,010	22.5	52.1	5.0	11.3	9.0	0.0
Connecticut	12,481	16,923	9.6	50.5	1.8	2.5	30.9	4.6
Delaware	2,065	2,894	25.4	39.4	2.6	8.6	16.2	7.8
District of Columbia	3,210	4,916	8.3	75.9	0.0	1.9	0.0	13.9
Florida	79,086	82,119	15.2	33.4	2.1	5.9	2.4	40.9
Georgia	34,120	24,567	14.3	62.3	4.6	8.3	4.1	6.5
Hawaii	1,974	2,185	10.4	8.3	1.1	6.6	2.0	71.5
Idaho	2,667	7,936	31.1	47.5	0.0	16.3	0.0	5.1
Illinois	37,539	35,657	9.9	39.2	3.1	8.8	1.1	37.8
Indiana	26,818	18,962	17.0	66.1	3.0	13.9	0.0	0.0
Iowa	8,215	7,311	21.3	63.0	2.8	12.8	0.0	0.0
Kansas	–	5,312	21.3	33.8	1.8	14.3	8.3	20.5
Kentucky	22,239	22,875	25.1	57.6	0.0	7.2	10.1	0.0
Louisiana	15,383	13,773	19.5	69.5	0.0	6.6	4.0	0.4
Maine	4,133	3,579	20.6	34.1	0.0	12.0	33.3	0.0
Maryland	–	14,234	–	–	–	–	–	–
Massachusetts	28,621	27,559	–	–	–	–	–	–
Michigan	25,774	22,744	18.7	43.5	2.2	6.4	5.6	23.7
Minnesota	9,256	10,572	24.2	64.2	3.3	7.5	0.8	0.0
Mississippi	7,584	6,079	19.7	62.0	0.0	13.4	2.5	2.4
Missouri	21,732	12,556	19.8	49.9	2.5	16.7	1.8	9.3
Montana	–	3,292	13.0	54.3	2.5	9.7	15.9	4.7
Nebraska	5,595	4,219	27.3	62.1	0.0	10.7	0.0	0.0
Nevada	7,703	8,014	13.1	44.1	2.4	2.5	2.9	34.9
New Hampshire	1,056	1,159	21.9	52.9	0.0	22.2	3.1	0.0
New Jersey	19,546	9,851	22.5	63.2	3.4	8.0	2.9	0.0
New Mexico	4,379	4,241	24.9	52.3	2.7	6.3	13.7	0.1
New York	57,931	83,537	10.9	9.5	2.5	2.7	0.8	73.7
North Carolina	24,880	37,357	3.9	87.2	2.6	4.1	0.4	1.8
North Dakota	2,893	n/a	–	–	–	–	–	–
Ohio	49,434	33,552	27.4	55.2	0.0	14.1	3.1	0.2
Oklahoma	–	16,584	16.4	61.6	2.2	5.6	7.2	7.0
Oregon	8,126	10,147	11.4	17.9	3.4	11.3	6.0	50.0
Pennsylvania	7,951	5,392	40.4	3.7	2.7	45.6	1.9	5.7
Rhode Island	5,393	3,448	22.4	65.6	1.9	6.9	0.5	2.6
South Carolina	9,632	8,432	11.6	36.6	3.4	6.6	0.7	41.0
South Dakota	4,132	2,647	20.3	63.3	0.0	7.2	9.2	0.0
Tennessee	11,473	9,930	19.6	43.0	3.1	22.4	1.8	10.1
Texas	53,939	39,925	25.9	49.8	4.2	13.7	3.4	3.0
Utah	8,524	7,990	14.6	25.8	1.1	18.1	31.4	9.0
Vermont	1,500	887	24.3	33.7	2.5	38.4	1.0	0.0
Virginia	14,174	9,766	24.0	55.7	2.2	13.8	3.5	0.8
Washington	–	12,926	24.4	53.4	4.0	9.1	8.0	1.1
West Virginia	–	7,793	25.3	39.5	1.1	9.5	7.5	16.9
Wisconsin	14,165	8,168	21.6	36.3	0.7	26.4	0.9	14.1
Wyoming	2,478	807	24.0	61.7	1.6	10.3	1.4	0.9

*Substantiated and indicated cases.

— Data not available.

Note: Because of changes in definitions and reporting requirements, data may not be comparable from year to year, or from state to state.

Source: U.S. Department of Health and Human Services, Children's Bureau, *Child Maltreatment 1996: Reports from the States to the National Child Abuse and Neglect Data System* (1998), Table 2; and U.S. Department of Health and Human Services, Children's Bureau, *Child Maltreatment 1998: Reports from the States to the National Child Abuse and Neglect Data System* (2000), Appendix D, Tables 3.2 and 4.1. Calculations by Children's Defense Fund.

TABLE B21

Number of Adoptions from Foster Care, 1995-1999

	1995	1996	1997	1998	1999	Percent change, 1995-1999
Alabama	128	153	136	115	153	19.5%
Alaska	103	112	109	95	136	32.0
Arizona	215	383	474	–	760	253.5
Arkansas	84	185	146	258	278	231.0
California	3,094	3,153	3,614	4,418	6,251	102.0
Colorado	338	454	458	575	713	110.9
Connecticut	198	146	278	314	403	103.5
Delaware	38	46	33	62	33	-13.2
District of Columbia	86	113	132	139	166	93.0
Florida	904	1,064	992	1,549	1,355	49.9
Georgia	383	537	558	714	1,098	186.7
Hawaii	42	64	150	301	281	569.0
Idaho	46	40	47	57	107	132.6
Illinois	1,759	2,146	2,695	4,656	7,028	299.5
Indiana	520	373	592	795	759	46.0
Iowa	227	383	440	525	764	236.6
Kansas	333	292	421	411	566	70.0
Kentucky	197	214	222	206	359	82.2
Louisiana	292	321	310	311	356	21.9
Maine	85	144	96	112	202	137.6
Maryland	324	413	290	470	583	79.9
Massachusetts	1,073	1,113	1,161	1,095	922	-14.1
Michigan	1,717	1,950	2,047	2,257	2,446	42.5
Minnesota	232	239	302	429	540	132.8
Mississippi	109	101	131	170	237	117.4
Missouri	538	600	533	640	847	57.4
Montana	104	98	143	149	186	78.8
Nebraska	208	168	180	–	197	-5.3
Nevada	155	145	148	–	210	35.5
New Hampshire	51	59	24	51	63	23.5
New Jersey	616	678	570	813	729	18.3
New Mexico	141	148	152	197	258	83.0
New York	4,579	4,590	4,979	4,819	4,719	3.1
North Carolina	289	417	694	882	949	228.4
North Dakota	42	41	57	111	139	231.0
Ohio	1,202	1,258	1,400	1,014	1,868	55.4
Oklahoma	226	371	418	505	822	263.7
Oregon	427	468	441	665	765	79.2
Pennsylvania	1,018	1,127	1,526	1,515	1,451	42.5
Rhode Island	216	341	226	222	292	35.2
South Carolina	231	220	318	465	456	97.4
South Dakota	42	72	55	55	84	100.0
Tennessee	458	330	195	335	382	-16.6
Texas	804	746	1,091	1,597	2,030	152.5
Utah	283	124	268	334	369	30.4
Vermont	62	83	80	118	139	124.2
Virginia	320	298	276	235	326	1.9
Washington	645	521	656	854	1,040	61.2
West Virginia	139	188	220	211	312	124.5
Wisconsin	360	511	530	643	642	78.3
Wyoming	10	20	16	33	44	340.0
United States	25,693	27,761	31,030	36,466	45,821	78.3

Source: U.S. Department of Health and Human Services, Administration for Children and Families, Children's Bureau, Adoptions of Children with Public Child Welfare Agency Involvement, unpublished, data as of 2/28/01.

Calculations by Children's Defense Fund.

TABLE B22

Firearm deaths of children and teens ages 0-19, by manner, 1996-1998

	Total*			Homicide*			Suicide			Accident			Unknown Intent		
	1996	1997	1998	1996	1997	1998	1996	1997	1998	1996	1997	1998	1996	1997	1998
Alabama	104	93	86	59	57	47	25	23	24	14	10	11	6	3	4
Alaska	22	23	16	6	9	3	12	10	10	4	2	3	0	2	0
Arizona	120	117	102	64	53	49	47	52	43	4	5	6	5	7	4
Arkansas	63	55	69	27	28	36	26	18	24	9	7	3	1	2	6
California	672	594	493	508	457	372	108	106	102	52	26	13	4	5	6
Colorado	43	57	60	15	22	29	23	31	26	4	4	4	1	0	1
Connecticut	36	21	23	29	17	15	6	4	6	1	0	2	0	0	0
Delaware	5	7	2	4	2	2	1	5	0	0	0	0	0	0	0
District of Columbia	62	65	30	59	59	27	1	4	3	0	1	0	2	1	0
Florida	190	165	154	116	108	80	57	44	65	12	12	8	5	1	1
Georgia	160	129	111	79	70	61	51	35	39	24	20	10	6	4	1
Hawaii	3	3	4	2	2	2	1	1	2	0	0	0	0	0	0
Idaho	27	26	27	11	2	3	11	21	18	4	3	5	1	0	1
Illinois	308	254	264	263	211	206	33	29	40	7	10	13	5	4	5
Indiana	98	79	92	55	47	57	30	21	27	8	8	7	5	3	1
Iowa	22	33	26	8	8	6	13	20	15	0	3	5	1	2	0
Kansas	53	53	54	24	28	28	22	17	22	7	7	3	0	1	1
Kentucky	52	57	44	23	34	17	20	16	23	9	7	3	0	0	1
Louisiana	192	154	124	133	98	74	43	39	35	15	15	15	1	2	0
Maine	5	13	10	1	3	2	4	10	7	0	0	1	0	0	0
Maryland	106	104	108	88	91	89	13	11	13	3	2	2	2	0	4
Massachusetts	32	24	28	26	17	19	5	6	8	0	0	1	1	1	0
Michigan	157	156	135	96	103	87	42	41	43	13	10	3	6	2	2
Minnesota	56	55	34	25	26	12	21	25	22	6	4	0	4	0	0
Mississippi	77	81	55	38	41	28	19	28	19	18	11	7	2	1	1
Missouri	101	97	89	63	48	52	33	34	32	5	13	4	0	2	1
Montana	20	16	17	4	4	3	12	8	12	3	3	2	1	1	0
Nebraska	28	26	30	8	12	13	17	13	15	3	1	2	0	0	0
Nevada	36	34	48	25	21	26	8	13	20	3	0	1	0	0	1
New Hampshire	7	2	9	1	1	0	6	1	9	0	0	0	0	0	0
New Jersey	66	53	49	55	43	35	6	7	13	4	3	1	1	0	0
New Mexico	43	40	47	22	22	25	17	14	14	2	3	8	2	1	0
New York	199	146	123	150	107	88	43	33	28	6	4	5	0	2	2
North Carolina	135	92	88	70	45	43	49	37	30	15	9	13	1	1	2
North Dakota	9	8	7	0	0	2	8	8	4	1	0	1	0	0	0
Ohio	126	95	100	75	49	48	31	36	41	17	8	11	3	2	0
Oklahoma	61	82	61	30	48	22	25	29	30	5	3	6	1	2	3
Oregon	39	38	30	9	13	10	24	19	13	6	3	4	0	3	3
Pennsylvania	181	167	123	113	108	79	59	49	34	4	9	4	5	1	6
Rhode Island	6	4	5	5	2	4	1	2	1	0	0	0	0	0	0
South Carolina	78	54	60	39	32	30	27	16	23	9	5	7	3	1	0
South Dakota	10	12	12	1	0	2	9	7	9	0	5	1	0	0	0
Tennessee	123	117	109	66	64	53	32	37	38	23	12	16	2	4	2
Texas	359	377	322	202	194	176	121	139	108	27	39	29	9	5	9
Utah	37	35	32	11	10	12	24	24	19	0	0	1	2	1	0
Vermont	5	4	5	1	2	0	2	1	5	1	0	0	1	1	0
Virginia	109	114	97	54	68	46	43	39	39	12	5	9	0	2	3
Washington	67	83	66	31	35	28	31	36	32	4	8	5	1	4	1
West Virginia	16	23	19	6	9	5	8	10	12	2	3	1	0	1	1
Wisconsin	76	58	53	35	31	30	32	26	18	8	1	5	1	0	0
Wyoming	11	10	9	1	1	1	7	7	6	2	2	1	1	0	1
United States	4,613	4,205	3,761	2,836	2,562	2,184	1,309	1,262	1,241	376	306	262	92	75	74

*Total firearm deaths and homicide firearm deaths exclude firearm deaths by legal (police or corrections) intervention and deaths by air rifles.

Source: U.S. Department of Health and Human Services, National Center for Health Statistics, unpublished tabulations, Table III: Deaths from 282 selected causes. Calculations by Children's Defense Fund.

TABLE B22

State Budget Balances, Unspent TANF and CHIP Funds, and Tobacco Settlement Money in Millions

	Total balance, FY 2000	Unspent TANF funds, through FY 2000		Total unspent funds	Amount of FY 1998 CHIP funds unspent after three years	Tobacco settlement payment	
		Unobligated funds	Unliquidated obligations			2001	through 2025
Alabama	$ 68	$ 69.2	$ 2.7	$ 71.9	$ 28.7	$ 111.9	$ 3,166.3
Alaska	2,889	2.9	6.8	9.8	0.0	23.6	668.9
Arizona	609	35.1	65.5	100.6	78.6	102.0	2,887.6
Arkansas	NA	21.1	0.0	21.1	45.7	57.3	1,622.3
California	7,828	0.0	1,636.5	1,636.5	597.6	883.7	25,007.0
Colorado	1,024	0.0	94.2	94.2	17.8	94.9	2,685.8
Connecticut	564	0.0	0.0	0.0	9.9	128.5	3,637.3
Delaware	243	1.1	0.1	1.2	5.8	27.4	774.8
District of Columbia	NA	18.2	79.9	98.1	5.8	42.0	1,189.5
Florida	1,795	3.6	432.3	435.8	87.2	0.0	*
Georgia	545	96.8	100.4	197.2	68.5	169.9	4,808.7
Hawaii	272	14.3	5.8	20.1	8.5	41.7	1,179.2
Idaho	75	17.4	9.0	26.4	3.1	25.2	711.7
Illinois	1,517	0.0	0.0	0.0	69.1	322.2	9,118.5
Indiana	1,638	40.6	91.4	132.0	0.0	141.2	3,996.4
Iowa	609	12.0	5.2	17.2	6.1	60.2	1,703.8
Kansas	378	0.0	0.0	0.0	9.1	57.7	1,633.3
Kentucky	415	0.0	4.7	4.7	0.0	121.9	3,450.4
Louisiana	79	169.0	0.0	169.0	66.1	156.2	4,418.7
Maine	445	0.0	12.1	12.1	0.0	53.3	1,507.3
Maryland	1,518	49.5	54.2	103.7	0.0	156.5	4,428.7
Massachusetts	1,687	102.7	0.0	102.7	0.0	279.6	7,913.1
Michigan	1,264	124.8	0.0	124.8	39.9	301.3	8,526.3
Minnesota	1,533	95.5	83.5	178.9	28.4	0.0	*
Mississippi	290	62.9	58.2	121.0	26.8	0.0	*
Missouri	338	0.0	0.0	0.0	0.0	157.5	4,456.4
Montana	172	29.0	0.0	29.0	6.9	29.4	832.2
Nebraska	458	9.6	0.0	9.6	5.0	41.2	1,165.7
Nevada	292	0.0	27.7	27.7	17.3	42.2	1,195.0
New Hampshire	24	8.2	0.0	8.2	8.9	46.1	1,304.7
New Jersey	1,170	0.0	379.7	379.7	18.4	267.7	7,576.2
New Mexico	214	57.7	0.0	57.7	58.8	41.3	1,168.4
New York	1,167	761.0	546.7	1,307.7	0.0	883.6	25,003.2
North Carolina	38	6.0	80.1	86.1	0.0	161.5	4,569.4
North Dakota	60	11.5	0.1	11.6	3.2	25.3	717.1
Ohio	1,199	216.7	504.9	721.6	18.2	348.8	9,869.4
Oklahoma	438	94.4	0.0	94.4	34.4	71.7	2,030.0
Oregon	137	0.0	21.4	21.4	19.0	79.5	2,248.5
Pennsylvania	1,708	0.0	437.3	437.3	0.0	397.9	11,259.2
Rhode Island	164	4.9	0.0	4.9	0.0	49.8	1,408.5
South Carolina	566	0.0	33.8	33.8	0.0	81.4	2,304.7
South Dakota	37	14.3	2.4	16.8	3.9	24.2	683.7
Tennessee	313	100.0	27.6	127.6	24.4	169.0	4,782.2
Texas	1,606	141.2	41.6	182.8	480.1	0.0	*
Utah	223	33.4	0.0	33.4	3.4	30.8	871.6
Vermont	41	3.2	0.0	3.2	1.6	28.5	805.6
Virginia	1,228	0.0	36.8	36.8	44.8	141.6	4,006.0
Washington	1,239	88.0	141.2	229.3	46.1	142.2	4,022.7
West Virginia	221	135.2	25.6	160.8	12.8	61.4	1,736.7
Wisconsin	836	40.7	284.6	325.3	17.2	143.5	4,059.5
Wyoming	95	40.7	16.3	57.0	6.7	17.2	486.6
United States	41,269	2,732	5,350	8,083	2,033.5	6,923.7	193,598.6

NA — Data not available.

*Florida, Minnesota, Mississippi, and Texas did not participate in the larger tobacco settlement; they settled in individual suits and received lump-sum payments. These lump sums are: Florida, $12.7 billion; Minnesota, $6.1 billion; Mississippi, $3.6 billion; and Texas, $5.3 billion.

Sources: National Association of State Budget Officers, *The Fiscal Survey of the States: December 2000* (2000), Table A-11; Ed Lazere, *Unspent TANF Funds at the End of Federal Fiscal Year 2000* (Washington, DC: Center on Budget and Policy Priorities, 2001), Table III; U.S. Department of Health and Human Services, Health Care Financing Administration, SCHIP Federal Allotments and Application of Expenditures FFY 1998; Status @ 9/30/00; Preliminary, File ST011701.xls, sheet a1198 (unpublished); and National Association of Attorneys General, Annual Payments to Each State (November 16, 1998), at http://www.naag.org/yearly.rtf . Calculations by Children's Defense Fund.